DORSET
in the Civil War
1625–1665

Tim Goodwin

DORSET BOOKS

First published in Great Britain in 1996 by Dorset Books

Copyright © Tim Goodwin 1996

*The map on page viii has been specially drawn
for this volume by Penny Brown*

British Library Cataloguing in Publication Data
CIP data for this work is available from the British Library

ISBN 1 871164 26 5

DORSET BOOKS
Official Publisher to Dorset County Council
Halsgrove House
Lower Moor Way
Tiverton EX16 6SS
Tel: 01884 243242
Fax: 01884 243325

Printed and bound in in Great Britain by Bookcraft Ltd, Midsomer Norton

CONTENTS

ACKNOWLEDGEMENTS

It is impossible to write a book like this without using and building on the work of literally hundreds of other people, both living and dead, who have researched, catalogued and written about this time, and whose work I have consulted. I would like to thank them all.

I would also like to express my thanks to the Society of Authors, whose generous grant to me, from the Authors' Foundation, helped to cover the expenses of all the research work I had to do. Without that grant it would have been very difficult for me.

Other people to thank include the staff at the Dorset County Record Office and the Dorchester Reference Library, who were always helpful and friendly, Dorset Books for agreeing to publish this book, and of course my family, Penny, Eleanor and Sam, for putting up with me while I disappeared into the seventeenth century.

INTRODUCTION

The role of Dorset in the Civil War is not particularly well known, probably because none of the great battles were fought within the county's borders. However, balanced between the royalist heartlands in the West and Midlands, and the great population and manufacturing centres of the South East, Dorset was of crucial importance, as were its ports – Weymouth was the nearest place to London where Charles could reasonably hope for his long-awaited French allies to land. Furthermore, probably more than any other county in England, Dorset was the weathercock of fortune. Whichever party controlled Dorset dominated the war, so the story of Dorset at the time is the story in miniature of the whole Civil War. In 1642 the royalists made great efforts to crush all resistance as fast as possible, and their narrow failure, both in Dorset and elsewhere, was what condemned Britain to civil war. Parliament subsequently tightened its grip, only to be scattered in defeat the next year. Royalist control of Dorset was almost total by the end of 1643, though the resistance of a few centres reflected the king's national failure to penetrate the parliamentary strongholds of the south and east. From the summer of 1644 onwards the story of Dorset, as of the rest of the country, is of gradual parliamentary advance – with occasional set-backs – until the king's final defeat in 1646. Nevertheless military victory was not enough, and Dorset demonstrated the unease of the country at large with a series of plots and conspiracies, culminating in the uprising of 1655, and the enthusiasm with which Charles II was finally welcomed back by royalists and parliamentarians alike.

Dorset had more than its fair share of exciting, heroic, brutal and, occasionally, even comic episodes that make the story more real and more human: everything from the stupendous resistance of little Lyme Regis to the full strength of the royalist western army – a tale of endurance and courage among men and women that deserves to be far better known – to the panic at Sherborne, the slaughter at Abbotsbury, the tricks used to take Portland, and the fascinating and often-ignored rising of the clubmen – one of the very few true peoples' rebellions in British history.

Virtually all the great characters of the Civil War spent time in Dorset – Cromwell, Charles I, Fairfax, Warwick, Essex, Prince Maurice and many others – while the story of Charles II's flight through the county after his defeat at the battle of Worcester is one of the great romances of British history, on a par with the wanderings of Bonny Prince Charlie. The Civil War in Dorset also made famous two men who were to become key players in subsequent British history: the Somerset-born Robert Blake, who made his name at Lyme Regis, and went on to forge the British navy; and Sir Anthony Ashley Cooper, he of the shrewdly timed changes of side, who as the Earl of Shaftesbury dominated the first twenty years of Charles II's reign and more or less invented modern party politics. Many other less well-known figures of the war in Dorset have fascinating stories: Lady Bankes and her stubborn resistance at Corfe Castle; Sir Lewis Dyve who escaped from the Tower of London; Colonel Sexby the parliamentarian revolutionary who tried to assassinate Cromwell; John White the Puritan preacher who helped settle New England; Denzil Holles, one of the foremost parliamentarians in England, later impeached by Cromwell for secretly dealing with the king; William Wake, the grandfather of an archbishop of Canterbury, who was imprisoned 19 times; and John Penruddock who led two uprisings in ten years. People and events like these come together to make the history of Dorset in the Civil War a fascinating tapestry.

ABBREVIATIONS

Bayley: A.R.Bayley, *The Great Civil War in Dorset, 1642–1660*, (Taunton, 1910).

CJ: *The Journals of the House of Commons*.

Clarendon: Edward, Earl of Clarendon, *The History of the Rebellion and Civil Wars in England*, ed. Bulkeley Bandinel, 8 vols, (Oxford, 1826).

CSPD: *Calendar of State Papers, Domestic*.

DCRO: Dorset County Record Office

Dorset Proc.: *Proceedings of the Dorset Natural History and Antiquarian Field Club* (under various titles).

DSC: C.H. Mayo, ed., *Minute Books of the Dorset Standing Committee, 23 September 1646 to 8 May 1650*, (Exeter, 1902).

HMC: Historical Manuscripts Commission.

Hutchins: John Hutchins, *The History and Antiquities of the County of Dorset*, 4 vols, (1861–74).

LJ: *The Journals of the House of Lords*.

MRBD: C.H. Mayo, *Municipal Records of the Borough of Dorchester*, (Exeter, 1908).

SDNQ: *Somerset and Dorset Notes and Queries*.

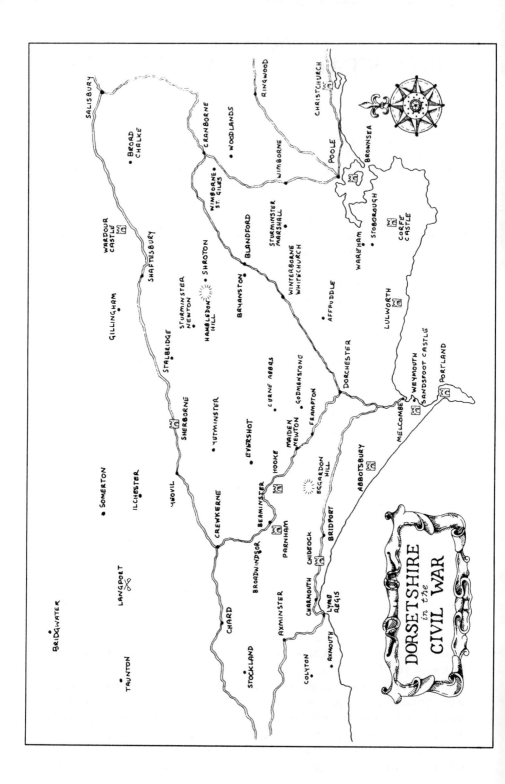

DORSETSHIRE in the CIVIL WAR

⊷ Chapter One ⊶
THE STAGE AND SETTING
1625–1640

The Civil War and the subsequent Restoration were the most important events in English history between the Norman Conquest and
the present day, laying down the basic shape of parliamentary
democracy.

For well over a century and a half, beginning in the reign of Edward IV
(1461–83), the strength of the English monarchy had been slowly growing,
tightening its grip on English life. The same gradual shift towards royal
absolutism was visible in almost all the nation-states of Europe: France,
Austria, Spain, Sweden, Prussia, Denmark. England was the only seventeenth-century monarchy where this expansion of royal power was
stopped in its tracks. And this was because of the defeat and execution of
King Charles I. When Charles's son, James II, also tried to impose
absolute rule in 1685–8, memories of the Civil War ensured he never had
a chance of success. No subsequent ruler dared even make the attempt.
In contrast when the French *parlements* and nobles rose against the Crown
between 1648 and 1653, they were crushed.

Dorset was not one of the most significant counties of England in the
1620s and 1630s. It had no great cities, no great manufacturing base, and
its population was only about 2 per cent of the country's. Yet it provides
an almost perfect microcosm of much of the nation, a complex mosaic of
rural, urban and maritime life. Arable and pastoral agriculture dominated the county, as it did the whole of England. However there were also
medium-sized inland towns like Sherborne and Dorchester with their
small-scale industries and the important ports of Poole, Weymouth and
Lyme, which had regular links with the continent, the New World, and
even further afield. Dorset illustrated the very England which each side
in the coming conflict had to win over, and Charles's failure in Dorset was
his national failure.

Much of England suffered relatively little fighting during the Civil War.
The country below a line joining Portsmouth and the Wash remained
solidly parliamentarian, and the same was largely true of the Midlands
triangle outlined by Nottingham, Warwick and Bedford. Wales, the
south-western peninsula and the Oxford area were consistently royalist.
In the North the fighting was fierce but short-lived, effectively over by
summer 1644. However in Dorset royalist and parliamentary garrisons
were simultaneously present for well over three and a half years, making
the county a constant battlefield. Skirmishes and sieges made up nearly
all the engagements of the Civil War and inflicted the vast majority of
casualties. They also characterised events in Dorset. The lack of major
set-piece battles, which has often caused the war in Dorset to be ignored,

demonstrates just how representative it was of the nation as a whole.

In the same way the transformation of Dorset from a county that was solidly, if unenthusiastically, behind Cromwell in 1655, to one that celebrated the Restoration of Charles II five years later, demonstrated the swing of attitudes throughout England, as did the lingering on of a fierce independence in religious matters.

On the accession of King Charles I the biggest source of conflict in Dorset was religion. The vast majority of the population was solidly Protestant, with a small minority of Roman Catholics, well-off papists like the Arundells of Chideock, the Turbervilles of Winterborne Whitechurch, and George Penny of Toller Whelme. However it was within the Protestant majority that the vital break was coming, for increasing numbers of people were being drawn towards the more extreme form of Protestantism that became known as Puritanism.

As the Puritans were Independents, their beliefs were by definition hard to generalise about, but they all shared a conviction of the complete and literal accuracy of the Bible, disapproval of what they considered trivial pleasures, a belief in some form of predestination, and enthusiasm for prolonged religious services. A typical Sunday service:

> begins at eight of the clock, and continues till twelve of the clock. The like courses and exercises are observed in the afternoon, from two of the clock unto five or six.[1]

The most important, and most subversive, tenet of Puritanism was that religion was at heart a direct communion between God and the individual, and therefore did not need the medium of priest, bishop, or formal religious services. This led to a concept entirely alien to pre-Reformation society: that people were solely responsible for themselves and their own actions. By raising the status of the individual, Puritanism provided a crucial source of resistance to the established church, and to the state. However the new King of England, like most European rulers of the time, believed that he stood between God and the nation as a sort of lieutenant and mediator. The creeds of Puritanism and the divine right of kings could scarcely have been more diametrically opposed.

The leaders of Dorset in the 1620s and 1630s included several Puritans, notably John Browne of Frampton, Sir Thomas Trenchard of Wolfeton and Sir Walter Erle of Charborough, a Dorset M.P. for forty-eight years from 1613 to 1661. It was this strong Puritan tendency among sections of the Dorset gentry that prevented the county from meekly following most of the South West into the royalist camp. Not that the Puritans were dominant, as they were in East Anglia. The determined royalism of the Bankes family in Corfe Castle governed the Isle of Purbeck. Similarly George Digby, John Hele and Richard Rogers ensured that the north of Dorset was a royalist stronghold. Though even in royalist Shaftesbury there was a moderate Puritan minister, Edward Williams, who was often in trouble for not wearing his surplice, using unauthorised versions of parts of the Bible, and preaching against the 'King's Book'.

Most of the county was rural, dominated by the political and religious affections of the local landowner, and the minister he had probably appointed. However along the sea coast matters were different. The ports of Weymouth, Poole, Lyme, and Bridport generally leant towards Puritanism and Parliament. Only Weymouth had a strong royalist party, and men like George Churchey and Fabian Hodder, respectively the mayor and treasurer of the town in 1639–40, would work hard for the King's cause during and after the war.

Dorchester was the largest town in the county, only Sherborne was comparable in population, and crucially the county town was devoted to Puritanism. Under the guiding hand of the Calvinist rector of Holy Trinity church since 1605, John White, 'usually called Patriarch of Dorchester or Patriarch White',[2] and 'one of the wisest and subtlest of that sort of men',[3] Dorchester became, in the words of one leading royalist, 'the magazine from whence the other places were supplied with the principles of rebellion'.[4]

The attitude of local ministers was of crucial importance in forming opinions. For the vast majority of the population weekly sermons were almost their only link with a wider world and with national politics, and religious radicalism was not confined to the towns. On 7 March 1626 Sir Francis Ashley examined Nicholas Day, parson of the little West Dorset village of Hooke, who was accused of having preached a sermon saying that:

> the land was not governed by justice, but by bribery and extortion and that kings could not contain themselves in their own kingdoms, and that they seek to make invasions of other countries and to sack their goods, ravish their wives, deflower their daughters, and all other villainy.[5]

Although Day denied he had made most of the statements attributed to him, there were witnesses to the contrary, and there is little doubt that the sermon was a direct attack on King Charles. Nevertheless, two highly respectable Dorchester men, Richard Williams and Matthew Butler, both of them churchwardens and constables, and probably of Puritan leanings, went surety for Day.

Not that all ecclesiastical troubles stemmed from the clash of ideologies. Sometimes it was simply the standards of the minister in question that raised problems. William Bartlett, the vicar of Yetminster, was accused of having bought the vicarship of Church Knowle, and then putting in charge 'as his curate, Thomas Jacob, a litigious and debauched character'.[6] The Bishop of Bristol attempted to put one Valentine Minge in his place, but Bartlett and Jacob resisted, and the case dragged on for years.

When Charles ascended the throne in March 1625, freedom from invasion, and the determination of his predecessors to avoid entanglement abroad, meant England was probably the most under-taxed country in Europe. There was no sense of irony in the Earl of Clarendon's comment that:

> this Kingdom, and all His Majesty's dominions, enjoyed the

greatest calm, and the fullest measure of felicity, that any people in any age, for so long time together, have been blessed with; to the wonder and envy of all the other parts of Christendom.[7]

Among the aristocracy the same feeling was common. John Aubrey said of the time 'there had been a long serene calm of peace, and men minded nothing but peace and luxury.'[8]

However, the fierce wars that ravaged mainland Europe cast their shadows even over Dorset. Refugees arrived in the county during the 1620s, and three eminent German Protestants settled in Blandford, where one at least, Frederick Saggitary, became friendly with the influential Richard Rogers of Bryanston. More surprising were the events of 1624, when Oliver Lawrence of Affpuddle and his uncle, Edward Williams, caught a Spanish spy who was apparently working with an Englishman named Henry Cotton, for which they were rewarded by the King with £20.

The young King of England was determined to help his brother-in-law, the King of Bohemia, whose loss of his throne to the Catholic Habsburgs in 1618 had sparked off the Thirty Years War. But such was Charles's ineptness, that within two years of his accession he was simultaneously at war with two mutual enemies, Spain and France. The wars went disastrously, and conscript soldiers roamed the southern counties, unpaid and uncontrolled by their inexperienced officers. Any traveller might find himself in sudden danger, as Sir William Waller recalled:

In Dorsetshire...being somewhat wearied and alighting to refresh myself at the descent of a hill, and my men staying with the horses a little behind, I walked down alone, suspecting nothing, when suddenly out of a lower hollow way, there crossed upon me a man on foot, with his hat under his arm as covering something with it. I demanded what he was, but he returned only a soft, grumbling answer which I heeded not, and so walked on, and he kept on a little way by me. But my men showing themselves near upon the coming down of the hill, he parted from me into the woods which were close by; but my men, in his passage near them, observed he had his sword drawn under his arm, with his hat covering the hilt, so that in all probability, if in that instant of time he had not discovered my men, I had been assaulted by him[9].

Not that it was only soldiers who prowled the roads. John Clavell of Wootton Glanville, deep in debt to a money-lender, became a horse-thief and highwayman. After being caught and sentenced to death, he was given an amnesty for Charles I's coronation, and eventually freed in about November 1627. Subsequently he reformed, and made a living by combining writing, medicine and the law.

Nonetheless, the breakdown in public order was largely blamed on the army, and martial law was introduced. On Boxing Day 1626 Sir Francis

Ashley began investigating an incident at Mr Brereton's house in Benville, near Corscombe. It was alleged that eleven soldiers, guided by Giles Fisher, tapster of the Swan in Evershot, had gone 'to a papist's house to fetch out a seminary priest'. Once there the soldiers, 'whose purpose was to get money from the people in the house', threatened the household with their muskets, attempted to break down the doors, and fired a musket into the hall, until Mrs Brereton 'threw out at the window £4 10s.' The soldiers were then arrested, 'whereof when some other soldiers heard, they assembled themselves together, threw stones at the windows and attempted their rescue, but prevailed not'.[10] Three weeks later:

> was held an extraordinary commission for the trial of some soldiers, in which Sir Francis Ashley sat judge, and condemned seven soldiers and one tapster to death for burglary, but six of the soldiers had a pardon.[11]

The pardoned men were sent to join several hundred Dorset troops that took part in Charles's ill-fated attack on the Isle de Rhé off the Atlantic coast of France, where English losses ran at over 50 per cent. John Mason, a carpenter from Netherbury, was badly wounded there and returned home to find his brother had taken possession of the copyhold that should have been his. At Bere Regis there were several payments 'for maimed soldiers'.[12]

Next year Sir Walter Erle was still complaining of the soldiers:

> In my county, under colour of placing a soldier, there came 20 in a troop to take sheep. They disturb markets and fairs, rob men on the highway, ravish women, breaking houses in the night and enforcing men to ransom themselves, killing men that have assisted constables that have come to keep the peace.[13]

Even if the soldiers and sailors did not degenerate to theft and murder, they still had to be given food and places to stay, and rather than pay them Charles made them chargeable to local inhabitants. A thousand soldiers from Devon and Cornwall were quartered in Dorset at a cost of from 3s. a week for a private to 7s. a week for a lieutenant, and the treasurer of Shaftesbury received just £10 for the passage through the town of 300 soldiers marching to Wiltshire. The Earl of Dorset himself complained that it did 'much unsatisfy the county to have the soldiers there, and no money in their hands to pay them',[14] while one village wrote a desperate letter to John Browne and Sir Walter Erle:

> We, the inhabitants of Stockland desire your worships will please take into consideration our present condition, first in that our parish being the common road way out of Devon towards London, has for a long time been charged weekly in the passage of soldiers, especially of the sick and weak sort, and now likewise with mariners, every day coming from the King's shipping destitute of all means and money; moreover our weekly rate for the billeting of soldiers is 46s., the burden

whereof we, being all husbandmen and the most of us but of mean estate, shall not be able long to undergo.[15]

Bridport too was constantly visited, and the town accounts of the time are full of references such as: 'gave three soldiers that were returned from the fleet 3d... one sick soldier that came from the fleet 3d.'[16] and so on. The same probably applied to Shaftesbury, where the fragmentary accounts include a reference to 4s. 5d. 'laid out upon the soldiers by the way and at Dorchester'.[17] One company of soldiers that had left Dorchester was ordered back again, but the more influential people flatly refused to accept any more billeting upon them. Nearly five years later the inhabitants of Dorchester were still protesting about £260 9s. 10d.:

which they have expended and been at charge for the passage and billeting of his Majesty's soldiers in the second and third year of his Majesty's reign...whereof they have yet received no manner of satisfaction.[18]

As late as 12 November 1633 the town council bitterly objected that they could not receive 'one penny of money'[19] from the local magnates who were supposed to have paid out loan money to cover the costs.

Lyme Regis probably adopted the shrewdest plan by bribing the soldiers to go somewhere else and had 'given to ensign of soldiers for avoiding the town £1 0s. 4d.'.[20] However even that did not always work, and in 1627 Lyme paid out £2 7s. 7d. for expenses connected with the passage of a troop of soldiers, followed by another 8s. 2d. 'towards hose, shoes and shirts, and conduct money, and horse for them to Bridport'.[21]

The wars brought other expenses. The Spanish were expected to invade, and not only was Weymouth ordered to fortify the harbour and town, but also if there was 'apparent argument of an enemy',[22] beacons were to be lit and warning sent to neighbours and to the royal court.

At the time it was widely thought that England was overpopulated, containing more people than she

can well nourish or well employ... Not only innholders and shopkeepers, of both which we need not the third person, but even handicraft men, such as shoemakers, tailors, nay masons, carpenters and the like, many of whom with their families live in such low conditions as is little better than beggary, by reason of the multitudes that are bred up and exercised in those employments.[23]

It was not only unemployment and underemployment that troubled the nation. Prices were rising rapidly. In 1624 Richard Eburne, vicar of Henstridge on the Somerset border, complained that 'the prices of all things are grown to such an unreasonable height, that the common, that is the meaner sort of people, are even undone.'[24] Between 1621 and 1630 the price of wheat in the South West had risen almost year on year, despite seasonal variations. Other grains were rising too, 'barley and oats were very dear'[25] commented William Whiteway, and the poor harvest of 1630, followed by 'the last wet winter',[26] led prices to more than double again, which represented enormous suffering for the majority of the population. In November 1631, though, the Dorset J.P.s complained that the price rises were partly artificial, caused by panic, 'the interference of the justices and the suspicion of want thereby excited'.[27]

The profits of merchants and traders may have increased with inflation, but many landowners were under financial pressure from rising prices because the rents they could charge were fixed by law. To add to shrinking incomes, martial law and billeting, came another grievance: Charles's attempts to introduce arbitrary taxation. Only a year after his accession, the King had already dissolved two parliaments and ordered a forced loan, a tax unapproved by Parliament. Most of Dorset paid without complaint, indeed the Earl of Suffolk reported from Blandford the 'people very well inclined to lend',[28] though Bridport sent three representatives to Dorchester to discuss the matter, and begged to be excused because of a 'twenty weeks visitation of plague',[29] which killed 80 people out of a population of perhaps 2000.

Disease was ravaging much of the area. In Beaminster the death rate rose alarmingly, while Exeter, where one-sixth of the city's population died, saw riots. After Agnes Hoble of Toller Porcorum developed a mysterious, apparently deadly sickness, the local court ordered that £8 should be collected from the parish to pay 'to the party that shall undertake the said cure, taking from him good caution for performance thereof'.[30] Smallpox also struck periodically, notably at Sherborne in 1626, 1634, 1642–3 and 1649–50.

There was some resistance to the King's demands for money. The lawyer William Savage of Bloxworth 'desired to see the Act of Parliament under which he was called upon to pay',[31] and was one of about 80 people who were brought up before the Privy Council for resisting the forced loan. He ended up in prison, as did two of the leading magnates of the county, Sir Walter Erle and Sir John Strangways, who were only freed in January 1628.

The King did not take kindly to increasing criticism. Furious at 'the disobedient and seditious carriage of certain ill-affected persons', such as 'our kingly office cannot bear, nor any former age parallel',[32] on 2 March 1629 he issued an order that Parliament should adjourn, and the Speaker rose to leave. One of the two MPs for Dorchester was Denzil Holles, the younger son of the Earl of Clare and son-in-law of the Dorchester Recorder Sir Francis Ashley. Shortly after Charles's accession he had been invited by the King to take part in a royal masque, but Holles was a Presbyterian, and his instincts were firmly against the court. Now, with another member, he

> laid violent hands upon the Speaker, to the great affrightment and disturbance of the House. And the Speaker being got out of the chair, they by violence set him in the chair again, so that there was a great tumult in the House.[33]

As Parliament continued sitting, the King's officers hammered on the fastened door of the chamber, and Holles put forward three resolutions against changes in religion and arbitrary taxation.

Two days later Holles was arrested with three other M.P.s. One of them was a relation of Sir Walter Erle, named William Strode, of whom the King's Attorney General said 'he behaves himself so passionately and violently...forcibly and unlawfully'[34] that he even struck one of the King's officers. Despite the King's comment that 'he was sorry with all his heart for the miscarriage of his old companion and bedfellow',[35] Holles was put in the Tower of London, but he had not been forgotten by his constituents. Two months later the governor of the Tower wrote:

> one John White, minister, preacher of Dorchester, and Ferdinando Nicholls [White's former assistant] of Sherborne, came under the window of Mr Holles and would have spoken unto him, but were prevented by his keeper and put out of the Tower.[36]

The Dorchester corporation defiantly voted to present their M.P. with 'a standing cup of plate which cost 20 marks, for his service done the last Parliament'.[37] Next year Holles was fined a thousand marks (£667) for the offence and ordered to be imprisoned until he apologised for his behaviour. 'I made an escape, and lived a banished man for the space of seven or eight years, and then at last was glad to pay my fine'.[38] William Strode stubbornly refused to pay, and was released from prison only in 1640.

King Charles now began to rule without a parliament. Unable to use the normal methods of taxation, he invented or developed other sources of money. One was the knighthood compositions tax, an ancient law revived in 1630, by which everyone who held land worth £40 per annum or more was fined if they had not taken up the responsibilities of knighthood. Oliver Lawrence of Affpuddle and his half-brother Edward Lawrence, who would be knighted by Charles in 1643 for his devoted royalism, had to pay £10 a head.

July 1632 saw the J.P.s of Dorset complaining that 'this little county' was having to pay as much tax as Hampshire and Wiltshire, even though:

> they had performed the service of many thousand loads of stones in the Isle of Portland, for building the Banqueting House [at Whitehall], and that service is still continued upon them towards His Majesty's buildings, besides that there is £5000 and upwards due this county for billeting soldiers.[39]

The best-known of Charles's taxes, ship money, was first levied in 1634. The ports of the county were traditionally liable to this charge and Denis Bond, shortly to become mayor of Dorchester, simply remarked: 'a taxation upon the sea coast for the setting out of a fleet of ships for the King and I paid for Lutton, Carrance and Bucknoll £18'.[40] Dorchester was assessed at £100 and Wareham at £30, but some areas suffered more than others. 'The Islanders of Purbeck, when Sir Thomas Trenchard came thither of purpose, told him they could not pay it,'[41] and that it was 'a place which time out of mind has been a nursery for mariners and sailors,

8

on account whereof they have hitherto been exempt from charges of this nature',[42] while it was resolved that the town clerk of Weymouth should travel to London to petition for a reduction in the sum of £220 towards 'setting forth a ship of war for His Majesty's service'.[43] William Whiteway, another of the Puritans who dominated Dorchester, reported 'this rate was paid with much grudging...many refused and were sent to Newgate, but were released again shortly after.'[44] In fact the tax was, initially, very successful.

Encouraged, Charles extended ship money to cover the entire kingdom, and Dorset was assessed at £5000 a year. The village of Long Bredy got a bill of £21 6s. 8d., and 38 inhabitants had to pay anything from 1s. to £4 1s. 7d. In contrast Charles II's unpopular hearth tax of 1664 charged 29 inhabitants between 2s. and £1 2s. for a total of £6 16s. Discontent grew steadily, and in 1636 Thomas Leddoze, the mayor of Weymouth rode to Blandford to meet Sir John Freke, the sheriff, and other county mayors to discuss the matter. Poole's tax bill in 1634 had been £60, almost as much as the total annual cost of running the town, and the inhabitants objected so much that the tax demand was halved for the next year and dropped again in 1637. Shaftesbury was excused the tax altogether in 1636 after a severe outbreak of plague.

The hardship in Dorset was made worse by the weather:

This year was dry all the first part of the year and little rain, so that they did cut rye, barley and oats in the latter end of June in several places. In Purbeck this year they had little rain from the first day of this year until 6 July. Not all the rain they had was not six hours.[45]

A chronology of Netherbury also complains about the almost complete lack of spring or early summer rain over the years 1634-6.

It was almost certainly this drought that led to charges being brought against Richard Chafin and Henry Phelips in 1635 for 'diverting water out of the Hungerhill River' in East Stoke, 'to the damage of George Savage.'[46] Too dry a spring was usually catastrophic, destroying much of the harvest before it could grow. But sometimes the problem was different: '1638 was a sickly and feverish autumn' and a few miles over the Wiltshire border at Broad Chalke 'there were three graves open at one time in the churchyard'.[47]

Increasing numbers of people were having their goods seized for non-payment of the King's taxes. John Freke, who even distrained the possessions of his own son 'that he would not seem partial' objected that:

the greatest part of the arrear falls among the poorer sort who pay like drops of blood, and some sell their only cow, which should feed the children, and some come to the parish.[48]

Sir Walter Erle again refused to pay, as did Denzil Holles and other leading Puritans like William Strode and John Browne, and in 1637 the defaulters had their goods seized by the fiercely loyalist sheriff of the year,

Richard Rogers. This treatment of 'some great ones reduced the rest to conformity',[49] for a while. But still the unpaid arrears mounted. Robert Hancock, alias Randell, of Maiden Newton was too poor to pay what he owed and 'indulged in railing upon the governors, officers, and others, his neighbours, in such an open, foul, common and usual manner as was insufferable',[50] for which offence he was sent to the house of correction at Dorchester for a month.

Other financial pressures were also being brought to bear. Many of the leading merchants of Dorset were accused of 'great frauds' and that they 'refused to pay customs and transported their goods at their own pleasure, beating His Majesty's officers'. A court case was brought against several of them, including Thomas Waltham of Weymouth, two members of a well-off Dorchester family the Blachfords, and James Gould of Dorchester. Gould, who later became if not a royalist, certainly no parliamentarian, was acquitted, but the rest were fined heavily. John Blachford fled to France, while Thomas Waltham subsequently gained a name as a religious radical. Eight years later John Gardiner, the collector of customs at Poole, complained of the men in question that 'ever since which time they have studied his ruin'.[51]

North-east Dorset had its own problems. Gillingham Forest belonged to the Crown, but Charles leased it to his former tutor, Sir James Fullerton for £11 a year, in exchange for an assurance that Fullerton would disafforest, enclose and improve the land. Initially there was no resistance, but over the winter of 1626-7 the true impact of Fullerton's plans became clear as the deer were destroyed, trees cut down and enclosures laid out. Local people complained bitterly that the land they were being offered in exchange for their traditional grazing rights was poor, far away, and sometimes without access. Furthermore some roads through the forest were being made unusable, and areas were being enclosed that should not be. Many echoed the complaint of a yeoman, Mark Hastell, that the enclosures 'must needs be to the great hindrance if not to the utter undoing of most part of the inhabitants of Gillingham'.[52] In face of growing resistance, commissioners looked into the matter and recommended changes, but Fullerton took no notice.

Early in 1628 discontent exploded into open resistance:

> Several people, sometimes a hundred, sometimes more, armed and disguised by day and nights, threw down the fences, filled up the ditches three miles in length, sawed off the rails and carried away or burnt them, threatened to kill the workmen and burn their houses if they came any more to work.[53]

A regiment of soldiers sent to suppress the disturbances refused to take any of the rioters prisoner. Messengers from the Privy Council itself were whipped at the post, and official documents they carried were burnt. A fresh attempt to bring order to the area in November, when the Sheriff of Dorset brought in more troops, also failed, with the local people defiantly declaring, 'here we were born and here we stay.'[54] That winter yet more soldiers were sent in and the rioters were at last overcome. Eighty-seven people were arrested and taken to London, and in February 1629 the court of Star Chamber fined and censured eighty of them. Many of the fines, which were not particularly heavy, were never paid, and unsuccessful efforts were still being made to get the money ten years later. As for the officers of the rebellious regiment, they were ordered to be set in the pillory, with papers on their heads declaring their offence.

Two and a half years later there was fresh trouble over 'breaking up enclosures in Gillingham Forest'[55] by John Phillips, a well-off tanner of Gillingham, who had been one of the leaders of the original revolt. The sympathy many in the county must have felt for the local people was symbolized when Joseph Paty, a leading figure in Dorchester, went surety for Phillips. There was further trouble in the late 1630s, but the enclosures went on, even though Shaftesbury market experienced a sharp, if temporary, slump because the narrowing or blocking of roads had made it less accessible to many local farmers.

The enclosure of common land was still in its infancy, but scattered examples occurred throughout the county, notably at Loders, Bere Regis, Piddlehinton, and Fordington. John Churchill proposed to enclose the common waste of Wootton Glanville in 1639, and the Marquis of Winchester, Sir Francis Fulford, Sir Thomas Trenchard and Roger Preston agreed to divide up and enclose the wastes of Hooke, Poorton, Wytherston, Toller Porcorum and Kingcombe, though the plan was not carried through. Enclosure was widely regarded with deep suspicion, if not hostility, and even in the 1620s there were complaints about 'the covetousness of some private men that to increase their domains have depopulated whole parishes'.[56] Many of the aristocracy themselves spoke against its evil consequences:

> the revenue of too many of the Court consisted principally in enclosures and improvements of that nature...which brought much charge and trouble upon the people.[57]

From 1631 the King actually took some action against the enclosers, fining them up to £4000 and ordering them to reverse their enclosures and rebuild depopulated farms. This certainly lessened Charles's popularity with many landowners, but probably without any corresponding increase in his popularity among the poorer sort, especially because he himself and his courtiers continued enclosures themselves. Meanwhile the King's parallel attempt to reimpose medieval forest laws also caused widespread ill feeling. In 1630 especially there was a sudden outburst of cases over 'killing of deer in Cranborne Chase'.[58] The prosecutions were mostly against local husbandmen and yeomen, but even local gentry joined in poaching, and there were occasionally pitched battles between keepers and poachers in which people were killed.

Despite this slowly rising tide of unrest, day-to-day life rolled on, broken only by rare moments of drama and disaster. The combination of

11

wooden houses, thatch and open fires meant every seventeenth-century town and village faced the ever-present danger of fire, and Dorset had more than its fair share. The great fire of 1613 that destroyed around 170 houses, half the whole town of Dorchester, is well known, but there were others. A fire in Wimborne in 1634 burnt down only five houses, but one at Bere Regis cost 50 houses at a claimed cost of between £7000 and £20,000, and left 306 people destitute; 83 houses were destroyed in Yeovil in 1640 when Dorchester contributed relief of £40, while Dorchester itself suffered a second fire that cost 30 houses in 1623. Not surprisingly fire was a regular preoccupation of local councils. Shaftesbury paid John Freke £1 'for looking to the chimneys about the town',[59] while Steven Kent, a blacksmith of Pimperne, found himself in trouble for improper use of his forge, endangering the houses of his neighbours. Eventually the court ordered:

> he shall not make any fire to come in the said forge, save only with seacoal, and that for the necessary use of his trade only, or to be committed to the county gaol if he do not obey this order.[60]

Dorchester town council, not surprisingly, was especially aware of the danger. In June 1640 several councillors were asked to look over a house and faggot pile which were said to be 'exceeding dangerous for fire'.[61] Several years later it decided that 'every one will contribute towards the raising of £30 or £40 to buy a brazen engine or spout to quench fire in times of danger.'[62]

Off the coast pirates infested the seas. In 1636 the merchants and shipowners of the South West petitioned for help against the Barbary pirates of Tunis and Algiers, as well as against the Englishman, T. Purser, who preyed on ships around Weymouth. On the other hand, disaster at sea could mean unexpected wealth for people who lived on the coast. Mr Endymion Porter, a gentleman of the King's bedchamber, was travelling home from Spain in December 1628 when his ship was wrecked at Burton Bradstock. All the people aboard were saved, but 'the goods of the ship were pillaged,'[63] though most things were said to have been restored eventually. This certainly did not happen with regard to the *Golden Grape*, driven ashore at Wyke Regis in December 1641, and plundered of 2000 barrels of raisins, 400 jars of oil, 12 butts of wine, and an assortment of other luxuries. An inquiry into what had happened to the cargo was held, but little of value was ever recovered.

Justice at the time was fairly rough and ready, and the list of crimes was long, including swearing, fathering a bastard, sabbath-breaking, even idleness and gossiping. Thomas Rawlings, a tailor of Bere Regis, was riding towards Affpuddle in September 1638, when he overtook Thomas Joyner and gave him a lift on his horse. Joyner began to talk about a local woman, Ann Neale, and said she was more common than the highway, and that John Dyett of Bere Regis had more use of her than her husband did. For spreading these stories, Dyett was sentenced to public penance for slander. Some years before Ursula Greene had to come to Charminster church dressed in a white sheet and confessed in public to 'committing the wicked and detestable offence of fornication with Christopher Harbyn'.[64]

At the assizes there were nearly always a few public executions, often of women. Eleanor Galpin of Dorchester was put to death for killing her ten-day-old baby, whereas Elizabeth Johnson, alias Stevens, was hanged at Bridport in 1635 simply for being an incorrigible vagrant. Even more scandalous must have been the case of Mary Shepherd. During the hearing at Wareham in 1638, Jane Coward testified that Mary Shepherd had pulled one of her stockings, and within two hours she 'was taken in all her limbs that she could not stir either hand or foot'. Coward's mother appealed to the mayor of Wareham, who forced Shepherd to shake Jane Coward's hand, and she recovered. A similar seizure three days later was also cured by a pull of the hand from Shepherd. Other evidence came from Ann Crew, also of Wareham, who said

> she saw Mary Shepherd come into the house of John Gillingham, and likewise saw Edward Gillingham come down bare-footed very well, without any lameness of sickness at all, and presently after the said Mary Shepherd had pulled on a legging upon the leg of the said Edward Gillingham, he fell instantly both lame and sick.[65]

Four years earlier two witchcraft cases had been dismissed at Dorchester, but after the Civil War John Aubrey saw a poor schoolmistress, Ann Bodenham, tried for witchcraft at Salisbury, and executed.

The Calvinist archbishop of Canterbury, George Abbott, died in 1633, and Charles appointed William Laud, a fierce high-church Anglican, as his successor. Laud was determined to root out Puritanism and Presbyterianism, and he cracked down severely on all ministers who showed Calvinistic tendencies, while introducing many changes in the Church of England that moved it closer to Roman Catholic practices. When Robert Skinner, the Bishop of Bristol, visited Dorchester in 1637 his insistence that 'ceremonies (believe it) do not only set off, but moreover fortify and secure even the substance of religion'[66] was unlikely to have gone down well with the local Puritans. Eight years earlier Walter Erle had warned in Parliament of the danger of Catholicism and Armenianism [anti-Calvinist high church Protestantism] allying to bring in a Spanish tyranny. As the 1630s passed, the combination of Laud's reforms and the influence of the King's Catholic wife, Henrietta Maria, must have made his speech seem more and more prophetic, until by the end of the decade much of England was possessed by growing fear of a papist conspiracy.

Two years before Charles's accession John White had founded the Dorchester Company, which was governed by his friend Erle, and included most of the leading Puritan lights of the county among its members, men such as Richard Strode, John Browne, John Hill, William Whiteway and Sir Francis Ashley. The Company's 120 members included 21 clergy,

and its aims involved the religious instruction of fishermen, as well as:
the settling of a plantation in New England in America, for
the better and more convenient taking and saving of the fish
in the seas of those parts, and also for bartering and
exchange of commodities transported from the Kingdom of
England with the natives of New England.[67]

The first boat sent out, the *Fellowship of Weymouth*, cost over £300, but arrived at the fishing banks several weeks too late, so the voyage ended with a loss of £600. Subsequent ventures were also dogged by bad luck and bad judgement, and at last, 'the said joint adventurers having spent and lost about £3000',[68] the Dorchester Company was swallowed up by the better known Massachusetts Bay Company. But a link between New England and Dorset had been established, and in 1630, 140 West-Country Puritans founded the settlement of Dorchester, Massachusetts, just a few miles from Boston, from where they soon spread to Hartford, Connecticut. Among their leaders was Roger Ludlow, uncle of the Wiltshire regicide Edmund Ludlow. John White himself considered leaving, but eventually decided to stay with his flock in England. In 1635 he and John Browne were accused of illegally sending money for the support of Puritan ministers in New England, but nothing could be proved.

Over the next few years, the emigration accelerated:
...numbers to avoid these miseries and mischievous
molestations departed out of the Kingdom, some into
Holland, some into New England and other desert and unin-
habited parts of America, thereby exposing themselves, their
wives, children and estates to the great dangers of wind and
waves by sea and many other inevitable hazards by land.[69]

Of roughly 120 Dorset emigrants whose movements can be traced over the years 1620–50, about a third went to Dorchester, with another 20 to Salem. The rest went elsewhere in Massachusetts, except for a scattering to the more religiously tolerant settlements in Rhode Island, Maine, Long Island and Connecticut.

The emigrants came from all over the county, but the main movement was from Dorchester, Weymouth and the nearby villages, with another cluster along the coast from Lyme to Bridport, where, in 1635, the village of Symondsbury alone provided nine emigrants, aged up to sixty. Few people came from those areas, like Sherborne and Blandford, that would show royalist leanings.

In spite of the difficulties of the ten-week Atlantic crossing, links remained open between New England and Dorset. For example, in 1637 Richard and John Derby from Askerswell, and John Chipman of Briantspuddle, sailed to Barnstaple, on Cape Cod Bay. The two Derbys were younger brothers of the successful mercer, William Derby, who was one of the close-knit largely Puritan clique that ran Dorchester, while Chipman was a friend of Oliver Lawrence of Affpuddle. Richard Derby returned to England but was back in America by 1641, while John

Chipman conducted a twenty-year long campaign from his home in Massachusetts to get some money he claimed he was owed by the English members of the Derby family. As the Civil War grew closer, there are signs that the rate of emigration slackened. Gabriel Ludlow, the brother of Roger Ludlow, gave up his planned departure in about 1639, and a certain number of emigrants returned to England in the 1640s, such as John Humphrey of Dorchester and Roger Derby from near Bridport.

The Puritan-influenced parliaments of the 1620s consistently supported the extension of the voting franchise in elections, but one town where this extension occurred, Bridport, still elected Sir Lewis Dyve, who was related to the Digby and Strangways families, and would be one of the leading supporters of the King. In practice elections were always open to corruption. At the Dorset county election of 1626 the main support seems to have been for John Browne, but Sir John Strangways had his own candidate, Sir George Morton of Milborne St Andrew, 'large, strong, stout, generous and plain-hearted'.[70] The sheriff overseeing the election was the seventy-five-year-old Francis Chaldicott. He and his wife were apparently 'liberal constant housekeepers, bountiful relievers of the poor, careful breeders of their children in piety and virtue',[71] but Chaldicott was clearly under the control of the Strangways family, for he moved the whole election down to the George Inn, shut out most of Browne's supporters, and took votes for Morton until he had enough to win. The House of Commons overturned the election, but Morton won the rerun, apparently because of a variety of other tricks by Strangways, who subsequently took Morton's place himself. Morton lost much of his money after indulging in some risky ventures with Sir George Horsey, and later suffered for his loyalty to the King, his sequestered estates not being returned to him until 1653.

Not all the Dorset aristocracy were involved in politics. Henry Hastings of Woodlands, the son of the Earl of Huntingdon and owner of the manor of Christchurch, was a famous eccentric whose clothes were 'always green cloth and never worth, when new, five pounds'. Hastings spent all his time hunting except:

> what he borrowed to caress his neighbour's wives and daughters, there being not a woman in all his walks, of the degree of a yeoman's wife or under, and under the age of forty, but it was her own fault if he was not intimately acquainted with her. This made him very popular, always speaking kindly to the husband, brother or father, who was to boot very welcome to his house, whenever he came there he found beef pudding and small beer in great plenty.[72]

When finally forced to take sides Hastings joined the royalists and had to pay a fine of £500. But even civil war did not stop him enjoying his main interests and shortly before his death, aged well over eighty, he still 'rode to the death of a stag as well as any'.

The Puritans unquestionably represented the forces of change in early

15

Stuart England, but it would be wrong to consider all their demands progressive. Sir Walter Erle had been described as a sectary and disturber of the peace as long before as 1621, only it was for trying to pass a bill that would ban dancing, church ales [festivals] and May games. Several Dorset towns, including Bridport and Lyme, actually paid companies of actors not to visit their towns, and at Beaminster in October 1630 there were complaints that a travelling company, which had already been refused permission to perform in Dorchester, had:

> set up their shows of puppet playing, and there do exercise their feats not only in the daytime but also in the night, to the grievance of divers of the inhabitants who cannot keep their children and servants in their houses by reason that they frequent the said shows and sights late in the night in a disorderly manner.[73]

Members of the company were also accused of arguing with the town preacher, who had probably given a sermon attacking them, and of brawling with local inhabitants.

When Parliament was recalled in 1640, Erle demonstrated the hostility of many Puritans to improving the lot of the great mass of the population, remarking 'it was proved that mechanic men's children should not be brought up in learning.'[74] This was notably in contrast to John Browne, who built a school at Frampton for boys and girls. Browne also left £20 a year for the relief of the poor of Frampton, where Erle, who was almost certainly substantially richer than Browne, left only a total of £15, 'to the poor of the parish of Morden £10 and to the poor of Sturminster Marshall £5'.[75] Both those rich Puritan landholders were outshone by less well-off men. Bernard Mitchell of Weymouth left 'to the poor of Weymouth 33s. and 33s. yearly, to the poor of Wareham 20s. yearly' and bequests to many other Dorset towns, including Bridport, Wimborne, Abbotsbury and 'the poor widows of Melcombe';[76] while Gilbert Adams, a mercer of Beaminster, left £200 for the poor of Beaminster and another £40 'for the building of a house for the poor of Beaminster'.[77] Money from the Adams bequest was still being used in the twentieth century.

The largely Puritan rulers of Dorset's towns went to some lengths to protect their own commercial interests. One of Poole's newest industries was the making of silk stockings, which had been introduced 'to the great benefit of the town and relief of the poor'. However 'some ill-disposed persons that desire rather the impoverishing of the place than the relief of the poor'[78] had encouraged the people of Poole to work for employers from outside the town. The businessmen of Poole reacted rapidly to this threat to their monopoly. In September 1625 the town council passed a regulation fining any Poole inhabitant who helped make silk stockings for 'strangers' 2s. 6d. a pair.

The Puritans' initial reaction to the increasing persecution they faced was not aggressive. Those who did not emigrate, generally conformed as far as they could, and on 7 March 1633 John White preached that:

to beguile the King is not only base robbery but sacrilege, to scandalize him is not a simple slander but a degree of blasphemy, to violate his person is not an ordinary murder but treason and parricide in the highest nature.[79]

As late as 1636 the churchwardens of White's church paid out 8s. 6d. for a copy of the hated Book of Common Prayer, and three years later spent 3d. 'for a prayer for the King'.[80]

The Civil War itself would later be blamed for the increasing militancy of the Puritan preachers, and of John White it was said:

He was for the most part of his time a moderate, not morose or peevish Puritan...before the rebellion broke out he, by his wisdom, did keep the inhabitants of Dorchester in good order and obedient to the church, and also proved eminently useful in reforming the dissolute manners of the people thereof, it fell out that after the turn of the times, it was by his means stocked with such a factious and fanatic crew, that all endeavours could not reform it, nor ever, as it is thought, will.[81]

However in that same sermon of 1633 White had also made a fundumentally subversive point which underlay the entire Puritan rebellion: 'obedience to the will of God discharges a man from performing the will of the ruler.'[82] The same theme was repeated a year later by Mr Spratt, the minister of Beaminster: 'I do advise you rather to obey God's laws rather than the laws of the King.'[83]

The link between resisting Archbishop Laud's vision of the Church of England and resisting the established government was still only notional, but it was strengthening. The chief thorn in the side of the Shaftesbury corporation in the 1620s and 1630s was Nicholas Gower. What his religious views were we do not know, but it is probably significant that his son-in-law, William Hopkins, was described as 'a Brownist and will not come to church'.[84]

Repressing the Puritans meant attacking many of the leading men in Dorset. In 1634 Sir Richard Strode, elder brother of the imprisoned William Strode and former M.P. for Bridport, was involved in a long-running dispute over the Parnham estate near Beaminster. At the same time he was feuding with the minister of his local church at Cattistock. Eventually he refused to pay tithes and was put on trial because he 'was and is reputed a schismatical person'. The court decided there was a strong suspicion that Strode was 'a man ill-affected to the state and government ecclesiastical and the orthodox true religion here by law established',[85] and warned him to behave peaceably and according to the law. The same year there was trouble over the ceremonial followed in the parish churches of Charminster and Stratton, which were under the sway of that 'very honest, well-natured, worthy man, a favourer of Puritans',[86] Sir Thomas Trenchard.

Archbishop Laud himself complained angrily of the infiltration of Puritans:

in most parishes in Wiltshire, Dorsetshire and the western parts, there is still a Puritan and an honest man chosen churchwardens together. The Puritan always crosses the other in repairs and adorning the church...and in the issue puts some trick or other upon the honest man, to put him to sue for his charges, he has been at for the church. You shall find it at this instant in the parish of Beaminster.[87]

Certain parishioners of Beaminster were forced to a humiliating apology 'for not bowing or using lowly reverence in the time of divine service when the blessed name of the Lord Jesus is mentioned',[88] and they had to promise complete obedience in future. Other local church problems were more mundane. In Fordington eight people were reported 'for that they have played at a game called fives in the churchyard, and thereby have broken the glass of one of the windows of the church',[89] at a cost of 5s. Similarly the churchwardens of Wimborne complained:

> our church and churchyard were not well kept, for our church was much abused by children playing in it and defiling it; and that the churchyard was often turned and mined up by pigs the last year.[90]

The Dorset gentry were said to be 'endowed with much friendship one towards another, which has been the cause of their frequent matching among themselves'.[91] On the whole that seems to have been more true among the Puritans, who probably felt themselves a coherent minority who had to support each other. Not that there was no intermarrying between the two sides, for example in 1640 Giles, the son and heir of Thomas Strangways of Muston married Margaret, the daughter of Sir Henry Ludlow of Maiden Bradley and sister of the regicide Edmund Ludlow. The year before Sir John Strangways had been a witness at the marriage of Sir Walter Erle's son and heir, Thomas Erle, but the royalist aristocracy of Dorset was split by feuds and rivalries.

The King made a lot of money from wardship, running or leasing out the estates of minors to his own advantage, and also selling off parts of them. After Anthony Ashley Cooper of Wimborne lost both his parents at the age of ten, he became a ward of the Crown, and men like the wealthy John Tregonwell of Milton Abbas and Cooper's own great uncle, Sir Francis Ashley, seized the opportunity to buy up some of the young orphan's lands. At the same time Sir John Bankes, to whom King Charles had just granted Corfe Castle, enclosed part of Holt Heath which Cooper claimed belonged to him. The victim himself many years later remarked 'thus was my estate torn and rent from me before my face by the injustice and oppression of that Court, near relations, and neighbours.'[92] John Tregonwell also seems to have done very well out of his wardship of the estate of Troilus Turberville of Winterborne Whitechurch. So well that when his wardship ended, Tregonwell bought up the whole estate, which he claimed was heavily in debt to him. Tregonwell may well have 'enjoyed his nightcaps, his poached eggs, his chamber pleasures' but it seems unlikely he 'thought no further of the world'.[93]

One of the most powerful men in Dorset was Richard Rogers of Bryanston:

> a proper handsome man, and indeed a very worthy noble gentleman, and one that thought so well of himself as gave him a value with others. The Earls of Hertford had married into his family, which filled his sails with no small vanity.[94]

Rogers tried to woo Ashley Cooper's intended wife, Margaret, the daughter of the moderate Lord Keeper Thomas, Lord Coventry. His attempt to cut out the young Cooper failed, but 'the offer and attempt was so open and avowed that it began a never reconciled feud betwixt us, he having offered me the highest injury, and merely out of malice.'[95] The result was a deep split among some of the leading aristocrats of the county, a split that Ashley Cooper himself deepened by using other men's jealousy of Rogers and

> ...my design to make him to be understood by his greatest and most potent neighbours, Sir John Strangways, Sir Gerard Napier, and Sir John Hele, that all justly thought themselves at least his equals, and were easily brought to apprehend him as one who expected to command us all, and valued himself to the court as already doing so.[96]

The aristocracy of Dorset entered the 1640s deeply divided. Those divisions reflected the situation in the country at large, but the future would soon show that the problems of the nation were far more than a simple power struggle within the ruling class. John Browne cannot have been alone in brooding on 'that evil to come which our sins give us just occasion to fear will speedily overtake us'.[97]

STUMBLING INTO WAR

1640–1642

W hen the eighteen-year-old Anthony Ashley Cooper finally married Margaret Coventry, a detailed inventory was made of everything in his home at Wimborne St Giles. An inventory of the same house sixty years later contained no arms or ammunition at all, but that was far from true in 1639:

> In the chamber out of the kitchen...a fowling piece, four petronels [long horse pistols] one with a velvet case, one bullet piece, two pistol cases... In the hall...eleven halberds, twelve picks, one loading halberd, seven muskets, five pairs of bandoliers, four petronels, three musket rests... In the loft where the armour was...two petronels, one buff coat, three jacks [soldiers' coats].[1]

Over the border in Wiltshire the Earl of Pembroke had an armoury at Wilton House that 'was very full...here were muskets and pikes for [several] hundred men, lances for tilting, complete armour for horsemen, for pikemen etc'.[2]

It was not only the aristocracy that was armed. When Francis Pester, a dairy farmer of Halstock with eight cows and some arable land, died in 1631, his possessions included 'one birding piece, one pike and head piece, one halfmusket furnished'.[3] The weapons were valued at £2 out of a total estate of £168. However around neighbouring Yetminster arms vanish from wills from 1603 until the first gun in 1671, with the possible exception of John Elford of Chetnole, who in 1637 left, among other things, 'a great chest, three pikes and three rakes',[4] though Elford's pikes were probably agricultural implements rather than weapons.

Every county in England had a local militia, the trained bands, who theoretically trained once a month in the use of pike and musket. Basic training for early seventeenth-century soldiers was not easy, with as many as 56 words of commands for a musketeer's drill, and a whole series of complicated manoeuvres to learn. In 1641 trained bands of Dorset, totalled about 3000 men, though for many 'the arms etc. not complete',[5] but in practice it is unlikely that they were any more conscientious than those described by Colonel Ward:

> After a little casual hurrying over their postures, the militia men would load their muskets to give their captain a brave volley of shot at his entrance into his inn, when after having solaced themselves for a while after this brave service, every man repairs home.[6]

Sometimes drunkenness came before drill. During one trained band muster at Poundbury in May 1635 Methuselah Notting, a blacksmith, had been drinking heavily. When his sergeant, William Paty, gave orders, he kept doing the exact opposite. Eventually the officer lost his temper and 'Notting was beaten at the drill by Paty...two or three blows'[7] with a cane. The blacksmith died some days later, though Paty escaped blame as Notting had played at cudgels the evening after the assault.

In September that year, during a muster 'in Fordington field', another member of the Dorset trained bands, John Cross, was unluckily struck on the head

> by shooting of a piece...which gave him a wound in his head the length of an inch and a half, whereof he languished until about three o'clock in the afternoon this day and then died of the wound.[8]

Certainly the performance of the Dorset trained bands when they first came under fire, at Sherborne in September 1642, said little for the quality of their training.

Nevertheless there was a ready supply of experienced soldiers. On mainland Europe war had been raging since 1618, and at least 20,000 Britons are reckoned to have served abroad between 1625 and 1642. Most of the men who would lead the armies of both sides in the Civil War, such as the Earl of Essex, William Waller, Ralph Hopton, Prince Rupert, and Prince Maurice, had learnt their soldiering skills in the Thirty Years War. Walter Erle also

> had been a Low Country soldier, valued himself upon the sieges and service he had been in; his garden was cut into redoubts and works representing these places, his house hung with the maps of those sieges and fights had been the most famous in those parts.[9]

Royalist and parliamentary armies alike also had a crucial stiffening of lower ranking veterans.

Much of the Civil War would be fought over relatively few strongholds that dominated their local areas. Sherborne Castle and Corfe Castle belonged to royalist aristocrats, as did most of the fortified country houses like Chideock House, Hooke Court, Lulworth Castle and Wardour Castle. Sandsfoot, Portland and Brownsea Castles were owned by the Crown, but although they all had heavy guns, none were in a good state, at Portland there was 'no place left for the ordnance but only the gunroom',[10] and the King had been advised to spend over £1000 on repairing them. When Walter Erle surveyed the state of the county's defences in May 1641 he also found an assortment of small cannon in the towns, five in Dorchester, seven in Lyme, 22 in Weymouth and four in Poole. Many towns still retained part of their medieval walls and, as Lyme Regis and Melcombe would prove, even the most indefensible-seeming places could be transformed into formidable bastions of resistance.

As well as weapons and soldiers, seventeenth-century war required one more thing – gunpowder. In point of fact there was a fair amount available in Dorset, as was revealed in 'a note of the store of powder in the magazine in the shirehall taken by Mr William Joliff and Mr Joseph Paty, 27 September 1639'.[11] The county store came to 4364 pounds, with a town store of another 364 pounds. So peaceful had England been that some of the gunpowder scattered through the county, and classified as 'very old but serviceable'[12] had been untouched for over half a century, since the Armada.

The spark that would lead to civil war was lit in Scotland. Charles's attempt to force Archbishop Laud's Book of Common Prayer on the fiercely Calvinist Lowland Scots was a dismal failure, so the King determined to subdue the country by force. His first attempt, in 1639, using the northern trained bands, failed miserably. A year later Charles resolved to try again, but this time with a fresh conscript army from the south. He was encouraged to do this by messages like that of the Lord Lieutenant of Somerset who assured the King that 'all things there are in a very good order, and the trained bands continually exercised and in a readiness to march for your Majesty's service.'[13] Subsequent events would show just how wrong he was.

Dorchester provided two tents for the Earl of Suffolk and his company, as well as three soldiers, however the three men in question were not enthusiastic about their service, and refused to leave:

> Whereas there was an agreement made last Friday that the
> three soldiers that were pressed for the King's Service to go
> away on Monday last, until which time we were content, in
> regard of their poverty, they had 8d. a day, but now seeing
> they are come about again, they are to have no pay at all by
> the day from the town.[14]

Two weeks later the town council heard that people were still being pressed for the army, and there was a warrant for 20 men from the Dorchester division, and 600 from the whole of Dorset. The Deputy Lieutenant 'called the trained companies together and offered them press money' but the men 'refused...saying they never knew the train to march out of their county'.[15]

Finally the Dorset troops marched north against the Scots, who had crossed the border. Among their officers were Troilus Turberville, who had gone to fight on the continent after losing the family estate, and Bullen Reymes of Mappowder, trained as a courtier but unable to find a place in Charles's impoverished court. But the men themselves were bitter and mutinous force.

Near Faringdon in Berkshire Lieutenant William Mohun, had an argument with one of the drummers, who disobeyed an order and struck the officer with his drumstick. Mohun, something of a martinet, drew his sword and cut the man's hand 'almost off'. The result was anarchy. The men turned on Mohun and attacked him, Captain Lewknor and an ensign. The three officers 'opened the window and got astride upon the sign post, where they were pelted with stones'. Lewknor and the ensign got down, but Mohun stayed up there until he was knocked to the ground, where he was beaten, pulled by the hair 'into a common sewer', then dragged about the town before being left for dead. In fact Mohun recovered, but the men returned, knocked his knife out of his hand and 'assaulted him again with their batons till they had knocked out his brains. Then they dragged him again through the town, and at last hanged him upon the pillory.'[16]

Most of the mutineers 'slipped away...towards their own county of Dorset',[17] but 52 were arrested of whom two were hanged and three more condemned to death but later freed. Only 340 of the county's 600 troops reached Yorkshire, and even there

> they thought to do as they want, but for disobedience to their officers in the field as they were mustering, I was forced to take out one of them and...we arquebused him in the sight of the rest, whereupon they were all quiet.[18]

Those who fled were offered a free pardon if they reported back for duty at Selby or Blandford.

Troops from other parts of England also resisted:

> uttering in bold speeches their distaste of the cause, to the astonishment of many, that common people should be sensible of public interest and religion, when lords and gentlemen seemed not to be.[19]

'The soldiers being raw and heartless in this war, and the commanders themselves inexperienced, they were vanquished,'[20] and Charles was left with no choice except to concede all the Scots' demands, as well as paying them a large indemnity. In April Parliament had finally been recalled, to vote money for the war against the Scots. The Earl of Suffolk requested that Dorchester should choose Sir Dudley Carleton as one of its M.P.s. Carleton was very much a man of the court, a former privy councillor and veteran diplomat. Dorchester's response was unenthusiastic and the Earl was told 'they resolve to choose townsmen and some refuse to declare their opinions.'[21] The members actually elected for Dorchester that April were Denis Bond 'very severe and resolved against the church and the court'[22] and Denzil Holles. After three weeks, as a petition was about to be organized against the Scottish war, Charles hastily dissolved Parliament 'and nothing done'.[23]

A few months later, to pay off the Scots, Charles recalled Parliament again. This was to be the most famous, and longest-lived, Parliament in English history, lasting with interruptions almost twenty years. On 3 November 1640, the very day the Long Parliament opened, the Trenchard family was dining in the great hall at Wolfeton. Suddenly the sceptre held by a figure of the King carved on the hall screen fell to the floor and smashed into pieces. Shortly afterwards Sir Thomas Trenchard replaced the excluded royalist Richard Rogers as one of the Dorset M.P.s.

Virtually the first thing the new Parliament did was to arrest Charles's chief advisor, Thomas Wentworth, Earl of Strafford. Archbishop Laud soon followed him into captivity and Parliament debated the entire abolition of the office of bishop, which inspired the bells of Holy Trinity, Dorchester, to ring out 'for the happy success of the Parliament'.[24]

The Roman Catholics were the first group to suffer from the recalling of Parliament. Francis Matthews of Woodsford was fined £40 for recusancy, as were his wife, two of his sons and two of his daughters. The fines helped bankrupt Matthews, who had to mortgage his estate soon after, and was arrested by creditors in 1642. Sir Francis Windebank, one of the two M.P.s for Corfe Castle and a principal secretary of state, was accused of helping papists, but mysteriously he was not instantly arrested and had time to flee. On 21 December William Aylesbury wrote to Edward Hyde, the future Earl of Clarendon:

> you said it was not in the wit of man to save Windebank, and the next day we heard he was at Calais...I am glad the poor creature is safe... He came over in a sloop and with much hazard. For besides that of so little a boat, it was so great a mist that they could not see a boat's length before them.[25]

The proceedings for the impeachment of Strafford opened on 23 March 1641. Denzil Holles was still one of the leaders of the Parliamentary party:

> as he deserved to be, being of more accomplished parts than any of them, and of great reputation... but he would in no degree intermeddle in the counsel or prosecution of the Earl of Strafford, who had married his sister.[26]

However two other Dorset M.P.s were to take important parts in the trial.

Among the 11 managers of the impeachment were Walter Erle and George Digby, the brilliant, handsome, ambitious and vain son of the Earl of Bristol, who was to become one of Charles's most trusted advisers. On 10 November Digby had presented a list of complaints from Dorset, which included objections against ship money and other taxes, pressing soldiers, and changes in religious practices. He then went on to attack the King for 'the deplorable state of this, his kingdom'.[27]

Initially Digby firmly supported the impeachment, and 'he became one of the eminent darlings of the people, as being a person discontented,'[28] but his contempt for the Puritans who made up the bulk of the Parliament soon became very plain. When he sneeringly asked who 'that slovenly fellow', the unknown Oliver Cromwell, was, Cromwell's cousin John Hampden sharply and prophetically retorted 'if we should ever come to have a breach with the King, (which God forbid), I say that sloven in such case will be one of the greatest men of England.'[29]

Digby was already moving from one side to the other over the proposal to end the office of bishop. In opposition to Holles, Erle and most of the other leaders of the House of Commons, Digby protested that 'a multitude of allegations'[30] was not enough reason to abandon episcopacy. The debate was heated. When Sir John Strangways said that to make a parity in the church would necessitate a parity in the Commonwealth itself,

24

Cromwell was so infuriated that only the support of Holles and John Pym prevented him being called before the House to apologize.

Walter Erle's job in the trial of Strafford was to accuse the King's minister of planning to bring over an army from Ireland to conquer England. His attempt to prove the charge crumbled because of lack of witnesses, upon which he 'was very blank and out of countenance'. Digby 'in a very witty and rhetorical speech took off Sir Walter,' and the Queen, who was present, asked who Digby was ridiculing. When she was told his name was Sir Walter Erle, she commented 'that water dog did bark but not bite, but the rest did bite close.'[31] In the circumstances it cannot have been unexpected when 'the bold and waspish young Lord Digby'[32] finally changed sides on the prosecution of Strafford, and declared 'I do before God discharge myself to the utmost of my power; and do, with a clear conscience, wash my hands of this man's blood.'[33] It made no difference, on 21 April 1641 the House of Commons voted 204 to 59 for Strafford's death. Copies of Digby's plea for mercy, which had been printed and circulated in London, were ordered to be burnt by the common hangman. Digby unconvincingly excused himself by saying that his half-brother, Sir Lewis Dyve, and his cousin John Digby, had had the speech printed without his permission.

The next move by the Commons was to draw up what came to be called the Protestation. The entire House swore:

> to maintain and defend, so far as lawfully I may, with my life, power and estate, the true Reformed Protestant religion...as also the power and privileges of Parliament, the lawful rights and liberties of the subject.[34]

Subsequently it was resolved that anyone in the country who did not make the Protestation was unfit to bear office. Between February and March 1642 most of the county of Dorset did so.

Under pressure from a mob that surrounded Whitehall, the King signed Strafford's death warrant. Two and a half weeks after Strafford's execution Sir John Strangways, 'a wise, crafty experienced man, but extremely narrow in expenses, a great enemy of the Puritans',[35] protested that he and the 59 who had voted in favour of Strafford 'went in fear of their lives, great threats being offered to them'.[36] Like almost half the House, Strangways had actually not voted, being at home in Dorset on the day in question. Nevertheless the man who thirteen years before had been put in prison for his resistance to the Crown, and had demanded a remonstrance of grievances against Charles, now had a reputation as one of the most fanatical royalists. His name actually stood at the top of a list read out by 'the rabble of apprentices and inferior persons of the city... under the style of persons disaffected to the Kingdom'.[37] Digby, in the meantime, was raised to the House of Lords as Baron Digby, and John Browne of Frampton took his seat in the Commons. Two royalist M.P.s, Rogers and Digby, had been replaced by two Puritans, Trenchard and Browne.

Meanwhile, to pay for the Scottish war, Parliament had voted for the lay subsidy. This was partly a tax on wealth, partly a poll tax, and it seems to have been much evaded. The commissioners, who in Dorset included Sir Walter Erle, Thomas Tregonwell and Thomas Erle, often let off their friends and neighbours very lightly. Oliver Lawrence and Thomas Thornhurst of Affpuddle were taxed on lands worth £2 a year, which was a ridiculous figure, almost certainly less than a hundredth of the true value.

October 1641 saw war erupt in Ireland. The persecuted Roman Catholic majority rose up and massacred several thousand Protestants, with many more drowning or dying of cold, hunger and ill-treatment. Both sides in England agreed that an army must be raised to reconquer the island, but the parliamentary leaders were terrified that the army raised for Ireland could also be used to crush them. They forced through the Grand Remonstrance, a history of the wrongs suffered by the kingdom under Charles, with suggestions for reform. Since the death of Strafford, Denzil Holles had resumed his place as one of the leaders of the House, and as well as carrying up to the Lords the impeachment of Laud, he made a major speech in favour of the Remonstrance. Then on 27 December, a day when fighting broke out in Westminster Hall, Holles pressed for the impeachment of Digby and his father, the Earl of Bristol.

Digby, who had 'a confidence in himself which sometimes intoxicated, and transported, and exposed him'[38] retaliated by giving Charles some catastrophic advice, which the King promptly followed. On 3 January 1642 the Attorney General rose in the House of Lords and accused Holles, four other M.P.s, and one member of the Lords, of high treason. That morning the lodgings of Holles and John Pym had been invaded and searched by the King's men. The next afternoon the King himself with armed men at his back, hurried to the House of Commons to arrest the five Members. When he arrived, the door was blocked open so the M.P.s could see some of the soldiers 'holding up their swords, and some holding their pistols ready cocked, near the said door'.[39] Charles demanded to know where the five Members were, but the Speaker, William Lenthall famously replied:

> May it please your Majesty, I have neither eyes to see, nor tongue to speak in this place, but as the House is pleased to direct me, whose servant I am.[40]

In any case it was too late, Holles, Pym, William Strode, Arthur Haslerig and John Hampden had slipped away. 'All my birds have flown'[41] said Charles at last, bitterly. Digby offered to search the City for the accused men, but the King refused.

Six days later the King and his family left London. The day after, the five Members returned to wild public enthusiasm. As for Digby, he fled to Holland, pursued by the invective of John Browne, who warned the House of Commons of 'the manifold eminent dangers which are likely to fall upon that county [Dorset] by reason of Digby's escape'. He went on to fulminate against 'papists, recusants and other of his confederates' and 'their multiplicity of armour, muskets and other ammunition, every particular man exceeding, having greater and larger store than any neighboring Protestant'.[42] On 4 February the sheriffs and justices of the peace in Dorset sent a petition to the House of Commons concerning gatherings of 'popish recusants' at the houses of, among others, Sir George Morton and John Arundell, 'which in these times of danger may prove to be very inconvenient'. The House of Commons responded with permission for Thomas Trenchard and others to search the said houses and 'seize such arms and munitions as they shall there find'.[43] Holles warned the House that Digby was gathering troops and arms, and everywhere came rumours of war.

While these epoch-making events were transfixing London, 'the sink of all the ill humours of the Kingdom',[44] most of the people of Dorset were probably more concerned with outbreaks of plague on the Somerset border. Although Dorchester sent a gift of £60 10s. to strongly Puritan Taunton, the council also made sure that

> a ward shall be put at every entrance into town to keep out
> and not admit into the town...all or any person or per-
> sons...from Langport, Ilchester or any other near place,
> because of the pestilence.[45]

Bridport too took measures to prevent the spread of plague.

Other problems were also increasing. In January 1640 it was remarked in Dorchester that 'beggars do now begin to go abroad about the town,'[46] while there were steadily worsening problems in getting people to pay their tithes. The collection of the royal taxes was even less successful. By 1640 the combined influence of ship money and other taxes, such as those 'upon all things of most common and necessary use, such as soap, salt, wine, leather, sea-coal and many others of that kind',[47] even including innkeepers cooking and serving meat, had inflamed such resentment that only £300 had been collected from the year's demand of £6000. Bailiffs were attacked and driven off, people would not buy distrained goods, and even the mayors themselves refused to pay. In January 1641 the town of Weymouth sent Matthew Allen 'to ride to London to solicit the House of Parliament concerning the grievances of the town, and he is to have 3s. 4d. the day for his expenses there'.[48]

After the outbreak of the Irish war there was also a steady flow of money to the Protestant refugees. On 27 June 1642 Milton Abbas paid out 6s. to 'poor Irish people',[49] and even a year later, when Dorset had enough problems of its own, the parish still paid out 1s. 6d. to 'Irish people'. Dorchester also contributed generously. In July 1642 the town authorities gave one Irishwoman £2, while on the same day the widow 'of a certain man in Wimborne killed by thieves and robbers'[50] only got 15s. Five months earlier £3 had been granted to the family of Captain Peter de Salanova 'which came lately out of the kingdom of Ireland for fear of the rebels'.[51] De Salanova, who had captured a ship which sank in Weymouth harbour in 1629, repaid the generosity of Puritan Dorchester by faithfully serving as 'apothecary and surgeon-general for all the garrisons and soldiers belonging to this county',[52] throughout the Civil War. In 1645 he was given a down payment of £20 for his services as well as his pay, while in March 1647 he was paid £6 'for salves and medicines which were used at Corfe Castle about wounded soldiers',[53] and at the same time his continuing value was clearly revealed when his pay, which had been cut to 20s. a week, was rapidly returned to 'his accustomed pay of £3 per week'.[54]

The Dorset trained bands had probably never been an impressive force, but in the winter of 1641-2 their condition was clearly not good, especially as many of the officers seemed, at least temporarily, to have lost their commands, perhaps because of political uncertainties. On 24 January 1642 Dorchester council:

> agreed that a letter be sent to Mr D.Bond, our burgess of
> Parliament, to desire him to procure Mr John Hill, alderman
> of our borough, to be made captain of our band of soldiers.[55]

John Hill was an ironmonger, a former mayor and investor in the Dorchester Company. He almost certainly had little or no experience of warfare, but the important thing was that he was reliable, one of the Puritan rulers of the town.

Military matters were coming more and more to the fore. Over the winter, Dorchester council had ordered protective shutters, or 'window leaves', to be made for the back parts of the shire hall, and that:

> one discreet person shall every Lord's day during service
> and sermon watch on the tower of St Peter's and view the
> country round about. And that the townsmen shall be
> moved to provide all their arms in readiness for defence of
> the town.[56]

Poole too was taking precautions, and in January 1642 an order was made for to be watched the town by three men, including a gunner, during the day, and eight men at night.

The following month the House of Commons received a petition from 'the Knights, Gentlemen, Ministers, Freeholders etc. of Dorset' remarking that 'Distractions and fears increase among us more and more' and 'the Kingdom is not yet put into such a posture of defence as these dangerous times require.' The petition ended by complaining 'we have no Captains appointed over our trained bands' and asking for 'more arms in supply of those many that were taken away and lost in the Northern Expedition'.[57] Then in May the House of Commons wrote to the mayor of Dorchester, John Allambridge, speaking of the inhabitants' 'affections for maintenance of the religion, laws, liberties and peace of the Kingdom' and requesting a loan:

> towards the present payment of the army [in Ireland], which
> are even ready to mutiny for want of money, and for the pro-
> vision of that sum...which is shortly to be paid to our
> brethren in Scotland.[58]

Dorchester demonstrated its fidelity to Parliament by raising a £200 loan.

Like every other county in the country except solidly parliamentarian Middlesex, Dorset's M.P.s were split between the King's party and Parliament's. The division of Dorset M.P.s seems at that time to have been 12 to seven in favour of Parliament, but large stretches of the county were to demonstrate fierce royalism. John Aubrey, who lived only a few miles from the Dorset border in Wiltshire, had his own theory as to exactly why people in different parts of his county divided so sharply into two sides:

> In North Wiltshire...(a dirty clayey country)...they are phleg-
> matic, skins pale and livid, slow and dull, heavy of spirit;
> hereabout is but little tillage or hard labour, they only milk
> the cows and make cheese...these circumstances make them
> melancholy, contemplative and malicious...and by the same
> reason they are generally more apt to be fanatics....On the
> downs where 'tis all upon tillage and where the shepherds
> labour hard, their flesh is hard, their bodies strong; being
> weary after hard labour, they have not leisure to read and
> contemplate of religion, but go to bed to their rest, to rise
> betime the next morning to their labour.[59]

Certainly there is little doubt that the downlands of Dorset, for example around Blandford, Purbeck and Portland, did incline strongly to the King.

Clarendon, however, had no doubt where the fundumental blame lay:

> this strange wild-fire among the people was not so much and
> so furiously kindled by the breath of the Parliament as of
> their clergy, who both administered fuel and blowed the
> coals in the houses too. These men, having crept into, and at
> last driven out all learned and orthodox men from the pul-
> pits, had, as before remembered, from the beginning of this
> Parliament, under the notion of reformation and extirpating
> of popery, infused seditious inclinations into the hearts of
> men against the present government of the church, with
> many libellous invectives against the state too.[60]

Whatever the cause, the spring and summer of 1642 saw England tottering on the brink of disaster. Parliament had made sure of London, with its great supply of arms. The two other major magazines in the country were at Hull and Portsmouth. It was with his eyes on the former of these that Charles arrived at York and set up his court there. Not long after, Sir Lewis Dyve, Digby's half-brother, entered Hull and announced that the King and a troop of horse were about to pay a visit. Sir John Hotham, the governor, hesitated, then took the first step of open rebellion by refusing to allow him in. Tension ratcheted up as the two sides exchanged recriminations. Elsewhere:

> fears and jealousies had so generally possessed the
> Kingdom, that a man could hardly travel through any mar-
> ket town, but he should be asked whether he were for the
> King or Parliament.[61]

Nevertheless one party was still trying to find a settlement, and one of its leaders was Sir John Bankes, Charles's Attorney General, the owner of Corfe Castle, and 'a grave and learned man'.[62] Over May and June he maintained a constant correspondence with several of the leading moderates in Parliament, trying desperately to find some common ground. On 21 May, Denzil Holles wrote blandly to him:

> I am confident the Parliament will most readily cast itself at the King's feet with all faithful and loyal submission, upon the first appearance of change in his Majesty, that he will forsake those councils which carry him on to so high a dislike and opposition to their proceedings.[63]

The same day Bankes wrote to Giles Green, the M.P. for Corfe Castle:

> I have adventured far to speak my mind freely according to my conscience and...the King is extremely offended with me...I have studied all means which way matters may be brought to a good conclusion between the King and the Houses, all highways and ways of force will be destructive; and if we should have civil wars, it would make us a miserable people, and might introduce foreign powers; therefore there is no other way left but the way of accommodation.[64]

Bankes's correspondence also included letters to several parliamentary leaders, not least the man who would be Lord General of Parliament's armies, the Earl of Essex, of whom Clarendon remarked:

> a weak judgement and some vanity, and some pride, will hurry a man into as unwarrantable and as violent attempts, as the greatest and most unlimited and insatiable ambition will do.[65]

However the Attorney General gained little in return except complaints about the great numbers of horsemen the King was gathering in the North. The strong Puritan, Viscount Saye and Sele, whose daughter was married to Sir Walter Erle's son and heir, Thomas Erle, wrote coldly from London:

> there is little hope of any accommodation in that way we are in; believe it my Lord, your cavaliers (as they are called) do much mistake in persuading themselves or others that there is any fear here.[66]

Bankes had also tried to persuade the King to return to London, and briefly looked like succeeding, but then Charles changed his mind.

Although the entire court in York, including Bankes, signed a declaration denying any intention of making war, few parliamentarians believed it. Probably not even the King himself did, for at the end of June he tried to place one of his men in charge of the navy. The move was foiled by Parliament, who promoted the Puritan Earl of Warwick, and the royalist cause suffered another blow. Gradually more and more people must have been realizing what was happening to the nation. Two years earlier Kenelm Digby had remarked that 'people are strangely disaffected and untoward,'[67] now there were:

continual rumours of civil wars in this Kingdom, no discourse almost stirring, but what has possessed the subjects' hearts with fear and terror by reason of the continual expectation of blood and mischief.[68]

The possession of these stores of arms and ammunition became absolutely crucial as the certainty of armed struggle grew. In Dorset many of these lay under the control of the great royalist-leaning families, but as most Dorset town councils were pro-Parliament, one source of weapons was available to Parliament: the town magazines. On 1 July the Dorchester store of powder, lead and match was moved to the town brewhouse for greater security. An ordinance demanding that Poole and other towns preserve their magazines for parliamentary use met with ready response, and on 19 July Parliament sent out another ordinance ordering:

that the mayor, aldermen and capital burgesses of the town of Dorchester, in the county of Dorset, or any three of them, shall have power to assemble and call together all and singular the inhabitants of the said town...and them array, weapon, train, exercise and put in readiness...for the suppression of all forceable attempts that shall be made against the said town, and to hinder the surprisal of the ordnance and magazine there.[69]

Nine days later Parliament 'being informed of divers warlike preparations lately made and many threatening speeches given out in the county of Dorset' gave Denzil Holles, Thomas Trenchard, Walter Erle and John Browne authority to 'arm, train and put in readiness all and every the inhabitant of the county fit for the wars'.[70]

The King, still poised outside Hull, had sent the Marquess of Hertford to the West as 'his lieutenant general of all the western parts of the kingdom, with power to levy such a body of horse and foot as he found necessary'.[71] William Seymour, first Marquess of Hertford was fifty years old, a quiet apparently rather uninteresting man:

conversant in books, both in the Latin and Greek languages...so wholly given up to a country life, where he lived in splendour, that he had an aversion, and even an unaptness for business.[72]

In his youth he had secretly married Arabella Stuart, a cousin of King James I. It was a marriage that showed either massive naiveté on Hertford's part, or else an ambition that never resurfaced, for both of them had tenuous claims to the throne. The King was furious and Arabella, who was caught fleeing in man's costume, died broken-spirited, if not mad, in the Tower of London. Hertford too spent time in the Tower, and never defied his monarch again.

Hertford's chief lieutenant in these early weeks, Sir Ralph Hopton, was a very different sort of man. A stern God-fearing disciplinarian who 'abhorred enough the licence and the levities with which he saw too many corrupted'.[73] He was an extremely wealthy Somerset landowner, and a fierce royalist who earlier in the year had justified the King's attempt to seize the five Members, and had been put in the Tower for two weeks by the House of Commons because he did 'contradict everything without scruple'.[74] In other words he accused the Commons 'that they seemed to ground an opinion of the King's apostasy upon a less evidence that would serve to hang a fellow for stealing a horse.'[75] Despite only limited experience in soldiering on the continent (which had included carrying King Charles's sister, the Queen of Bohemia, on his horse during her flight from Prague) Hopton was to be one of the ablest of all the royalist commanders.

Hertford's job was to raise forces by royal commissions of array, which allowed him:

> to levy and raise forces for the defence of the Protestant religion, our person, the two Houses of Parliament, and for the laws of the land, the liberty and property of the subject, and privilege of Parliament.[76]

However the commissions were rather ridiculously written in Latin, allowing his enemies to translate them 'into what English they pleased' and persuade people 'that all should be, upon the matter, no better than slaves'.[77] Not that Hertford himself was pessimistic. On 11 July he had written to Queen Henrietta Maria:

> His Majesty's affairs are now I hope in a prosperous way. And the affections of his people break out every day more and more, who begin to have their eyes open, and will I believe no longer be deluded with imaginary fears and jealousies.[78]

Once he had gathered an army Hertford's orders were to relieve Colonel Goring, who had been put in charge of the crucial garrison of Portsmouth by Parliament and had then declared for the King. Subsequently he lost the town with barely a fight, partly at least because he had wasted the money he was given (by both sides) to strengthen the fortifications 'in good fellowship, or lost it at play; the temptation of either of which vices, he never could resist'.[79]

However Hertford was sublimely confident in his own ability to come to Goring's help 'without any great difficulty...And hey then down go they'.[80]

It was not going to be so easy. Arriving at Marlborough, on his own estate, Hertford discovered that people had broken down the church doors and seized the magazine, which they refused to hand back to him. The royalists were too few to do anything about it, and rode on to Somerset. 'And now the fire began to break out in the West.'[81]

Chapter Three

THE FIRST SHOTS
JULY 1642–JULY 1643

Traditionally, the first blood of the war was spilt when a party of royalist horse was driven out of Manchester on 15 July 1642. The earliest outbreak of violence in Dorset took place soon after. One Sunday morning Robert Morton, who had been ordered to fortify the town of Wareham for Parliament, rode to the Town Cross and began to read a proclamation. The rector, William Wake, an 'honest, merry and true-hearted parson...both a good scholar and a good soldier, and an excellent drum-beating parson',[1] begged the crowd not to listen, and for his pains was hit with a pistol butt. Next day the quarrel flared up afresh and Morton shot Wake, then cut him on the head with his sword until, in the words of Wake's son, Captain William Wake:

> one Susan Bolke, a servant of my father's, being in a field
> hard by, fetching of peas, came and with her corn-pike made
> at Morton; who rode from her and was by her pursued into
> his own doors.[2]

Wake, whose 'blood was the first spilled in opposition to the rebels in the West of England', survived but after recovering he was arrested by Major Sydenham and, together with Mr Ware, Mr Gardiner and Mr Moon, put in the disease-ridden prison at Dorchester. Here the four men:

> taking a quantity of plague waters, threw out a slimy scab all
> over their bodies, which was supposed saved their lives; but
> nothwithstanding purging and what else they were advised
> to do, my father had for a year after several blotches and
> boils that rose and broke upon him.[3]

Another minister from Wareham, James Crouch, who was rector of Hinton Martel as well, was also imprisoned, first in the county gaol at Dorchester then at Weymouth, before escaping to join the King's army. On 4 January 1643 the congregation of St Mary's Wareham, petitioned Parliament that 'James Crouch, their curate, is now absent from his cure by reason of his restraint in Dorchester for traducing and scandalizing Parliament' and asking that he should be replaced by John Sacheverell 'he being a man both sound in doctrine and of unblameable life and conversation'.[4]

Serious bloodshed arrived in the region at the beginning of August 1642, after Hertford, Sir Ralph Hopton and Lord Digby's brother John Digby, (who would be one of the very last royalists to surrender and finally became a Roman Catholic priest in France), tried to use the King's commission of array to raise troops in Somerset. The House of Commons demanded that Hertford's men 'should return home to their houses if not, that then they would take it as an insurrection, and endeavour to repress it'.[5] On 1 August the short-tempered Hopton arrested two parliamentary leaders. 'And thus innocently began this cursed war in those parts.'[6]

There was widespread hostility to the royalists in Somerset, and despite Hertford's order to 'forbear any hostile act', between 80 and 140 of his men confronted perhaps 600 Parliament-supporters at Marshall's Elm, near Somerton. 'Sir John Stawell, using many sober persuasions to them that they would not by their advancing begin a civil war, but prevailed not.'[7] One cavalier volley and a cavalry charge was enough to inflict 27 deaths and take 60 prisoners, some of whose lives were only saved by Sir John Paulet, soon to be the Marquis of Winchester, telling his men not 'to spill the blood of the poor fellows'.[8]

This easy victory solved little, for the Somerset royalists were menaced by a huge and growing parliamentary force, at least 12,000 strong, who demonstrated their Puritan sympathies by lying 'all that night upon the hill, fasting and in cold, spending the time in prayers and singing of psalms'.[9] It was, to all intents and purposes, a popular uprising. Although this great army was almost entirely untrained and armed only with pitchforks and similar implements, the massively outnumbered royalists had little alternative but to scuttle hastily away south into Dorset, bringing war in their train.

Hertford, John Digby, the 'haughty and obstinate'[10] Sir John Stawell, and Hopton, all of whom Parliament wanted arrested as delinquents, led their 500 horsemen to the Digby stronghold of Sherborne, a 'finely seated and well watered' town which 'for largeness, frequency of inhabitants, and quick markets, gives place to none in these parts'.[11] Having garrisoned the Old Castle, Hertford wrote to Poole, promising

> to be so noble and generous as to spend £200 a week there,
> and fortify that town most strongly for their greater security
> and safeguard. But it seemed that those birds were too old
> than so easily to be caught with such chaff.

The mayor of Poole, Henry Harbin, answered briskly that 'they would not trouble his lordship to send any forces, but if he did send any without their consent, they would deny them entrance.'[12] Hertford received a similar reply to his blandishments from Dorchester, where the town council ordered 'that there shall be a strong watch kept in the town by night and ward by day, to hinder or stop any insurrection or tumults in the town' and that 'the gates and wards of the town shall be made fast every night at eight of the clock.'[13] Meanwhile the royalists damaged their reputation by getting involved in a scuffle at Sherborne market in which a townsman was killed.

The sheriff of Dorset, Edward Lawrence, had joined Hertford in Sherborne, but his efforts to raise the county in support of the King met with little success. When he ordered Dorchester to stop mustering forces and to demolish the fortifications that had been put up, Parliament swiftly countered with a letter to the mayor and aldermen assuring them that:

training and exercising and defending the said town and magazine, as aforesaid, shall be held by both Houses to do a service acceptable and beneficial to the King and Kingdom.[14]

After Lawrence ignored an order to explain his actions, Parliament demanded that he too should be arrested and sent to London. Meanwhile his son, Robert Lawrence, arrived in Wareham with a commission to raise and lead 100 men, but he was taken prisoner by the townspeople, though he subsequently escaped.

While both sides busily tried to establish themselves, collect money, raise recruits and gather information, the summer assizes in Dorchester took place as usual. But the already strained atmosphere grew fervid with the trial of two Roman Catholic priests. After an order that all Catholic priests should immediately leave the country, Lady Blanche Arundell's chaplain, Hugh Green of Chideock who used the alias Ferdinando Brooke, and Father Browne, tried to take ship from Lyme. But they had delayed too long and were arrested. Browne recanted at the foot of the gallows and was immediately released, but Green would not and, on 18 August, at Maumbury Rings he was hung, drawn and quartered by the local barber-surgeon, Matthew Barfoot. The crowd played football with the priest's severed head, put sticks in the eyes, ears, nose and mouth, and savagely attacked some local Catholics who tried to take away the dismembered corpse. There was however a widespread belief that the town had been punished by God with the plague of 1597 (in which 44 people died) after displaying a Catholic priest's head on the town gates, so eventually Green's mutilated head was buried.

The royalists at Sherborne, who had been joined by Sir John Berkeley, were growing steadily more confident, and one Dorchester man complained 'we dare not send seven miles abroad, for fear of the cavaliers, who lie at Sherborne, pillaging, robbing and killing like so many sons of Hell.'[15] Another Dorchester man, George Leddoze, was seized by the royalists and accused of being a spy. Having bravely made clear that he was a parliamentary supporter, and warned his captors of the great guns in Dorchester that would be used against them, Leddoze had to endure an anti-parliamentarian rant from Hopton, before being released.

Meanwhile the war had officially begun. King Charles, on his way south to try to help Goring in Portsmouth, the job Hertford had been supposed to do, stopped at Nottingham and, on 22 August, set up his standard and proclaimed the Commons and their soldiers as traitors. Few recruits joined him and the royal standard was blown down in the night and could not be set up again for three days.

Typically, Charles then had second thoughts and sent a fresh appeal for peace to Parliament 'in a softer and calmer style than his Majesty had been accustomed to for some months'.[16] The message was entrusted to the Earls of Southampton and Dorset, Sir John Colepepper the Chancellor of the Exchequer, and the Dorset knight Sir William Uvedale of Horton, 'whom his Majesty gave leave, under that pretence to intend the business of his own fortune'.[17] The King's message was rapidly rejected by Parliament. It was too late to turn aside from the road to war.

Aside from Hertford at Sherborne, there were scattered Dorset aristocrats prepared to hold their own areas for the King, notably Sir John Strangways at Abbotsbury, Sir Richard Rogers at Bryanston, and Lady Bankes at Corfe Castle. All of them probably agreed that 'the security of the nobility and gentry depends upon the strength of the Crown, otherwise popular government would rush in like a torrent upon them.'[18] However to join one of the gathering armies was another question. It was highly expensive to raise a troop of soldiers and few could afford to do it. Abraham Highmore, the son of the rector of Winterborne Stickland, apparently sold seven manors and a mansion house from his family estate in Cumberland to raise and equip a volunteer corps for the King.

Throughout rural England it was largely activist minorities that swung their counties either to King or Parliament. In Dorset the Puritan leaders had been better prepared and moved faster. Sir Walter Erle efficiently made sure of Weymouth, Lyme and Wareham, as well as arranging the handover of the royal castle of Portland. He may also have placed a garrison in Giles Strangways's manor at Bockhampton outside Dorchester. Giles Strangways, the eldest son of Sir John Strangways, wrote a letter to the parliamentary committee of Dorset, insisting that he had done nothing against the garrison, and claiming there was no significance to his 'opening a door in dead of night'. Whatever had actually been going on, the parliamentarians clearly took it very seriously, and Giles was left to complain bitterly that:

> Captain Starre has been here with me this afternoon to show me an order from the Council of War signed by the clerk alone, whereby he had power given him to put myself and all my servants out of my house on the morrow... I know not how to dispose of myself any otherwise, nor have means to do it, and I hope I shall not be put to such extremity as to lie in the streets.[19]

The idea that the heir of one of the richest men in Dorset would 'lie in the streets' must have impressed no one. Certainly the parliamentarians had every reason to suspect the inclinations of the Strangways family. Within a few weeks of the outbreak of war Giles, or more probably his brother James, was involved in fighting near Worcester, 'Sir John Strangways' son was taken prisoner, who is exchanged for Captain Wingate.'[20]

Meanwhile Sir Walter Erle and the Dorset trained bands marched to join the young Earl of Bedford, Lord Lieutenant of Somerset and descendant of a Weymouth wine trader. A few weeks before Bedford had been launching amateurish raids on the houses of his royalist neighbours in Hertfordshire, and sending the proceeds to Parliament. Now, with Denzil Holles as his second-in-command, he led a large parliamentary army, perhaps 7000 strong with 18 pieces of ordnance. However his soldiers were poorly equipped and entirely unready for the experience of battle. On 2

September this unwieldy force arrived before Sherborne Castle, where a thousand royalists awaited them, and where Bedford found himself face to face with a problem that was to prove all too common.

Especially during the first year or so, the English Civil War, unlike the wars that were currently raging in Germany, Ireland and Scotland, offered very little which could determine which side an individual would be on. Many changed sides, and one result was that the war was, by and large, fought in a relatively humane spirit. Another was frequent divisions among relatives. Among the heavily intermarried Dorset aristocracy probably as many as one family in three had split loyalties. The royalist Hertford was the brother-in-law of Parliament's Lord General, the Earl of Essex, while Holles had at least one royalist cousin and a wavering brother, but the immediate problem was that the Earl of Bedford's sister had married George Digby. One of the first things the parliamentary commander did on arriving at Sherborne was therefore to send a message to his sister Ann, telling her to quit her house, the New Castle built by Walter Raleigh, as he had orders to demolish it. Lady Digby, who would later become a highly successful wine importer, working almost to her eightieth birthday, reacted in a way that was to become typical of a host of Civil War heroines. She rode to her brother's tent and told him that 'if he persisted in his intention, he should find his sister's bones buried in the ruins.'[21] Bedford hastily backed down and, after replying to Hertford's improbable challenge to a personal duel with a promise that 'he would be ready, when the business of Parliament should be over, to wait upon the Marquis when he should require it,'[22] the parliamentary commander turned his attention to storming the Old Castle.

The initial prospects seemed good. Hertford's latest appeal for volunteers to fight for the King had exposed widespread inertia, netting only 12 men from Somerset and ten more from the Blackmore Vale. Then several little Sherborne boys were caught playing with fireworks and, on being asked how they had made them, a certain John Pelham led Bedford's men straight to a deep cellar containing Digby's secret arms cache, 'barrels of gunpowder to the number of 200, being overlaid and covered with abundance of old casks, faggots and other lumber',[23] as well as 300 muskets, 1500 assorted other guns, pikes and lances.

However, when the parliamentarians did attack, Hopton's musketeers, lurking in the town gardens, beat them off with some ease. Subsequent night raids by the royalists added to the confusion and panic:

> It is the terriblest thing in the world to have an enemy fall into one's quarters by night, and nothing more resembles the last Resurrection and judgement than to see so many people together rise up naked, and run to the hills and woods to hide them.[24]

An attempt to batter the castle into submission failed because the roundhead cannon were too far away to have much effect, and Hertford's men retaliated, using the castle guns to bombard the parliamentarian camp, which 'did some small execution upon them, but cast such a fright upon the rest that it was credibly reported 800 of their foot ran away from them that night'.[25] They were not the first to go, nor the last. In three days Bedford's force shrank to less than a quarter of its original size, 'not that they deserted the cause, but being men who had wives and estates, were loth to hazard their lives in an offensive war.'[26] On the morning of Tuesday 6 September, the parliamentary army cut its losses and fell back in disarray, harrassed by the triumphant royalists.

The embarrassed Bedford and Holles quickly wrote a letter to the Earl of Essex, attempting to explain away the fiasco. They claimed that few officers would obey commands, the moment bullets flew nearly everyone fell flat on their bellies, the royalist cannon made men run 'as if the Devil had been in them', and it only took five or six deaths to make half the troops flee, while the other half were about to follow. It was also 'the fourth extreme cold night we have been without any sleep'.[27]

Encouraged by news of 300 reinforcements from Blandford under his cousin, Sir Richard Rogers, Hopton resolved to pursue Bedford's retreating army. Shortly after lunchtime the next day he took up a position on Babylon Hill near Yeovil, where his men, who included a company led by Captain George Morton, spent the afternoon shooting down at the parliamentarians on Yeovil Bridge, without great effect. With the approach of sunset Hopton decided to retreat, but a party of parliamentarians had slipped out of Yeovil unnoticed, and now charged straight up the hill at the royalists.

The war was still very much an amateur affair. The royalists had carefully laid an ambush for the roundheads at a narrow place near the top, 'six musketeers on each side the way to entertain us, but they missed us all',[28] while a cavalier captain named Hussey had gone into battle 'clad in plush'.[29] One troop of attackers panicked after their leader was killed, but two other troops, supported by foot soldiers, drove the royalists back. 'The truth is in very short time, all the horse on both sides were in a confusion,' said Hopton. 'In this extreme confusion, Sir Ralph Hopton was enforced to make good the retreat with a few officers and gentlemen that rallied to him.'[30] The parliamentary view was very different: 'God cast upon the cavaliers a spirit of fearfulness, that they ran like mice into every hole.'[31] Only darkness saved the royalists from a sharp defeat, and as it was overconfidence had cost Hopton 50 or 60 men, including the overconfident Captain Hussey, compared with 15 or 16 parliamentary losses.

The fighting in Dorset was still focused almost entirely around Sherborne, and for twelve days the two sides fenced cautiously, trying to gather their own reinforcements and intercept those of their enemies. The cavaliers may have expected the war to spread rapidly as on 17 September the Roman Catholic Lord Paulet, 'a cunning crafty old fox',[32] was reported to have made a most bloodthirsty speech to his soldiers:

> when you come to the Puritanical towns of Taunton,
> Crewkerne, Bristol, Dorchester and Exeter, then let your

swords cruel it without difference of age, sex, or degree. Let
those three counties of Somerset, Dorset, and Devonshire be
fattened with the blood and carcasses of the inhabitants, that
they may not make head against us.[33]

Probably this report was completely invented, part of the anti-Catholic
propaganda being assiduously and successfully spread by Parliament
and its supporters.

From his headquarters in Dorchester Bedford opened the siege afresh
on 19 September. Three cannons sent from Weymouth proved decisive.
Having learnt from his previous failure, Bedford moved them as close to
the castle walls as he dared and was rewarded when they blasted away a
portion of the battlements, a cannon, and some of the wall. The cavaliers,
deciding 'the castle of Sherborne being indeed not at all defensible in
itself, nor in any measure provided for a real siege',[34] asked for a parley
and shortly afterwards a letter wrapped around an arrow was shot over
the wall to Bedford, offering to surrender the castle in exchange for a
peaceful retreat. If the offer was refused, Hertford threatened to 'place
Lord Bedford's sister upon the battlements, to serve as a flag of defiance
to him and all his followers'.[35]

Bedford accepted the peace terms, and Hertford fell back to Minehead,
from where he sailed to South Wales, while Hopton, Berkeley and John
Digby turned south with a small force to try to raise Cornwall for the
King. After an abortive attempt to destroy the military usefulness of
Sherborne castle by hiring Purbeck quarriers to break down the walls,[36]
Bedford and Holles rejoined the Earl of Essex and the main parliamentary
army.

With the departure of the royalist force from Sherborne, and the arrival
of autumn and, more importantly, harvest time, life in Dorset seemed to
return to normal. William Constantine, one of the M.P.s for Poole, wrote
to the House of Commons that

this county was in itself divided, for a main part of the chief
gentry laboured with all their industry to bring war into
their own houses, and to supply the Marquess of Hertford
with men, victuals and ammunition, but God...frustrated
their endeavours and we see their party vanished.[37]

But no one was taking peace for granted. At Wimborne bars were put on
the doors and windows of the minster, while Lyme raised a volunteer
company, and in Weymouth a garrison of 40 men was established and a
fourteenth-century church, commandingly placed 70 steps above the
street, was converted into the Chapel Fort. In Dorchester precautions
were made against street-fighting, the watch was armed with pikes, hal-
berds and muskets, and wardens of proven reliability were put on all the
gates of the town. The wardens were to 'open all the gates at break of day,
and to shut all the back gates at candle lighting, and the east, west and
south main gates between eight and nine at night'.[38]

The total cost of the defences of Dorchester was enormous: over £19,000.

Much was raised by loans from local merchants and dignitaries like John Fitzjames who lent £1300, William White £1100 and John Browne £420, but roughly a quarter of the total was paid by grants from Parliament. In contrast Wareham spent £60 on fortifying the town during the first month of the war, and Bridport a mere £10, though the council did turn aside from quarrelling over the neglect of the harbour to agree

> that the inhabitants that have muskets shall watch at night in turn...that a watch-house shall be created at each bridge, that eight of the commoners shall watch at night, eight by day, two at each of the three bridges.[39]

Even little Milton Abbas paid out £2 7s. 6d. 'for the town watching which was agreed upon day and night watching'.[40] As for the parliamentary forces, most were quartered on 'such towns here as had shown themselves violently ill-affected', where 'the foot are something violent upon the papists, several of whose houses they have endeavoured to plunder.'[41]

Many individuals too were taking precautions. When John Henley of Colway rode off to join the parliamentary garrison at Lyme, Mrs Henley's maid, Ursula Tanner, buried the family money bags, which contained at least £200, in a field, then took the Henley children to join her father, John Tanner, at their family house in Wootton Fitzpaine, where he was still living twenty-two years later.

Among the first victims of the Civil War in Dorset were those members of the clergy who had supported Archbishop Laud. Gilbert Ironside, rector of Winterbourne Steepleton and Winterbourne Abbas, was a fierce critic of Puritans and of John White in particular, whom he had accused of causing 'disaffection in the present government, turbulent commotions at home, needless fruitless plantations abroad'.[42] He was stripped of Dorset estates valued at £500 a year and 'imprisoned in Dorchester gaol, where he continued until the Restoration, almost starved to death',[43] his family relying on charity from those he had formerly helped. Nonetheless he can scarcely have been ruined as shortly after the Restoration he was appointed Bishop of Bristol, 'being wealthy he was looked upon as the fittest person to enter upon that mean bishophric'.[44]

John Strode of Beer Hackett, whose sister was married to Gilbert's brother Ralph Ironside, was 'sequestered of his living and robbed and plundered of five hundred pounds in money besides an incredible quantity of plate and jewels'.[45] After then being ejected from his vicarage, Strode flatly refused to hand over the key to the Dorset Committee's nominee, James Pope.

Ralph Ironside of Long Bredy and Little Bredy, suffered even more severely than his brother and brother-in-law. His wife was driven from her childbed just two days after giving birth to a son, while he was ruthlessly plundered by parliamentary soldiers:

> He having a fine lap-dog which he valued much was the same holding in his hands, which a common strumpet of the soldiers demanded of him. The old gentleman replied 'You

have taken from me my all excepting shirt and my lap-dog, pray don't rob me of this too.' At that the wench gave him a severe blow under the ear and said 'You confounded old rogue, I can keep a lap-dog now better than you can.'[46]

While raiding the house, some of the soldiers burst down into the lowest cellar, which was five or six feet deep in water, and only escaped drowning with the help of Ironside, 'more merciful to them than they were to him or any of his family'. Subsequently he was dispossessed of all his lands and fled to Portland. Here he earned a living 'picking of stones for two pence a day', and hid in Gorwell Coppice where he was secretly brought food by a certain Mary Bartlett.

A former chaplain to King Charles, Bruno Ryves, was also plundered by the parliamentarians and forced to take shelter with Lord Arundell of Wardour in Shaftesbury. Ryves became a leading royalist propagandist, and among his many works were the *Mercurius Rusticus* newsbooks. He survived until the Restoration when, in honour of his services, he was made a chaplain to King Charles II.

Reports reached London in October that plundering by parliamentary forces in Somerset and Dorset had angered the local people, so the House of Commons hastily ordered that the units involved be sent off to join Essex's army, and that the Somerset M.P. John Ashe go into the country to hear complaints.

As the autumn passed most people in Dorset probably believed the struggle between King and Parliament was about to be decided over a hundred miles away. At the end of October the local court at Wimborne was holding cases, and Christopher Charlton was fined 4s. 'for bloodshed upon Thomas Hillard'.[47] There would soon be bloodshed in profusion.

Two weeks earlier Charles had at last begun his long-awaited march on London, and on 23 October Essex and the parliamentary army faced him at Edgehill in the first great battle of the war. The royalist cavalry under Prince Rupert scattered their opponents, including Denzil Holles who 'planted himself just in the way'[48] and tried to rally his red-coated regiment without success. In contrast the King's infantry was roughly handled, and the day finished without a clear-cut decision, although Essex had suffered more and retreated the next day after a bitterly cold night in the field. Among those knighted by the King for bravery was Troilus Turberville of Winterborne Whitechurch, who was made Lieutenant of the King's Guards. He served throughout the war until his death three years later, during the King's march on Huntingdon.

King Charles was shaken by his losses, and missed the chance of a quick strike at London. Nevertheless by 12 November he was at Brentford, where Prince Rupert's cavalry came down upon the 'broken regiment of Colonel Holles, but stout men who had before done great service',[49] and drove them into the River Thames with some slaughter before enthusiastically sacking the little town.

Victory was just a few miles away for the King, but Essex's army, strengthened by the London trained bands, was drawn up among the orchards and kitchen gardens of Turnham Green. Charles hesitated, then retreated to Reading. The war had a long way yet to run.

That month Charles had issued a declaration offering a free pardon to all rebels in Dorset 'except Denzil Holles esquire, and Sir Walter Erle knight, against whom we shall proceed according to the rules of the law, as against traitors and stirrers of sedition against us'.[50] In Dorchester people were probably more concerned by the unseasonably cold weather, and on 2 November the poor of the town demanded access to the common store of peat turves. The council refused to make the fuel available until four days before Christmas because 'it has been found in former years that by means the turves having been sold out to the poor too soon in the year, the store has been spent long before the sharpness of winter has been past.'[51]

Although winter put an end to large-scale campaigning, fighting still flared up occasionally. In January a troop of horse from Dorset joined the parliamentary relief of Exeter, but next month Sherborne was recaptured for the King by Sir John Hele of Clifton, 'a personable well-natured honest gentleman, very generous, kept a great house; his fault was only that he loved the cup'.[52]

Peace talks were in the air. Denzil Holles, wounded and depressed by his defeats at Edgehill and Brentford and the consequent disintegration of his regiment, also responding, it was said, to the nagging of his 'bitchwife',[53] had left the field for the comforts of Westminster. Here he grew steadily hotter against those he would later call 'blood-suckers' and 'their design of perpetuating the war to an absolute confusion'.[54] His calls for negotiation struck a chord and eventually Parliament did talk to the King. The only concrete result was a brief truce, though Sir John Bankes did not give up his doomed search for peace until the summer.

Local truces had been established in many parts of England including Dorset. By late January 1643 the townsmen of Dorchester were beginning to question the necessity for quite such a well-prepared and well-paid garrison, and on 3 February the listed soldiers were told they only need muster once a week, and their pay was to be cut from 2s. a week to 8d. At the beginning of March local royalist and parliamentarian leaders signed a treaty, and Thomas Trenchard and John Browne wrote to Parliament

> concerning the disbanding of all forces of all sides in their
> county, and touching the opposing of all forces whatsoever
> that shall enter that county to the disturbance of the peace
> there.[55]

There was talk of a larger agreement, and a forty-day ceasefire was observed throughout Devon, Somerset and Dorset. Back in London the parliamentary high command grew increasingly worried, and their general Sir William Waller wrote:

> there can be nothing more destructive both to the kingdom
> and to your own county than these treaties...while this and

that county shall sit down and think to save their own stakes, leaving the burden of the war upon a few shoulders, His Majesty will with the more ease subdue our party in the field, and that done (being master of the field) march with ease through every corner of the kingdom, and then all the privilege those poor countries shall obtain that sat down first will be to be devoured last.[56]

To reinforce his words Waller arrived in Dorset with 3000 horse.

William the Conqueror as he was known, because of his early successes in Hampshire and Sussex and his shrewd use of sudden night marches, was one of the more enigmatic figures of the Civil War. A Presbyterian and 'little in person',[57] he was described as having

so eager a spirit against the court, that he was very open to any temptation, that might engage him against it, and so concurring in the House of Commons with all those counsels which were most violent.[58]

Nevertheless he was almost constantly at loggerheads with his commander, the Earl of Essex, while he had many royalist friends, notably Sir Ralph Hopton to whom he wrote movingly:

my affections to you are so unchangeable, that hostility itself cannot violate my friendship to your person, but I must be true to the cause wherein I serve... That great God, which is the searcher of my heart, knows with what a sad sense I go upon this service, and with what a perfect hatred I detest this war without an enemy... We are both upon the stage and must act those parts that are assigned to us in this tragedy; let us do it in a way of honour, and without personal animosities, whatsoever the issue be.[59]

Nonetheless Waller was also a man with an eye to the main chance. Badly in need of horses, (as both sides were throughout the war), he sent some of the royalists of Dorset and Wiltshire a summons to come speedily with their horses to serve Prince Rupert, and then unhorsed and disarmed all who arrived. His visit to Dorset was not unprofitable according to the royalists, who accused him of recklessly allowing his troops to plunder the county, of taking £30,000 as his own share. More significantly several leading royalists, including Sir John Strangways, 'fled away with all speed, whereby that county was fairly freed from those disturbers of their peace'.[60] Though John Churchill, a successful lawyer and father of the fiercely royalist Winston Churchill, was still more interested in negotiating a renewal of his lease at Minterne with Winchester College. John Churchill was eventually summoned to attend the Dorset Committee, ordered 'that restitution be made of the cattle driven by way of distress',[61] and fined for his royalist sympathies, but the fine was suspended because in 1645 he had lent £300 to the parliamentary garrison of Weymouth.

While in Dorset, Waller was joined by a new second-in-command, Sir Arthur Haslerig, famous for his regiment of 'lobsters', cavalrymen armoured from head to toe. Haslerig, a Presbyterian and one of the five Members, was apparently of 'disobliging carriage, sour and morose of temper, liable to be transported with passion, and to whom liberality seemed to be a vice',[62] but he and Waller rapidly forged a good working relationship. Frustrated by the truce, they soon departed for the Welsh borders, leaving behind 100 new muskets for the local forces, as well as a few bills. On 17 March Robert Burt demanded 10s. compensation from Dorchester council for 'work he did in making chests for muskets for Sir William Waller'[63] who had left without paying. The town agreed to pay 9s.

A certain amount of reorganization of the Dorchester garrison was taking place, and 'most of Captain Churchill's company' were put 'under the command of Captain Joseph Paty'. This might have seemed a sensible precaution as William Churchill would soon change sides; however, Paty too switched allegiance. The garrison was 'agreed to be 160 at least, besides officers',[64] and at the end of February, 28 fresh soldiers were enlisted, most from Bridport or Netherbury. They do not seem to have been a very impressive collection, only half were fully armed, six had no weapons at all, one was sick and another had 'gone home to return'.[65]

Spring came early in 1643, with mild and open weather, but there were bad omens. On 11 March the diarist John Evelyn reported 'a shining meteor that evening and night, resembling a naked sword, bright like the moon pointing to the North very dreadfully'.[66] At Wimborne Minster the churchwardens had to pay out 6d. 'for one of the surplices being taken by a soldier',[67] and the inscribed brass plate from the effigy of King Ethelred was removed and hidden to keep it from thieving soldiers.

Fighting was soon bubbling up again. In the middle of April Hertford and Digby set out from Oxford to try again to raise troops in Dorset. Parliament quickly forestalled the move by sending a strong force from Bristol under Colonel Alexander Popham, with orders to lance that constant sore, the 'very malignant town' of Sherborne. Popham sent his brother Hugh and 120 horse on ahead to spy out the land, but with specific instructions not to enter the town. However they did, and the local constable, who they told to find them quarters, rang the fire bell to raise the town against them. On hearing the alarm, the parliamentarians demanded what was happening, and were told it was just the nine o'clock bell. Shortly afterwards they found themselves facing the attack of 300 townsmen crying 'Kill the parliament dogs.' Hugh Popham was killed, but a parliamentary counter-attack by 40 dismounted dragoons drove the royalists back. During the struggle a parliamentary soldier was sniped at out of a window and 'in the heat of his blood shot up his pistol into the thatch of a house'.[68] The thatch caught fire, and only the prompt action of parliamentary troops, unaided by a single local, prevented a conflagration. Three days later Alexander Popham arrived with 3500 men and took the town and castle.

The fall of Sherborne had severe consequences for the inhabitants. John

Walcot, a relation of the Digbys, had to pay £300 to stop troops pulling down his house; while three houses belonging to Hugh Hodges, an attorney who compounded with Parliament for £200 in 1645, were actually pulled down; and a well-off mercer, Josias Cooth, who was one of the leaders of the royalist cause, was pillaged of property worth £2000. The parliamentary troops stocked up for the future by 'killing all the fat sheep and calves and taking away almost all the barley and malt in the town'.[69] The abbey church was spoiled, the accounts for the time including charges 'for mending the rails in the chancel that were broken down by the soldiers...for mending the church windows...for powder and workmen about the works and watchmen extraordinary' and 'for committing three soldiers to the gaol'.[70] The victors also discovered Lord Bristol's buried plate, worth a useful £5000. Several people paid to be left alone, only to find themselves plundered anyway, and even taken away as prisoners. As the roundheads finally left, they even took their revenge on the bell that had summoned the citizens to attack them by pulling it down.

Over the next few weeks the parliamentary commanders attempted to crush the remaining centres of royalist resistance in Dorset. Although Sir John Strangways had fled to Oxford, his wife Grace, who was 'of a most malignant spirit', held Abbotsbury for the King. When hidden arms were found there, she paid for her defiance with £200 worth of damage to the house, and a demand that she should pay £500 in ten days or else the troops would 'take all away from the house and land'.[71]

The beginning of May saw some of Alexander Popham's men joining the parliamentary garrison of Weymouth to force the surrender of recalcitrant Portland, where royalist gun runners had been busy all winter. The ardent cavalier rector of Portland, Humphrey Henchman, who had encouraged the royalist sympathies of the Portlanders, was ejected from his office, fined £200, and replaced by Henry Way. After the Restoration Henchman 'a discreet and learned divine, a firm confessor and an excellent person'[72] became bishop of first Salisbury, then London. Meanwhile Popham, loaded with booty, returned to Bristol, where he peremptorily refused to hand over any of his plunder to the governor, Thomas Erle's brother-in-law, Nathaniel Fiennes.

On 1 April 1643 Parliament had appointed 17 men to be in charge of sequestration, fines and confiscation of property, in Dorset. The list is a catalogue of the leading parliamentary supporters in the county at the time, including Denzil Holles, Thomas Trenchard, Walter Erle, John Browne, John Bingham, Denis Bond, Thomas Ceeley, John Henley, William Sydenham and Robert Butler.

On the border with Wiltshire Sir Edward Hungerford, the local parliamentary leader, sat down with 1300 men before the important stronghold of Wardour castle, which was 'very strongly built of freestone' and gained its name 'from the conserving there the ammunition of the west'.[73] It was garrisoned by Lady Blanche Arundell, her maids, and about 25 men. When the sixty-year-old Lady Arundell was summoned to surrender the castle, she 'bravely replied that she had a command from her lord to keep it, and she would obey his command'.[74] After a siege of six days, during which the roundhead cannon 'had done little other hurt, save only to a chimney piece, by a shot entering at a window',[75] the besiegers mined the building. Lady Arundell was offered quarter for the women and children but not the men. She and her daughter:

> scorning to sacrifice the lives of their friends and servants, who had no other crime...but their fidelity...choose bravely rather to die together than live on so dishonourable terms.[76]

But when the roundheads produced 'balls of wild-fire to throw in at their broken windows',[77] the tiny garrison had little choice but to surrender.

The victorious roundheads did damage that was estimated at £100,000, and sold the timber, fruit and fish they had stolen from the estate at bargain prices. The booty, which included five cartloads of rich hangings and furniture, was brought to Shaftesbury, together with Lady Arundell herself, her daughter-in-law and three of her grandchildren. The prisoners, who were allowed to keep only the clothes they had on and six serving men, were to be taken to Bath, but sickness had broken out there and the women refused to travel on unless the parliamentarians 'would take the old lady out of her bed and the rest by violence, and so carry her away, but the rebels fearing lest so great inhumanity might incense the people, declined,' and instead took two of her grandsons to Dorchester 'a place no less dangerous for the infection of schism and rebellion than Bath for the plague and smallpox'.[78] Lady Arundell, widowed by the death of her husband at the battle of Lansdown, was finally allowed to seek the protection of the Marquess of Hertford in Salisbury, where Henchman had also gone.

Although Parliament seemed on the brink of making sure of the whole county there was not much enthusiasm, for the war was encroaching more and more upon the lives of ordinary people. In Dorchester on 23 June the town council 'ordered that in respect of the danger of the times there be a strict course taken tomorrow at the Fair for fear of incomers'.[79] A fresh explosion of trouble also broke out in north Dorset. Mobs

> riotously assembled themselves in great numbers about Mere, Shaftesbury, Gillingham, Knoyle, Motcombe...being armed with muskets, fowling pieces, and other weapons as well offensive as defensive, and broken open houses, thrown down enclosures, and robbed and spoiled divers of the King's subjects and committed many outrages.[80]

Edmund Ludlow was ordered to arrest 28 named people and take them to Wardour Castle, but those rioters who were arrested were either bailed for assizes that never took place, or allowed to escape by sympathetic soldiers. Even those areas free of soldiers had to contend with prices and taxes that had been forced up by the war. In spring 1643 hay cost £8 14s. a ton, far above its normal figure and equivalent to the value of three fat bullocks. By summer Dorset was expected to pay Parliament £437 10s. a week, with Poole supplying another £5. Ship money had only cost the county £100 a week.

Sir Robert Poyntz, cousin of the Catholic George Penny of Toller Whelme, said of recruiting for the King in the Westcountry at that time:

the Gentry came in apace, but the commons not so heartily, not in any considerable number. The true reason is...my countrymen love their pudding at home better than musket and pike abroad, and if they could have peace, care not what side had the better.[81]

A young man who would eventually loom large in the history of England, was having similar thoughts. In July 1643 the twenty-two-year-old Anthony Ashley Cooper of Wimborne was introduced to King Charles. According to an account written many years later, Cooper claimed he 'could put an end to the war if his Majesty pleased', and went on to explain that in his opinion the people were tired of war and would be glad to be 'at quiet at home again if they could be assured of a redress to their grievances and have their rights and liberties secured to them'. To make his point, Cooper asked for the right to offer parliamentary garrisons in Dorset a personal amnesty and the promise of a free Parliament. Charles remarked that he was 'a very young man for such an undertaking',[82] but willing to try an experiment that could cost him nothing the King gave Cooper some vague powers.

Only one important centre of royalist resistance remained intact, Corfe Castle 'so ancient as without date, yet all her walls and towers...are all in very good repair...the walls round about her are very strong and large'.[83] In charge of Corfe was Mary, Lady Bankes, 'a virtuous and prudent lady',[84] whose husband Sir John Bankes, recently promoted to be Chief Justice of the Common Pleas, was in Oxford with the King. Lady Bankes was planning the traditional May Day custom 'to hunt, course, kill and carry away such stags as may be found in the western woods, to the which sport diverse gentlemen for their recreation resort'.[85] However the chatelaine then learnt of

some troops of horse from Dorchester and other places...intending to find other game than to hunt the stag, their business being suddenly to surprise the gentlemen in the hunting and to take the castle.[86]

Immediately she shut herself up in the castle. When early one morning 40 seamen from Poole demanded she hand over her four small cannons, Lady Bankes, her children, and the five men and assorted maidservants who represented the entire garrison prepared and fired one of the cannons 'which small thunder so affrighted the seamen that they all quitted the place and ran away'.

The parliamentary leaders were not amused. They banned the selling of supplies to the castle, threatened to burn down the house of anyone who helped the Corfe garrison, and undermined the resolve of those local men who were in the castle by bringing their wives outside the walls:

there they weep and wring their hands, and with clamorous

> oratory persuade their husbands to come home and not by
> saving others to expose their own houses to spoil and ruin.[87]

Unable to risk open defiance, Lady Bankes surrendered her cannons and was left alone for a few weeks. She profited from the time by amassing supplies, and

> began to raise a garrison against the Parliament, and collect-
> ed and maintained at her own charge 80 men or more, com-
> pletely armed, and also procured a gunner for the castle. By
> these means the whole island is ruined and the country
> brought into subjection to the King's forces.[88]

A troop also came from the Marquess of Hertford, under Captain Robert Lawrence.

The parliamentarians realized their mistake, and in June Sir Walter Erle gathered 500 or 600 men, seized the town of Corfe Castle under cover of a misty morning, and surrounded the castle itself, threatening no quarter even to women and children. To demonstrate the truth of his threats Erle plundered Captain Lawrence's family home at nearby Creech Grange, so that the captain's mother, Lady Lawrence (before her marriage Grace Brune of Athelhampton), had to save herself by fleeing into the woods.

Nevertheless the Corfe garrison defied him and the six-week siege that followed was a fierce one as Erle tried almost everything. The boar and the sow, engines like wheeled sheds, made bullet-proof with planks and wool, were constructed (at a cost of £2 3s. 4d.), but the garrison shot at the unguarded legs of the attackers and the assault failed.[89] The parish church was turned into the parliamentary headquarters, snipers shot from it, the lead roof was recycled into bullets, the priest's surplices were made into soldiers' shirts, and foreshadowing Parliament's 1644 ordinance remov-ing organs from churches, the organ pipes were used as cases for powder and shot. Erle himself, after a narrow escape when a musket ball pierced his coat, may have suffered a temporary psychological breakdown for a bizarre accusation was levelled at him that 'he put on a bear's skin, and...for fear of musket shot he was seen to creep on all fours on the sides of the hill to keep himself out of danger'.[90]

The parliamentary admiral, the Earl of Warwick, arrived off Studland to help the siege. Warwick was a popular and attractive personality, and the single most important figure in ensuring almost the entire British navy took the side of Parliament. Clarendon described him as

> a man of a pleasant and companionable wit and conversa-
> tion; of an universal jollity; and such a licence in his words,
> and in his actions, that a man of less virtue could not be
> found out... but with all these faults he had great authority
> and credit.[91]

However shortly after arriving in Dorset, the admiral received orders to relieve Exeter and sailed away again. But not before providing 150 marines as reinforcements and an assortment of ladders and explosive weapons, as well as promising 'his assistance to set this county right on his return'.[92] Subsequently there would be many regrets that Warwick had not left the main mass of his men 'to join with Sir Walter Erle, and by that means Dorchester, Weymouth and all that country might have been saved'.[93]

Outside Corfe several prisoners, even including some under sentence of death, were added to the parliamentary assault force. Financial rewards were offered, the first soldier up the walls would get £20 (over a year's wages for most men), the second £19 and so on down to £1 for the twentieth. Large amounts of alcohol were also handed round liberally. The treasurer reported £1 12s. spent on 'a firkin of hot waters for the soldiers when they scaled the castle',[94] while the royalists sneered that Old Sir Wat, as they called Erle, 'was the only man almost that came sober to the assault'.[95]

The attack failed, partly because Lady Bankes and her daughters enthusiastically heaved stones and hot embers from warming pans onto the heads of the enemy. Parliamentary sources blamed the men:

> such was the baseness and cowardice of the seamen and landmen both that scarce one man of five came on...Sir Walter Erle at first used all the arguments he could to persuade them, but those not prevailing he offered to lead them on himself if they would promise to follow, which they did; but before he was advanced 30 or 40 paces, the bullets coming thick about their ears, they shamefully ran away and left him alone to make a single retreat.[96]

Having suffered 100 casualties, and inflicted only two, the disheartened parliamentarians retired in disorder. Erle took a boat for Poole 'making more haste to convey himself...than generals use to do',[97] and then complained bitterly to the House of Commons that he had repeatedly warned them of the danger Dorset was in, and begged for help, 'that storm being now fallen upon us and having wholly crushed and overwhelmed us'.[98] Erle's second-in-command, William Sydenham was just sitting down to dinner when he was suddenly told the royalists were coming. He left the meal untouched in his haste to get away, and the Corfe garrison captured all the parliamentary artillery and ammunition, as well as a hundred horses.

It was not only this humiliating rebuff that had undermined parliamentarian morale. Since the beginning of the summer, the tide of the war had been running strongly in the King's favour. Sir Ralph Hopton had gathered an army of tough, disciplined Cornish infantrymen, and his victory at Braddock Down in January 1643 swept Cornwall free of roundheads. A second victory at Stratton in May did the same for most of Devon, and Colonel Were's attempt to block his advance at Tiverton was swept aside. Meanwhile Hertford was on his way west through Salisbury to Blandford. Waller and Parliament alike were warned that if Hertford's march was not intercepted the whole of Dorset, which was 'in a weak condition' with troops 'no way considerable for the opposing of such a force as was coming toward it' would be lost. Dorchester prepared to resist, magistrates and officers alike taking an oath 'to live and die together in defence of the place'.[99] But unexpectedly the royalists swung north and joined up with Hopton at Chard. This combined army was now ready to take on Waller and dispute the control of the South West.

◂◂ *Chapter Four* ▸▸
THE ROYALIST STORM
AUGUST 1643–APRIL 1644

The royalist army poised north of Dorset in the high summer 1643 had behind it over six months of almost unbroken triumph across the South West. Hopton's Cornishmen, having penetrated as far as Somerset, were reinforced by Prince Maurice's Oxford cavalry which, in the words of Captain Richard Atkyns:

> was accounted the most active regiment in the army...which gave me more proficiency as a soldier in half a year's time, than generally in the Low Countries in four or five years, for there did hardly one week pass in the summer half year, in which there was not a battle or skirmish fought.[1]

There were many tensions between the two halves of the army. Hopton complained that at the taking of Taunton on 9 June 'there began the disorder of the horse visibly to break in upon all the prosperity of the public proceedings',[2] while Atkyns remarked:

> the Cornish foot could not well brook our horse (especially when we were drawn up upon corn) but they would many times let fly at us: these were the very best foot that ever I saw, for marching and fighting; but so mutinous withal, that nothing but an alarm could keep them from falling foul upon their officers.[3]

Nevertheless the combined army was a formidable fighting force, which was also buoyed up by good news from elsewhere. John Hampden's cavalry had been routed by Prince Rupert at Chalgrove Field on 18 June, and Hampden himself, the most respected and spirited leader of the parliamentary party, was wounded in the shoulder and died six days later. On 30 June King Charles's affairs looked in even better shape, for the royalist commander in Yorkshire, the Marquis of Newcastle, destroyed a parliamentary army under Lord Fairfax and his son Sir Thomas Fairfax on Adwalton Moor. Except for the great fortress of Hull and the Puritan weaving towns of Lancashire, the whole of the north of England rapidly fell to the royalists. The Queen, 'Her She-Majesty Generalissima' as she now styled herself, had arrived in England and now came south to join her husband in Oxford with an escort of 3000 infantry, 30 companies of horse, and six good cannon.

A month after Prince Maurice and Hopton joined forces, the combined army, with Winston Churchill of Wootton Glanville as one of the captains of horse, took on Waller at the bloody battle of Lansdown north of Bath, of which 'some old soldiers said that the furious fights in France were but a play in comparison of this.'[4] Losses on both sides were heavy, and

Hopton himself was shot through the arm, then seriously wounded after the battle when an ammunition wagon exploded, but it was Waller, 'a wary man as he is, and well known not to be too apt to expose himself to danger',[5] who retreated. On his way east into Wiltshire Waller sent a message to Dorchester asking for two troops of horse and 100 dragoons to be sent to Colonel Norton in Hampshire, and the reinforcements duly set off, though Sir Walter Erle complained that that left him with only 500 men, and Dorchester and Weymouth 'by none of judgement can be thought tenable by twice that number'.[6] Reinforcements from Dorset were also joining Hopton, including Lieutenant George Jolyff of Gillingham, who later discovered the lymph educts, for which he 'got to himself a great name, and was for a time much retired to for his knowledge of physic'.[7] But there were losses as well, most notably Richard Rogers of Bryanston. His death was considered something of a disaster by the King's side because he

> had a wonderful great influence upon the county of Dorset...and had so well designed all things there that Poole and Lyme, (two port towns in that county, which gave the King afterwards much trouble), if he had lived, had been undoubtedly reduced. But by his death all those hopes were cancelled.[8]

Waller and Hopton clashed again on 13 July, at Roundway Down, Runaway Down as the Cavaliers christened it, where Waller's army was utterly destroyed. Ten days later, Maurice and Hopton linked with Prince Rupert and besieged Bristol, the second city of the kingdom. Nathaniel Fiennes and his garrison fought fiercely and inflicted heavy losses, especially on the Cornish infantry which had already suffered heavily at Lansdown, but on 26 July Bristol was stormed. Large numbers of the defeated roundheads 'were taken prisoners in Dorsetshire and so remain to this present',[9] though others escaped and fled in all directions. Back in London a native of Dorsetshire, Clement Walker, who had been born in Tincleton, led demands for the impeachment of Fiennes. Walker was a zealous Presbyterian and propagandist, who later became a fierce enemy of Cromwell and was imprisoned in the Tower of London, where he died in October 1651.

The fall of Bristol was a body blow to the parliamentary cause. Hopton became Rupert's deputy, and the triumphant Maurice took over sole command of the Western Army. Over the crucial following months he would be the most important single man in the south-western war. The Prince 'an addition rather of gallantry than strength to the King's side',[10] had been born in Germany in February 1621 and named after his great uncle, the brilliant Dutch general Maurice of Nassau, 'because he will have to be a fighter'.[11] His physical resemblance to his older brother, Rupert, gained Maurice the nickname of Rupert's shadow, but there was a wilder, less responsible streak in Maurice. At the age of fifteen the young prince took part in a fatal duel, and shortly afterwards was sent off to join the Swedish army. When civil war broke out in England his mother, Queen Elizabeth of Bohemia, did not want her sons to join Charles 'but I neither could nor would hinder them from going, seeing the King and Queen desired them'.[12] Maurice's first year as a cavalry commander had been efficient, if unspectacular, now he had a chance on his own. Not that Maurice was popular among the King's advisers. Clarendon was frankly contemptuous of him:

> the Prince never sacrificed to the Graces, nor conversed among men of quality, but had most used the company of ordinary and inferior men, with whom he loved to be very familiar. He was not qualified with parts of nature, and less with any acquired...and understood very little more of the war than to fight very stoutly when there was occasion.[13]

Nevertheless the change in command did not slow down the run of royalist triumphs. The dashing young Roman Catholic globetrotter Robert Dormer, Earl of Carnarvon, swept into Dorset with a force of horsemen, described by the royalists as less than a thousand, and by the parliamentarians as 2000, and when Sir John Hele sent a message to the magistrates of Dorchester ordering them to return to their allegiance to the King, there was little enthusiasm for resistance:

> The inhabitants of the town of Dorchester (as generally all the well affected people in those western parts) being by the disaster lately befallen Sir William Waller, and the loss of the city of Bristol, much dismayed; the richest and chiefest of them began to remove and carry away their goods to other places, which (amongst the inferior sort, especially the soldiers which were unsatisfied of their arrears) occasioned a kind of mutiny.[14]

Among those moving their belongings was Denzil Holles, whose servant Ezekias Lambe took all the M.P.'s goods from Dorset to the safety of the Isle of Wight.

As if the flight of the rich was not enough, the Somerset M.P. William Strode, who had failed to hold Sherborne for Parliament the previous February and was now fleeing from Bristol, viewed Dorchester's expensive new fortifications and informed the nervous corporation

> that those works might keep out the cavaliers about half an hour; and then told them strange stories of the manner of assaulting Bristol; and that the King's soldiers made nothing of running up walls twenty foot high, and that no works could keep them out.[15]

When Carnarvon's horse arrived the garrison of Dorchester, even without including armed private citizens, was fairly strong:

> well-nigh 600 Musketeers...with two troops of horse, and 14 or 15 great guns, or thereabouts ready mounted in the streets, and on the platforms; But such were their fears and distractions, that of all those there appeared scarce the tenth

man resolved to oppose, the soldiers that were of the garrison running away.[16]

Clarendon cuttingly remarked the town was:

> strongly situated, and might very well have been defended by the spirits of the people if they had courage equal to their malice; for a place more entirely disaffected to the King, England had not.[17]

Be that as it may, Dorchester hastily and ingloriously surrendered, the only terms being that it was spared pillage and punishment. In the corporation minute book appears a brief note, 'by reason of the wars this book was discontinued for four years and another book made use of for the town's business'.[18]

A few days later Prince Maurice arrived with the rest of the army, and immediately broke the articles of surrender by looting and destroying the town brewhouse and many private homes. Several years later Lady Grace Strangways asked Dorchester council to petition for her husband's release from imprisonment in the Tower of London because he had saved the town in 1643. The council were

> inclinable to certify that Mr Strangways had been the means of preserving their town from firing, but not to petition because they pretend he was the cause of bringing the Prince thither, by which occasion their town was fired.[19]

Among the victims of the plunderers was John White. The soldiers burst into the old preacher's house where 'they seized upon a great number of books, manuscripts of divinity, evidences, writings and other goods of great value.'[20] White fled to London where he was granted the sequestered parish of Lambeth, and remained for most of the next three years. Some of his library was sold to Roger Clark, the royalist rector of Ashmore, who fought in Hopton's army.

Dorchester had in fact been fairly gently treated in comparison with some other towns. Nevertheless the indiscipline of Maurice's troops may have lost a valuable opportunity to win over the inhabitants. John Fry of Tarrant Gunville had apparently intended to send two well-mounted men into the King's service, but then 'Prince Maurice came for the West and harshly stripped Fry of all he could carry off...this soured Mr Fry and he always after opposed the King's cause'.[21] As for Carnarvon, who had negotiated the terms with Dorchester, he was so infuriated with Maurice that he resigned his command in disgust.

Some local members of the Prince's army took the opportunity to enrich themselves quietly. Captain Barnaby Burleigh visited John Arthur's property and took 'three score and ten burstones [the best kind of stone for millstones], and appropriated them for his own use for his mills at Sydling'. Arthur did not forget, and three years later, as one of the leaders of the triumphant parliamentarians, he was granted the right to 'seize on the millstones and other implements of the mill'[22] up to their estimated value of £8 15s.

Portland castle was taken within a few days with the help of a gentleman named Bragg who was trusted by the parliamentary garrison. This turncoat, perhaps Richard Bragg whose lands at Childhay and Burstock were sequestered in 1645, arranged that he and 60 disguised cavaliers would gallop desperately towards the town, calling for help and apparently closely pursued by some of Carnarvon's cavalry. The trick worked perfectly:

> the credulous rebels...set open the ports, at which his Majesty's soldiers entered, and seizing on the guards, who looked not for such unwelcome visitants, made themselves masters of it [the castle] without further trouble.[23]

Melcombe and Weymouth also surrendered rapidly, and it must indeed have seemed that 'God was now turned Cavalier.'[24]

Anchored in Weymouth Roads at the time was 'a ship laden with rich goods belonging to several persons well-affected to the Parliament', which included the last £50 left from John Henley's buried money bags. John Ellis of Hazelbury Bryan opened fire on the ship and ordered it to surrender:

> which they being not able to resist did obey and came in, and there the said Ellis did (as himself now confesses) seize on the said ship and good being of a very great value, amongst which the state had therein plate to the value of six hundred pounds or thereabouts.[25]

Just over four years later Ellis was punished with imprisonment by the Dorset Committee.

Weymouth, 'the best port town of that country, and to be kept with great care',[26] was a fine prize for the royalists, and a royal mint was established there, possibly in Sandsfoot Castle. However the town also turned into a source of tension among its conquerors. Sir Anthony Ashley Cooper who had been promised the governorship of the town by the Marquess of Hertford learnt that Maurice planned to give it to someone else and, with the support of Hertford, appealed to the King. Eventually Charles granted Weymouth to Ashley Cooper, but privately he told Hertford that because of 'the importance of those places' and Cooper's 'youth...and the want...of experience in martial affairs', he should be persuaded to resign in a few months, and Weymouth and Portland put into 'the hands of more able soldiers'.[27] It was one of Charles's typical compromises that pleased no one and encouraged the growth of bad feeling.

The royalists had taken large supplies of arms and ammunition in Dorchester, and considerable wealth in Weymouth including much of the loot from the sacking of Wardour Castle. In a few short days virtually the whole county of Dorset had been won for the King, and Walter Erle wrote to the Speaker 'there is no place remaining that there is any hope of making it good but the town of Poole.'[28] Parliament hastily sent Poole £300 out of the money raised to help Plymouth, and ordered 'that it be referred to Sir William Waller to consider of some course for the present defence of

Poole'.[29] In fact Waller no longer had an army worthy of the name, and the Dorset roundheads were on their own.

In Germany the sacking of conquered cities was usually the only practicable way to pay soldiers, as well as a routine weapon of terror. Prince Maurice had learnt his soldiering in Germany, and now Cranborne was another helpless town he delivered over to his soldiers:

> His cavaliers are most of them addicted to such cruelties that they show themselves more like tigers or savage bears than humane men, and so they may gain wealth, they care not who they have it from, nor how they come by it.[30]

However, the weapon could prove counterproductive. The storming of Bristol helped bring about the surrender of Dorchester, but so did the good treatment the city received by and large after its fall. In contrast Rupert's sack of Brentford, with its 'unnatural inhumane and strange cruelties'[31] had helped stir up London to resist in 1642, and now Maurice's plundering of Dorchester also encouraged roundhead resistance.

Nevertheless, William Churchill, who had fought for Parliament at Sherborne the previous year, went over to the royalists, as did William Constantine, the M.P. for Poole and Denzil Holles's legal adviser, who sent his town a blood-curdling letter advising instant surrender otherwise:

> the parts about Poole will be laid waste houses burned and harvest turned to horsemeat, if it be taken by assault, no submission can pacify the fury of the soldiers.[32]

But the parliamentarians had had time to recover their nerve. When ordered to offer allegiance to the King, Lyme refused 'because their mercies are cruelties and their promises of security from plundering a certain assurance of a miserable condition, and inevitable poverty to ensue'.[33] Poole's response to the summons to surrender had been even more defiant, and abrupt: 'our answer was shorter than the message, we gave fire at a troop of horse at great distance and killed a white horse with his scarlet rider'.[34] A month later the magistrates of Poole wrote that:

> our men blessed be God are valiant and full resolved to fight...our town was extremely divided, by reason of fears, covetousness and false jealousies, but now all things fairly composed by God Almighty.[35]

Not that those 'two little fisher-towns',[36] worried Prince Maurice. His eyes were on the last remaining bastions of parliamentary resistance in Devon. He left Dorset in the charge of the Scottish Earl of Crawford and marched west to more rapid success. Exeter fell on 4 September, Barnstaple and Bideford soon after, and he finally advanced on Plymouth, the only interruption to complete royalist domination of the south-western peninsula.

It seemed it would need a miracle to save the parliamentary cause. Several leading supporters of Parliament hastily fled to Oxford to plead the King's pardon for their rebellion, among them the Earl of Bedford.

Hertford had not forgotten that at Sherborne Bedford had put off his challenge to fight a duel and it took considerable care to soothe the Marquess's ruffled feathers. Back in London the fast-shrinking House of Lords proposed fresh negotiations with the King, only for the proposal to be narrowly voted down by the House of Commons. A crowd of London women, who came to Westminster to demand peace, were scattered by Waller's horse and an innocent bystander was killed in the melee.

The King turned upon the great wool city of Gloucester. As the siege grew tighter and the city tottered on the edge of surrender, the Earl of Essex stirred himself from his lethargy, gathered his London-based army and marched to relieve Gloucester. It was a desperate gamble, but astonishingly it paid off. Gloucester was saved, and when the King caught up with Essex at Newbury, the parliamentary general managed to fight out a drawn battle, during which Lord Carnarvon was killed, and then escape with his army back to London. It was a crucial turning point in the war, reviving a cause which had seemed all but lost, and 'the Parliament that were very low before, began to prick up their ears again'.[37]

Captain Francis Sydenham, one of several parliamentarian brothers from Wynford Eagle, was quartered in Poole in the house of a royalist. Francis Sydenham was not a happy man, he complained frequently of the losses he had suffered from supporting Parliament, and eventually his host's wife arranged a secret meeting with the royalist Captain Thomas Phillips. It went well and Sydenham agreed to betray the town in exchange for a promise of pardon, replacement of his losses, and £40 in immediate cash with more to follow.

The plan was that one night when Sydenham was captain of the watch, the royalist commander, Crawford, would approach the town with a large force and break in through a gate which Sydenham would leave open. Sydenham himself would pretend to flee from the royalists, crying out he was betrayed, and seize the opportunity to capture the parliamentary ship in the harbour before it could escape:

> The earl liking the plot very well, sent the captain a hundred
> pounds, promising him a sergeant-major's place (at the least)
> in the King's army [in Civil War armies a sergeant-major was
> a commissioned officer outranking a captain] and the ship
> for his pains.[38]

Meanwhile Sydenham was told to continue fighting the royalists, an instruction he followed so literally that shortly before the day the city was to be handed over he captured several royalist officers and horses in a raid.

Finally, in the last week of September, came the night and the hour. Crawford with eight troops of horse and 500 foot, crept towards the agreed gate then charged with a cry of 'All is our own; on, on!.' It was a trap. Sydenham had told everything to the governor of Poole, John Bingham, and the royalist troops were mown down as they advanced. Crawford himself only narrowly escaped with his life. The slaughter would have been even greater if the parliamentary guns had been mounted lower, as it was 'the country reports there were divers cartloads of dead.'[39] Poole remained nervous of treachery, and early the next year their turncoat M.P. William Constantine was found in the town. He was arrested and sent to London together with George Hastings, the son of Henry Hastings of Woodlands, and Henry Harbin the former mayor. Harbin was soon released, after a payment to prove his loyalty.

The war in Dorset now quietened down again while the royalists tightened their control of the county, Lyme and Poole strengthened their defences and waited to see what would happen next, royalist Wimborne spent 2s. 'for beer on the King's coronation day',[40] and the ordinary people of the county concentrated on getting in the harvest. Something that could not have been easy for the weather in the South West was appalling, 'so violent a season of rain, and foul weather', that many of Prince Maurice's army before Plymouth fell sick and died 'with lying on the ground'.[41]

The Prince himself caught influenza, then known as the New Disease, and almost died. The King even sent his own surgeon, William Harvey, discoverer of the circulation of blood, to tend Maurice.

Scattered skirmishes continued. At the beginning of October a parliamentarian officer, Verney 'was so courteous to Lady Trenchard in Dorsetshire' that although his quarters were five miles away, he and a dozen or so soldiers

> lay at her house to guard it, his men were not to disturb her, and his interest with the other party was to be enough to save him and his from prejudice within her walls. But at midnight the house was lost to an irresitible party, and H. Verney was taken. His soldiers were furious, particularly threatening that lady's house, which they began to plunder.[42]

The royalists had been checked before Gloucester, Poole and Plymouth, but the initiative still lay with them. Shortly after the battle of Newbury Charles summoned Sir Ralph Hopton, and made sure he was 'reasonably well recovered of his hurts' suffered at Lansdown. He then made him a lord and ordered 'he should draw into the field for the clearing of Dorsetshire, Wiltshire and Hampshire, and so point forward as far as he could go towards London.'[43] Hopton's plan was:

> to have fallen suddenly upon Wardour, and so, upon reasonable success there, to have fallen upon Lyme and block up Poole. All of which, as he conceived, was very feasible, and by this means to have left no enemy at his back.[44]

However the unexpected seizure of Winchester by local royalists forced Hopton to press into Hampshire, 'against his own judgement, and to the future great prejudice of the service'. Having just failed to catch the heavily outnumbered Waller near Farnham, Hopton poised himself for a strike into Sussex, whose iron foundries were the source of most of Parliament's arms. But the royalist commander was still far from happy about Dorset.

Bernard Ashley, who had been intended as Major General of the county, was seriously ill, Anthony Ashley Cooper was in Oxford indulging his own ambitions, and 'the rest of the gentlemen, though intending very well to His Majesty's service, yet proving unsuccessful in their proceedings, the King's affairs impaired apace in that county.'[45] Then, in November, a fresh royalist force landed at Weymouth, one that carried alarming implications for the war in England.

Ever since the Catholic Irish had risen up in rebellion in October 1641, bloody religious war had raged through the island. One of the main accusations against Charles had been that he was plotting to bring over a huge army of papist Irishman to crush English liberties, and certainly the King had great hopes of Irish help. However, one important Irish chieftain had not joined the rebellion. The ambitious Murrough O'Brien, Lord Inchiquin, hunted the rebels with such ferocity that he received the nickname Murrough of the Burnings, though Pepys was later to say he 'seems to be a very fine person'.[46] On 15 September 1643 a truce was agreed in Ireland, and at the end of October came the news that 1000 Irish troops had landed at Minehead. So great was the fear and hatred of them that many of the cavaliers themselves wanted to 'cut those papish dogs' throats'[47] and had to be dissuaded from it by Edmund Wyndham. Shortly afterwards 800 of Inchiquin's troops, under his brother Henry O'Brien, arrived at Weymouth to help King Charles. Inchiquin himself hurried to the royal court in Oxford, expecting to receive the presidency of Munster for his loyalty. However, the King was more interested in the support of the very rebels Inchiquin had been fighting, and the presidency of Munster was earmarked elsewhere.

The Dorset parliamentarians, freed from the threat of Hopton's army, were cautiously going over to the attack again. For many years the port of Wareham had been declining in importance, 'the castle is wholly ruinated, the haven choked up, many of the churches demolished.'[48] So low had the town fallen that 'the soil that was in the very heart of the ancient town produces great quantities of garlic,'[49] and little else. Nevertheless the crumbling medieval walls had been strengthened by the parliamentary garrison the year before. Wareham fell to the royalists without bloodshed, but on 23 November Captain Lea of Bridport and 200 musketeers from the Poole garrison launched an attempt to recapture the town.

The attack was by water, but a little way up the River Frome some royalists manning a breastwork fired a volley before hurrying off to raise the alarm. Having been warned, the defenders prepared several ambushes in the hedges and guarded the crucial footbridge, but the roundhead attack was well planned. Captain Lea separated his force into three groups so as to attack from several sides at once, and ordered his men not to shoot until they reached the town. In the dark moonless night the royalist ambushers had nothing to aim at and fell back. Pressing into the heart of the town, the parliamentarians found the entire garrison drawn up, ready to fight. For a brief moment the two forces paused facing each other. The cavaliers defiantly shouted 'Now come on, ye roundheads if ye dare!' However when the attackers took them at their word 'and gave them a handsome volley of shot',[50] the royalists panicked and fled. Two hundred prisoners were taken and Wareham was back in the parliamentary camp. On the same day Francis Sydenham had raided as far as Wimborne to cover the attack on Wareham, and next day the roundhead navy captured five small royalist ships in Poole harbour.

Captain Francis Sydenham was proving a sharp thorn in the royalists' side. One of his raids through Purbeck collected 323 head of cattle, and in December he launched a highly successful attack as far as Dorchester,

> where he apprehended Captain William Churchill, deputy
> governor of that town, and his lieutenant Joseph Paty, both
> of which had been very active against the Parliament, and
> had compelled that town and county to yield obedience to
> the King's cormorants.

Sydenham broke open the prison and freed 'such honest men out of it as had been committed by those cruel cormorants for refusing their illegal command'. During the raid his men captured a supply wagon containing so many guns that the roundheads could not carry them all, but had to break some and throw them into the river. 'He also borrowed there of one Mr Coker, a malignant goldsmith, such plate as he had.'[51] Robert Coker was in his mid-sixties, an important well-respected figure in his profession, a former member of the council of freemen, and probably the maker of the 1630 civic seal of Dorchester, but that did not save him from plundering.

On the north-eastern borders another parliamentary outpost was causing trouble. Colonel Edmund Ludlow in Wardour Castle had realized he would soon find himself under attack and began laying in a stock of provisions, partly by the simple method of intercepting farmworkers on their way to Shaftesbury market and taking their produce 'paying for it the market price, at which they were not a little surprised'.[52] He also obtained ammunition in Southampton, as well as discovering some money, plate and jewels walled up in a cupboad.

The first royalist attack involved a kitchen boy, who 'was not above twelve years of age and yet, as I was afterwards informed, had already attempted to poison his grandfather'.[53] The boy, who was from Shaftesbury, had been recruited by Captain White, 'a papist of Dorsetshire' (possibly Ignatius White of Okeford Fitzpaine). His job was:

> to number the men and arms in the castle, to poison the
> arms, the well and the beer, to blow up the ammunition, to
> steal away one of my best horses to carry him back to them,
> for which service he was to receive half a crown.[54]

Not surprisingly this ambitious plot failed. The boy was caught and confessed after being threatened with hanging, though he did successfully 'poison' one gun, which exploded. Then the advance of the main royalist forces was spotted after some cattle stampeded, and the siege began.

The arrival of large royalist forces in north Dorset inevitably cost the local inhabitants a great deal. At Milton Abbas the village had to pay for such things as 'billeting of Captain Hoddinot's soldiers' (Hoddinot was eventually captured at Sherborne in 1645), 'two barrels of beer for Colonel Barnes's regiment' and 'a barrel of beer more for the same occasion',[55] while at Charlton Marshall there were charges for 'righting a knapsack...forty bullets...three pounds of powder'[56] and much else besides.

The first royalist commander was shot, to be replaced by George Barnes who, with 300 men he had raised locally, 'was more employed in plundering the country than in advancing the King's service'.[57] The siege ground on for two months, with the garrison running short of supplies and having to rely for water on the castle well, which ran dry every evening. Eventually reinforcements, including Irish yellow-coats, arrived under 'that bloody tyrant Sir Francis Doddington',[58] a man with a well-earned reputation for savagery who on another occasion 'hung up thirteen after quarter. He made a son hang his father or e contra.'[59] On 14 March, the day after Ludlow had rejected a demand to surrender, a royalist mine exploded.

> I was lifted up with it from the floor, with much dust suddenly about me; which was no sooner laid, but I found both the doors of my chamber blown open, and my window towards the enemy blown down, so that a cart might have entered at the breach.[60]

Although the initial royalist attack was beaten off and the breach barricaded, five days later Wardour Castle surrendered 'notwithstanding the obstinate courage of Mr Ludlow'.[61] John Aubrey visited the castle 'the day after part of it was blown up, and the mortar was so good that one of the little towers reclining on one side did hang together and not fall in pieces'.[62]

It had been a remarkably bloodless conflict. In the two months fewer than 20 men died, and even Doddington, a relation of Ludlow's, expressed joy at seeing Ludlow alive and well, though he also said 'he was sorry to find so much resolution employed in so bad a cause'.[63] Ludlow, who had several other relations among the royalists, including Robert Phelips and Henry Williams, repaid his friendly reception by showing Henry, the new Lord Arundell, where he had hidden the castle's silver plate. In return he was well treated and soon exchanged, but the terms of surrender were not kept and two roundhead soldiers were executed.

The long resistance of Wardour Castle had badly held up the royalists, nor were things going particularly well elsewhere. Prince Maurice came within a whisker of taking Plymouth, but failed and raised the siege on Christmas Day. Next month part of Hopton's army under Lord Crawford was caught utterly unawares by Waller at Alton and suffered a sharp defeat, 'the lord Hopton sustained the loss of that regiment with extraordinary trouble of mind, and as a wound that would bleed inward.'[64] Further afield there was a roundhead victory at Nantwich, and most important of all, Parliament had come to a deal with the Scots. On 18 January, along roads thick with snow, a large Scots army crossed the border. The balance of the war seemed to be swinging again. It was almost unprecedented in European history for armies to remain in the field all winter, but even a great blizzard over the south did not put an end to military activity.

The garrisons of Poole and Wareham continued their raids, despite the heavy snow cover. In February they ambushed Colonel Edmund Wyndham and 150 of his horse, then defeated Lord Inchiquin's regiment near Poole. The Irish troops had been guarding a convoy to Weymouth from Rupert 'the most notorious Prince of Robbers...Duke of Cumberland and Plunderland',[65] and the roundheads collected £3000 in gold and silver, as well as horses, arms and ammunition.

The Irish soldiers in Hopton's army were described as:

> very mutinous and shrewdly infected with the rebellious
> humour of England, being brought over merely by the vir-
> ture and loyalty of their officers, and large promises which
> there was then but small means to perform.[66]

In November a party had mutinied near Shaftesbury, but Hopton fell upon them swiftly and hanged two or three of the ringleaders, after which he had no more trouble.

Not that they were always unreliable. On 27 February Francis Sydenham and 300 men of the Wareham garrison clashed with 45 of Inchiquin's men at Holmebridge, and the outnumbered Irish resisted stubbornly for five hours:

> The captain and lieutenant were both shot, and ordered their
> men to lay them on the brink of the bridge where they
> encouraged their men...the lieutenant bled to death, encour-
> aging his men with great cheerfulness'.[67]

Finally royalist reinforcements drove off the parliamentarians, who lost 40 men and eight loads of hay.

About this time Stoborough was destroyed. Royalist forces from Corfe and Weymouth were probably trying to fortify the village to act as a block on raids from Wareham. Eleven years later the inhabitants of Stoborough, supported by William Sydenham, Anthony Ashley Cooper, John Trenchard, John Bingham, John Fitzjames and Denis Bond, petitioned Oliver Cromwell on the grounds that:

> we willingly permitted our town of 100 families to be burned
> to preserve the parliamentary garrison at Wareham, even
> when the King's forces were most prevalent in the county,
> and thus we lost £3000, and are ruined.[68]

On 29 December, just before he gave up the governorship of Weymouth as the King had wanted, Anthony Ashley Cooper wrote a letter to Clarendon complaining of 'the want of those Irish foot were promised', and the great expense of trying to keep in the enemy garrisons 'so that we shall be eaten out before we come to reducing them. We have no help from any other county towards the pay of our soldiers.'[69] He asked for permission to leave the county, and several weeks later did just that, going over to the parliamentary garrison at Hurst Castle in Hampshire.

Why exactly the twenty-two-year-old aristocrat, with so many close links to the royalist leaders, changed sides, and at such a relatively unpromising moment, is not clear. The immediate cause of his decision was probably Parliament's offer of a pardon to all who came over to them before 1 March; possibly he distrusted the growing Roman Catholic influence on the King, especially through Queen Henrietta Maria. Ashley Cooper himself merely said he had come to see 'the King's aim destructive to religion and the state'.[70] Another possible explanation is that it 'proceeded from some secret suspicion which his Majesty had conceived of his fidelity, perhaps occasioned by the malicious whisperings of some about the King, who grew jealous of him'.[71] Certainly the envy and back-stabbing among royalist leaders, especially back in Oxford where the King had just opened his short-lived anti-parliament, was very great.

Whatever the reason, it was a massive gamble, for Ashley Cooper had received promises of great things from the King, and by defecting he was leaving almost all his estates at the mercy of the royalists who occupied them. With him went his neighbour Sir Gerard Napier, the recently-expelled M.P. for Melcombe who 'had one of the best estates in the county...and of a temper inclined to envy, not obliging, and to speak as ill as he could of the absent'.[72] It was a menacing forewarning of the influence young Ashley Cooper would wield against his erstwhile allies. The royalists were furious at his treachery and included his name in a widely circulated satire:

Ashley Cooper knew a reason
That treachery was in season
When at first he turned his coat
From loyalty to treason.[73]

Despite the setback at Holmebridge, the increasingly confident depradations of the parliamentary outposts in Dorset were causing concern further and further afield. On 11 February the King himself sent a letter to Sir John Stawell, the governor of Taunton, ordering him 'to send two hundred of your foot together with their arms and pay' for the subjection 'of the rebellious town of Lyme'.[74]

Although there had been little serious fighting in many areas of the county over the past year, war was gradually eating deeper into the fabric of day-to-day life. At Sherborne the churchwardens' accounts reveal the increasing expenses that came from ever-present soldiers, for candles, wood and coal, as well as more unusual payments, such as 2s. 6d. 'for altering the treble bell into a fire bell', presumably to replace the one destroyed by Popham's men in April 1643, and 1s. 'for mending the lock of the poor man's box'.[75]

The village of Hermitage in north-west Dorset was an example of a small rural settlement feeling the effect of war. The farmer George Fox, who was still working there twenty years later, paid out 5s. 'for quartering of soldiers' and smaller amounts 'for fortification'.[76] Expenses directly related to the war make up less than five per cent of Fox's 1644 accounts, so the economic pressure does not seem to have been very great, although the harvests had not been good, and most people lived only a little above subsistence level. In such circumstances any extra cost might prove catastrophic. Nicholas Goffe, a farmer of Sturminster Newton, suffered so much from 'quartering soldiers and other heavy taxes and pressures'[77] that he was finally forced off his farm and, to avoid being imprisoned by his creditors, served for a year as a footsoldier for Parliament.

Matters were about to get worse. 1644 was to prove the crucial year of the war, and also the most bloody.

On 20 March Prince Rupert won a crushing victory at Newark, but it was more than cancelled out a week later when Waller, reinforced with 2000 of Essex's cavalry, inflicted a crucial defeat on Hopton at Cheriton in Hampshire. Cheriton was the first major parliamentary victory, Waller's reputation once more soared and the Lord General Essex, writing a few days later admitted 'last week there was but a step between us and death and (what is worse) slavery'.[78]

The royalist attempt to penetrate Sussex and the South East had failed and the pendulum of war in the south was about to swing back westwards into Dorset. Waller underlined the point by immediately marching 'towards Poole to relieve it, and in the way has taken Christchurch... where was about 300 soldiers and officers'. Among the prisoners was 'a valiant lady Captain' and to have taken the town 'would have been sharp work, had all the rest had that magnanimous spirit she had, but God be thanked this was without the loss of blood'.[79] Three days later, on 7 April, Waller was poised at Ringwood. Prince Maurice and the royalist western army had crossed the Dorset border, and the stage was set for the next act.

Chapter Five

THE SIEGE OF LYME REGIS
APRIL 1644–AUGUST 1644

T he port of Lyme, at the westernmost tip of Dorset, had a long history of religious radicalism, and the coming of the seventeenth century had seen the growth of an ever stronger Puritan influence. When war broke out Sir Walter Erle and Sir Thomas Trenchard had made sure of the town, which at the time was completely defenceless, and had set in motion the building of some defences.

After Lieutenant Lea had garrisoned Bridport for Parliament in June 1643 west Dorset was firmly in Parliament's hands. But just two months later, after the royalists had seized Dorchester and Weymouth, Sir Walter Erle wrote 'the towns of Lyme and Bridport being shut in between these places and Devonshire cannot hold out.'[1] At the time Lyme was garrisoned by ten companies, theoretically 1000 men, but in practice probably half that number.

The fall of Bristol had temporarily filled Dorset with fleeing parliamentarians. The panicky William Strode clearly helped undermine the morale of the Dorchester garrison. Lyme, under its governor and mayor, Colonel Thomas Ceeley, gave shelter to a very different sort of man. Lieutenant Colonel Robert Blake was the eldest of 12 sons of a Somerset merchant. He had spent nine years at Oxford University, where he was 'an early riser and studious, but withal he did take his pleasure in fishing, fowling etc. and sometimes in stealing of swans'. However he failed to get a fellowship, 'whether it was for want of scholarship, or that his person was not handsome or proper (being of stature little)'.[2] More likely it was his personality and political views:

> He was of a melancholic and a sullen nature, and spent his
> time most with goodfellows who liked his moroseness, and
> a freedom he used in inveighing against the licence of the
> time, and the power of the Court.[3]

Subsequently Blake became a merchant like his father, and in July 1629 he was probably the Robert Blake who paid the fairly large sum of £20 to become a freeman of Dorchester. He was elected M.P. for Bridgwater in 1640 and threw in his lot with the parliamentarian side, but he had made little mark in public life, except for the stubborn defence of 'a little fort at Bristol'.[4] On his arrival at Lyme he immediately set about improving the fortifications, and tightening the line so as to make it more defensible.

After Prince Maurice had summoned Lyme to surrender and received such a determined refusal, the town was left in peace until December 1643, when the royalists forcibly conscripted several hundred men in Devon and told them they were to attack Lyme. The conscripts objected, and when faced with a threat to hang the first who refused, 'they all cried, "Hang one and hang all," and grew to a mutiny, that the commissioners were forced to shift for themselves.'[5] Many of the mutineers joined the Lyme garrison and encouraged by these reinforcements the parliamentarians began to imitate their allies of Poole and take the initiative. On 18 January a party from Lyme marched to Ashe House near Axminster in response to a plea for help from a widow, Lady Eleanor Drake, but they arrived too late. Lady Drake, despite having a royalist son-in-law, Captain Winston Churchill of Wootton Glanville, had been driven from her home by Lord Paulet, whose soldiers 'stripped the good lady who, almost naked and without shoe to her foot but what she afterwards begged, fled to Lyme for safety'.[6] After each side burnt down a country house belonging to their enemies, they both retreated.

A month later parliamentary troops from Lyme seized Axmouth. Then, in the beginning of March, Captain Townsend fell upon Bridport, only to come unexpectedly on more than 100 cavalier cavalry, who drove him back in disorder. Colonel John Were, who had been captured at Exeter the autumn before, then exchanged, had arrived from London ten days before with 200 reinforcements for parliamentary force. He blamed the rout on another officer:

> we had returned safe to Lyme had not Major Orme there
> basely run, saying 'retreat, the hedge is lined with muske-
> teers, or we are lost' which occasioned a disorderly retreat, so
> that I lost some men.[7]

Orme was subsequently accused of talking to the enemy without permission and sent to London. Freed on the way by royalists from Weymouth he changed sides, only to change back again after being captured by the parliamentarians.

A few days after the defeat for Parliament at Bridport Captain Thomas Pyne stormed the Arundell stronghold of Chideock Castle, took 50 prisoners and two pieces of ordnance and garrisoned the place, from where he was able to levy contributions on Bridport and 11 adjacent parishes.

Life was growing more and more dangerous as royalists and parliamentarians skirmished all over the county. Gamaliel Chase, rector of Wambrook, was in Exeter when it was under royalist control and as a result he was 'thoroughly plundered, partly by the garrison of Lyme, partly by his own neighbours' and was finally driven to begging, 'forced to eat cabbage stumps'. Trying to avoid a roundhead patrol, he even hid in a heap of wool, 'where the soldiers soon discovered him by thrusting in their swords, one of which wounded him in the thigh'.[8] Religious life especially suffered, as an ever increasing number of parishes found themselves without vicars due to flight, sequestration or death. This could lead to other problems, for example in Cranborne a 'base-born' child named Elizabeth was not baptized 'till she was of age to call for parsons at the font'.[9] In March 1644 the Earl of Warwick asked the House of Lords that 'both the navy and many congregations which want ministers may be timely furnished',[10] but with the war flaring towards its climax there was little time for such things.

The next raid launched by the Lyme garrison was more ambitious. Major William Butler marched north with 60 horse to collect recruits and took Hemyock Castle, near Chard, but then 'contrary to the order' stayed too long. Royalist troops rapidly gathered from all over the region to counter-attack, and Butler 'delivered the castle so dishonourably that three honest men were hanged, and himself and the rest carried prisoners to Exeter'.[11] Shortly after, as the cavaliers 'to express their joy for this victory fell a-drinking and carousing',[12] Colonel Were, Captain Pyne and the Lyme cavalry launched a surprise assault on Colyton, took 250 prisoners and freed some of their men.

The parliamentarians must have been hoping for great things in the spring of 1644. Waller, fresh from his victory at Cheriton and reinforced from Poole, was poised for an advance into Dorset. A thousand roundhead cavalry from Salisbury swooped down on royalist recruiters at Winterborne Whitechurch, then pursued their enemies to the very walls of Weymouth, taking 300 prisoners. Royalist Shaftesbury was showing signs of panic, laying out money 'to raise a stock for powder and to pay poor men that go on the alarm', not forgetting 'four quarts of wine for Captain Barnes',[13] whose men seem to have had an incomparable thirst! Even royalist leaders were rapidly losing confidence. In the spring of 1644 Lord Arundell of Chideock was hurriedly 'carrying his goods into Cornwall'.[14] Then, suddenly, Waller's London regiments insisted on returning home, and the general was left without most of his army.

The Dorset royalists counterattacked. Three weeks earlier Sir Thomas Aston had defeated the Poole horse and briefly penetrated as far as the port 'where the cannon and small shot played thick upon them from the walls'.[15] Next the cavaliers persuaded Captain Morton, the man who had struck the first blow in Dorset's Civil War, to betray Wareham to them. On 11 April, when captain of the watch, he did what he was asked, and William Ashburnham, Ashley Cooper's replacement as governor of Weymouth, and the Irish commander Henry O'Brien took Wareham with the loss of only two men. Afterwards the royalists were accused of putting most of the parliamentary garrison to the sword, including the wretched Morton himself, and of raping many of the women of the town. The war was getting dirtier.

After the disaster of Cheriton, the King had sent letters to Prince Maurice warning him 'not to engage himself before Lyme or any other place'.[16] Nevertheless the Prince's army of the west, five or six thousand strong, advanced on Lyme from the north. The town was of crucial importance for a variety of reasons. It was the only port available to the parliamentary fleet between Poole and Plymouth, the garrison's raids were damaging royalist control of the West Country, and taking it would complete a chain of strongholds stretching from Bristol to the Channel, providing added protection for royalist Devon and Cornwall.

On 7 April Maurice quartered his men in the 'pretty market town'[17] of Beaminster, where he was joined by fresh reinforcements. A week later, on Palm Sunday, there was a quarrel among the royalist troops. The result was catastrophe:

> The fire was first kindled in John Sargent's house in North Street and it was a musket discharged in the gable, and it was wild fire and the wind being directly with the town, so that the whole town was all destroyed in two hours; and those goods for the most part which were carried out of the fire, were carried away by the soldiers.[18]

Except for East Street and part of Church Street the town was burnt to the ground. The cost was estimated at £21,080 and 144 houses were destroyed, which made it the most destructive fire in England since the conflagration at Wymondham thirty years before.

The inhabitants of Beaminster subsequently appealed to 'the renowned and illustrious Prince Maurice':

> that, notwithstanding their weekly tax, they have been much charged with the free quarter of your Highness's army, while it was at Beaminster, as also, in providing of provision for your Highness and your said army. Besides the great loss that the inhabitants of the said town have lost by that late unfortunate fire, your petitioners are in continual charge in relieving the poorer sort, which have been burnt out of all that ever they had.[19]

They went on to beg that the costs of quarter and provision could be met 'out of the weekly contribution paid to Colonel Strangways'. It seems unlikely that they got much satisfaction from the royalists. When Joshua Sprigg visited Beaminster almost fifteen months later, he described it as:

> a place of the pitifullest spectacle that man can behold, hard-
> ly a house left not consumed with fire, the town being fired
> by some of the enemy in five places at once when Prince
> Maurice was there, by reason of a falling out between the
> French and the Cornish.[20]

Maurice left the ruined place and on 20 April came down upon Lyme, where he was awaited by a garrison of about 1000, and a population no doubt swollen by refugees to three times that size.

The defences of Lyme consisted of a trench known as the Town Line with a rampart perhaps six feet high connecting four strong points, forts made of earth, stones, turfes and timber. The mile-long rampart ran to the sea, completely surrounding the town, and building it must have been a huge communal task involving most of the population.[21] The time had come to see if the effort had been worth it.

Having reached Uplyme Hill Maurice, who was still recuperating after influenza, so much so that his ghost was said to be leading the siege, ordered his entire army to parade before the town. The attempt to over-awe resistance seems to have had little effect; Edward Drake said that the garrison, of which he was part, 'were not a jot dismayed at the sight of the enemy but rather longed to have dealt with them'.[22] Having failed to terrify the garrison into rapid surrender, Maurice turned to practical measures, seizing outlying farmhouses at Haye House and Colway Manor, the home of Henry Henley, and quartering his troops around them.

Bullen Reymes of Mappowder had been with Maurice for almost a year, and on 10 August 1643 he had received a commission as the Captain of a company of 100 foot. Now he led an attack on Sir Walter Erle's country house at Stedcombe, about 3 miles from Lyme, which was garrisoned by part of Colonel Were's regiment. Some of the defenders managed to fight their way back to Lyme. The rest, under Captain Peter, resisted Reymes' attacks for twenty-four hours, then 135 men and officers surrendered and were sent as prisoners to Taunton and Exeter. The royalists also captured 'six colours, one piece of cannon and two murderers [small cannon], good store of ammunition and one seditious lecturer'.[23]

The next day, Easter Sunday, Maurice launched his first assault. His troops attacked the western end of the town, trying to seize some cottages just outside the Town Line. The defenders retaliated by setting fire to the cottages, but the royalists used the cover of the smoke to assault the defences proper, lying among the hedges and ditches and 'very boldly shooting at us every hour the remainder of the same day with very great courage within very near pistol shot of our line'.[24] The next day the royalists sited some of their 'excellent train of artillery'[25] and began to bombard the Town Line and the forts. At the same time snipers picked off any of the garrison who were unwise enough to emerge from cover, but Lyme's own cannons replied from the forts. The day after, a ship from Poole carried news of the siege to Captain Sydenham, begging for Waller to send them relief.

On St George's Day 190 men 'who longed to fight with their enemies more than for a good breakfast',[26] launched a sortie from the town and took one of the royalist batteries, as well as 35 prisoners and a cavalier captain, before being driven back. Despite a fresh sally from the town, Maurice set up other batteries, which included a cannon which fired 'bullets' which weighed 32 pounds, though the steepness of the hill down into Lyme partially neutralized the fire of the royalist guns.

Two days later 'very little powder was by this time left in our town,'[27] while 15 royalist prisoners overpowered their guards, seized the ship they had been incarcerated in, and sailed it triumphantly off to Weymouth. A fresh royalist battery threatened Davy's Fort, which was considered the most important point of the defensive line, and the garrison had to build up the walls until they were 6 or 8 feet thick. At the same time the most easterly of the four forts was given up and the royalist siege lines grew closer and tighter.

The first full-scale attempt to storm the town came on Sunday 28 April. It was now that one of the weaknesses of Maurice's army showed itself, for many of the men had been forced to join and they showed little enthusiasm for the attack. Maurice's horse even attacked their own conscripts from behind 'slashing and hewing them when they were put on any hard service else they would have run away to their homes'.[28] In contrast all the parliamentary garrison were volunteers.

The noise of the battle, and especially of the royalist guns which 'bestowed powder and shot freely on us, insomuch as their firing seemed a continual blaze',[29] was so great that it could be heard off Portland Bill by two parliamentary ships on their way from Portsmouth to resupply the garrison. Not that the bombardment was particularly effective, despite using up 200 barrels of powder. 'The enemy had made above 1000 great shot against the town, and yet had slain with them but one old man, that was making his will just as the bullet hit him.'[30]

Having lost between 60 and 80 men and failed to take the town by frontal assault, the royalists tried shooting fire arrows into the town, though without much effect. Reinforced by 100 men from the ships, the garrison sallied out again, blocked up some royalist guns and 'slew 50 or 60 men and two or three women of the Irish'.[31] They also 'lost Major Harrington, unhappily killed by one of our own men, but so many of the enemy were slain that the water that served the town was coloured with blood'.[32]

A fresh attempt to storm the town was launched on the evening of 6 May. All day a thick sea fog had lain over the town, and the defenders had waited for an attack. When it had not come by seven p.m., most of the garrison went off to eat their suppers. It was exactly what Maurice had anticipated, and he unleashed his troops. 'Fall on, fall on, the town is ours, the day is ours,' cried the royalists, to hear their enemies reply: 'Come on you rogues, we are ready to receive you'. Savage hand-to-hand fighting erupted, and one party of royalists penetrated the defences and forced their way deep into the town before being cut off and killed or captured. At length the attackers were driven back, and many of the royalist conscripts took the chance of the dark misty evening to run away.

Among the royalist dead was Captain Francis Blewett, and next day the royalists asked for his body back. It was returned to them by Blake who:

> demanded of them that came for the corpse whether they had any order or command to pay for the shroud or coffin. They answered no. He replied nevertheless 'Take it, we are not so poor but we can give it you.'

During the parley, Blake also told a royalist commander:

> Here you see and behold how weak our works are; they are not things wherein we trust; therefore tell the Prince that, if he desires to come into the town with his army to fight, we will pull down 10 or 12 yards so that he may come in with ten in a breast, and we will fight with him.[33]

Repulsing this attack bought the Lyme garrison several days of comparative peace, broken by bombardment from the guns. Governor Ceeley took the opportunity to send the Prince a message saying that:

England that had fed him and his brother with bread, they in requital came to consume with fire and sword; but he hoped to see them both rewarded with a halter or made shorter by the head.[34]

It was becoming more and more clear that Lyme's survival depended on help from the sea, so Maurice, christened Sennacherib by the people of Lyme, moved a large part of his artillery to the west of the town. From there it could cover 'the rare and unparalleled harbour called the Cobb',[35] and prevent the landing of supplies and reinforcements. The garrison continued to launch sallies with varying success, during one of which Prince Maurice lost his own colours, though a boy belonging to the besieging army retaliated by stealing the garrison's colours from the Cobb. There were also rumours of treachery in the town, and a gun and 12 muskets were found to have been sabotaged.

It was a local man, George Bird of Westhay, who gave the royalists the vital clue to how to deal with their enemies: 'he advised Prince Maurice to burn the ships in Lyme Cobb, which was the way to take the town.'[36] On 22 May a supply boat full of malt and peas was sunk, and attempts to rescue some of the supplies cost the garrison several casualties. That evening the royalists attacked the harbour, and 60 men burnt most of the supply barges there with fire balls. A sally by the garrison drove the cavalier musketeers back, but Maurice's cavalry counterattacked and the destruction in the Cobb continued. The day's fighting also cost the life of one of the parliamentary leaders, Thomas Pyne: 'more ships might be got again, but such a man was rarely to be found.'[37]

At the royalist headquarters in Oxford:

His Majesty, notwithstanding his former order to Prince Maurice not to engage himself before Lyme, was yet content (the possible and sudden gaining of that place being daily presented thence) that his Highness should continue that siege.[38]

But Parliament too was aware of the vital importance of Lyme, both strategically and in terms of morale country-wide. The very day after the disaster at the Cobb the Earl of Warwick arrived in Lyme Bay, with eight ships and 36 fresh barrels of powder. A few days later he wrote:

I was fully informed of the gallantry of the defendants...who though they wanted shoes, stockings, clothes and pay, and had been kept on the line from the beginning of the siege without relief, yet were every of them resolved to hold out to the utmost point of time, and when all failed, to make way through the enemy with the sword.[39]

Such determination impressed the sailors of Warwick's fleet so much that:

they lent them above 30 pairs of boots, 100 pairs of shoes, 160 pairs of stockings, some linen and old clothes, and some quantity of fish and bread that they had formerly saved out of their sea allowance. They did also unanimously give one-

> fourth part of their bread for the next four months...which
> their hard labour and constant duty might advise them to
> have reserved rather for their own bellies.[40]

The royalists reacted to Warwick's arrival by intensifying their bombardment of the harbour so that all communication between fleet and town had to be at night. The town itself was also the victim of a constant barrage, which was now wreaking considerable damage. A fresh attack, combined with the continual gunfire, inflicted on the defenders the heaviest losses of the siege so far and both Were and Blake were wounded, the former in the belly, the latter in the foot. Sensing that the crisis was at hand, on 28 May Warwick reinforced the garrison with 300 seamen, and next day tried to lessen the pressure on the town with a seaborne feint threatening a landing near Bridport.

The royalists were not taken in. On the contrary, a massive attack on the town was unleashed. A breach was made and Warwick's mariners, unused to this savage hand-to-hand fighting, were on the edge of a flight that would probably have lost the town. Then a seaman named Moizer, 'a stout man, both of person and courage' took his stand in the very centre of the breach, raising high the colours, and single-handedly resisting the royalists. The man's heroism, for which he was later recommended for promotion, gave fresh courage to the defenders:

> he never giving a foot of ground until such time as the staff
> of the colours was shot off in his hand with two or three of
> his fingers, saying to another of his fellows standing by him
> in those or the like words 'Here take you the colours, while I
> go to the surgeons to be dressed.'[41]

Once again Lyme had managed to survive.

It was almost certainly during this attack that the women of Lyme established their heroic reputation:

> in these assaults they relate that the women of the town
> would come into the thickest of the danger, to bring powder,
> bullet and provisions to the men, encouraging them upon
> the works.[42]

Some are said to have worn men's clothes to make their enemies think the garrison was larger than it was, and others even joined in the fighting itself:

> One woman shot off sixteen muskets upon the enemy, and
> the women of the town generally did fill the soldiers' ban-
> doliers while they fought. And...a maid that had had one of
> her hands cut off in the fight, being asked what course she
> would take to live, now she had lost one of her hands.
> 'Truly' (said she) 'I am glad with all my heart that I had a
> hand to lose for Jesus Christ, for whose cause I am as willing
> and ready to lose not only my other hand, but my life also'.[43]

The garrison were also inspired by 25 Puritan preachers, including James Strong, who was married to a niece of John Browne of Frampton.

Subsequently Strong wrote a rather poor 200-line poem comparing the women of Lyme to Joan of Arc and detailing their heroic acts:

> As well by defying the merciless enemy at the face abroad, as by fighting against them in garrison towns; sometimes carrying stones, then tumbling of stones over the works on the enemy when they have been scaling them, some carrying powder, others charging of pieces [reloading guns] to ease the soldiers.[44]

The poem included the lines:

> Alas! who now keeps Lyme? Poor female cattle
> Who wake all night, labour all day in battle
> And by their seasonable noise discover
> Our foes, when they the works are climbing over.

It was later published as a satire by the royalists, who prefaced the piece with a series of savage attacks on Strong, who was accused of everything from having stinking feet to breath so bad that spiders fell dead 3 yards from him, and lice ran from his body. However, the real cause of their attacks was surely Strong's claim that 'to most 'tis known, the weaker vessels are the stronger grown.' The idea that women might be stronger than men was close to heresy. It is ironic, but scarcely surprising, that in the very year that the women of Lyme so distinguished themselves, entries appear in the town account book: 'paid two soldiers to attend the whipping of a woman 2s. 6d.', 'for whipping four women 4s. 10d.' and 'for whipping a woman 4s. 4d.'.[45]

Fresh ships were continuing to arrive offshore from the town, until more than a third of the entire parliamentarian fleet lay at anchor in Lyme Bay, though many passed by without providing fresh help.

> Intercepted communications warned the parliamentary command what a dangerous condition the town of Lyme was in, and how much the royalists esteemed of that place, so as to account the keeping or loss of a great part of the West to depend on their taking or being repulsed from thence.[46]

But the besieging army was also growing desperate, and it was asserted that 'the villainous town of Lyme had destroyed more brave gentlemen of the West and men of honour than had been lost in all the West since these wars began.' And if the royalists retreated, there was another danger, that 'the country people would cut their throats, they were so bent for the Parliament at Westminster.'[47]

On 28 May Charles had written to Maurice from Oxford, ordering him:

> As soon as you shall have finished what can be done upon Lyme, or shall plainly see that it is not to be taken, we desire you to draw with all your forces to Bristol, to be there in a readiness to meet with us or come to us.

A postscript was added in the King's own handwriting.

> This is of so much importance for my service that I desire you to take notice that this is not an ordinary dispatch from

a secretary, but a particular direction from me upon mature deliberation.[48]

Maurice's response was to make fresh efforts to set the town alight with fire arrows. The weather was unusually hot and dry, and 20 or 30 houses were destroyed, despite the efforts of the fire fighters many of whom were women, before the wind blew the fire northwards, away from the rest of the town. Four days later the garrison, calling from their defences, persuaded two royalist N.C.O.s to change sides and come over to them. The same day Warwick wrote that the enemy 'seem to have their former spirit and fury much abated, their railing language being not so frequent, nor have the besiegers confidence of their own relief'.[49]

A few days later there was a fresh attempt to burn the town down, using:

> red-hot bullets and iron bars crooked at the ends that they might hang on whatsoever they lighted, one of which kindled a house where the ammunition was and likewise several thatched houses which were saved by the diligence of the people who took care to fill their vessels with water for that purpose.[50]

It was even said that a witch had been hired by the royalists to help burn the town and sink the fleet. Warwick once again grew worried and wrote 'the enemy continues his siege, and brings his approach daily nearer the town's lines so that they are in some places within a pike's length of each other.'[51] But the long-expected parliamentary relief force was finally approaching.

On the night of 14 June the royalists began taking down their tents. At two the next morning, some shots at the besiegers' works received no reply. The siege had been lifted. The garrison of Lyme had lost about 120 men, Prince Maurice was said to have suffered up to two or three thousand casualties. The figure must be an exaggeration, though even the royalists admitted they had lost more men than before Bristol or Exeter, including Colonel Barnes's only son, and still failed to take 'a little vile fishing town, defended by a small dry ditch', the Prince 'having lost much reputation in those parts by his unsuccessful attempts'.[52] Maurice's repulse before Lyme had been a disaster for the royalists, psychologically more important than Hopton's defeat at Cheriton, for the propagandists of both sides had made sure that the eyes of much of England had been turned on Lyme for the past two months. The anniversary of Lyme's deliverance was celebrated locally as a day of public thanksgiving until the Restoration, and in 1648 the town received 2000 oak trees from the Paulet estates for 're-edifying and building of their houses and ships, mills and fulling-racks for cloth, burnt and lost in the siege by Prince Maurice'.[53]

At Haye House and Colway Manor the men of Lyme found so many supplies that they had a market there and sold everything, while 'others walked into the fields and green meadows to refresh themselves...and to enjoy the benefit of the fresh air'.[54] More grimly an old Irishwoman, left behind by the retreating royalists was chased through the streets, beaten, robbed, and finally cut to pieces. Sources differ as to whether the crime was committed by the seamen, or by the women of Lyme.

At noon on 15 June Warwick came ashore. The same day he wrote to Speaker Lenthall:

> It is little less than a miracle they should hold out so long and so violent a siege, the town standing at the bottom of two hills, and their works being so low...that I myself could in many places run over them, and a strong hand may in many parts thrust them down...there are many houses burnt, yet the other day a grenade, falling in a room and breaking on a bed whereon lay three children not one of them had any harm. There is scarce a house in the town that is not battered, and scarce a room is not into which shot hath not been made.[55]

Among the houses destroyed was the vicarage, later rebuilt at a cost of £12. Lyme had survived untaken because of, 'next to the protection of Heaven, the courage and honesty of the officers and soldiers'.[56]

Four days later Warwick and his fleet withdrew to Weymouth. There was a rumour that the cavaliers would try a surprise attack on Lyme, which had been emptied of all the seamen and some of the garrison, but it came to nothing. In fact the retreating royalists were falling out among themselves. Lord Paulet, who had led a regiment of Devonshire men on the west side of the town, quarrelled with Maurice and the Prince seems to have caned him, then refused to fight a duel in satisfaction. Meanwhile Parliament rejoiced, 'other garrisons have slain their thousands, done very proudly, but this of Lyme its ten thousands, far outstripped them all.'[57] The town was awarded £2000, £1000 a year from Lord Paulet's sequestered estate, and granted a collection throughout Parliament-controlled territory for the relief of its poor and ruined people.

The royalists themselves confessed that:

> the besieging of this place was very destructive to His Majesty's affairs, although the reasons for attempting it were very probable, and according to the humours of that army not to be avoided. And it is possible, had it been more actively attacked, it might have been had, especially when his Highness first lay down before it. But it was not then thought fit (and perhaps with good reason) suddenly to hazard many men when in all probability it might be got in few days without the loss of any.[58]

Puritan preachers rejoiced, 'Thou gavest not the day to the strong, nor measured out success according to the numbers, but madest the weak chafe the mighty, and a handful overthrow a host.'[59]

One of the strongest cards the roundheads had was their complete control of East Anglia where Cromwell and others had organized the Eastern

Association, whose men and money proved a backbone of the parliamentary cause. So the royalists planned a Western Association of their own under Maurice, covering Cornwall, Devon, Somerset and Dorset. This Western Association, which was organized on 1 May 1644, was to provide the King with money, and a large new conscripted army. The resistance of Lyme temporarily blocked the plan, but it remained a serious threat, even though according to Warwick the people of Dorset 'appeared generally well affected to Parliament, in respect of the great pressures laid upon them by a beggarly and cruel enemy'.[60]

While Lyme fought for its life, and with Poole too in great distress so that £500 had to be borrowed for the town, the armies of Essex and Waller, 'with their prodigious number of cockneys',[61] had been trying to catch the King's army around Oxford. At one point it seemed certain Charles must be trapped between them, but when urged to surrender, the King replied, 'possibly he might be found in the hands of the Earl of Essex, but he would be dead first,'[62] and managed to slip away into the Cotswolds. Parliament grew impatient, and wrote irritably to Waller that he should concentrate on relieving Lyme, 'considering that the safety of the Western forts is committed to your care, and many of your forces designed for that end'.[63]

It was probably in response to this letter, and to the constant prompting of Warwick, that on 6 June the two parliamentary generals met at Stow-on-the-Wold. But Essex, as the senior, insisted Waller should follow the King while he himself marched south-west. Three reasons encouraged Essex to strike down towards Dorset and Devon: to join his cousin, Warwick, in relieving Lyme; to try to catch Queen Henrietta Maria, who on 16 June gave birth to her last child, Henrietta, in Exeter; and to break up Maurice's Western Association.

It was the news that Essex's army had arrived in Dorset which drove Maurice from his lines outside Lyme. However the same news had angered the parliamentary high command, who sent Essex a sharp letter recalling him and insisting that Waller, not he, must go into the South West. The Lord General received the letter at Blandford on 14 June, and replied petulantly:

> in truth I do not see how well Sir William Waller can take care of all the countries along the seaside from Dover to St Michael's Mount... if you think fit to set him at liberty and confine me, be pleased to make him general and me the major of some brigade, that my soldiers may have free quarter, free plunder, and fair contributions besides, as his have without control.[64]

Faced with such recalcitrance the politicians in London could do little. After objecting weakly to the vehemence of his phrasing, and admitting, 'they find themselves much discomposed by your lordship's going into the West,' Parliament merely asked Essex to use his best 'endeavours for the reducing of the West'.[65] The Lord General's march was initially highly successful. Wareham, strengthened by 500 of Maurice's men, defied him, but 1500 royalist cavalry, which included French mercenaries, were put to flight by 400 parliamentarians. When the fleeing royalists tried to take shelter in Dorchester the inhabitants closed the gates, and they had to ride on to Sherborne.

Lord Hopton had tried to gather an army at Dorchester to stop Essex, and asked Maurice for 'five men out of every company, which he promised to make good by an equal number of pressed men, but they were denied him'.[66] He then conscripted a force, but almost every man ran away, and Hopton had to fall hurriedly back into Devon.

On 16 June came Essex's greatest prize so far when the townsmen of Weymouth and Melcombe rose up and surrendered their town to him, followed three days later by the capitulation of Sandsfoot Castle. Essex made an elegant speech to 300 men who came to Weymouth to join up as soldiers, for which he received general applause, while the worried royalists complained he was:

> endeavouring by a counterfeit civility to draw people to his
> party, and to speak truth of him and his army, they are not
> guilty of those barbarous and ungentlemanlike qualities
> which most of Waller's army are possessed with.[67]

Although Portland still resisted, Warwick was delighted by the surrender of Weymouth, 'it having been most serviceable to the enemies' designs and supplies of any port in England'.[68] He spent some days planning the defences, and declared that £1200 and 500 men and 200 horse stationed there would be enough to hold 'the county of Dorset thereabouts in awe'.[69]

The royalist governor, Colonel Ashburnham, subsequently had to face a council of war in Oxford to explain the loss of the town. Sir Lewis Dyve, then the King's commander in Dorset, recognized Ashburnham's difficulties and wrote that 'all the ill accidents happening to this county...are to be attributed rather to his misfortune than his fault'.[70]

Essex's army spent little time in Dorset, though its brief passage from Blandford to Dorchester and Weymouth, then looping north via Bridport to Crewkerne, was enough to hand almost the whole county back to the parliamentarians, except for isolated strongholds like Corfe, Wareham, Sherborne, Portland and Abbotsbury. In late June Essex arrived at Chard, where Colonel Were later objected that he stayed too long: 'had there been a speedy advance, we had beaten Maurice and Grenville, and returned soon enough to beat the King also.'[71] Essex's delay was understandable, as hundreds of volunteers from Somerset and Dorset flocked to the parliamentary army, though there were difficulties because the troops wanted to be commanded by their own countrymen, and the year-long royalist control of the area meant there were few local men available as commanders.

The speed with which Essex left Dorset was good news for the county, for his army brought camp fever in its train. Camp fever was probably a variety of typhoid, and it seems to have first broken out first among Essex's men the previous year while they were stationed in the marshes of the Thames valley around Reading. It became endemic in his army, whose arrival in Devon sparked off a major outbreak near the Dorset border at Ottery St Mary, where there was 75 per cent mortality. The disease lingered long after the army had passed by.

While Essex, supported by Warwick's fleet, pursued Maurice towards and past Exeter, Parliament 'taking into their consideration the necessity of speedy raising money for the maintenance of the army and garrisons',[72] appointed county committees throughout the Westcountry. That for Dorset listed 31 men, including Denzil Holles, Sir Walter and Thomas Erle, John Browne, John Trenchard, John Fitzjames, William Sydenham, Denis Bond, Henry Henley and Thomas Ceeley. There was a separate list of six names for Poole, led by John Bingham and William Skutt. These were the men who would rule Dorset for the next few years.

Military affairs still predominated, however, and the Lyme garrison demonstrated the siege had not exhausted their determination by seizing Taunton on 10 July. Blake was made governor of the town. A day later Colonel O'Brien, the royalist governor of Wareham, retaliated by sending 240 horse out to plunder Dorchester. However the population of the county town was now behaving with far more resolution than it had a year earlier, and the women of Dorchester had clearly learned a lesson from those of Lyme, for they:

> did now the second time behave themselves as gallantly as
> they did lately when they beat out the French by pelting
> them with stones; and defending themselves with their spits
> and other such weapons.[73]

The royalists then found themselves up against a strong parliamentarian force who drove them back to Wareham.

Another of the formidable Sydenham brothers, Thomas Sydenham, had 'left Oxford while it was a garrison for his Majesty's use, and did not bear arms for him as the other scholars then'.[74] He was captured by the royalists and imprisoned in Exeter for nine or ten months before being exchanged. Returning to the war he:

> behaved himself very bravely in this action, which was per-
> formed with the loss of only one man who, being taken pris-
> oner by the enemy in the town, as they were carrying him
> away, one of them rather than he should escape, butchered
> him.[75]

The defeat of O'Brien's attack on Dorchester cost the royalist garrison of Wareham 160 men taken prisoner. Of those, eight were 'Irish rogues' who 'had such quarter given them as they gave the Protestants in Ireland, viz. that they hanged them up presently'.[76] One of the eight was spared in exchange for executing his fellows. Less than a week later Sir Francis Doddington attacked a roundhead prisoner so brutally he broke his skull, and then included him among 12 to be hanged upon the same tree in revenge for the Irishmen. During the execution another man's noose broke, and he pleaded 'that what he had suffered might be accepted, or else that he might fight against any two for his life, notwithstanding which they caused him to be hanged up again'.[77] About the same time Essex captured a certain Captain Howard who some time before 'ran away with 19 horse to the King's party' and had him executed. Sir John Berkeley's retaliated by hanging Captain Turpin, a parliamentary sea captain who had been part of Warwick's attempt to relieve Exeter the year before. 'The Parliament took this man's death very ill, alleging that his case was quite different from Howard's, the latter being a runaway, the former a fair prisoner of war.'[78] There was grave danger of a self-perpetuating spiral of reprisals until the business was sharply brought to an end by the stern common sense and humanity of Lord Hopton.

As Essex pressed deeper and deeper into the royalist heartlands of the far South West, the war in Dorset continued to go well for the parliamentarians. Portland, under blockade since the fall of Weymouth, was suffering from lack of 'beer, salt and other supplies',[79] while yet another raid on Dorchester, this time by Doddington, was foiled by Francis Sydenham. In Weymouth they were hard at work making light cannon for Essex's army, using timber taken from royalist estates, including that of Sir John Strangways.

The King and Waller had finally clashed on 29 June at Cropredy Bridge north of Oxford. Waller's attack was repulsed, and after being almost surrounded, he only just managed to extricate his badly mauled army. It was only three and a half months since Waller's victory at Cheriton had been hailed as the turning point of the war and he had been the parliamentary hero par excellence. Now his forces withered away from desertion, and one after another of his colleagues wrote to complain of him.

Just as the royalist victory at Newark in March had been within a week more than cancelled out by Hopton's defeat at Cheriton, so the King's success at Cropredy Bridge paled next to what happened three days later, the largest battle ever fought on the British mainland.[80] On the evening of 2 July, with a storm threatening, Prince Rupert and the Marquis of Newcastle clashed with three parliamentary armies on Marston Moor. The struggle was long and savage. Cromwell was wounded and his men only saved from disaster by the Scots cavalry, two parliamentary generals fled the field convinced of royalist victory, and Sir Thomas Fairfax barely escaped capture by tearing off his parliamentary insignia. Finally the discipline of Cromwell's cavalry, who regrouped for a second charge as the battle hung in the balance, decided matters. By midnight the royalists had lost 4000 men, and the North.

The King was faced with a grim decision. Destruction had struck down both his northern and south-western forces, he must use his own victorious army to repair the damage. Eventually he resolved to pursue Essex, even though it meant plunging into hostile territory, as Aubrey revealed:

Major John Morgan fell sick of a malignant fever as he was

> marching with the King's Army into the West, and was
> brought to my father's at Broad Chalke, where he was
> lodged secretly in a garret.[81]

Wiltshire and Dorset were not safe places to leave royalist officers.

After failing to catch Queen Henrietta Maria, who escaped to France, Essex made the mistake of pressing on after Maurice. Behind him came the King, who had learnt a lesson from the roundheads and hanged several of his own men for plundering. But the King's troops did not pass unchallenged. The indefatigable Lyme garrison ambushed a regiment at Colyton 'before the enemies had well digested their supper', then raided Chard just after Charles had left it, capturing '11 gallant horses, all with rich saddles and furniture, conceived to be the King's own stable horses'.[82]

Arriving on the Cornish border, Charles joined Maurice and hemmed in the parliamentary army around Lostwithiel. As the stranglehold on the trapped Earl of Essex grew tighter, Parliament in desperation detached 2000 men from Waller's battered army, put them under Lieutenant General John Middleton, and sent them to the relief of the Lord General. Middleton penetrated as far as North Petherton in Somerset, where on 14 August he was soundly defeated by Sir Francis Doddington. He gave up the attempt to save Essex and instead helped William, eldest of the Sydenham brothers and the new governor of Weymouth, to attack Wareham. Henry O'Brien, the royalist commander there, had written to Charles a month earlier, welcoming 'the long looked-for arrival of His Majesty and his army into this country' and assuring the King:

> I have not been wanting to let my officers know what an
> especial care His Majesty has to encourage and reward them;
> and they every one resolve to sacrifice their lives to God and
> His Majesty in this cause.[83]

However, since then O'Brien had received a letter from his brother, Lord Inchiquin back in Ireland, telling him that he had changed sides. After the outworks had been stormed, O'Brien hastily surrendered and 500 captured Irish soldiers agreed to travel back to Munster to fight for Parliament.

In Cornwall Essex's cavalry cut their way through the royalist lines on 31 August, and the next day Essex himself got away by sea. The roundhead infantry surrendered, and having been stripped of most of their possessions were allowed to march away 'pressed all of a heap like sheep, though not so innocent. So dirty and so dejected as was rare to see'.[84] Two months after the fortunes of war had seemed to have swung irrevocably, the royalists had fought back.

⊷ Chapter Six ↠
THE BATTLE FOR WEYMOUTH
AUGUST 1644–MARCH 1645

T he survivors of Essex's cavalry from Lostwithiel arrived in Dorset and Somerset in early September, taking out their anger at defeat by smashing the windows, monuments and organ of South Petherton church. Among these beaten men must have been the 'Lord General's cook',[1] who was buried at Dorchester on 11 September. In the first fifteen months of the war, church records had generally recorded the names of buried soldiers, but by 1644 few bothered any more.

Essex's disarmed and unprovisioned foot suffered a nightmare march through hostile countryside:

> especially through Cornwall and Devonshire, which were great enemies to them...they found the same also in Dorsetshire, the country people being usually for the strongest party, and the King's affairs at that time run very smoothly.[2]

Six thousand soldiers had surrendered to the King. Desertion and death were costing 300 men a day, and by the time they reached Poole 'they were reduced to the number of 1000, and those in no very good condition, most of their officers by that time had left their charges and were gone to London.'[3]

The parliamentary high command considered the disaster of Lostwithiel 'a plain piece of treachery to the state and Parliament...but who the persons were was not then so clear'.[4] The first blame was cast on Middleton for his failed march, but then a new scapegoat was found, one of the heroes of the siege of Lyme. Colonel Were had joined Essex on his ill-fated march into Cornwall and, when attacked by a small force of royalist cavalry, his whole regiment of foot 'at first made a stand, but presently after began to stagger, and in great disorder to quit that field and run back with their cannon and colours towards the main body'.[5] Subsequently Essex himself described Were as 'the renegade'.[6] After escaping from the royalists Were, bitterly protesting his innocence, was imprisoned and not released until November 1645, when he was bailed to the Committee of the West to be 'employed in such a manner as they think fit'.[7]

Waller and Haslerig arrived in Dorset in September, and attempted to gather what new forces they could while stiffening the garrisons of Weymouth, Poole and Lyme with fresh infantry. The fort on Brownsea Island was strengthened by the delivery of four heavy guns from the Isle of Wight, and four more were sent to Poole. Six weeks later the Brownsea garrison was also provided with four large chests of muskets from Weymouth.

The parliamentary generals had been joined by a fresh recruit that August. After being fined £500 for fighting against Parliament (he never paid and thirteen years later the debt was cancelled by Cromwell), and despite his almost total lack of military experience, Anthony Ashley Cooper was appointed Field-Marshal-General of the parliamentary army in Dorset, and took part in the capture of Wareham. The next month he and Waller reorganized the parliamentary troops of Dorset, bringing them together into a single force of ten regiments of horse and foot.

The King and his victorious army were on their way back eastwards. He paused for four or five days of unsuccessful demonstrations outside Plymouth, but had greater success with Barnstaple, which surrendered at the mere rumour of his coming. On 18 September Charles arrived in Exeter to face a problem that had long plagued the royalists of the South West: 'the troops of Lyme, which were grown more insolent by the success they had had; and made incursions sometimes even to the walls of Exeter.'[8] But the King dared not tie down his army in a fresh siege. Instead he sent out Sir Edward Waldegrave with a regiment of horse to quarter at Bridport while a hundred of Sir John Berkeley's foot seized Chideock House. William Sydenham sent out his cavalry from Weymouth to try to ambush Waldegrave:

> But the vigilant old Colonel, instead of being taken, got between the rebels and home, and at Portesham near Abbotsbury fell upon them; where some few horse were slain, 40 horse and a cornet taken.[9]

From Exeter the royal army marched to Chard. Waller, who had cautiously advanced as far as Bridport trying to raise men, hastily fell back, his cavalry having been mauled by Sir Robert Howard. From Shaftesbury he wrote to Essex, who had arrived sick and disheartened in Portsmouth: 'I am so heartily weary of this war that I shall submit to anything that may conduce to the despatch of it.'[10]

The royalists were not in particularly good shape either and the King's army 'through the flux and other diseases, does much decrease. The Cornish will not come out of Cornwall, nor the Devonshire men out of their county.'[11] Nevertheless, despite the detachments sent to block up Plymouth, Taunton and Lyme, the King still wielded a formidable fighting force of over 10,000 men that had crushed two parliamentary armies in two months. It was the last great undefeated royalist army left in the island.

Waller's outlying cavalry skirmished with the King's advance guard around Yeovil, but were brushed aside and on Monday 1 October Charles entered Dorset. He spent the night at South Perrott while the main mass of the army were at Evershot. The next day the army moved on to Kingcombe, while Charles himself stayed at Maiden Newton with the rector Mr Osborne, who was later to be 'unjustly turned out of the living by the Rumpish Triers and afterwards restored by the just hand of Providence'.[12] It was here the King had his first meeting with Prince Rupert since the catastrophe of Marston Moor.

Although Maiden Newton is only 7 miles from Dorchester, the King did not immediately risk an advance on the county town. Instead he swung back north, into the areas where the royalist cause had always been popular, staying at Sherborne, Stalbridge, and Sturminster Newton, where he received a petition from the clergy, gentry and freeholders of Somerset begging 'to embrace your Majesty's gracious offers of peace, and put an end to the calamities of this distracted and almost ruined nation'.[13] Charles promised he would do all he could to bring back peace, but at the same time he gave permission to the sheriff and county comissioners to raise men. A general impressment seemed so probable that many people 'were forced to fly from their dwellings'.[14]

Supplies were a nagging problem for any Civil War army, and the local farmers rarely had any choice as to whether they helped. While in Sturminster Newton, John Payne, 'wagon-master to His Highness, Prince Maurice' provided a pass for '23 men with three score oxen and three horses' who had been pressed into the King's service, 'and have performed it and are discharged and are to pass quietly with their cattle to their several dwelling places'.[15]

From Sturminster Newton Charles rode to visit Richard Rogers's widow at Bryanston, and then stayed in the Blandford area for four days, while 3000 men were ordered south to break the parliamentary siege of Portland, quartering at Dorchester on the way. After Portland had been relieved, Ashburnham was replaced as governor by Sir Walter Hastings, and the castle was freshly provisioned.

As the tides of the war turned against Charles, he trusted more and more to foreign help to win it for him. Much royalist energy had been spent on fighting for control of the ports of Ireland such as Pembroke, Chester and Bristol, but the Irish troops had proved a disappointment. That left the French. Early in 1644 French mercenaries began to join Prince Maurice. Then the Regent of France, Anne of Austria, signed a formal treaty of friendship with Charles. But to land any French army in England, Charles had to have control of a large Channel port, and the only ones he possessed, Falmouth, Dartmouth and Topsham, were a long way from both the French coast and the parliamentary heartlands in the South East. Portland was far more promising. It was within easy reach of Normandy, and during the royalist control of Dorset there had been a regular weekly shipping service between Portland Harbour and Cherbourg. But Portland was useless as long as his enemies held Weymouth.

Before he broke the siege of Portland, Charles left a regiment of 150 veterans in Sherborne castle under Sir Lewis Dyve, who was married to Sir John Strangways's daughter Howard, (she had previously been married to Richard Rogers's cousin, Edward Rogers of Bryanston). With Dyve were some horse, under Giles Strangways. Dyve was 'made commander-in-chief of Dorsetshire; in hope that he would be able shortly by his activity, and the very good affection of that county, to raise men enough to recover Weymouth'.[16]

The fast-retreating Waller was in serious trouble. His army numbered only 1500 men rather than 3500 as the royalists thought, and men he had were not trustworthy. One of Ludlow's officers openly insulted Waller, and

> the like disobedience I met with in the Dorsetshire troops, where I could never draw above one small regiment of Colonel Fitzjames, and one troop of Captain Starre's into the field when the King's whole army advanced upon me.[17]

After staying Sunday at Blandford to attend church, the royal army set forth again. 'His Majesty marched before the foot on foot...and with his whole army marched that night over the downs to Cranborne.'[18] In more peaceful times Charles had often visited Cranborne, where he 'did chiefly delight to hunt in the said walk or chase, as the late King James had done'.[19] There was no time for such relaxation now, nor for the King's cousin, Lord Bernard Stuart, to appreciate staying at Woodlands with the eccentric Henry Hastings. The next day, which was wet, cold and windy, the army marched on to Salisbury. The King's two weeks in Dorset were over. He would not return. The ever-optimistic Digby described the situation to the Earl of Ormonde, Charles's commander in Ireland:

> We are now marching eastward, victorious and strong...so that you may confidently esteem His Majesty's affairs here are in the best posture that they have been at any time since these unhappy wars.[20]

Charles's pursuit of Waller, and his hopes of lifting the sieges of Basing House and Donnington Castle led the King straight into a trap as three parliamentary armies closed in around him. The roundhead force was twice the size of the King's army, but the high command was torn by dissension. Manchester wanted to make peace, and was at odds with his cavalry commander Cromwell; Essex was sick, or said he was; and his rival Waller's reputation was in tatters. Nevertheless, on 27 October the parliamentarians attacked, north of Newbury. The survivors of Essex's infantry recaptured some of the guns they had lost at Lostwithiel, but the cavalry was badly handled, and after the royalists had fought their enemies to a standstill, they slipped away to Oxford for the winter. The second battle of Newbury was a mirror image of the first one fourteen months before: this time it was the parliamentarians who had missed the chance of crushing their enemy and had to settle for a draw.

The departure of the royal army from Dorset opened the way for parliamentary retaliation, and Waller rapidly resupplied the troops there, first sending them 'fifty barrels of gunpowder with ball proportionable',[21] then appealing for 'a fortnight's pay for those poor foot I left in

Dorsetshire, which will be a great encouragement'.[22] Suitably encouraged, the garrison of Poole attacked the Queen's Regiment near Blandford, then Ashley Cooper skirmished with Lewis Dyve. Two or three hundred royalist horsemen based round Colyton and Beaminster were indulging in extensive cattle rustling, until they were caught up by Ceeley and the Lyme garrison, 'who soon discovering the plunderers fell upon them...all the plundered cattle were mercifully restored to their owners'.[23] For the next few months the county was roughly split into two and fighting was incessant.

The wretched people of Dorset complained against first one side then the other. Parliamentary troops under Middleton were said to have plundered around Shaftesbury, and demanded up to 60s. a day from the inhabitants; while French soldiers fighting for the royalists were accused of committing a whole series of outrages including six of them raping a woman 'she having been but three days before delivered out of childbed'.[24] Even churches were not free from fighting. A royalist party who took shelter in Maiden Newton church found themselves under fire from their roundhead pursuers, and 300 years later their bullets were discovered embedded in the wood of a Norman door in the church. In Wimborne the bars on the church windows and door were mended and 2d. was 'paid to a soldier for taking up of the latch,' with another 1d. 'for pay'.[25] People took what precautions they could, but not necessarily successfully. In November 1644 John Hodder of Melcombe Regis gave most of his valuables to John Vincent, a potter of Broadway, to hide for him. When he demanded them back some time later, Vincent told him that soldiers had come to his house, dug up the floors, and taken everything except 22s. 6d. he found in the dirt the next morning. Hodder accused Vincent of having stolen the goods himself, but the truth was impossible to prove.

The propaganda war was also in full flow. Ashley Cooper and Thomas Erle accused Lewis Dyve of having a force of 'French papists and other outlandish monsters for the destroying of religion, laws and liberties'. Dyve responded hotly that it was the 'most notorious falsehood, and invented by themselves to colour their foul and unnatural rebellion'. He also charged that the parliamentarians had 'destroyed and defaced our churches, burnt the houses of their neighbours, driven away their cattle, plundered them of all their horses and goods, and imprisoned their persons'.[26]

Gradually the town of Lyme was being repaired and the scars of the siege healed. The town accounts include payments 'for mending the Cobb...for mending the prison wall...for work about the schoolhouse' and several for 'removing the rubble in the town'.[27] However the garrison remained the most active in the region, as is reflected by frequent references to wounded soldiers. Varying in size between 320 and 700 men, it was clearly well supplied, 'each man his two pounds of beef a day',[28] and raided constantly. In November an attack was launched on a royalist force in Axminster who 'betook them to the church which they had fortified, on which we were loath to cast our men',[29] and the parliamentarians retreated after setting fire to part of the town. A few days later the Lyme men joined with Sydenham's force from Weymouth to attack Axminster again. Their attempt to surprise the royalist stronghold in the church failed, so they decided to:

> set the houses on fire, that were not burnt in the first firing,
> which accordingly we did, and burnt down the whole town,
> unless it were some few houses, but yet they would not come
> forth of the church.[30]

The same day a ship from Brittany, bound for Topsham, was blown ashore near Lyme loaded with £3000 worth of linen cloth belonging to royalists in Exeter. Next the roundheads turned on the royalist garrison in Chideock,

> but they refused to yield, whereupon our soldiers were all
> willing to storm it, which we did, but we were forced to
> leave it, and lost in the storming nine killed and seven
> wounded, and in the night marched to our garrison again.
> Had we but 500 horse, we should, through God's mercy,
> clear all the country.[31]

About the same time Ashley Cooper covered Weymouth's northern approaches by attacking the Strangways mansion at Abbotsbury. Twice he offered quarter if the garrison would surrender, but Colonel James Strangways hung out a bloody flag, meaning they would fight to the end:

> they were so gallant that they would admit of no treaty, so
> that we prepared ourselves for to force it, and accordingly
> fell on. The business was extreme hot for above six hours;
> we were forced to burn down an outgate to a court before we
> could get to the house, and then our men rushed in through
> the fire and got into the hall porch, where with furze faggots
> they set fire on it, and plied the windows so hard with small
> shot that the enemy durst not appear in the low rooms: in the
> meantime one of our guns played on the other side of the
> house, and the gunners with fire balls and grenades with
> scaling ladders endeavoured to fire the second storey but,
> that not taking effect, our soldiers were forced to wrench
> open the windows with iron bars, and, pouring in faggots of
> furze fired, set the whole house in a flaming fire, so that it
> was not possible to be quenched and then they cried for
> quarter.[32]

The aftermath was bloodier than the initial fight. Cooper was resolved to refuse quarter, partly because the parliamentarians had already lost 15 men, partly to terrify other royalist garrisons, but Colonel Sydenham ordered his men to give quarter, a disagreement that may have helped spark off a long hostility between the two men. Despite warnings the roundhead troops charged inside the blazing house looking for plunder.

A few minutes later the royalist powder store exploded, and 50 or more of the looters were killed instantly. The house was burnt to the ground.

From Abbotsbury Cooper marched east, and the royalist garrisons of Sturminster Newton and Shaftesbury fled at his approach. He may have been fighting for Parliament for less than three months, but there was no doubting his determination, nor his ruthlessness, as is evidenced by a memorandum he sent to Colonel Bingham, the governor of Poole, in which he suggests:

> whether it be not absolutely necessary to pluck down the town of Wareham, it being impossible for us to victual; if Sir W.Waller ever draw away his foot the town is left naked and exposed to the pleasure of the enemy, who will certainly possess it unless it can be made no town; and there can be no argument against the demolishing it, being extremely mean-built and the inhabitants almost all dreadful malignants.[33]

Fortunately for Wareham Bingham did not take Cooper's advice to obliterate the town, nor his alternative proposal that the garrison should be all cavalry, so if they were attacked they could simply set fire to the town and escape. However Bingham did follow some of his other suggestions, including the garrisoning of Lulworth Castle as a check on Corfe, and perhaps also putting men in the Marquis of Winchester's Hooke Court, which was later burnt down by parliamentary troops.

Cooper's success stung the royalists into action, and Major Strangways and Captain Walcot defeated a party from Poole near Blandford. Next Sir Lewis Dyve tried the usual raid on Dorchester, but was double-crossed by some townsmen who had called for his help and then attacked him. However, Dyve drove them off. A few days later Dyve was involved in another skirmish near Dorchester, after the:

> renowned Colonel Sydenham, impatient of the double flourishes of a vapouring enemy, that night drew out a party of between 50 and 60 horse, double-pistolled, and with them marched himself in person, desirous to show Sir Lewis Dyve some action.[34]

During this fight a vicious family feud came to a head. One of the Sydenham brothers recognized Major John Williams at the head of the charging royalist cavalry:

> This Williams had formerly basely and cruelly killed Colonel Sydenham's mother, whom so soon as Colonel Sydenham saw, he spoke to his men that were next to him, to stick close to him; for, said he, 'I will now avenge my mother's innocent blood;' and so he most valiantly made his way to Major Williams, and slew him in the place, who fell dead under his horse's feet.[35]

Mary, daughter of Sir John Jeffrey of Catherston and mother of the Sydenham brothers, died in August 1644. However, it is possible the feud might not have been started by Major Williams at all, for on 27 April 1644 there was an 'Arendell Williams buried'[36] in Bridport.

Dyve was seriously wounded during the fight at Dorchester, and had to retreat hastily back to Sherborne.

To the north Robert Blake was tightly besieged in Taunton, 'one of the chief towns in Somersetshire, and though it was an open and unfortified place, it was very strong against the King in the natural disaffection of the inhabitants'.[37] From behind feeble defences, Blake and his men threw back two major royalist assaults. Eventually Major General James Holborne was sent out from the main parliamentary army to relieve Taunton. Holborne was joined by Edmund Ludlow and his Wiltshire cavalry and Ashley Cooper with a strong detachment of troops from Dorset. On 9 December the parliamentarians arrived in Somerset. Ludlow's report reveals something of a slowly growing royalist reluctance to fight:

> when we advanced near the enemy, my troop was ordered to
> a quarter of which they were in possession, but quitted upon
> our approach, as they did also the siege soon after, contrary
> to our expectation.[38]

Five days later Taunton was relieved. Although Holborne was the commander of the relieving force, the ambitious Cooper seems to have taken over as the effective leader, calling himself commander-in-chief and writing the dispatch to Parliament to announce their success:

> Last night we brought all our carriages safe to Taunton with
> our horse. We find the castle in no great want of victual, only
> of powder and salt. The town began to be in great distress,
> and it almost a miracle to us that they should adventure to
> keep the town, their works being for the most part but pales
> and hedges, and no line about the town.[39]

The straits Taunton had been in were confirmed by the royalist Edmund Wyndham, a veteran from the Low Countries who would shortly be made governor of Bridgwater. Wyndham wrote that the garrison of Taunton had been so hungry that after the royalists retreated:

> they could not follow us by any house but that they sought
> for bread, and by that means they gave us the better oppor-
> tunity of coming off, and lost some of their own men with
> the bread in their mouths.[40]

Wyndham blamed the relief of Taunton on Sir Lewis Dyve's failure to arrive with his cavalry. Certainly Dyve was worried enough by the resurgence of the roundheads to pull the cavalier garrison out of Chideock Castle to strengthen his own position in Sherborne. The garrison at Lyme, reinforced by some of Holborne's men, hastily reoccupied Chideock a week before Christmas.

Back in London the seeds of future strife were beginning to sprout. Arguments had flared between the Scots and Presbyterians on one side, and the Independents on the other over how much religious toleration Parliament should permit. The Independents argued vehemently in favour of toleration, but the M.P. for Lyme Regis, Edmund Prideaux, 'among the ablest of the House of Commons, opposed them to their face'.[41] Another Dorset M.P., Denis Bond, was more cautious, and when a vote was taken in committee, he abstained, allowing the Independents to win by just one vote. The question of toleration looked set to tear apart the parliamentary side, but the furious Scots had just proved the worth of their army by taking the last major royalist stronghold in the North, Newcastle, and the differences were, temporarily, smoothed out.

It was in the winter of 1644/5 that the Westcountry first became acquainted with George, Lord Goring, a dashing and experienced cavalry commander with a string of successes in the north to his name.

> a person very winning and graceful in all his motions, and by a hurt in his leg, which he had nobly and eminently obtained in an assault of a town in Holland, and which produced a lameness not be concealed, he appeared the more comely and prevailing. He had a civility which shed itself over all his countenance...his courage was notorious and confessed; his wit equal to the best...and his language and expression natural, sharp and flowing, adorned with a wonderful seeming modesty, and with such a constant and perpetual sprightfulness and pleasantness of humour, that no man had reason to be ashamed of being disposed to love him, or indeed of being deceived by him.[42]

This paragon would bring such ruin and destruction to the people of Somerset and Dorset that 'Goring's Crew' would still be spoken of with fear and loathing after almost a century. After being improbably appointed the King's Lieutenant General for Hampshire, Sussex, Surrey and Kent, counties where the royalist presence was minimal or entirely nonexistent, Goring suddenly struck eastwards with astonishing speed and bravura. Edmund Ludlow's cavalry was badly mauled at Salisbury on 31 December, and Ludlow himself was wounded, had a horse killed under him and narrowly escaped capture.

A party of royalist horse also advanced on the 'little unfortified fishertown'[43] of Christchurch. The parliamentary governor, Major Philip Lowther, hastily loaded the garrison's ammunition into boats and sent it across to the Isle of Wight. He himself retreated to Hurst Castle, harrassed by the cavaliers. Goring drove on as far as Farnham, spreading brief terror in London, then turned back and attacked Christchurch, which had been reoccupied by the roundheads. The townsman who had guided in Goring's 1000-strong force was the first killed, and this time there was a fierce struggle. The parliamentary garrison was driven back into a few strongholds, the church, the castle and one Mr Hastings's house, and was on the point of being overrun when the cavaliers noticed a bright beacon fire in the direction of Poole. Assuming wrongly it was a relief force Goring retreated to Lymington, stripping the local farmers of all their corn, not even leaving them any for seed so they had to leave their land or starve.

Ludlow, who had taken refuge on the Isle of Wight, was hastily gathering reinforcements, but just as they were about to put to sea 'news was brought that the enemies were beaten off, and so saved our men that trouble,'[44] It was probably this attack that required the expenditure which appears in an undated account of the time, including 'paid to the constable of the castle' and 'for mending the gate'.[45] Goring's army of 4500 retreated westwards until they found winter quarters around Crewkerne and Chard, from where they took part in the re-established siege of Taunton.

A spell of savage weather descended at the end of January 1645, with a heavy snowfall and weeks of freezing rain and sleet, while 'Lord Goring's forces equally infested the borders of Dorset, Somerset and Devon, by unheard of rapine, without applying themselves to any enterprise upon the rebels.'[46] In fact, as well as mercilessly plundering the rich villages around Bruton, Goring's troops also raided into roundhead-controlled Wiltshire, from where Waller, uncomfortably stationed in Salisbury, wrote wryly: 'Noble lord, God's blessing be on your heart you are the jolliest neighbour I ever met with.'[47] When the two generals met at Shaftesbury to negotiate an exchange of prisoners Waller, who clearly knew his man, presented Goring with a gift of fine wine from London, and the whole gathering was carried out with such splendour and courtesy on both sides that 'the country people, believing we were appointed to make a peace, flocked in great numbers to Shaftesbury.'[48]

South Dorset had been so quiet over the winter that when Weymouth council met on 29 January, its main concern was cleaning up the town, and a full meeting agreed:

> that all the dirt in the several streets and lanes of this town shall be made up into heaps by the inhabitants of the town before their several and respective houses, grounds, lands and dwellings before Saturday morning next upon pain of every man making default 3s. 4d.[49]

Dirt collection would be on Wednesdays and Saturdays, and Robert Hawkins and William Winter would take it all away 'with their horses and pots', for which they would be paid £8 a year. The minister to the parliamentary garrison, Peter Ince, was equally sanguine:

> In the beginning of February we were in as sweet and quiet security as any garrison in the kingdom. No enemy near us but one at Portland, and they not very considerable being but about 300 or 400 men.[50]

The peace would not last. Several Weymouth townsmen, led by Fabian Hodder, had been intriguing since Christmas to betray the town to the royalists. Hodder had enrolled a variety of supporters, paid them £5 each, and made them swear to secrecy. His wife, Anne, wrote a letter to Sir Lewis Dyve telling him the town was ready to be handed over, and the letter was carried to Sherborne by a widow, Elizabeth Wall. At midnight on Sunday 9 February a royalist force from Portland was ferried over the narrow strait and advanced silently on Weymouth, to be joined by Hodder's conspirators, who used the obscure password 'Crabchurch' and wore white handkerchiefs on their arms. The parliamentary garrison was caught utterly off their guard, and before the alarm could be given the cavaliers had penetrated the defensive forts that ringed the town. The attack had been carefully planned to take place when there were no ships in the harbour, and the northernmost fort was taken from the sea by a boat guided in by a local fisherman, Walter Bond.

The parliamentarians, 'finding such dangerous guests possessed of those places which above a half year's pain and sweat had endeavoured to make our security',[51] counter-attacked. Outside the town Mr Wood, the curate of Sutton Poyntz, and thirty men armed with cudgels, waited in vain for Sir Lewis Dyve to arrive, and finally went home. It was not until Monday morning that Dyve arrived with 1500 men to complete the seizure of Weymouth. Among the dead was Major Francis Sydenham, whose fall sparked off something of a panic among the parliamentarians: 'his death was no small joy to our enemies, to whom he was a perpetual vexation and terror, and no small grief to us who had our eyes too much upon him.'[52]

While the royalists mopped up the last resistance, the defeated round-heads fled across the 'fair arched wooden drawbridge'[53] that connected Weymouth to its twin town of Melcombe. Weymouth at the time was much the smaller of the two settlements, 'consisting chiefly of one street, which for a good space stands open to the sea' while Melcombe had 'a market place and convenient streets, and also yards for their wares, by means whereof most of the merchants have chosen this for their habitation'.[54] Nevertheless it was Weymouth that had all the defence works, Melcombe was entirely unprotected.

Despite this, and the death of his brother, Colonel William Sydenham did not consider surrender, and after raising the drawbridge, his men began to throw up a rough earthwork. The royalists used the guns they had taken in the Weymouth forts to bombard Melcombe, but without much effect. The parliamentarians grimly continued making fortifications and waited for help.

The fall of Weymouth, and all it implied for the King's hope of French reinforcements, sent a shudder through the parliamentary command. Waller tried to get his foot to march to the relief of Melcombe, but the weather was bitter and his men, short of arms, knapsacks and stockings, were very reluctant to move. On 14 February Essex's cavalry were ordered to join Waller's relief force, and instantly mutinied, sending a message to Parliament declaring, 'we will rather go under any the Lord General shall appoint than with Sir William Waller – with all the money in England.'[55] There were other mutinies among Cromwell's men in Portsmouth, and at Henley-on-Thames. The parliamentary high command, in near-panic, wrote feebly to the commanding officer at Henley, 'sorry to hear that your officers and soldiers are not in so good a temper as we could wish'.[56]

Sixteen days before, a truce had been agreed between the King and Parliament, and peace negotiations had begun at Uxbridge. Neither side seems to have taken them very seriously, and the King's main aim was to split the Scots and their allies, the Presbyterian M.P.s led by Denzil Holles, from the Independents like Cromwell.

While the negotiations were going on, Sir Lewis Dyve intercepted a letter from the Somerset parliamentarian John Pyne to Edward Popham, a leading member of the parliamentary navy, who was 'of a passionate and virulent temper'.

> The subject of the letter was a bitter invective against the Earl of Essex, and all who advanced the treaty of peace, and a great detestation of the peace, with very indecent expressions against the King himself, and all who adhered to him.... The Scots were likewise as inveighed against as anybody else.[57]

Charles made sure Essex saw the letter, but the Lord General's influence was rapidly waning.

The Scots, worried by the growing power of the Independents, dropped hints that if the King softened his line on religion, they might change sides and support him. But Charles's complete refusal to get rid of the bishops ended his last chance of peace with honour. With a week of the truce left to run, the war party in Parliament used the mutinies to force through a series of measures that would entirely reform the parliamentary army.

Back in Dorset the battle at Weymouth was coming to a head. The royalists appear to have thought they had done all the hard work, and on Wednesday 12 February a party visiting Radipole were confident enough to concentrate on getting 'distempered with beer'.[58] However by the end of the week, the royalist commanders had realized their enemies in Melcombe were not going to give in, so they tried to burn them out, firing fire red-hot slags into Melcombe, and setting a thatch on fire. Colonel Sydenham sent Dyve a letter demanding that he 'cease this useless burning', but Dyve replied scornfully, 'we scorn to parley with you, and will do what we please.'[59] Thereupon Sydenham retaliated by sending a band of men across the river to set several houses in Weymouth alight, he also launched a fire ship at the royalist boats in Weymouth harbour. The fire bombardment ceased. Shortly afterwards a roundhead sally netted 900 sheep and a royalist captain, who mistook the parliamentarians for his own men.

Once again parliamentary control of the sea came into its own. A ship from Poole brought 80 reinforcements, then on 18 February the vice admiral of the parliamentary navy, William Batten, arrived with two more ships:

> we landed out of our ships a 150 seamen (for the better keeping of Melcombe till some relief came) with what ammunition I could spare. The enemy continually played upon the town with great and small shot, day and night, who were accordingly answered by the town in a plentiful manner.[60]

A hundred Dorset cavalry, under the command of Colonel James Heane who had escaped from Portland Castle only ten weeks earlier, also managed to slip in by land. But the royalists were being reinforced too. At that moment Weymouth was the crux of the war in the south, and both sides recognized it.

While Dyve asserted, 'the business is of that importance as little less than the Crown depends upon it,'[61] Goring demanded help from Devon and arrived at Dorchester with his entire army of close on 5000 men. His plan was to storm Melcombe, then sweep up towards Salisbury and break Waller, whose army he regarded with contempt. Once he had done that, the road to London might open up. Meanwhile ordinary Dorset people suffered from this fresh quickening of the war's momentum. Thomas Clark of Hazelbury Bryan had been 'reduced to such necessities that he could scarce get bread for his family'. His son, William, 'who was in orders and a person of great courage and loyalty,' was travelling between Hazelbury and Weymouth on 13 February when he 'was shot to death upon the road'.[62]

On Sunday 23 February, two weeks after the seizure of Weymouth, Goring began to build an earthwork, partly to prevent the landing of any more assistance from the ships in Weymouth Bay, partly to give his troops cover before they attacked in earnest. Next day the parliamentarians sallied out, seized all the working tools and drove off Goring's men. The battle flamed towards its climax on 25 February when the heavily outnumbered parliamentarians again sallied out and captured a royalist provision convoy and 25 horsemen. Goring angrily sent out infantry from Weymouth to recapture the convoy.

It was the moment Sydenham had been waiting for. With most of the royalist garrison of Weymouth fighting to the north of the town, Sydenham suddenly lowered the drawbridge and unleashed 150 musketeers across the river into the heart of Weymouth. The tactic was a brilliant success, and the roundheads seized back the Chapel Fort, 'a strong place, and the greatest annoyance we had, because it overlooked Melcombe and shot into all the streets'.[63]

Among the men who took Chapel Fort was probably Thomas Sydenham. 'A person of a florid style, of a generous and public spirit, very charitable',[64] he would become the greatest physician of the century. By a strange coincidence, practising for the royalists in Weymouth was another man whose importance in the history of medicine can scarcely be overstated, Richard Wiseman 'the father of English surgery'. The total surprise achieved by the attackers was witnessed by Wiseman:

> I was dressing a wounded man in the town almost under the Chapel Fort, and hearing a woman cry 'Fly! Fly! The fort is taken!' I turned aside a little amazed...I saw our people running away and those of the fort shooting at them. I slipped down this work into the ditch and got out of the trench; and as I began to run, hearing one call 'Surgeon!' I turned back,

and seeing a man hold up a stumped arm, I thought it was an Irishman whom I had absolutely dismembered [amputated], whereupon I returned and helped him up. We ran together, it being within half a musket-shot of the enemy's fort; but he outran me quite.[65]

Captain Alexander Keynes, a Catholic from Radipole Farm was not as lucky as Wiseman and was captured while carrying a 'portmanteau, a parcel of Holy beads, a commission for a ship to play the pirate with at sea, which lay blank at Dunkirk'.[66] Keynes's wife Sarah was subsequently ordered to bring their daughter up in the Protestant religion, for which £10 a year was taken from Keynes's sequestered estate. Along with Keynes the parliamentarians took 60 prisoners, including eight commissioned officers. Dyve immediately wrote to Sir John Berkeley about 'the disaster that happened to us this day, by negligence of some of our horse', though he assured him that taking Melcombe 'we are confident cannot be a work of many days'.[67]

Nevertheless, with the parliamentarians back in control of Chapel Fort, the royalist hold on Weymouth was suddenly precarious. Goring must either give up, or launch a full-scale attack. He chose the second course. At one in the morning on 28 February a simultaneous assault was launched on the Chapel Fort and Melcombe. Among the local people were many royalist sympathisers, and 'these treacherous townsmen within let in many of the enemy's forces through their back doors.'[68] Others used false keys to try to free cavalier prisoners and seize a fort. The royalists swept over the defensive works and drove into Melcombe as far as Weymouth bridge. But Sydenham had been warned of Goring's plans by an escaped prisoner, and he and Batten had prepared hidden barricades and batteries in the heart of the town. The royalists were suddenly exposed to a savage counterattack, and after two hours struggle they turned and fled with a loss of 250 men slain or drowned. In Batten's words 'the streets were well strawed with their dead bodies.'[69]

Clarendon was not impressed by the royalist commanders at Weymouth:

that place of so vast importance was, by most supine negligence at best, retaken by that contemptible number of the enemy, who had been beaten into the lower town, and who were looked upon as prisoners at mercy. The mysteries of which fatal loss were never inquired into.[70]

The next morning Goring's men fell back to Wyke Regis, leaving behind some of their colours and many guns. Shortly afterwards they retreated to Dorchester and wrought characteristic destruction, as is evidenced in the Dorchester town records:

Forasmuch as the stock of the hospital brewhouse of this town was almost quite lost and destroyed in the late wars by the violence of the soldiers (230 quarters of malt by estimation spent and spoilt by Goring's men at one time, £1000 and more was lost in bad debts) and bad debts.[71]

Three hours after Goring's precipitate retreat, a royalist ship, the *Endeavour*, arrived in Portland Harbour, with 12 cannons and a supply of salt and other vital commodities. The ship took shelter from Batten under the guns of Portland Castle, which was still held by the royalists, but the seamen mutinied and braved cannon fire from Portland to join Batten.

'My soldiers, horse and foot, have all had very hard service of it,' commented Sydenham. 'They have neither money nor clothes, and yet unwearied in this business.'[72] Nine hundred parliamentarians had fought 'eighteen days and nights together, during all which time our valiant soldiers put off neither arms nor clothes',[73] and defeated 4000 royalists, despite the hostility of many of the townsmen. The hostility would cost the population of Weymouth dear, for the implacable Batten lined up prisoners on board H.M.S. *Reformation*, ready for hanging. A Melcombe alderman and former royalist sea captain, John Cade, confessed to Batten and was immediately hanged, but Thomas Samways, a Melcombe tailor, regretted his actions and was reprieved at the very foot of the gallows, as was Walter Bond, the two of them being taken back to prison 'to make a further discovery of their partners'.[74] Another of the plotters, an Irish Catholic, knew his nationality and religion left him no chance of mercy and so hanged himself. As for John Mills, a Weymouth constable, he died:

> without any sign or token of sorrow or repentance...when he was upon the ladder he most desperately threw himself off not showing any signs of humiliation, or calling upon God for mercy on his soul, but carelessly in a most desperate manner died, not so much as praying to God to receive his soul.[75]

The chaplain, Ince, remarked with grim satisfaction that 'there be not many of the villains left, but their sin has found them out.'

From Sherborne Dyve sent Sydenham a letter accusing him of barbarous inhumanity, declaring, 'were all my children under the power of your cruelty, I would not be diverted from justice to save their lives,'[76] and saying he intended to hang one of his prisoners, Paty, a royalist who had changed sides. Sydenham's reply was that if Paty was hanged, he would 'make a halter of your letter to hang Hodder with'.[77] It seems likely that Sydenham's threat had some effect, as Fabian Hodder was not put to death.

Less than a week later Parliament showed the importance they attached to the victory by voting £2000 to the officers, soldiers and sailors of Weymouth, and declaring 12 March a Solemn Day of Thanksgiving in London. The recapture of Weymouth provided another bonus when a ship from Rouen in France, bringing cannons and supplies of arms to the royalists, who were still thought to hold the port, was seized on 8 March. The parliamentarians gratefully accepted the rewards of their triumph, and prepared for the campaign of summer 1645 that would decide the war.

-+ Chapter Seven +-

THE CLUBMEN
MARCH 1645–AUGUST 1645

On the last day of February 1645, the eyes of the great must have been firmly fixed on Weymouth. But in the little village of Godmanstone a few miles north of Dorchester a largely unnoticed event took place that briefly threatened to tear control of the war from the hands of the generals and politicians. Provoked by the demands of some of Goring's men, the villagers of Godmanstone turned on their tormentors and killed several soldiers. Next day nearly a thousand men gathered 'with guns and clubs to resist the French and Irish among the cavaliers'.[1] The country people of Dorset had had enough, and soon their example would be followed by the inhabitants of a great crescent from East Sussex through Hampshire, Wiltshire and Berkshire to Dorset, then north into Somerset, Gloucestershire and the Welsh Borders, areas which had 'more deeply...tasted the misery of this unnatural intestine war',[2] and where civilian government had utterly collapsed. One of the rare rural uprisings in English history was about to explode.

The next month was published 'The Western Husbandman's Lamentation', which reflected the detestation felt by many for both sides:

I had six oxen the other day
And them the Roundheads fetched away
A mischief be their speed.
And had six horses left me whole
And them the Cavalieros stole
We poor men be agreed.

How I do labour, toil and sweat
And bear the cold, with dry and heat
And what dost think I get?
Faith just my labour for my pains
The garrisons have all the gains...

There goes my corn and beans and peas
I do not care them to displease
They do so swear and vapour.
When to the Governor I do come
And pray him to discharge my sum
Gave nothing but a paper...

If all this be not grief enough
They have a thing called quarter too

O 'tis a vengeance waster.
A pox upon it, they call it free
I'm sure they make us slaves to be
And every rogue our master.[3]

The borough of Weymouth was concentrating on the return to day-to-day life. On 21 March, just three weeks after the end of the siege, the council meeting was once again dominated by the problem of cleanliness. The eventual decision was to appropriate litters 'by warrant from the vice admiral [Batten] for the carrying away of the soil which now lies in the streets and lanes'.[4] Something must have happened to Robert Hawkins and William Winter, who had been chosen to clear up the town seven weeks earlier, for new men were appointed.

However the war seems to have brutalized some inhabitants of the town. The following year Mary Chiles, the wife of a Weymouth innkeeper, John Chiles, testified to a particularly unpleasant crime. She said that on the Thursday after the siege a middle-aged trader from Taunton Deane named William Courtney, with flaxen hair and a yellow beard, spent the night at Chiles's inn. He had with him a canvas bag containing £300, most of it in gold, the rest in silver. At midnight Chiles asked his wife to agree to Courtney's murder. When she said she was frightened of being caught, Chiles replied: 'it was no matter for killing a man now, it was a time of war.' Chiles killed the man by hitting him twice on the forehead with a hammer while he slept, threw the body into the sea, then:

> struck fire and lighted a candle and told [counted] the
> money in their low room, on the bare table which stands by
> the window next the street, and laid the gold by itself, and
> the white money by itself, and then put it up again into the
> said bag.[5]

The couple then went to bed, Chiles confidently claiming the 'money would make them both.' When the case was investigated, Chiles denied everything. Evidence was provided that Courtney was still living even though he and another man, who was also still alive and who fitted the description of the murdered man much better, had indeed been in Weymouth at the time. On the other hand if there had been no murder there seemed no reason for Mary Chiles to put herself in serious danger of being executed for collaborating in a murder, nor for her to provide such extensive detail. The mysterious case was considered for four months before being sent to the assizes. John Chiles must have been found innocent of the charges as he was still an inhabitant of Melcombe in 1664.

That spring King Charles sent his fourteen-year-old eldest son, Charles, Prince of Wales to Bristol to, in his own words, 'unboy him',[6] providing him with a council that included Edward Hyde (the future Earl of Clarendon) and Lord Hopton. Within days Prince Charles was met with complaints about:

> the riots and insolencies of the lord Goring's soldiers, and

that those parts of the country which were adjacent to Sherborne and Bridgwater were compelled to work at those fortifications.[7]

Prince Charles promised he would do what he could, but in practice that was very little. The troops were unpaid and almost out of control as they closed back in around Blake in Taunton. Blake's response was typical. Knowing he did not have enough supplies in the town for a large garrison, he sent away Holborne and the men who had relieved him the previous December, and prepared to face Goring's entire army with only his original garrison.

Parliament too was on the move. Waller was marching into the West to relieve Taunton and ruin any hopes the royalists still held of establishing a Western Association. Waller's army was roughly the size of Goring's, perhaps 5000 strong, but its cavalry commander was a man already famous throughout England, Oliver Cromwell. Waller's description of 'this eagle in his eyrie' provides an intriguing glimpse of Cromwell when he arrived in Dorset in the spring of 1645:

> although he was blunt, he did not bear himself with pride or disdain. As an officer he was obedient, and did never dispute my orders nor argue upon them. He did, indeed, seem to have great cunning, and whilst he was cautious of his own words, (not putting forth too many lest they should betray his thoughts), he made others talk, until he had as it were sifted them, and known their inmost designs.[8]

On his way into the Westcountry, near Andover, Cromwell captured Lord Harry Percy, the former head of royalist ordnance, and a group of cavaliers. Among them was 'a youth of so fair a countenance' that Cromwell, with wellfounded suspicion, ordered the captive to sing:

> which he did with such a daintiness that Cromwell scrupled not to say to Lord Percy that being a warrior, he did wisely to be accompanied by Amazons. On which that lord, in some confusion, did acknowledge that she was a damsel.[9]

Cromwell, who had reported to the House of Commons that his regiment 'were sorry for their former mutinous carriage',[10] arrived in Dorset as the county threatened to dissolve into anarchy. Four thousand Dorset clubmen, as they had been christened, had gathered and 'threatened to plunder all who did not join with them to extirpate the cavaliers'.[11] The parliamentary governors of Poole and Wareham, sensing possible allies, sent some horse to join the clubmen, but

> it was evident, though the avowed ground for the rising was the intolerable oppression, rapine and violence exercised by the Lord Goring's horse, that in truth they received encouragement from many gentlemen of the country, some of them...believing it would be a profitable rising for the King.[12]

The Prince of Wales and his council, worried by this unpredictable new force, told Goring to crack down on the clubmen, but Goring ignored their orders.

The siege of Taunton dragged on while the rival armies spent the next three weeks skirmishing around Dorset and the Somerset and Devon borders. Goring and his men were ambushed by Holborne near Crewkerne, and next day retreated back to Exeter 'where they stayed three or four days in most scandalous disorder, a great part of his horse lying upon free quarter, and plundering to the gates of the city'.[13] The roundhead forces of Holborne, Cromwell and Alexander Popham joined together at Cerne Abbas on 19 March, where 'the enemy came within three miles of them undiscovered'.[14] But neither side was ready for a battle. Waller, encouraged by a possibility of seizing Bristol through bribery, hurried north but the plot failed. His response was to write to London complaining about his lack of infantry:

> if I had but those 3000 that were assigned unto me, you might be Masters of the West, and of the places of the greatest importance in it, the people being universally disposed to receive us, but unwilling to engage till they see me with such a body as may give them assurance I mean to stay with them, and not to be gone tomorrow.[15]

On 26 March Holborne was at Bridport and Cromwell on the Hampshire border at Ringwood where he was joined by Colonel Norton, while Goring was poised at Shaftesbury, threatening their lines of communication. Royalist reinforcements under Sir Richard Grenville were on their way, and Goring sensed a chance to trap his enemies between the two royalist armies, especially as Waller's army was in a fairly bad way with a 'smoke of discontent' among its officers. Cromwell hastily rejoined Holborne and, strengthened by reinforcements from Taunton, Poole and Weymouth, some of which had arrived by sea, he reoccupied Dorchester. Goring's response was to launch a sudden cavalry attack, scattering 800 roundhead horse. Tradition says Cromwell himself only escaped by climbing a tree in Came Park, and that Tupp's Corner at Fordington was so named in memory of the superhuman speed of a fleeing parliamentarian named Tupp. Within a week Waller's forces were rumoured to have shrunk by 1000, mostly from desertion.

Not for the first time, nor the last, Goring was unable to profit from his success. Grenville had quarrelled with both Berkeley, who was besieging Taunton, and Goring. After he was wounded his troops from Cornwall and Devon refused to co-operate with other royalist forces. Despite apparently losing a large force of foot in a wreck off Weymouth, Waller marched north and Goring fell back towards Bruton with his 'smart army of old soldiers'.[16] The two sides circled each other warily for some days, threatening a major battle, but finally Cromwell and Waller resolved their army was too weak in foot and that they would not risk 'a too unequal engagement'.[17] Goring seems to have come to the same conclusion, and battle was postponed.

The passage through parliament on 3 April of the Self-Denying Ordinance, by which members of Parliament, Lords and M.P.s, would no longer be able to hold commissions, was about to revolutionize the round-head army. The old warleaders, Essex, Warwick, Manchester and many others, including Anthony Ashley Cooper, had to surrender their com-mands, and Waller's army retreated after what Richard Mayor (whose daughter later married Richard Cromwell) described to Colonel Norton as 'your late unhappy western march'.[18] Waller, who claimed that fight-ing for Parliament had cost him over £30,000, was relieved of his com-mand, and the New Model Army came into existence under the com-mand of Sir Thomas Fairfax, described by the King as the 'rebels, new brutish general'.[19]

There was still much unfinished business in Dorset and Somerset, and at the end of April Fairfax marched west from Windsor, to be joined by Cromwell at Newbury. It was not before time. Goring, with increased powers, was prowling the area, Hopton and Sir John Berkeley and their army of over 6000 men were besieging Taunton ever tighter and Chideock had been reoccupied by the royalists. Not that they were unchallenged. A skirmish near Oborne led to the death of 'Morice Lee, an Irish soldier'[20] on 29 April, but just eight days later Thomas Ceeley of Lyme wrote to the Speaker begging for help before 'an utter ruin come upon this garrison'.[21]

The New Model Army that marched into Dorset for its first-ever cam-paign was perhaps 10,000 strong, the product of combining the three roundhead armies that had fought at the second Battle of Newbury. The weapon Parliament had forged to win the Civil War was to become one of the most famous British armies ever, and never lost a major battle in the fifteen years of its existence. Denzil Holles, no friend of army reform, commented that Parliament 'have the sword where they would have it, and resolve with it to cut all knots they cannot untie'.[22]

Fairfax arrived at Sixpenny Handley on 6 May, and Blandford the next day. Along the march his army demonstrated 'wise and christian-like dis-cipline...as was admired by the country people. Proclamation having been made that it should be death for any man to plunder anything from any person.'[23] By the time the New Model Army reached Witchampton it had covered an impressive 78 miles in nine days. But it still might not be fast enough, Blake's situation in Taunton had become desperate, and he was unthatching the houses to feed his few remaining horses. The royal-ists confidently wrote 'if they should have no succours within three days, we shall certainly have it, and with it all the West except two or three small things.'[24]

Guessing that Blake and his men knew relief was on the way, the besiegers staged a fake battle with blank ammunition outside the walls, in an attempt to lure the roundheads out of the town. The imaginative plan failed, so they launched attack after attack, though Blake and his men 'gave them such showers of lead as filled the trenches with their dead car-casses'.[25] On 7 May the East Gate was stormed, but the royalists failed to fight their way up the long slope of East Street. Next day, at noon, came a general assault. The defensive line around the town was breached, the walls scaled, and the exhausted roundheads driven back to their final redoubt, a triangular line of barricades and trenches in the heart of the town. An attempt to burn them out failed because the wind was blowing in the wrong direction. Next day a fresh assault was launched. By that evening one-third of Taunton was a smoking ruin and Blake's men were still holding on only in the castle, the church, a blockhouse called Maiden's Fort and an entrenchment that ran across the market place. The attackers announced triumphantly 'the governor of the place was yesterday slain by the breaking of a gun...with him we conceive the malice of the place died'.[26] But Blake was still very much alive, and when summoned to surrender, he replied he would eat his boots first.

The defence of Taunton was fast becoming one of the epics of the war, and Fairfax knew he must come to Blake's help. But if he committed his entire force to the relief he risked being crushed between the royalist forces outside Taunton and the armies of Goring and Grenville. Fairfax decided to gamble, and detached 600 horse and 1200 foot as a relief force, while he himself with the main mass of the New Model Army feinted to continue west, advancing to Puddletown then doubling back to Blandford again. The relief force arrived within a few miles of Taunton on 11 May and gave the agreed signal, firing ten pieces of artillery to warn Blake of their approach, but the defenders heard only the sound of the royalist guns.

The besiegers first thought the relieving force was reinforcements for them. Realizing their mistake, they assumed Fairfax's whole army was upon them, and panicked. Within hours the cavaliers, with at least twice the numbers of the relief force and Blake's men combined, were in headlong flight. The Taunton garrison sallied out and harrassed their enemies, but the royalists blocked the roads behind them by chopping down trees from the local orchards. Back in London news of the relief was greeted with enthusiasm, and the House of Commons voted a day of public thanksgiving, £2000 for the garrison and £500 for Blake himself.

It was a little premature. The royalists had been outwitted not defeated, and within days Berkeley and Hopton joined up with Goring, and the combined army of 10,000 men drove Blake and the relief force back into Taunton. The siege was renewed, and Blake wrote to Parliament:

if relief comes not speedily we shall be put into great straits
for provisions and ammunition. We assure the House we
have never accepted a parley from the enemy but scorned it,
and we have some ammunition left, and are resolved to feed
upon our horses.[27]

But the threat of Fairfax on Goring's rear was too great, and on 14 May the siege was finally raised after fifty-four days. Six days later Goring missed an easy chance to destroy the Taunton relief force which was on its way to rejoin Fairfax. So anarchic was the royalist command structure becoming that two units of Goring's army spent two hours fighting each other near Crewkerne 'to the loss of many of their men; both the chief officers being dangerously hurt, and one of them taken, before they knew their error'.[28] Goring casually dismissed the event as 'the most fantastical accident that has happened since the war began'.[29]

Fairfax, having achieved his short-term aims in the West, turned northeast to attack Oxford. He left behind a local parliamentary leadership radically changed by the war, a transformation that reflected on a local level the transformation of the aristocrat-led armies of Essex and Manchester into the New Model Army. The Puritan gentry were being superseded. Walter Erle, Denis Bond, John Browne and their peers still wielded influence in London, but the day-to-day running of Dorset was in the hands of men, many without aristocratic pedigree, who had risen through the war: officers like George Starre, John Fry, John Lea, Walter Foy, John Arthur and James Dewey. These men were not only more likely to have revolutionary views about society and religion, they were also, by and large, more ruthless prosecutors of the war than their predecessors, even when family ties cut across the party divide.

Walter Foy's sister was married to a major in the King's horse. The royalist major's father was Richard Fitzherbert, archdeacon of Dorset and rector of Cheselbourne. When Foy arrived in the village, his sister begged him to spare her father-in-law's house, but Foy refused. He even warned his sister that 'if he could catch her own husband, he would make him an example to his brethren, the cavaliers'.[30]

Fairfax's departure left the parliamentary garrisons in Dorset still nervous. On 30 May Edmund Butler wrote to Anthony Ashley Cooper from Wareham, complaining

> the 50 men you sent to this garrison are mutinous and unruly...the enemy is still about Dorchester and have doubled their numbers...we have but 30 horse and they but meanly armed, and we have no money to buy more, there is a great want of swords both for horse and foot, besides other arms.[31]

The King had meanwhile struck east and stormed the parliamentary stronghold of Leicester. Fairfax hastily raised his ineffective siege of Oxford and on 14 June Fairfax and the King clashed south of Leicester, at Naseby. Had Goring followed Fairfax into the Midlands and linked with the King's army, as he had been repeatedly ordered to do, the battle might have had a very different result. But Goring insisted

> he was certain in few days to be master of Taunton, and should leave that country free from any enemy, excepting Lyme (which was then and had been for some time blocked up), whereas if he should leave the siege, the enemy would be masters of that country.[32]

The outnumbered royalist veterans initially drove the New Model Army back, but the huge parliamentarian advantage in cavalry proved decisive. Cromwell's ironsides broke the northern horse that faced them and by one o'clock in the afternoon the battle was over. The royal army that had won the victories of Cropredy Bridge and Lostwithiel was utterly destroyed, and 4000 prisoners were marched to London. The King's secret correspondence was also captured, and Charles's constant efforts to bring Irish and French armies into England provided a huge propaganda coup for Parliament, which published selected highlights in *The King's Cabinet Opened*.

Back in Dorset the clubmen were rapidly increasing. Three thousand gathered between Shaftesbury and Blandford on 12 May, and sent a letter to Colonel Bingham, the governor of Poole referring to the 'late unhappy greeting between some of your garrison and of our neighbourhood, occasioning the dangerous (if not mortal) wounding of some, and the death of another'.[33] The clubmen asked for an investigation into the clash, and five days later Bingham wrote politely back 'to my noble friends, the inhabitants of the county of Dorset near Shaftesbury', promising to look into the matter when he could, and to bring their grievances to the notice of Parliament.

Two weeks later the meeting place was Badbury Rings, near Anthony Ashley Cooper's seat at Wimborne St Giles, where there gathered 'near four thousand armed with clubs, swords, bills, pitchforks and other several weapons'. A certain Thomas Young, 'an attorney more eloquent than honest', read out their declarations that 'our ancient laws and liberties...are altogether swallowed up in the arbitrary power of the sword' and agreeing 'to join with and assist one another in the mutual defence of our liberties and properties against all plunderers and all other unlawful violence whatsoever'.[34]

Gradually the clubmen movement was growing more organized. Each parish was to have a committee of three with two constables to raise the alarm. Arms and ammunition were stockpiled, and villages rang the church bells to warn each other of the approach of soldiers. The clubmen themselves wore white silk ribbons in their hats, and carried banners with mottos like 'Peace and Truth' or 'If you offer to plunder or take our cattle, Be assured we will bid you battle.'[35] The clubmen were not only poor rural workers, but also farmers, craftsmen, minor gentry, and knights. There were even several ministers among their leaders, including Samuel Forward, a curate of Edward Davenant, the royalist vicar of Gillingham. Davenant, whose valuable library was seized by Waller's soldiers, and which he had to pay to redeem, was a well-known mathematician who left all his parish work to his curates. In 1645 his vicarage was sequesterd.

As the summer wore on, there were fresh gatherings in many parts of north and east Dorset including Buxbury and Sturminster Newton, as well as on Salisbury Plain. The clubmen, who represented a provincial conservatism supported by neither side, claimed to be neutral but in practice they tended to lean one way or the other. Sir Lewis Dyve, from his stronghold at Sherborne, warily watched the rise of the clubmen and complained to them of 'a backwardness in some of your parts of the country, and a denial from others, in payments of contribution', while warning them of the behaviour of the roundheads who 'have abused our churches by making stables thereof, and by robbing and defacing the same'.[36]

The majority of Somerset clubmen had parliamentary sympathies, and eventually Fairfax would enrol large numbers of them in his army. However the clubmen of Dorset and Wiltshire contained many ex-royalist soldiers among their leaders.

In late May Ashley Cooper received a warning after some of Colonel Bingham's troopers at Blandford

> were beaten and kept prisoners but at length set at liberty... God bless our forces in the West, otherwise we may easily guess which way their clubs will be employed. You shall do well to haste a relief, otherwise the forces in the West are like to be endangered, and the country, if not the garrisons lost.[37]

A few days later the Prince of Wales accepted a petition from a deputation of clubmen and spoke pleasantly to them, while Goring made more efforts to win them over. The inhabitants of Dorset also petitioned the King himself that they had:

> in a deeper measure than other subjects of this Kingdom suffered, by means of the many garrisons within this little county (they being ten in number) and the armies yearly drawn into these parts by reason thereof.

The petition was signed by 'above ten thousand of your Majesty's loyal subjects of this county, not in arms on either party in the present wars'.[38] On 8 July the King replied with a carefully-worded proclamation which said the matter was receiving attention, and assuring them of his favour.

West Dorset was not immune to this new phenomenon. In April there had been meetings and Thomas Ceeley persuaded 500 clubmen to take the Covenant. A fresh outburst of activity at the beginning of July saw Ceeley enrol 150 of them as cover for his own troops, many of whom had been taken to fight Goring. It seemed the clubmen of West Dorset, like those of Somerset, favoured Parliament, but this was about to change sharply. The next day, in very hot weather, a fresh crowd gathered near Bridport, possibly at the hill fort of Eggardon Hill. Ceeley's messenger was roughly handled:

> they rudely tore his papers and increased their seditions, whereupon he made toward them to disperse them, which he did with the loss of 50 or 60 clubmen, who, it seems, will not understand reason till it be beaten into them. These clubmen were led by an officer of the King's, and we understand that Goring has lent them divers of his men to seduce them to disaffection and destruction.[39]

The clubmen had actually given a good account of themselves, Ceeley's brother was captured, and the governor of Lyme himself 'a stout man, hardly escaping',[40] as well as being slightly wounded. Roundhead forces in South Dorset were also coming under increased pressure from the clubmen, who were harrassing the pro-Parliament fishermen of the coast.

This growing support for the King was about to bring the Dorset clubmen into direct confrontation with the New Model Army.

After the triumph of Naseby Fairfax resolved to strike immediately at the one significant remaining royalist field army, that of Goring. Meanwhile Grenville's plan to use the garrisons of Exeter, Dartmouth and Barnstaple for 'the blocking up of Lyme which, he resolved, should bring him in plenty of money',[41] was ruined by the Prince of Wales, who forbade the use of the Barnstaple garrison. By 2 July the New Model Army was back in Dorset, marching from Bowerchalke to Blandford. The area had seen several outbreaks of disorder, and at the end of June the clubmen had 'forced the Parliament's quarters at Sturminster Newton, divers slain and wounded on both sides'.[42]

The clubmen were entirely unimpressed by the New Model Army and between four and five thousand gathered near Blandford. 'They come into our quarters and steal horses where they find them at grass' objected Fairfax, who considered them 'abundantly more affected to the enemy than to Parliament'.[43] Nevertheless the general had no intention of provoking the clubmen, so after capturing two leaders, John Penruddock of Compton Chamberlayne in Wiltshire and John Fussell of Blandford, Fairfax released them in exchange for a promise that they would stop their unlawful assemblies. On the road from Blandford, during a very hot day, Fairfax spoke politely to a deputation of clubmen, and promised that if parliamentary troops committed disorder of any sort 'justice shall be done and satisfaction given'.[44] He also warned them of the danger of a French or Irish invasion if the King was not quickly defeated, while reporting back to London that the clubmen

take upon them to interpose between the garrisons of either side, and when any of their forces meet in places where they have a sufficient power...they will not suffer them to fight but make them drink together and so make them part.[45]

Fairfax, despite leading a victorious army, was being typically careful. The clubmen:

were so strong at that time that it was held a point of prudence to be fair in demeanour towards them for a while, for if he should engage with General Goring, and be put to the worst, these clubmen would knock them on the heads as they should fly for safety.[46]

The clubmen requested that all men who desired it should have the liberty to return home, but in reply the parliamentary general asked how he could maintain his army if everyone went home.

The New Model Army passed by without trouble, probably because Fairfax's men actually paid for their quarters, a source of utter disbelief to the villagers of Dorset and Somerset as John Lilburne reported to the House of Commons, 'divers of them telling us that they never knew what it was to finger soldiers' money'.[47] Nevertheless Colonel Sydenham met Fairfax and warned him of 'the great danger of the club risers who would not suffer (so high were they grown) either contributions or victuals to be carried to the Parliament's garrisons'.[48]

Fairfax was now hot on Goring's trail. From Blandford he made his way to Dorchester, where he offered the army a rest. But the New Model Army had a morale and enthusiasm that were almost unprecedented:

> our poor Foot, being impatient of the relief of their friends at Taunton marched 62 miles in five days; and offered at Dorchester, after 12 miles march that day, to march all night to relieve Taunton – hearing that Goring was fallen on again.[49]

From Dorchester Fairfax pressed on to Beaminster, and on 5 July the New Model Army came to Parnham House. The estate, valued at £200 a year, had been the cause of a legal battle between Sir Richard Strode and his uncle Sir John Strode that stretched back thirty-five years. John Strode died before the beginning of the war, but his wife Lady Anne Strode, one of the royalist Wyndham family, had clung on to the estate with the help of the King's forces

> until the end of the first war, when this Lord General, then Lieutenant General, had totally routed the enemy in the West; and near that day one of his soldiers with his sword casually killed Lady Strode in that same place, Parnham, which she so unlawfully kept against Sir Richard.[50]

The estate was sequestered and never came to Sir Richard Strode, who had to settle for compensation.

Nearby Hooke Court, the decaying house of the Marquis of Winchester, was also stormed and burnt to the ground. In March 1646 Richard Munden of Colway would be ordered 'to view, fell, sell and dispose of' all the timber fit to be felled 'in the old park at Hooke...for and to the use and benefit of the state'.[51] The following year 10s. would be paid to a mason sent to Hooke to dig for lead among the ruins, which he did so successfully that he found 15 hundredweight of the metal.

Fairfax next swung north to Crewkerne, where there was a brief clash with some royalist troops who fell back hastily. Goring was trying to protect his outnumbered army by hiding behind the rivers of the Somerset levels, among 'those rotten unhealthy moors',[52] but Fairfax's sudden seizure of Yeovil, which Goring thought was guarded by Sir Lewis Dyve's Sherborne troops, opened the way to pursuit. Goring responded with a brilliantly effective feint towards Taunton that entirely deceived Fairfax, and cost him Colonel Massey and a strong force sent off in the wrong direction. Massey did manage to catch Goring's brother-in-law, George Porter, 'the best company, but the worst officer that ever served the King',[53] entirely unawares near Ilminster, 'all their horses at grass, and some of the men asleep, some swimming, and the rest carelessly walking in the fields'.[54] But there was no time for Massey to rejoin the main parliamentary army, nor for Colonel Montague and 2000 musketeers, unnecessarily sent to reinforce Massey. So when Goring and Fairfax faced each other on the morning of 10 July between Langport and Long Sutton, the numerical advantage of the parliamentarians was far less than it might have been. Fairfax's weakness as a general lay in strategy, and Goring had comprehensively outwitted him, but in tactics the parliamentary leader was formidable.

Goring had placed his army with some care, at the top of a narrow green lane lined with overarching hedges. Royalist musketeers covered the lane from both sides, and Goring's cannon were at the top of it. It seemed it would be easy for Goring to slip away to the protection of the royalist fortress of Bridgwater, and his infantry were already starting on their way. But Fairfax was not going to let them escape so easily.

Under the command of Major Bethel, the roundhead cavalry heroically charged straight up the lane, where 'they could not march above fourabreast, and up to the belly in water.'[55] Having burst through the crossfire they clashed with three times their number of Goring's horse at the top, and were flung back. But Cromwell's brother-in-law, John Desborough, joined in a second charge and the royalist cavalry began to break. Goring's infantry took to their heels, and the general's attempt to cover his retreat by setting Langport alight failed as Cromwell's Ironsides relentlessly followed 'although the fire was flaming very hot on both sides of them'.[56] The royalists lost perhaps two hundred killed and ten times that number of prisoners. The King's last field army had been effectively destroyed in one of 'the most supine and unsoldierly defeats that were ever known'.[57]

Fairfax, Cromwell and the New Model Army had, in just twenty-six days, marched over 200 miles, fought two major battles, and effectively won the war. 'Thus you have the Long Sutton mercy added to the Naseby mercy,' wrote the transported Cromwell, 'and to see this, is it not to see the face of God!'[58]

While the Somerset clubmen picked off stragglers and his men deserted en masse, Goring retreated to Barnstaple and 'gave himself his usual licence of drinking...and discoursing much of the revenge he would take upon those who had affronted him'.[59] Meanwhile the New Model Army closed in on Bridgwater. Several leading Dorset royalists, including Hugh Wyndham and John Hele, were present in the garrison of over 1000, which had been established by Hopton and held the vital link between the royalist strongholds of Cornwall and Devon, and the King's largest remaining source of income, the port of Bristol. Bridgwater, bombarded with red-hot shot and grenades, surrendered after just a week. Among those who died, of a gangrened arm wound, was John Digby, brother of the occult royalist philosopher Sir Kenelm Digby, and a distant cousin of George Digby, described by Aubrey as 'the best swordsman of his time...such a hero'.[60] Cromwell himself was also nearly killed by one royalist volley. The contrast between the rapid surrender of Bridgwater, partly caused by the insistence of the townspeople, and the stubborn resistance of Puritan Taunton with a much smaller garrison and weaker defences, shows more clearly than anything else the complete disintegration in royalist morale:

> The taking Bridgwater, which the King had been persuaded to believe a place impregnable, could not but make great impressions upon him, to think that he was betrayed, and consequently not to know whom to trust. It was in truth matter of amazement to all men.[61]

Six days later the Lyme garrison, for the third and final time, stormed Chideock Castle, taking 100 prisoners and seriously damaging the church, which had to be repaired after the war. A skirmish 'in the court at Folke House' cost the life of 'a soldier of the parliamentary side', while another, Will Robertson, was 'slain in Alveston'.[62] Nevertheless, the only important royalist strongholds remaining in Dorset were the castles of Sherborne, Corfe and Portland.

Fairfax's opinion was that the King could no longer expect anything from his forces, as he wrote to his father, 'his greatest hopes now seems to be in the clubmen.'[63] Some roundhead regiments, which were not part of the New Model Army, had been taking free quarter and plundering the area, which further strengthened the pro-royalist stance of the clubmen. They now presented a serious threat, endangering Fairfax's communications, stopping messengers and preventing his army being supplied with arms or food. Rather than pursuing the royalist leaders into Devon, Fairfax was forced to return into Dorset. In the general's own words: 'It is more considerable than to force Goring into Cornwall for the clubmen of Wiltshire, Dorsetshire and Hampshire is like to be of dangerous consequence if not prevented.'[64]

The royalism of the Dorset clubmen, 'a disorderly rabble and rude company of mongrel malignants and rotten-hearted nauseous neutrals',[65] meant that Sir Lewis Dyve's garrison of 400 men at Sherborne acted as a focus of resistance, so it was to Sherborne that Fairfax marched, arriving on 1 August. However, after the non-stop campaigning of the last months his men were almost out of ammunition, and unable seriously to threaten the castle until their supply lines were freed from the clubmen.

The day after Fairfax's arrival, the clubmen met at Shaftesbury to discuss what to do about the siege of Sherborne and Sir Lewis Dyve's appeal to them for help. The defiance was too blatant to be ignored, and Fairfax sent out Cromwell, who was 'well satisfied of the danger of their design',[66] with 1000 horse, to deal with 'that giddy-head faction in Dorsetshire'.[67]

On 3 August Colonel Fleetwood attacked the club stronghold on Castle Hill at the western end of Shaftesbury, and soon returned with 50 ringleaders, many 'of good or fair estate',[68] and including John Saint Lo 'a notable agent for the King' who had carried the clubmen's petition to Charles a month earlier. Another prisoner was Edward Williams, the minister of Shaftesbury. During the 1620s and 1630s Williams had been considered a Puritan sectary, but attitudes had hardened since then, and now he found himself on the other side. The next year he was removed from his living for being 'very unfit for the ministry by reason of his old age, natural defects and scandalous conversation'.[69]

The clubmen continued to mass, planning to attack the parliamentary camp and free their leaders. There were rumours that Hopton himself would come to command them, and claims that they would soon have a well-supplied army of 10,000 with which to raise the siege of Sherborne. Fairfax reported:

> Lieutenant-General Cromwell is gone out with some horse to hinder the clubmen's meeting which I hear they have appointed to come and demand their leaders. We must not neglect this business for their violence is probable to lead them to some foolish attempt which I hope may make them repent their errors if they will not be advised.[70]

The first gathering Cromwell came upon was at Duncliff Hill just west of Shaftesbury, 'a high hill, full of wood and almost inaccessible'.[71] Cromwell assured the clubmen that they could defend themselves and that plunderers would be treated very severely, 'upon this very quietly and peaceably they marched away to their houses, being very well satisfied and contented.'[72] However the second gathering, between two and four thousand clubmen on the ancient earthwork of Hambledon Hill, was not so obliging and refused to disband.

At the bottom of the hill Cromwell's men came upon a musketeer and asked him where he was going. He replied 'to the club army'. When questioned as to what he was going to do there, the man replied that it had nothing to do with them:

> Being required to lay down his arms, he said he would first lose his life, but was not so good as his word, for though he cocked and presented his musket, he was prevented, disarmed and wounded but not killed'.[73]

Cromwell asked to speak to the clubmen in peace, but his men were shot at. He made a second request, but:

> they still (through the animation of their leaders, and especially two vile ministers) refused. I commanded your captain-lieutenant to draw up to them, to be in readiness to charge, and if upon his falling on they would lay down arms, to accept them and spare them. When he came near they refused his offer, and let fly at him; killed about two of his men, and at least four horses...whereupon Major Desborough wheeled about; got in the rear of them, beat them from the work, and did some small execution upon them; I believe killed not 12 of them, but cut very many, and we have taken about 300, many of which are poor silly creatures, whom if you please to let me send home, they promise to be very dutiful for time to come, and will be hanged before they come out again.[74]

The most striking thing is Cromwell's comparatively gentle treatment of a large and potentially extremely dangerous force, most of whom suffered no more than that they humiliatingly 'slid and tumbled down that great steep hill to the hazard of their necks'.[75]

Sixteen roundhead prisoners, some of whom had been threatened with hanging, were freed, and among the clubmen taken were four vicars and curates, who had been 'at no divine service I can assure you'.[76] The 'malignant priests, who were the principal stirrers up of the people to these tumultuous assemblies',[77] were Thomas Bravell of Compton Abbas, who had threatened to pistol any clubmen who ran away, John Talbott of Milton Abbas, who remarkably was still in his living ten years later, and, apparently worst of them all, Lawford of Child Okeford. Together with the other prisoners, they were herded into the recently-rebuilt Shroton church and kept there for the night. Next morning Cromwell took a list of names and examined the leaders. Then he lectured the entire group, warning them not to stop any soldier who was going about his business, before sending all but a few away on promise of good behaviour.

August and September saw further clubmen risings in Devon, Cornwall, Berkshire, Hampshire and Sussex, but after the events of Hambledon Hill the clubmen would never again be a serious threat. Before then Fairfax's army had been in danger of slow strangulation, afterwards 'a man might ride very quietly between Sherborne and Salisbury',[78] through what had been the heart of the uprising. Because the clubmen never inflicted any major defeat on the warring parties, their significance is probably underestimated, but Fairfax's chaplain, Joshua Sprigg had no doubt about the threat they represented: 'if this had not been crushed in the egg, it had on an instant run all over the kingdom, and might have been destructive to the Parliament'.[79] As it was, Parliament had broken the back of both the royalist resistance, and that of the local people. Now came the mopping up.

⊷ Chapter Eight ⊶
THE LAST STRONGHOLDS
AUGUST 1645–APRIL 1646

Cromwell returned swiftly to the parliamentary camp before
Sherborne Castle. Now the threat of the clubmen had been
removed, it was time to concentrate on what John Bond called 'that
first western nest of the cockatrice's eggs, the cradle of cavalierism, the
very bag of the western imposthume'.[1]

Sherborne castle was a formidable fortress with a garrison of about 400,
18 heavy guns and a mortar, and walls 12 feet thick, 'a malicious mischievous castle like the owner',[2] the King's chief adviser, George Digby. It was
situated close by the main road to the South West, in the centre of the area
of Dorset most sympathetic to the royalists. The garrison contained several of the most vehement and influential local cavaliers, Sir Lewis Dyve,
his uncle Sir John Walcot, several members of the Strangways family,
including Colonel Giles Strangways, who had been with the King at
Lostwithiel, James and George Strangways, and the vehement anti-
Puritan priest, William Wake whose ill-treatment at Wareham had
marked the beginning of the Civil War in Dorset.

Fairfax's original intention was to storm the castle immediately, but the
lack of recruits dissuaded him, and not until Tuesday 5 August, the day
of Cromwell's return, did the parliamentarians made their first aggressive
move, a party creeping along in the shadow of a stone wall to seize a
haystack within a stone's throw of the garrison's outworks. The next day
the garrison had built a fresh work on which they could plant cannon to
blast the parliamentarians from their newly-won haystack. However the
roundhead troops attacked first and drove the garrison from their defensive work. The attack was not without losses. Among Sir Lewis Dyve's
men were two gamekeepers armed with long, high-quality fowling
pieces. These men acted as highly efficient snipers, shooting through
loopholes, and on this day alone were said to have picked off a major and
four captains.

Fairfax still intended to storm the castle that day or the next, but first
sent a fresh demand that the castle should be surrendered. Dyve's courteous reply seems almost to belong to some mythical world of chivalry:

> Sir, I have received your second summons this day for the
> surrendering this castle of Sherborne into your hands for the
> use of the Kingdom. I shall endeavour to purchase a better
> opinion with you (before I leave it) than to deliver it up upon
> such easy terms. I keep it for His Majesty my sovereign, unto
> whom this Kingdom belongs, and by the blessing of the
> Almighty am resolved to give such an account thereof, as

becomes a man of honour to do who is, Sir, Your humble servant, Lewis Dyve.[3]

On consideration the parliamentary leaders decided any attempt to storm the castle before a breach was made would cause very heavy losses. Furthermore the castle walls were so strong that Fairfax decided his own guns were unable to do sufficient damage, so he sent for special heavy cannon from Portsmouth, as well as for some Mendip miners.

The next day two of the snipers' victims, captains John Horsey and Robert Clements,[4] were buried in the church at Sherborne. John Horsey, whose brother Ralph appears also to have died in the siege, was the son of Sir George Horsey, a Dorset M.P. under James I, and many of his family were already buried at Sherborne.

George Horsey had been famous for wild schemes, including a project for smelting iron with coal, and a ludicrous attempt to drain the Fleet 'to make pasture land, whereon was spent great sums of money in making of sluices, trenches and other inventions to keep the tide from coming in',[5] and which brought him 'only some small quantity of fish'.[6] After Sir George Morton, who owed him money, absconded, he was sent to the debtor's prison, and sold off his entire estate for £28,000, much of it to Sir John Hele. Horsey subsequently had to live on water, oatmeal and three-pennyworth of sprats, took shelter with his brother-in-law Sir John Freke at Shroton, and was finally sent to the county gaol for a debt of £10, where he died. It is scarcely surprising that his disinherited sons took up arms for Parliament.

On Friday 8 August Fairfax himself came within a whisker of death. He was on his way to see the progress of the mining when a man close beside him was shot dead. This time it was not the royalist sharpshooters who were to blame, but parliamentarian soldiers shooting deer in the nearby park.

Sherborne Castle is built on soft rock and the attempt to undermine the walls made rapid progress:

Very freely did the soldiers work in the mines and galleries
and making of batteries, every man being rewarded 12 pence
apiece for the day, and as much for the night, for the service
was hot and hazardous'.[7]

There was another, more unusual, way in which Fairfax's men could supplement their income. Although the clubmen were no longer cutting off parliamentary supplies, the New Model Army was still desperately short of ammunition, and men were paid sixpence for every cannon ball they retrieved from under the castle walls. Meanwhile the royalists tried to interrupt the mining by sudden sallies and hurling down great stones.

On Sunday 10 August a small breach was made in the walls by gunfire, but it was not big enough to allow a full-scale attack. The next day the morale of the besiegers received another boost when the army's pay arrived. One of the crucial ways the New Model Army differed from any other army of the time, or indeed any English army at all up until then, was the fact that it was paid regularly, over three-quarters of the time in the case of the foot.

In fresh attempts to stop the mining, the Sherborne garrison threw down blazing faggots, while the gamekeepers concentrated their fire on the gunners, and picked off two in a day including the chief gunner of the army. Fairfax and Cromwell offered to allow the women in the castle to leave:

> Sir Lewis thankfully acknowledged the favour, seemed to incline to accept of it, but gave no positive answer, expressing withal his resolution (soldier-like) to hold out to the last. But under favour it was a madness rather than valour, seeing he despaired of relief.[8]

Presumably Dyve thought that if he allowed his wife to leave the castle, the garrison would assume he had given up hope and would soon stop resisting.

On 13 August Fairfax and Cromwell inspected the works and mines, and then oversaw the positioning of the newly-arrived great guns from Portsmouth, which weighed 32 tons apiece. The barrage began next morning at eleven o'clock, firing shot of 63 pounds each, though Sir Lewis and his wife refused 'to startle at the impression which the shock of our cannon made'.[9] By six in the evening the cannon had proved their worth, making a fresh breach and beating down one of the towers, even though another gunner was picked off. By now the two sides were so close to each other that it was often no longer practical to use muskets, and the garrison's chief weapons were stones and rocks, while the besiegers pulled the wool out of the woolsacks that lay on the defensive works.

The roundheads now launched a sudden attack under Colonel Richard Ingoldsby, later famous as the regicide who escaped execution by very unconvincingly claiming Cromwell had dragged him to the table and forced him to sign his name on the King's death warrant. His men seized one of the corner towers, and then demonstrated their own marksmanship by picking off one of the royalist gamekeepers. Inside the castle the garrison were frantically lighting fires in an attempt to find the mines, but without success.

In the small hours of the next morning Sir Lewis Dyve accepted the inevitable and offered to surrender in his usual outspoken way:

> Sir, I must acknowledge the advantage you have of me, by being master of my walls. If I may have such conditions from you, as are fit for a soldier and a gentleman with honour to accept, I shall surrender this castle into your hands; otherwise I shall esteem it a far greater happiness to bury my bones in it, and the same resolution have all those that are with me.[10]

Fairfax called Dyve's bluff and offered the garrison nothing but their lives, and that only if they surrendered immediately. As the royalist leader hesitated, Fairfax ordered his men to prepare to storm the castle.

Yet again there was no questioning the morale of the New Model Army. 'Without any order to fall on, our soldiers were in an instant both over the castle walls and works.' The besiegers had amassed 6000 faggots to fill the royalist trenches, and they threw them in front of them as they swept into the attack. Another tower was seized, and from inside it the round-heads were able to enfilade the garrison in relative security. Dyve's sec-retary was shot down, and as the roundheads continued to advance, it rapidly became clear that further resistance was useless. Dyve reluctant-ly pulled down the bloody flag that had flown over Sherborne for two weeks, put up a white one, and asked for quarter.

According to custom, once the besieger had begun to storm the castle he was not required to give quarter, especially when his men had suffered heavy losses, in this case 200 deaths in the sixteen days of the siege. Typically the humane Fairfax did agree to quarter, but it was not just their general's orders that persuaded the parliamentary troops to show mercy: 'There was such plenty of riches and plunder within, which took up and busied the soldier[s], otherwise it would have been difficult to have got them quarter.'[11]

The looting lasted all day and most of the night. The roundhead sol-diers had a point to make because they had been promised 10s. each for taking Bridgwater, but the money had not been paid, so they were deter-mined to get everything they could from Sherborne. But the soldiers also had great satisfaction from plundering:

five shillings gotten in way of spoil from an enemy, gives them more content than 20s. in a way of reward in an order-ly manner...there was not a man but got plunder, some two and three times over, as soon as they had been at home, came back again and returned loaded with booty in my presence.

Every member of the garrison, except Sir Lewis Dyve, Lady Howard Dyve, and a few others, was stripped of all they had, even most of their clothes, and the castle itself was emptied. It had been a short but savage siege, 'this business of Sherborne having tried the skill and resolution of the soldier more than in any things has yet fallen out'.[12] Nevertheless such was the discipline of Fairfax's men that although there were 60 men in the garrison who had families in the town, not a single house in Sherborne town was plundered.

The day after the surrender was conveniently a Saturday, so the soldiers held a great market in Sherborne at which they sold their loot. Five days later Parliament ordered the castle should be slighted, which was effi-ciently done that October. Two months later the town must have been back to some sort of normality as the governors of Sherborne School met to discuss money 'for the use of the free grammar school in Sherborne'.[13]

The parliamentarians took 344 common soldiers, together with a good collection of officers and others, including the indomitable William Wake who was:

stripped naked and led with several others, men and

women, in triumph through all the town, which was near half a mile...and from thence sent a prisoner to Poole, where the plague then was.[14]

Most of the prisoners were taken up to London, together with the leaders of the clubmen. Some months later the Dorset Committee dealt with one of the Sherborne garrison, Henry Burland of Abbotsbury, 'a very dangerous malignant, and does go up and down from garrison to garrison as a foe and enemy to the state'.[15] Burland had apparently gone from Abbotsbury to Portland to Bridgwater, and finally to Sherborne, before he was 'put into the custody of the marshal until further order'. Sir Lewis Dyve was brought to the bar of the House of Commons, where he 'demeaned himself very superciliously and proudly, refusing to kneel on both his knees till he was compelled to it'.[16] Dyve and Giles Strangways were then both committed to the Tower of London on charges of high treason, and the lieutenant of the Tower was told

to take especial care of the safe and strict custody of Sir Lewis Dyve and Mr Strangways...and that he suffer them not to come together, nor any of the other prisoners to come to them.[17]

Not long after they were joined in the Tower by Sir John Strangways, who had been travelling with the King, and was taken prisoner at Cardiff on 20 August.

That autumn the pregnant Lady Dyve wrote to her mother from the Tower, where she must have been trying to visit her husband:

Madam, I confess there could not anything have happened to me in the condition I now am in which I should have thought could have been an addition to my sufferings but this misfortune of my father's unfortunate taking.[18]

A few months later, when Lady Dyve begged to see her husband, she was not allowed to:

She, then in travail, said unless she saw her husband she could not be delivered, or if she was, both herself and her infant must perish – the blood of mother and infant (for they both died) will cry aloud for vengeance.[19]

The late summer and autumn of 1645 saw steadily growing tensions in London. As victory became more and more certain, the manoeuvring for control of the peace became ever fiercer and more overt. In July Denzil Holles, because of his enthusiasm for a settlement with the King, and his growing belief that 'the rights of the nation were barbarously invaded by that army which the Parliament levied to secure them',[20] found himself accused of being 'well-affected to the King and his cause'.[21] Despite a speech vehemently protesting his innocence, he was investigated by Parliament. There had long been bad feeling between Holles and Anthony Ashley Cooper, probably because Holles's father-in-law, Sir Francis Ashley had taken some of Cooper's lands during his minority. But when Cooper was asked if during his time as a royalist he had heard anything about the loyalty of Holles, his answer was a perfect example of maturing political skills. He said nothing at all, on the grounds that 'whatever answer he made, it would be a confession that, if he had known anything to the disadvantage of Mr Holles, he would have taken that dishonourable way'.[22] Holles was cleared, and there was a reconciliation between the two men, though both things were to be fairly temporary.

Religious matters were also assuming greater importance in the capital. A year earlier Parliament had issued an order for Wiltshire, Dorset, Devon, Cornwall and Somerset, against

> any ministers that are scandalous, either in life or doctrine, or any others that have deserted their cure and joined themselves actually with and are assistant to the forces raised against the Parliament'.[23]

The committee for plundered ministers handled these questions, and Sir Walter Erle joined in July 1645, reflecting its growing importance. Shortly afterwards the Assembly of Divines, of which John White was the assessor, presented a petition to Parliament that all 'scandalous' persons should be banned from the sacraments. White had no doubts of the vital importance of the petition:

> there is not a matter of higher concernment for the glory of God and peace of this church than the matter of this petition, nor was anything ever presented to the House with more zeal and tenderness of conscience.[24]

Back in Dorset there remained just two important royalist strongholds, Portland and Corfe Castle, but neither was strategically as vital as Sherborne. The parliamentarians in Weymouth did make a surprise attempt to seize Portland just a week after the fall of Sherborne, but it failed. Meanwhile the New Model Army, having freed its communication and supply routes from the dangers of Sir Lewis Dyve's raiding, swung north towards the biggest prize in the South West, the second city of the kingdom, Bristol. Prince Rupert had been preparing Bristol for a siege for more than a month, but there was little enthusiasm for resistance. Blockaded by sea as well as land, Rupert hung on for three weeks, then on 10 September, to the King's fury, surrendered on terms. A month later Cromwell, marching back into Hampshire, stormed the fortress of Basing House with great ferocity. John Paulet, the Marquis of Winchester, who had heroically defended Basing for over two and a half years, was taken prisoner and sent to the Tower, while two of the finest artists of the time, Wenceslas Hollar and Inigo Jones, only just escaped with their lives. Shortly afterwards Goring left his post in the South West without permission, saying he would return from France in two months. He didn't. The royalist cause was falling apart.

Throughout Dorset, Somerset and east Devon two horsemen of the apocalypse, war and death, had opened the way for the others, disease and famine. Bubonic plague carried off 458 people from Colyton alone that winter, while in Beer three-quarters of the entire population was said to have died. Dorchester was far less hard hit and 'it gleaned only a few among you, here and there, at that time when some other towns were almost laid waste by the same stroke of God's hand.'[25] There were other outbreaks in Yeovil, Sherborne, South Perrott, Wyke and Poole.

Anthony Ashley Cooper wrote to the Speaker about Poole

where the plague and famine busily contend for pre-eminence, and the distressed inhabitants, impatient of either of their reign, threaten to break out to the inevitable danger of the garrison and ruin of the places adjacent.[26]

The town windmill, which stood outside the built-up area, was used as an isolation hospital, and the mayor's account, which soared to five times its usual total, contains items such as:

pitch and tar for the sick people to burn in their houses – 4s. 9d... Paid William Young for a load of turfs and for his horse to draw dead corpses – 6s... For the box of drugs had from Salisbury – £3.[27]

Haviland Hiley, a former and future mayor of Poole, charged £12 'for my expenses in riding to the Committee, to Weymouth, to Cerne, to Dorchester and many other places to get in money and provisions in the sickness time'.[28] Hiley lost one horse and lamed another during his seven-week-long search for help. Fortunately for Poole a total of £493 9s. 102d. was voted by the Parliamentary commissioners or donated by private individuals, to help pay for the plague costs.

The parishioners of Christchurch sent £9 13s. 7d., and several subsequent gifts including 'six bushels of Hampshire corn, which made but five bushels Poole measure'.[29] In mid-December the mayor of Poole wrote to the people of Christchurch to thank them

that the good Lord has been most graciously pleased to stir up your hearts to consider and commiserate the miserable and sad depressed condition of the poor and needy sick people of this time and garrison of Poole, by raising a free and charitable benevolence towards their relief.[30]

By then the plague was gradually lessening its grip.

Next February Poole complained of 'its great suffering by loss of trade' and appealed for permission to confiscate certain lands, including those of the Bishop of Bristol in Fifehead Magna, to support

two able, orthodox and learned ministers, since it is well known to you and the whole kingdom with what courage and fidelity the town has held out during this unnatural war, the inhabitants freely and unanimously exposing their lives and fortunes when the whole country round about has been for near two years under the power of the enemy. For it we are most confident that they shall not receive a denial in a matter highly importing their eternal good, and without which 3000 souls must be as sheep without a shepherd.[31]

There was still a war on. At the end of September the New Model Army came marching back into Dorset, through Shaftesbury, Milton, and Beaminster to Chard, where it rested for eight nights. Fairfax paid a visit to Lyme:

where he was honourably entertained by the Governor, Colonel Ceeley, and stayed there that night. It was wonderful to think, considering the situation of the place, and the meanness of the works about it, that it should possibly hold out as it did against such a force as laid siege to it.[32]

During the army's passage six of Cromwell's men were convicted of robbing some cavaliers they had been escorting in Blandford. One was chosen by lot to be executed for the crime of all of them, and died penitently. Nevertheless the army was restless and mutinous talk flourished until the pay arrived on 11 October. Even then things were not going particularly well, and the army was 'much wearied out with the extreme wet weather, and their carriages broken'.[33]

Other roundhead troops, notably those of Edward Massey, were behaving much worse. A Presbyterian like Waller, Massey briefly had joined the royalists in 1642, then switched sides. He had gained a great reputation from his heroic defence of Gloucester in 1643, and in May 1645 had been made general of the parliamentary forces of Cornwall, Devon, Somerset, Dorset and Wiltshire, but his men rapidly became notorious for their poor discipline and crimes. John Fitzjames, whose mother had entertained King Charles eighteen months earlier, was among Massey's colonels, and it was his men, who in March 1646, assaulted and robbed Hugh Peter, the celebrated Puritan preacher and for a while Cromwell's own chaplain, this even though Peter and his companions had special passports signed personally by Fairfax.

Remarkably some troops seem to have been used for private concerns. Lady Alice Lawrence, stepmother of the royalist Sir Edward Lawrence, had retired to the Isle of Wight which remained in parliamentary hands throughout the war. She had sold a farm to John Gould of Evershot, but when he fell behind on his payments in 1645, she apparently sent armed soldiers to seize his cattle until he paid what he owed. Subsequently the Dorset Committee charged Lady Alice £20 for money she received from her first husband's estate, which was being run by her sister-in-law, Elizabeth Bishop. When Lady Alice boldly refused to pay, goods worth £20 were taken from Mrs Bishop. Eventually the sisters-in-law may have been reconciled as Lady Alice left Mrs Bishop seven silver spoons in her will.

Back in London, Sir Walter Erle, who had become lieutenant of the ordnance after the death of John Pym in 1643, demonstrated an unusual talent by managing to decipher some intercepted letters in code that had been captured at Dartmouth, and 'he had the thanks of the House for it.'[34]

The end of the year saw a sermon to the House of Commons by William Strong. Strong had been a mininster first at Fordington, then More

Crichel, until like John White he had fled the royalists in the summer of 1643 and taken shelter in London, where he was given the parish of St Dunstan's-in-the-West. Strong warned his congregation 'that all the vipers have not eaten themselves out of our bowels.'[35] He went on to reassure the Commons:

> there are many scandalous imputations cast upon you, and many a wilful misinterpretation put upon most of your actions; all is said to be done in rebellion, humour, for self-end, and out of a desire to rule... And you, like wise Physicians, have many times heard your patients say 'you will kill me.' when your utmost endeavour hath been to cure them.[36]

The time was fast coming when it would be seen if Parliament could indeed cure the nation.

Occasional flare-ups of violence continued here and there in Dorset. Captain Winston Churchill, who had been in the royalist garrison of Bristol, was still fighting in December, despite having been shot through the arm by Starre's men, and Thomas Leonard, 'a foreigner and horse-trooper of the parliamentary army,'[37] was buried at Hazelbury Bryan on 29 December. Most of the garrison of Lyme joined the siege of Exeter, which had begun on 28 October, while Colonel Sydenham blocked up Portland at the beginning of November, then joined Blake to attack Francis Wyndham's garrison of Dunster Castle, the last royalist stronghold in Somerset. The initial attack was not a success, neither was the attempt to starve it into surrender. On 3 January they tried to mine the walls, and despite making a breach were unable to penetrate the defences. After the Dorset troops were pulled out of the siege to join the attack on Corfe Castle, a sizeable band of royalist horse broke through to reinforce Dunster, which finally surrendered on 19 April 1646 after a one-hundred-and-sixty-day siege. It probably could have held out even longer, but Wyndham saw no point in continued resistance.

By January Colonel Bingham was confident enough to give a forty-day safe conduct pass to the royalist Sir Thomas Chaffin 'for the endeavouring the settling of his affairs as well in this county as in Surrey'.[38] Chaffin, 'a personable, well-carriaged man of good estate, wanted neither understanding nor value for himself',[39] had married one of the daughters of Sir Thomas Trenchard, while his son married Anne, a daughter of the dedicated royalist John Penruddock. After paying a fine of £900 for raising money for the King, Chaffin kept his head down and 'has lived very peaceably at his habitation within this county, and has readily conformed himself to all the orders and ordinances of Parliament'.[40] A few months later Ensign William Wake, teenage son of that dyed-in-the-wool royalist clergyman William Wake, received a pass from Fairfax himself permitting him to travel 'to Blandford or Wareham, there to remain – he having engaged himself not to bear arms against the Parliament without first rendering himself prisoner to the Parliament's forces'.[41] It was a promise

Wake did not keep.

A remarkable tribute to the peace in Dorset was made on 10 November when elections were held at Weymouth. Sir John Strangways, Gerard Napier and Richard King had been disabled, and seven men stood for the three vacancies. The Somerset M.P. John Ashe wrote to the Speaker:

> so many speeches made against strangers and unknown persons that if three townsmen had stood they had carried it against all that interposed; for they rejected four able men and chose a poor simple townman.[42]

Ashe was exaggerating. Two of the winners were very predictable, Colonel William Sydenham and John Bond the son of Denis Bond. The third was more suprising. Matthew Allen, a brewer, had been in constant trouble in the 1630s for not having a proper quay on the edge of his land so that the rubbish there had been washed into the port. Certainly he was much more than a poor simple townsman, having been rich enough to pay the poor of Melcombe Regis £54 in 1635 and another £21 three years later. He had also been the mayor of Weymouth in March 1643 when it was under parliamentary control.

Nonetheless, there does seem to have been a strong feeling in favour of local people at the time, and the same attitude was evident in what happened in Wimborne around the turn of the year. The arrival of parliamentary troops had clearly caused much concern, and at the Minster the glass was removed from the windows, and 1s. was paid 'for saving the old glass that was brought down by the minister'.[43]

When the roundheads did arrive, under the command of Colonel Bingham, a captain named Ford who was known as 'the fighting preacher', resolved to preach twice in the minster on Sunday. When Ford climbed into the pulpit he was met with jeers and demands for the local priest, William Stone. Ford shouted back at the congregation, and eventually Anthony Ashley Cooper ordered soldiers with muskets into the church. 'But the soldiers, seeing the people's resolution, and foreseeing what a bloody day such action would make, are wiser than their commander and sit still.' At which the local people's fury turned on Ashley Cooper himself and he was 'told the truth by the people that he had already starved their bodies, for he is a racking landlord, and now took a course to starve their souls'.[44] Without the support of the soldiers, Ashley Cooper and Ford had to give up, but shortly afterwards Stone was expelled and served as a chaplain to the King's army. Eventually he fled abroad to return at the Restoration.

Wimborne remained determinedly anti-Puritan, and as late as 1647 the churchwardens were still paying out 3s. 'for washing three surplices'.[45] The minister during most of the Interregnum was Constantine Jessop, who although originally pro-Parliament was forbidden ever again to visit or preach in Bristol after a sermon there against the government in 1650. There was also trouble in the area in March 1646, with fresh activity from the clubmen, furious at the free quarter of troops on them.

During most of the war Purbeck had been the scene of constant skirmishes and raids between the rival parties. For example in June 1645 Colonel Robert Butler came from Wareham and with the help of a shrewd diversion, contrived to seize the Corfe garrison's herd of cattle from under the very walls of the castle. A month earlier Denzil Holles, Thomas Erle, Denis Bond and Anthony Nicoll for the committee for the associated western counties had told Anthony Ashley Cooper:

> you are desired forthwith to repair to the Isle of Purbeck, and
> to draw together as speedily as may be, out of the garrisons
> of Poole, Wareham, Lulworth and Weymouth, such numbers
> of foot and horse as are sufficient to block up Corfe Castle.[46]

Gradually the siege was tightened, and on 18 December Fairfax sent 400 infantry 'for the reducing of Corfe Castle',[47] but a month and a half later the reinforcements were taken away again to rejoin the New Model Army in Devon. Dorset was also expected to supply another 600 recruits to Fairfax's men (compared with 1500 from Somerset, 1000 from Hampshire and Wiltshire, and 500 from Gloucestershire).

This stripping away of troops from the area gave the royalists a chance. Not far from Wareham was a party of roundhead troops from Massey's command, under Colonel Cooke, who fifteen or twenty years later would become a favoured crony of Charles II, who called him 'Honest Ned Cooke'.[48] On 29 January he was entertaining Edmund Ludlow when 120 soldiers, wearing the scarves of Fairfax's horse, passed by. No one showed any mistrust of these unexpected arrivals, and the cavalry force contined on to Wareham, where one of them told the sentries that his name was Dr Hudson, and he had authority to collect the King's rents and use them for Parliament. The bridge was immediately let down, and they entered the town. The intruders were in fact disguised cavaliers under Colonel Cromwell, a distant relation of Oliver, who had just ridden all the way from Oxford.

The first man to show any suspicion was Colonel Butler, the parliamentary governor:

> who seeing them, shut his door and with his son fired upon
> them, and made good his lodging three hours together, till
> the enemy fired the house to which the magazine was near,
> and then they were forced to yield upon quarter.[49]

During the fight one of Ludlow's uncles, Benjamin Ludlow, was badly wounded. He was taken prisoner, together with Butler and his son, but died the next day.

Although the local roundhead forces heavily outnumbered the cavaliers, they fell back, and Colonel Cromwell and his men 'took a mortar piece of the rebels, and made a safe retreat without any loss'[50] to Corfe Castle. Shortly afterwards the royalists returned to Wareham to try to re-establish control of it, but the roundheads had recovered their nerve, and Cooke drove them from the town, even though Michael Hudson had 'told Secretary Nicholas that 200 horse would take both Poole and Wareham'.[51]

Butler did not remain a prisoner in Corfe long. He came to a deal with the royalist leader, Colonel Robert Lawrence, and the two of them escaped together. Lawrence was replaced as governor by Henry Anketell, 'the priest and malignant doctor'.[52]

Colonel Cromwell's daring escapade had thoroughly alarmed the parliamentarians, and the committee for both kingdoms in London ordered Colonel Fitzjames to watch Corfe carefully as the 'incursion of the enemy' had resulted in 'some disaffection discovered to exist in that country'.[53] The next day the Committee nervously remarked 'in regard of the late accident at Wareham and the increase of the garrison in Corfe Castle, we conceive it would be very dangerous to leave that county without some convenient force.'[54] Five days later the governor of Chichester was ordered 'to send forthwith 100 foot to the siege of Corfe Castle, the town of Wareham having lately been endangered by the absence of their forces at the siege'.[55]

Corfe Castle, as Walter Erle had found two and a half years earlier, was a tough nut to crack. Nor, despite the promised reinforcements, did the local parliamentary leaders have anything like enough forces to launch the sort of full-scale assault Fairfax had unleashed at Sherborne. However Colonel Lawrence was not the only man whose loyalties were cracking as it became obvious the war was lost. Lieutenant Colonel Pittman, who had previously served under Lord Inchiquin in Ireland, came to Corfe as part of the royalist force that had briefly taken Wareham. Within a week or so of his arrival, he secretly offered to hand the castle over to Parliament. In exchange he was promised £200, amnesty for his previous behaviour, and a commission to raise a regiment for Ireland. Having told Colonel Anketell that he could gather another hundred men in Somerset to join the garrison, and also mentioning his hope of exchanging a prisoner in Corfe for his brother who was held captive by Parliament, Pittman left Corfe. He collected a pass from the parliamentarians dated 16 February, and returned to Corfe a week and a half later with a picked force of between 140 and 200 men from the garrisons of Weymouth and Lulworth.

Among the parliamentarians was at least one other ex-royalist who, like Pittman, had changed sides, for a few weeks after the fall of Corfe the Dorset Committee sent out an order that the sequestrators do not molest Corporal Jones for former delinquency in regard of his good service and hazard of his life as a guide in the taking of Corfe Castle.[56] This was almost certainly Richard Jones of Corfe Castle, who seems to have done quite well out of the civil war, as he owned three houses in Corfe in 1664.

Led by the turncoats, the parliamentarians made their way to a sally-port on the north-east corner of the castle, where Colonel Anketell 'stood to welcome them with much courtesy'.[57] When part of the force, variously described as between 50 and 140 men, had entered Anketell must have grown suspicious for he ordered the gate shut. Pittman pretended to be angry and accused him of treating the other men very badly when they had risked their lives to help him. While the argument was going on, the men who were already in the castle 'very gallantly and resolutely possessed themselves, in an instant, of the strongest wards in the Castle'.[58] This was not as hard as it sounds as the upper part of the castle was considered so impregnable that there were only six men guarding it.

It was about two in the morning of 27 February and the attackers must have expected the besieging forces outside would attack instantly, but nothing happened. For about four hours the intruders in the castle had to hold on against fierce attacks from the garrison who 'shot often and threw down great stones from the wall'.[59] At last, as the sun rose, the parliamentary forces outside began to advance. The royalists hastily demanded a parley and accepted the conditions they were offered, but then two besiegers hungry for plunder used a ladder to climb over the wall. The garrison fired on them, and there was brief danger of a savage battle to the end, until Colonel Bingham who led the besiegers managed to calm the situation.

It may have been now that, according to a long-lived tradition, Lady Bankes threw all the family plate into one of the wells of the castle, where it is still supposed to lie. Eventually the garrison received quarter, and the local men who had been in the castle were allowed to return quietly to their homes. The man who brought the news of Corfe's fall to Poole was given a shilling, while, more oddly, there was a payment of 2s. 8d. 'for 4 pounds of prunes to the gunners on taking of Corfe Castle'.[60] The Houses of Parliament were delighted and ordered 'that £20 be bestowed upon the Captain that brought the news of taking in Corfe Castle and another £10 upon the messenger that brought the news thereof'.[61]

The victory had been almost bloodless, with one parliamentarian and two royalists dying in the last fight, and total losses during the forty-eight day siege only 11. The roundheads captured 140 prisoners, including yet again William Wake who had been exchanged after his imprisonment at Poole, and freed 30 of their own men. They also looted the castle, especially the weapons they found there: 'many arms in the magazine and hall of Sir John Bankes's own, all there to the value of about £400 pillaged by the soldiers'.[62] It was probably as well that the besiegers had not been forced into any hard fighting as John Fitzjames, the Sheriff of Dorset, gives a harrowing glimpse of the state of the victorious parliamentary forces at the time in a letter to Major General Massey:

give me leave to tell you, with what earnestness your ragged, poor, yet faithful officers and soldiers expect you. They must have either your own self or money speedily, or their hearts will break. Truly sir I never saw such dejected spirits in my life as those of the officers as well as the common soldiers.[63]

Nor was it only the troops outside Corfe who were in such a bad way. Just after the fall of the castle, the Dorset Committee too was searching out money for 'Captain Richard Yardley and Captain William Harding and others of the garrison of Weymouth and Melcombe Regis, and now in great distress for want of money'.[64]

The fall of Corfe Castle was all the more welcome to Parliament as there had been rumours that 'the King had an especial eye upon Corfe Castle and would within three weeks be there in person for the relief thereof,'and that a royalist landing was planned at Swanage, while local commanders testified to 'the readiness of the country here to rise and join with the King's part'.[65] A week later Parliament voted to slight Wareham and Corfe. So well was the castle built that, despite costing well over £300, the slighting left large parts still standing.

Meanwhile the Dorset Committee turned its attention to taking control of the newly conquered area of Purbeck. No one whatsoever was to 'presume to intermeddle with any of the woods and coppices which lately belonged to Sir John Bankes, deceased, within this county without special order from this Committee'.[66] There was also the question of rewarding loyal supporters.

Five months earlier Henry Brine, who was 'more cordially for Parliament than other men' petitioned Parliament that he:

has been utterly undone by the garrison of Corfe, who have taken away his goods to the value of £200, and pulled down two of his houses in the town, and carried the stones into the castle.[67]

He begged for satisfaction out of Lady Bankes's estate, and just two weeks after the fall of Corfe the Dorset Committee gave their reply:

taking into consideration the great loss and sufferings of Mr Henry Brine by the garrison at Corfe Castle, whom they have burnt down and demolished his house and laid his other estate waste, and also taking into consideration his service for the Parliament in the garrison of Weymouth, do order and appoint that the sequestrators of the Blandford division do let unto the said Mr Brine, at some moderate rent, the castle waste, vineyard and mill with their appurtenances in Corfe, and also 12 acres of wheat now grown on the land of George Loope of Bucknoll in the Isle of Purbeck, a known delinquent and taken in arms in the said castle.[68]

Bearing in mind the poor weather of the 1640s, one wonders how profitable the vineyard was.

Portland was now the sole remaining royalist stronghold in Dorset. After the failed attempt to storm the castle on 23 August 1645 a fort had been built facing the island but nothing more had been attempted. As ever it was the navy who had the greatest interest in Portland, and on 24 March 1646 Vice Admiral Batten arrived offshore and began negotiating for a surrender. On Monday 6 April Colonel Thomas Gollop accepted Batten's terms and handed over the castle and island. Gollop of Candel Marsh clearly got on well with the roundhead victors as within a few months he became a member of the Dorset Committee.

Batten's terms were exceptionally generous. The garrison were allowed

to keep their weapons and march out with drums beating and colours flying; they were permitted to join the King at Oxford; and Batten promised
to beg Parliament to take off sequestrations on everyone in the garrison.
Not surprisingly Batten felt called upon to justify his leniency, and he
explained that 'not five of them' went to Oxford 'but are gone to their
homes or have taken up arms on our side', no one except the governor
was worth any money, and 'the island was very strong and would have
cost much blood to have reduced it by force...there is more to be done on
the island with a fair carriage than by violence.'[69] The royalist magazine
supplied Batten with 21 cannons, 28 barrels of powder, 120 muskets and
plenty of shot and match.

A week after the surrender of Portland, Exeter surrendered to Fairfax.
The West, from which the royalists had hoped for so much, had finally
fallen, although one soldier, John Hancock, was buried in Bridport as late
as 22 April. The New Model Army marched swiftly back through Dorset,
visiting Dorchester on 19 April and Blandford the next day, as it headed
towards London in triumph. On 5 May the King gave himself up to the
Scots, and seven weeks later Oxford surrendered. To all intents and purposes the war was over.

On 26 November 1645 John White had preached in Westminster Abbey
to the House of Lords. White warned against those who might take
'advantage of our present unsettled condition... poisoning the hearts of
the unstable with their pernicious doctrine'.[70] Drawing comparisons with
the ancient Jews, White spoke of a people:

apt to rise in rebellion against the King, which might turn to
his great damage. And that Satan and his instruments (as in
all former ages, so at present) have made use of the same pol-
icy to hinder our work of a thorough Reformation, is as clear
as the light. And I wish that jealousy were at this time so
thoroughly removed out of men's heads, that they might no
more fear that the Reformation of the church, according to
the pattern laid down in God's word, will prove... a means to
break all other kingdoms (that is, as too many conceive) all
civil power and government in pieces.[71]

Not for the first time White had proved a shrewd judge of the times.
And yet whatever he might hope, the old political order had indeed been
broken into pieces. What could be put in its place?

Chapter Nine

PICKING UP THE PIECES
MAY 1646–1650

Dorset might be rid of the organized forces of the King, but there were still soldiers and ex-soldiers all over the county, many of whom were not behaving with the discipline expected of members of the New Model Army. In July 1646, as the last royalist garrisons in the country were being snuffed out, the Committee of Dorset complained to the Speaker about:

> the great insolencies and disorders committed by the soldiers under the command of Major-General Massey, who (their superior commanders being absent) do in great numbers quarter on this county and levy money to very great value. The good subjects they spoil of their goods by plunder, their persons they assault on the highways...unless a speedy remedy by your wisdom be applied, the good beginnings of a happy settlement in these parts will be wholly crushed.[1]

However next year Massey's men complained in their turn that they were 'wading through deep wants and extremities...occasioned by that slender provision has been made for us, none receiving since the general reducement, above six weeks pay'.[2]

It was the first of a whole raft of similar complaints and counter complaints, though some disciplinary action was taken, and several soldiers were court-martialled for murder, cursing and swearing, and highway robbery. Anthony Ashley Cooper's diary of the immediate post-war period, when he was a justice, reads grimly:

> Nine hanged, only three burnt in the hand...three were condemned to die, two to run the gauntlet, two to be tied neck and heels...seven condemned to die, four for horse-stealing, two for robbery, one for killing his wife, he broke her neck with his hands...four burnt in the hand...five condemned to die, two women for murdering their children...[3]

And so on.

It was a brutal time, but Ashley Cooper was still willing to reprieve one horse-thief 'because he had been a Parliament soldier'. As late as March 1647 Ashley Cooper twice raised the county in an attempt to drive away soldiers who were destined for Ireland but 'quartered on the county without order, and committed many robberies'.[4]

There was trouble also at sea. Without a navy worthy of the name, the royalists had early in the war turned to piracy. Now, from their strongholds in the Scillies and the Channel Islands, they harrassed the southern coasts, and special watch had to be kept along the coast of Purbeck, and from Fleet to Burton Bradstock, 'for preventing the hurt which may be committed by rogues and pirates'.[5]

Religion was a further source of friction. The garrison preacher of Weymouth, Peter Ince, was accused of being a knave and not long afterwards left the post, though apparently to general regret. Parliament was well aware of the vital importance of ministers in shaping local opinion and the new minister for Melcombe was James Strong, the admirer of the women of Lyme, who received a grant of £15 towards his food. Subsequently Strong held the living of Bettescombe.

The Dorset Committee came down heavily on ministers they considered hostile. William Bartlett of Yetminster, despite having been vicar for thirty-nine years, was one of many stripped of office and subsequently imprisoned. In a letter of 18 October 1646 he complained

> my body is committed to prison where I have remained
> these two and twenty weeks, and cannot be ransomed with-
> out the loss of my soul in swearing against my conscience,
> which I will never do.[6]

Bartlett, who finally regained his post after the Restoration, blamed a variety of people for his treatment, notably John Mintern of Newland 'my old adversary', Mintern's father-in-law John Browne, and Walter Foy.

When John Pitt of Chardstock was interrogated in 1647 'he was very refractory, and gave them just such satisfaction as they deserved, that is none at all'. In the circumstances it was scarcely surprising that he was dispossessed of his vicarage and 'plundered of his household goods and books'. But perhaps we will never know the truth behind the 'one circumstance which did in a peculiar manner add to the sharpness of his sufferings, but for certain reasons I forbear to relate it'.[7] Such was the discontent that there was even talk of a second and greater war if the Independent clergy were not put down, but in fact it was the Independents who were increasing their power all over the land.

On occasion the Committee changed its mind over its clerical appointments. William Douch, the rector of Stalbridge, and the man who taught the famous physicist and chemist Robert Boyle, died in 1648. The influence of Boyle, who lived at his manor there until 1650, may have ensured that the new rector was John Douch. But the next year John Douch, and his whole family

> were pulled out of their houses by a troop of horse, who also
> plundered them both within door and without, and scarce
> left them a bed to lie on, insomuch that had it not been for
> the charity of an honest neighbour he must with his wife and
> five small children, have lain under a hedge.

Douch was replaced by Samuel Fairclough, who had little time for his predecessor. When Douch 'used to come and knock at his own door for a piece of bread (i.e. for the fifths which were allowed him by ordinance) to keep his poor wife and children from starving' Fairclough 'would take him by the shoulders and bid him go thrash for his living'.[8]

The first aim of the new rulers of Dorset was to disband the vast majority of soldiers, so saving the troops' pay as well as opening the way for a return to peacetime life. The problem was that most of the men were still owed enormous sums in back pay. The minute books of the Dorset Standing Committee are full of decisions about payments to parliamentary veterans, especially officers.

Just what proportion of their pay disbanded soldiers had received varied hugely. Maurice Murphy, a lieutenant in the Wareham garrison, was owed £120 and had been paid £36 4s., whereas another lieutenant from Wareham, Nathaniel Tyre, had received only £65 7s. 8d. out of £470 7s. 6d. One of the worst-paid officers in Dorset was James Heane, who was owed £992 11s., and in just under two years service had received the princely sum of £10. In the circumstances it is remarkable how little rather than how much plundering there was during the wars.

Many civilians were also clamouring for their debts to be paid, from John Crabbe of Bridport who was owed half of the £100 he had lent during the siege of Melcombe, to Richard Bury, the county treasurer, who was owed £600. Giles Green, the M.P. for Corfe Castle, produced evidence that during 1643 and 1644 the parliamentary governor of Wareham had taken away from him for the garrison '47 kine, one bull, five young beasts and 49 loads of wheat (amounting in the whole to £350 10s.)...for which he got nothing'.[9] The Committee promised to pay him, together with interest of 8 per cent. The owners of various houses on the outskirts of Poole which had been burnt down to prevent enemy approach were also paid for their losses. Not that many of these payments were sorted out swiftly. It took until February 1648 for the overseers of the poor in St Peter's parish, Dorchester finally to agree to accept £20 to cover the £30 they had lent:

> for victualling of the town for five years ago, in regard that the fish, which was bought with the said money, was bestowed amongst the poor of the town after the surrender of this town to the King's party.[10]

Colonel Sydenham's debt of £58 to 'the brewhouse for beer while he lived at Weymouth'[11] was only cancelled in July 1650.

Expenditure also included help for some of the victims of the war. The daughters of Captain Robert Turpin, executed at Exeter in 1644 by Sir John Berkeley, got £30 out of Lady Bankes's estate. The widow of Jeremiah Pond of Sherborne 'who was most cruelly and unjustly put to death by the command of Sir Lewis Dyve, and his goods taken away'[12] received £10 from the Digby estate. Widows and maimed soldiers received 12d. each if they attended the Committee, and Richard Squire and Edward Norwood got 10s. and 20s. respectively 'they having lost their limbs in the siege of Lyme Regis, and therefore need charitable relief'.[13] Humphry Masters 'a maimed soldier (and in great distress)' was paid 'the sum of £3, he having at this time a rotting leg'.[14] Another soldier was compensated for breaking a leg while trying to escape from Corfe Castle. There were even cases of the Committee helping wounded soldiers to find employment. If the parishioners of Holy Trinity, Dorchester raised 40s. to send James Stagg to London to learn the trade of a barber, the Committee promised it would pay £5 to enable him to be apprenticed.

Other work for the Committee included safeguarding vital military supplies. In December 1646 George Borman had received a commission 'for the making of saltpetre for the use of the state, and for converting the same into powder'. The manufacture of gunpowder was, of course, of great importance. When two men, Robert Williams and James Bishop 'endeavoured the hindrance of him in this work, and incited others to threaten the demolition of the works, and invited divers soldiers to set fire on the houses'[15] the Committee had to sort the matter out rapidly.

To cover all this massive extra expense, the Committee was forced to take drastic measures. The easiest source of income lay in the sequestered estates of royalists. In Dorset these included the lands of such rich aristocratic families as the Digbys, Paulets, Strangwayses and Bankeses. Almost equally wealthy must have been the Roman Catholic, George Penny of Toller Whelme, who in June 1649 was one of 95 people, mostly Catholics, indicted for absenting themselves from divine service on Sunday.

The inhabitants of fire-ravaged Beaminster were assigned '£2000 out of the lands of the said George Penny in this county to be paid toward the repair of the said town'.[16] One hundred and sixty people were relieved, according to need rather than loss, while another 15 who had refused to sign the petition to Parliament got nothing. Other people must have left the town and returned too late to receive any money, as the churchwardens paid out occasional amounts from 1647 to as late 1652 when 1s. was given 'to a man who was burnt in the fire'.[17] The last £400 of the relief funds had been given to the Beaminster workhouse to buy 'hemp and wool for employing their poor, who were both numerous and idle'.[18] However, spending the money was easier than raising it, as Penny had shrewdly leased Toller Whelme out to Sir Robert Poyntz just before the estate was sequestered. After a legal squabble, it was eventually agreed that the lessee should contribute £100 a year until the fine had been paid. Much of Penny's money had previously been allocated to Lieutenant-Colonel Lacey to cover his back pay, but the claims of Beaminster were considered more important, and Lacey had to make do with an assortment of other bits and pieces, including a share in the *Mary*, a ship that lay in Weymouth harbour and was partly owned by the betrayer of Weymouth, Fabian Hodder.

The sequestrators were much hated, but there was always a chance of escaping lightly. Renaldo Knapton, the keeper of Dorchester gaol was that rare thing in Dorchester, a royalist. After the Restoration he complained that he was the only person in the town who had suffered sequestration or imprisonment because he had 'served his majesty in the late wars'.[19] In fact he was treated leniently because of a certificate from the mayor and aldermen of the town in which: 'they expound very favourably of him, making him a friend and not an enemy while lately the King's party was in this county'. As a result 'the Committee is fully satisfied of his fair carriage before the coming of the Earl of Essex into this county'.[20] If an accused could not provide a certificate like Knapton's, the best move was probably to follow the example of the fairly well-off William Bragg of Littlewindsor, whose land had been seized 'upon information of his delinquency'. At Bragg's appearance before the Committee, he 'manifested his good affection to the Parliament by freely giving the sum of £20 to the service of the state',[21] on which his land was given back to him and he was ordered to be left in peace.

The sequestrators did not take every penny from an estate, usually it was two-thirds of the income, and there were endless quarrels about just how much the original owner was entitled to. After Peregrine Percotey of Beaminster was sequestered, his wife appealed to the Committee and after 'the weak condition of the said woman (deserving pity) was set forth',[22] she was granted £5 10s. out of her husband's estate. More surprising was the Committee's relative generosity to the widow of John Cade, who had been executed for his part in the royalist seizure of Weymouth in 1645. Mrs Cade was granted an allowance of 40s. a year for three years to clothe her children.

The royalist aristocracy were naturally the chief victims of the sequestrators, but they often had influential relations on the parliamentary side to appeal to. Lady Grace Strangways was the sister of that resolute parliamentarian Sir Thomas Trenchard, and she wrote to him about her husband's sequestered estates, complaining bitterly against the Committee:

you may well judge by their inclinations what justice I could expect from them if I had not [a] friend to stand for my right... I thank God I am not guilty to myself that I have deserved it from any of them to be so strict against me, and should be very glad to know what they could allege against me that I might clear myself in it.[23]

Lady Bankes, Lady Weld and Lady Grace Strangways all petitioned the Committee that they might receive back part of their husband's estates to support themselves and their families, their jointure as it was called. The same was true of Giles Strangways's wife, Susanna, who also wrote pleadingly to Sir Thomas:

I am confident you are sensible of the sad condition we are in, and therefore am a suitor to you that you will use all your power to procure our children the fifth of their father's estate.[24]

Humphrey Weld's wife received her jointure very rapidly, on 9 March 1646, but in the case of Lady Bankes the sequestrators were not sympathetic: 'we, finding her active in the defence of Corfe Castle against Parliament...have not granted her desire, but conceive we ought to continue the sequestration'.[25] Before she finally received her jointure, Lady Bankes had to pay a composition of £1340 for herself and her children.

In contrast Lady Grace's appeal to her brother was at least a partial success. On 9 March 1646 the Dorset Standing Committee recommended 'that the mansion house and domain lands of Melbury Sampford', together with several other farms, 'shall be returned to the said Lady Strangways for her fifth part which ought to be allowed her by the Ordinance of Parliament',[26] and Lady Grace, just recovered from serious illness, responded by writing to her sister-in-law, Lady Trenchard to:

> present my humble thanks unto himself [Sir Thomas Trenchard] and to the rest of my friends which joined with him in the letter which was sent in my behalf to the Committee...and to let them know that upon the receipt of it they did allot my fifth part here unto me about the house, but I think not the full portion... they deal upon harder terms with me than anybody else.[27]

She then took the chance to object to having soldiers repeatedly quartered upon her, at one time at least 40 of them, and always having to buy oats for their horses. That appeal too seems to have had an effect as some months later the Dorset Committee allowed her '16 pence, day and night, for so many horse and men as she shall quarter of the county troop'.[28]

Besides sequestration and ill health, Lady Grace had another cross to bear, the imprisonment of her sixty-two-year-old husband, Sir John Strangways, in the Tower. Within a short time of Sir John's capture in Wales she was writing to Thomas Trenchard begging for his 'best assistance' so that her husband 'may have the liberty to come home to his own house, there to end his days, though poorly, yet in peace and quietness'.[29] But Trenchard was unable, or unwilling, to help in this matter. Even the House of Lords, who wanted to pardon Strangways in March 1646, did not move the new rulers. In May 1647, a couple of months after the joint composition for Sir John and Giles Strangways was set at a hefty £10,000, money that would be used for the navy, Sir John was still in prison, and his wife was still trying to get him freed. The sequestrations on the Strangwayses' estates were only finally lifted in June 1648.

The Committee did not allow its victims to get away with much, when the sequestration on Sir John Hele was lifted in December 1648, he not only had to pay £1400, but also unspecified 'charges, interest and damages'.[30] Robert Lawrence of Creech Grange may have deserted his post as the royalist governor of Corfe Castle, and helped Robert Butler to escape, but he was still ordered to pay a heavy fine, being ordered 'to settle £140 per annum for ever upon such places as the Parliament shall appoint: for which he is allowed £1400 and so his fine is reduced to £28 15s.'[31] A similar way of extracting payment was used with John Crook of Motcombe, whose lands around East Stour had been sequestered in 1645. In March 1647 he was ordered to settle £50 a year for ever on the minister of Christchurch, together with another £70 a year on two small rectories in

Hampshire, 'for which he is allowed £1200 out of his fine of £4855'.[32]

Robert Napier of Puncknowle, the younger brother of Sir Gerard and a lawyer who spent much of the war in Exeter collecting money for the royalist forces, had to pay £505 11s. The war and the fine either left him very poor, or else he was a tight-fisted man, for in 1655 a resident of More Crichel, Richard Gregory, wrote in his will that Robert Napier 'owes me for his daughter's bodice, and lent his son at Oxford'.[33] Winston Churchill of Wootton Glanville had to take shelter with his wife's roundhead relations at Ashe House. Perhaps finding his fine of £446 18s. too high to repay easily, he was still at Ashe in 1650 when his son John was born. John Churchill would become one of England's most famous generals, the Duke of Marlborough.

Nonetheless, most royalists were a long way from being bled dry. Humphrey Weld who had bought the Earl of Suffolk's estates around Lulworth for between £25,000 and £30,000 shortly before the Civil War, seems to have hesitated between the two sides before plumping for the King. Despite spending most of the war in Oxford, he was restored to his estates in December 1647, after paying 'the sum of £990 11s. in full of £1981 imposed on him by the Lords and Commons as a fine for his delinquency to the Parliament'.[34] He still owed £400 in August 1650, yet the very next year he bought the magnificent Weld House in London's Drury Lane.

Just how much money was made out of sequestration is highly debatable. Certainly the costs of the war and subsequent reconstruction were astronomical, and taxes went soaring up and up, to far beyond what had been considered unbearable a few years earlier. Denzil Holles asserted that the little finger of Parliament was 'heavier than the loins of the monarchy', and dismissed ship money and the rest of Charles's arbitrary taxations as 'but flea bitings' compared with the exactions of Parliament. 'At the worst one may say, we were then chastised with whips, but now with scorpions.'[35] In 1647 Dorset was expected to pay £935 10s. 10³/₄d. a month, more than twice the amount of ship money ten years before.

It was widely believed that the leaders of the parliamentary party had done extremely well for themselves. A contemporary royalist publication, *A List of the Names of the Members of the House of Commons...together with such sums of money, offices and lands as they have given themselves for service done and to be done against the King and Kingdom*, even gave specific, if unsubstantiated figures. Thomas Trenchard was supposed to have been given £1200, 'William Bingham' and 'John Sydenham' (the christian names of these two have clearly been confused) £1000 apiece, while Thomas Erle is less specifically described as 'a great Committee man, [who] punisheth his and his father's enemies, and rewards himself and his friends'. John Browne is accused of having 'seized £1000 worth of the stock and goods of Farmer Wade's in Portland' (Thomas Wade of Wyke Regis was described as a pauper in 1664), while Walter Erle is said to be 'worth £1000 per annum in time of peace, but in time of war worth £5000 per annum'.[36] One of the highest payments in the whole kingdom, £5000, was supposed to have been given to Denzil Holles, even though within three years Holles was describing the sequestrators as 'worse than any Spanish Inquisition, few escaping that were ever questioned'.[37]

There is no question that some did very well. John Lea made enough money to buy up Sir John Stawell's estates in Chilfrome and Rampisham, and Roger Hill, a lawyer with no family wealth, bought up 'the Bishop of Winchester's manor of Taunton Deane, reckoned the best in England and worth £1200 per autumn'.[38] Other parliamentarians grew rich by a variety of dubious practices. Richard Rose, the M.P. for Lyme Regis, and John Trenchard of Warmwell, the father-in-law of Colonels Bingham and Sydenham, apparently let out lodgings at high rates to old royalists, then seized their furniture and possessions, claiming that malignants could have no right to such things. One of their victims was a Mr Bailey, previously the glazier to King Charles, 'but he with a prudent perserverance, taking advantage of their disagreement in sharing their plunder which belonged to him, recovered it'.[39] John Trenchard's brother, Sir Thomas Trenchard, had married one of his several daughters to a royalist whom he promised to befriend to Parliament. However Trenchard had his son-in-law's estate first sequestered, then took it himself to cover an unpaid debt.

Anger against the sequestrators and taxmen was always likely to flare up into violence. One time when the Committee sat at Blandford Henry Flewell and William Chapman led a mob who 'came in a tumultuous and rebellious manner to withstand our proceedings', but the outburst was soon dealt with and the ringleaders put in prison 'they being very dangerous persons and suspected for robbers, desperate enemies to honest men, etc.'[40] Conspiracies, too, flourished. In May 1647 the Committee reported that 'under the pretence of football matches and cudgel playing and the like, there have been lately suspicious meetings and assemblies at several places,' while new taxes meant that 'the minds of many were never so exasperated as now against the Parliament.'[41]

The doubts and mistrust that were the legacy of war flourished throughout Dorset. Informers must have been common, and every town or village was likely to be split into hostile factions, sparring over who was to dominate in the new world opened up by the King's defeat. On 19 March 1646 Richard Alford, a merchant and three times mayor of Lyme Regis, demanded restitution 'having suffered many damages to his estate as he always occasioned, by his being sent away from his dwelling, during the siege before the town, by Colonel Ceeley'.[42] However there were serious doubts about Alford's commitment to the parliamentary side. Edward Drake had described him as:

> supposed by some to be a malignant and a desperate one because he was very rich and not very forward in advancing the Parliament cause, and especially because he had a son in arms against it and at this time before the town.[43]

133

Such was the distrust of Alford that, during the siege, he was forcibly put in a ship bound for Portsmouth. The ship was intercepted from Weymouth, then royalist, and the captain, Ceeley's brother-in-law Harvey, was imprisoned, but what happened to Alford is not clear.

Alford's royalist son, Captain Gregory Alford, was treated with kid gloves by the Dorset Committee and fined a puny £10 for his royalism. Another former mayor of Lyme, Anthony Ellesdon, had also had a son in royalist service, William Ellesdon, and his fine too was noticeably light, just £33 6s. 8d.

The Committee's reaction to the doubts concerning Richard Alford was to appeal directly to the people of Lyme:

> we have thought fit hereby to desire you that at your public meeting, you call together the inhabitants of the town, and to inquire of them whether the said Mr Alford before his send-ing away manifested himself disaffected to the Parliament or did adhere to the contrary party'.[44]

What the public meeting decided we do not know, but in January 1647, despite Colonel Ceeley's fresh accusations of delinquency against Alford, he was completely cleared by the Committee, and even given permission to search for his goods and take them back from any house or cellar where he found them. This laid the way open to repayment of the £3602 14s. 6d. Alford said he was owed, partly for his ships destroyed during the siege, and partly for supplies of salt and iron to the garrison of Lyme in the last year of the war. It also permitted him to become mayor of the town again that August. Alford's caution in not entirely committing himself to either side had paid a rich dividend, but it must have angered many more ded-icated people who had risked their lives and wealth during the war.

That summer Thomas Hogan returned to Lyme from London with an order to pay the local garrison £500. It was nothing like enough. 'The sol-diers in the garrison, having intimation of it, ran into a mutiny...saying they would have all their pay to a day.'[45] A few days later the governor of Plymouth arrested Daniel Lewes, an army agitator who had just been in Lyme and was now attempting to subvert the Plymouth garrison. Shortly afterwards the defensive works about Lyme were dismantled and the gar-rison disbanded. The heavy guns were sent away, leaving only enough metal to make an iron bell, now in the town museum.

The same month, July, the garrison of Weymouth, who six months ear-lier had still been owed £2636 17s. in unpaid back pay, also mutinied. Robert Coker, the sheriff of the county wrote to the House of Commons in panic:

> the extreme poverty and necessity of the soldiers (contrary to mine or any of their officers' apprehensions), hunger breed-ing through stone walls, caused them mutinously to gather together; and the most part of them, armed, broke forth of the garrison, marched to Dorchester, and there very rudely seized upon some of gentlemen of the Committee... Myself

being present, endeavoured by threats and persuasions to appease them; but, unless I would engage myself they should have their pay assured to them, I could not prevail, which to stop their violence I was compelled to do (but which way to get money to make good my promise, God knows). They are still out of the garrison in a mutinous posture with their arms; there is no way to quiet them but money.[46]

Presumably enough money was found, for the mutiny faded away. But Weymouth was a troubled town. This stemmed partly from the retention of a substantial amount of power in the hands of a group of royalist-leaning aldermen led by George Churchey, and partly from the radicalism of Captain John Arthur, the governor of Portland in 1643, and his supporters. Arthur was so loathed in certain circles, that the terms signed for the surrender of Portland in 1646, included a specific clause, 'that the late governor of the Island for Portland who was there when the island was lost to the King's forces, shall not be governor there any more during these wars'.[47] A merchant, John Waltham, who insulted, threatened and struck Captain Arthur was imprisoned 'for his lewd carriage',[48] while John Fawne, a seaman, had to pay £20 for calling Arthur a French dog, a cur and a toad. George Churchey, himself described by one of the constables as a drunken, malignant knave, accused Arthur of evading customs, and of conniving at the illegal seizure of goods by soldiers.

Churchey feuded with several of the parliamentarian rulers of Weymouth. As late as 1649 he was complaining he had been robbed of canary wine and other goods worth over £1000, by virtue of a warrant signed by William Sydenham. Though at the same time he also tried to distance himself from the royalists by claiming to have been 'in great trouble and fear as well in the time when the garrison was for the late King as when it was reduced for the Parliament, lest the same wines or goods should be plundered from him'.[50]

More revealing was Churchey's quarrel with Lieutenant Peter Peeke of the Weymouth garrison. Peeke had been a mere clothworker before the war, while Churchey had long been one of the leading men of the town. On 13 October 1646 Churchey complained that Peeke was trying to force him to quarter three soldiers even though he was already paying sixpence a week towards one and had a house full of children. Churchey was put in prison for some hours until he agreed to pay 1s. 6d. and was released. Twelve days later Peeke sent two more soldiers with 'provoking and urgent terms' who accused Churchey of swearing. At seven that night Peeke himself arrived together with Captain Harding, two sergeants and many musketeers 'with matches burning and ran into my house in a hostile manner and affrighted my people and in a special manner a sick son in a dying condition'.[51] After another argument, the soldiers left, but more soon arrived and insisted on searching the house to check that every bed was full. At last Churchey's wife 'gave them a groat and so they went'.

The episode illustrates the huge tension that must have existed between the new military and the old-established civil authorities of towns throughout Dorset, and further afield. However much civilians might object, ultimate power lay with

> this broad spreading tree, the army; a dismal cypress, the shadow and dropping whereof were so pernicious as to darken all the comfortable beams of our sunshine of peace and suffer no good thing to prosper near it.[52]

Shortly before the King's execution six Weymouth aldermen, including Churchey, all resigned.

An election in Shaftesbury in autumn 1646 to find a replacement for William Whitaker resulted in the army man, George Starre, comfortably defeating a moderate member of the gentry, John Fitzjames. After Starre's death a year later, the new M.P. was another radical, John Fry. Some time before Fry had been recommended to Anthony Ashley Cooper by Edmund Butler:

> it is pity but he should be in employment, for it cannot but give offence and be a prejudice to the state, when three-penny fellows shall be in places of honour and trust, and men considerably more worthy left out.[53]

Despite complaints that the election had been held on the wrong day and in secret, Fry took his seat in 1648.

Many parts of the army had been infected with revolutionary political and religious views, most notably 'that all degrees of men should be levelled, and an equality should be established, both in titles and estates, throughout the Kingdom',[54] which led to these fledgling democrats being known as Levellers. When faced with a Leveller-inspired mutiny among the army rank and file Cromwell reacted in a way reminiscent of his rough and ready treatment of the Dorset clubmen, though harsher:

> he knocked two or three of them in the head with his own hand, and then charged the rest with his troop, and took such a number of them as he thought fit; whereof he presently caused some to be hanged, and sent others to London to a more formal trial.[55]

Nevertheless, Leveller views remained influential in the army, and even among the officers. When some leading inhabitants of Poole petitioned against their governor, Lieutenant Colonel Rede, in 1651, their first accusation was:

> that being disaffected to the present government he promoted the designs of the Levellers against the state, not only in his command but in the County of Dorset and elsewhere. That in March and April 1648, being a time of great danger when the Levellers rose in actual arms against the state, he did absent himself from Poole.[56]

Up in London the indefatigable Sir Lewis Dyve sent secret letters to the King from the Tower, using as his messengers two Dorset royalists 'of most approved fidelity',[57] George Strangways and John Fussell. Dyve assured Charles that his enemies:

> are so distracted, their courage so sunk, their ends so contrary, their divisions so great, their jealousies among themselves so multiplied, the hearts of the people generally so alienated from them, and their minds so amazed and affrighted with their own guilty consciences, as are apparent evidences of their approaching ruin.[58]

Dyve, charged with high treason and with his lands sequestered, did what he could to spread mistrust among the King's enemies. One of the leaders of the Levellers was John Lilburne, and Dyve worked especially hard at widening the breach between Cromwell and Lilburne.

Although charged with high treason and with his lands sequestered, the restraints on Dyve had been loosened. He was allowed to see Giles Strangways, indeed a fellow prisoner described the pair of them as 'ne'er asunder',[59] and in exchange for his word not to try to escape, Dyve was allowed to live unwatched in a lodging place. However he was still regarded as a dangerous person, and changing their minds his captors resolved to put him in 'the common gaol'. Getting wind of this, Dyve hurried off to visit his warden, Sir John Lenthall the older brother of the Speaker of the House of Commons:

> I fell into a strange passion and in great heat told him I would not longer be engaged on my word...and so thrusting the chair from me whereon I sat, I made a short turn in the room, taking a candlestick in my hand which stood upon a side table and striking it with violence upon the board did much bruise the fashion thereof.

Lady Lenthall was infuriated by Dyve's rude behaviour, and accused him of striking her:

> The truth is had not Sir John Lenthall himself and some of his daughters in the room interposed between her and me, I verily believe it would have fallen to my share to have complained of a beating.

Having freed himself from his parole, Dyve organized a dinner party next evening, the day before he was to be imprisoned afresh, pretended to get drunk then slipped away 'leaving my friends to be merry without their host'.[60]

Dyve's brother-in-law, James Strangways, had also fled the country, leaving a letter behind for his mother, Lady Grace, promising that 'my sudden (and to you unexpected) departure' was

> not ever to take up arms again (for that were to forfeit both my promise and obedience to you), but to escape such writs (as in relation to some pretended irregularities during my late bearing of arms) do now by the report of fame attend me.[61]

Six months later James wrote to his mother again from La Rochelle.

Except for a brief reference to 'the afflictions I fear you are daily in' and a query 'if my father be safely delivered of his captivity', James was only really interested in 'whether I may safely return or no' and the fact that 'the allowance your Ladyship is pleased to give me...truly Madam I find it much too short.'[62] In March 1648 James's quarterly allowance was '£20 of lawful English money',[63] while in January 1650 it was £25. James might have done better to have stayed in England as his fine for compounding was only £40 10s.

James's father, Sir John Strangways, had been released from imprisonment and seemed fairly confident of his returning influence. In 1650 he wrote to a relation, Dr Wood: 'I will use my best endeavour to take off the sequestration from Berrow parsonage.'[64] But Parliament was not going to underestimate one of its richest and most formidable opponents in the South West. When Strangways asked permission to tour his estates that year, it was refused. The frustrated Sir John, who fancied himself as something of a poet, and had written a piece entitled 'Upon a private and retired life' during his time in the Tower, took solace in poetry:

> The lands which do belong to me
> I did resolve this spring to see
> But since the State hath me denied
> Above five miles from home to ride...

The poem continues for almost 250 lines of relentless rhyming couplets, minutely detailing virtually every tenement he owned in half a dozen counties, together with the rents and rights connected to them, before his visitation of the mind finally comes to an end:

> ...To Melbury Sampford thence I come
> And blessed be God am there at home.[65]

Five years later his main interest, rather than royalist uprisings, was the establishment of one of the first duck decoys in the country on his estate at Abbotsbury.

There was fresh trouble around Blandford in March and April 1648. The minister of Bryanston had been sent away for delinquency, so William Wake, himself sequestered from his parish in Wareham, seized the opportunity to preach there against the Parliament. Wake had apparently been imprisoned in the marshalsea of Melcombe for some months after December 1646, even though in June 1648 Colonel Heane complained that 'there is as yet not convenient house appointed for a marshalsea.'[66] The Dorset Committee ordered Wake to be arrested again, and responded to the 'mutinies and uproars' with an order to 'disarm all and every the inhabitants of the said town that are turbulent and ill-affected to the Parliament'.[67]

The first attempt to arrest Wake failed, even though the parliamentarians:

> brought a troop of dragoons to seize him and such as frequented the prayers of the church and barbarously murdered one Walter Elkins, a cutler, who made good his house and refused to be their prisoner.[68]

Subsequently Wake was seized and mounted behind a dragoon to be carried prisoner to Dorchester, but 'being market day, town and country rose and pursued them'. Eventually Major Edmund Uvedale and Wake's nineteen-year-old son, William Wake the younger who had been 'carried very young into the King's army',[69] rescued him. On 25 March the committee of both Houses wrote of 'an insurrection there to hinder the execution of a warrant, and the actual rescue of Wake',[70] and ordered some of Fairfax's men to the town to help sort matters out. On 28 April Major Uvedale, who had been in command of the royalist garrison at Langford House north of Salisbury, was ordered to 'be committed to the Fleet for making an insurrection in county Dorset'.[71] Subsequently Uvedale had to enter a bond of £1000 with the Speaker, and eventually compounded for 'having violently rescued a prisoner from the Parliament's soldiers'.[72]

A few weeks later the Dorset Committee referred to 'the present distempers of the kingdom'[73] and ordered that all the arms and ammunition in Lyme should be gathered together and transported to Weymouth.

Even in Dorchester there was waning support for the parliamentary party. John White had left Lambeth in July 1646 to return to the town, and in his valedictory work, *The Way to the Tree of Life*, he reminded his parishioners 'your very lives did hang in doubt before you, and you feared day and night,' before going on to reassure them:

> though your estates were wasted, yet your dwellings were preserved, that you might not be as Sodom, or like unto Gomorrah, as some other places are; as it was often threatened, and as often really intended by your enemies, and had questionless been executed, had not the Lord...almost miraculously prevented it.[74]

Shortly afterwards a royalist newsbook confidently reported:

> From Dorchester we understand good news of the loyal party there, who now begin to express themselves for the King and cry out for Common Prayer, and for setting the King on his throne.[75]

The parliamentary leaders regarded the situation in the region with deep distrust. Fairfax made sure there were still three troops of the New Model Army in Dorset 'for the security of the garrisons there, which are very weakly manned, and for suppressing insurrections',[76] while Cromwell wrote to him: 'You hear in what a flame these western parts are.'[77]

War was indeed about to burst out afresh. Charles, with the help of Sir John Berkeley, fled from Hampton Court to the Isle of Wight in November 1647, and from his loose imprisonment in Carisbrooke Castle he spent the winter summoning everyone he could think of to rise up. Infuriated by the ever-growing power of Cromwell and the Independents, and encouraged by Charles's concessions on religion, the Scots and the English Presbyterians finally agreed to ally with the royalists. The result was the second Civil War, a much smaller-scale conflict but fought with greater ferocity than its predecessor.

Even as large cuts were being made in the standing army, there were demonstrations and riots in London; then Kent, Essex and South Wales burst into outright rebellion. Royalists seized scattered fortresses, and a large part of the navy mutinied. However the New Model Army was more than a match for the rebels. Except for the dogged resistance of Colchester, the uprisings in the south were rapidly snuffed out, and when the Scots invaded in July, they were crushed by Cromwell in a running fight at Preston in mid-August. Among the prisoners taken was Sir Lewis Dyve. He had been free for scarcely seven months. Starving Colchester surrendered to Fairfax ten days later. In Dorchester a thanksgiving day for success against the Scottish army raised £5 11s.

Virtually all the fighting in the second Civil War took place in counties that had seen little, if any, fighting during the first Civil War. Nevertheless the royalists had done all they could to raise Dorset. On 15 June 1648, during the siege of Colchester, a *Declaration of the County of Dorset*, which claimed to be 'subscribed by above 10,000 inhabitants of that County', was brought out. It demanded, among other things: the speedy return of the King from imprisonment; the election of a new Parliament; the end of the power of the county Committee; and that everyone who had suffered for their allegiance to the King should have their estates restored and a right to seek reparation. There was also a specific paragraph requiring that Thomas Ceeley 'the late imperious governor of Lyme' should no longer 'glory in the innocent blood of the well-meaning countrymen he has so unlawfully spilt; nor live upon estates they have thievishly taken from the rightful owners'. The declaration ended:

> as heretofore on less encouragement, we engaged our lives,
> liberties and estates on the same grounds, under the slighted
> and unprosperous notion of clubmen...our ends are still the
> same and our endeavours shall be now vigorous and active,
> and we doubt not more prosperous and successful.[78]

Despite the declaration and a scattering of food riots, attacks on excise-men and outbreaks by the clubmen, war-weary Dorset showed little enthusiasm for a fresh conflict. Nevertheless the Committee took no risks and, having disbanded most local troops the year before, money and fresh soldiers were hastily raised:

> for as much as there is great and present occasion of two
> troops of horse in this county for preserving the peace there-
> of against the enemy who threaten to rise and disturb the
> same peace'.[79]

John Browne, Thomas Trenchard, Henry Henley and John Whiteway lent the money for three companies of foot and one troop of horse, and John Arthur was ordered 'to procure or cause all such arms as he has in his custody (belonging to the state) to be with all convenient speed to be well and sufficiently fixed and amended' as well as to 'deliver unto the commander-in-chief of Portland Castle 20 muskets, 20 pairs of bandoliers, 10 swords and belts more for the service of the garrison'.[80]

On 10 August Parliament ticked the Dorset Committee off because the garrisons of Poole and Brownsea were not 'so well supplied as such places in these dangerous times require to be', and reminded the Committee of 'the disaffection of the people, not long since manifested in your county'.[81] A week and a half later there were were rumours of royalist 'designs on Weymouth, Melcombe and Portland',[82] and next day came warnings that many royalist soldiers disguised as ordinary people were planning to slip into the West for a muster of 8000 somewhere in Somerset or Dorset. The authorities took care to watch the roads, ready to arrest all strangers who could not explain their business. A garrison also returned to Sherborne where it stayed in the school until 1649. After they finally departed the school had to pay out 5s. 6d. 'for mending the glass windows in the school after the soldiers (who made it their post of guard) went' and another 3s 6d 'for three days work and for straw and besoms to make clean the school after the removing of the soldiers'.[83]

In the middle of the second Civil War, on 21 July 1648, John White died. Old and sick, struggling to keep pace with the revolutions that convulsed the nation, he had never again wielded the same authority he had done before the war. Eight months earlier the corporation of Dorchester had voted for 'an assistant minister to help master White in his weakness',[84] and by May White could no longer guarantee his ability to preach on Sundays, so William Benn was chosen to cover for him 'which we understand also will give very good satisfaction to the town in general'.[85] In his will White left 40s to the poor of Dorchester, and begged the people of the town to 'suffer not themselves to be carried up and down with every wind of doctrine'. He also added, 'as I have never liked the affected solemnities thereof...may my funeral be solemnized with all privacy, without any sermon or ringing of bells.'[86] Nevertheless the council ordered that 'Mr Savage do cause the porch to be hung with black at the funeral and for one month after, and if it be stolen the company will satisfy him for it.'[87]

Even before the Scots' defeat at Preston, several former parliamentary leaders fled, including William Waller and Denzil Holles, who had challenged Cromwell's nephew, Henry Ireton, to a duel in the House of Commons itself, and then retired to Dorset. After riding to the Essex coast, they took a boat only to be caught near Calais and taken to Vice Admiral Batten's flagship. But as Batten himself was then in rebellion, they were allowed to complete their journey to France. Shortly afterwards Batten persuaded Prince Charles not to fight Warwick and the parliamentary navy and the mutiny died out. Batten himself was given indemnity by Warwick, and returned to England in peace.

Others would not be so lucky. Defeat in the second Civil War was the direct cause of King Charles I's trial in January 1649 'for levying war against the Parliament and people of England, for betraying their public trust reposed in him, and for being an implacable enemy to the

Commonwealth'.[88]   Only three of Dorset's M.P.s were named among the 135 judges to try the King. John Browne, who apparently Cromwell called the 'Old Roman' for voting to put Charles on trial, was not among them. Denis Bond and Roger Hill, the M.P. for Bridport, were listed but neither took any part in the trial. John Fry, the MP for Shaftesbury, was the third, and he seems to have been an assiduous judge. However after the first six days of the trial he was involved in a religious argument with another of the judges, John Downes, who accused him of denying the divinity of Christ. Faced with a charge of blasphemy Fry was 'suspended from sitting in this House and executing of his duty here as a member, till he shall give better satisfaction to this House'.[89]

Although he was later called a regicide, Fry was banned from taking part in the final stages of the trial, or signing the King's death warrant, and some time later he was disabled as an M.P., and had his two offending books burnt for being 'erroneous, profane and highly scandalous'.[90]

Cromwell seems to have been remarkably calm about the trial, for on the very day it opened, he was busying himself with an entirely unconnected matter concerning a former leader of the Dorset clubmen, John Fussell. Fussell had clearly been under suspicion during the troubles of the previous year, for a warrant was issued on 13 June 1648 'for apprehending John Fussell and William Wake'.[91] However, a few months later he was given ten days liberty from gaol 'with his keeper'[92] to deal with some legal business. Cromwell, with characteristic interest in the detail of government, accepted a bond of £500 from Fussell on condition that he 'shall not raise any forces or arms against Parliament, but live peaceably'.[93]

Edmund Prideaux of Lyme Regis had been appointed Solicitor General in October 1648, but he resigned the post shortly before the trial of the King. His caution cannot have been held against him as in April 1649 he was made Attorney General, and held the office for the rest of his life. The same year he used his office as Master of Post Messengers and Carriers to reinstate the national postage system, with conveyances to every part of the kingdom, which had been established in the 1630. Prideaux was said to earn a massive £15,000 a year from the post.

A month after the King's execution on 30 January 1649, Warwick was replaced as Lord High Admiral by those stalwart Somerset parliamentarians, Edward Popham and Robert Blake. While manning his flagship, the *Triumph*, Blake specifically sent for three men from Lyme Regis, one of whom was the Richard Squire who had lost an arm during the siege.

Like much of the rest of the country, Dorset had suffered one of the wettest summers of years, so the harvest had been very poor. On 30 September the governor of Weymouth, who was in charge of all the extra infantry raised that summer, was writing that he must disband the companies 'or see them perish for want of bread'.[94] Perhaps it was because of the hard times that the Dorchester corporation determined on 'setting the poor to work in spinning of worsted and knitting of stockings, and also of setting up a trade of making sackcloth',[95] which required advice from the sackcloth weaver of Toller Porcorum.

At the same time there was a fresh wave of refugees from Ireland. Wimborne made several payments, notably 'to an Irish woman and her children',[96] while the Beaminster churchwardens ungenerously paid out 'to 40 Irish people 1s. 6d.' in 1648, then revealed just how much England still was a class-based society the next year by granting 2s. 6d. 'to one Irish gentlewoman'.[97]

The inhabitants of Dorset also suffered from fresh outbreaks of piracy. Fleets of up to 30 Irish pirates patrolled the south-western seas, and in July 1649 there were reports that 400 men from the royalist base in Jersey were planning to join up with 600 more from France to seize Portland and Weymouth for Charles II, and 'to put all the soldiery to the sword, and other inhabitants that adhered to them'.[98] The plot was discovered and five people were arrested: two soldiers from the garrison; a woman named Mrs Gallot, and two Portlanders, one of whom was 'a very active treacherous fellow'[99] named 'King' Gardiner, who had been imprisoned in Dorchester in January 1643, one of the royalist garrison of Portland in May 1643, and was perhaps the William Gardiner whose estates at Monckton Wyld and Marshwood were sequestered in 1645. Forty small boats did appear around Portland, but then sailed away without attacking.

Perhaps the feeling that Dorset was growing ever more pro-royalist helped explain the drastic redistribution of local parliamentary seats planned by John Lilburne and Cromwell in 1648. Aiming to enlarge the electorate enormously, Lilburne also wanted to redistribute seats nationwide in a way that would not happen again until the Reform Bill of 1832. The intention in Dorset was to cut the county's representation from 20 M.P.s to just six, but special pleading from Dorchester enabled it to keep an M.P. the next year. In 1653 Dorset had ten M.P.s, but stubbornly royalist Sherborne, the second town of the county, was given no representation.

On 15 December 1648 it was resolved that Sir Lewis Dyve, back in the Tower, 'be brought to speedy justice'.[100] However, yet again Dyve escaped, as had several other royalists. Despite Fairfax's urgent order that Dyve, who was 'of a middle size, and hath a flaxen hair, in sad coloured apparel'[101] should be apprehended, he got away to Ireland, where he fought for the King again. On 6 September 1651 Dyve had dinner at Saint Germain, near Paris, with John Evelyn, who recorded how he:

> entertained us with his wonderful escape out of prison in Whitehall the very evening before he was to have been put to death, leaping down out of a jakes two storey high into the Thames at high water, in the coldest of winter and at night; so as by swimming he got to a boat that attended for him, though he was guarded by six musketeers. After this he went about in women's habit, and then in a small-coal man's, then travelled 200 miles on foot.[102]

It was an impressive story, not least as Dyve, whom Pepys described as 'a great gamester in his time',[103] was almost fifty when he escaped. Evelyn clearly regarded his escapades with some scepticism: 'this knight was indeed a valiant gentleman, but not a little given to romance when he spoke of himself.'[104] A few months later Evelyn met Dyve again. While telling yet more of his adventures, Dyve 'showed me divers pieces of broad gold which, being in his pocket in a fight, preserved his life by receiving a musket bullet on them'.[105]

Back in England Dyve's family paid the price for his adventures. After his wife Howard's death in 1646, Sir Lewis's children were looked after by a certain Mary Gresley, but she seems to have been heavily dependent on help from Lady Grace Strangways. Clearly Lady Grace was not suffering as much from sequestration as she claimed, for in May 1647 Mary Gresley thanked her for her generosity to her grandchildren: 'your Ladyship has so bountifully recruited them with so many fine things that I fear they will grow proud.'[106] As late as August 1650 Gresley was also appealing to the Bedfordshire Committee for part of Sir Lewis Dyve's estate to pay for the upkeep of his children, but

> they would not yield to allow anything for the maintenance of the children...so that I was forced to go to London and follow the business myself, not having any other body to employ.[107]

The compounding committee in the capital was more generous than the Bedfordshire Committee, but only a little. It gave her a fifth of Sir Lewis's estate, but in land not money, and Mary Gresley feared that after she had paid for someone to collect the rents in Somerset 'it will not be worth the sending for.' Dyve was lucky to have such devoted carers for his children as Mary Gresley and Richard Goodridge, who had looked after them for 'above nine years'[108] when he wrote to Sir John Strangways expressing his sorrow at the death of Lady Grace in 1652.

It had been a bitter time for the royalists, with the execution of the King, climaxing

> a year of reproach and infamy above all years which had passed before it; a year of the highest dissumulation and hypocrisy, of the deepest villainy and most bloody treasons that any nation was ever cursed with or under; a year in which the memory of all the transactions ought to be erased out of all records, lest by the success of it atheism, infidelity and rebellion should be propagated in the world.[109]

✦ *Chapter Ten* ✦
THE FLIGHT OF
THE PRINCE
1650–1651

E ngland was not at peace with itself. The famous engraver,
Wenceslas Hollar, who had recently returned to the country after his
unpleasant experiences at the hands of Cromwell's soldiers during
the fall of Basing House, described the change to John Aubrey:
> he told me that when he first came into England (which was
> a serene time of peace), that the people, both poor and rich,
> did look cheerfully, but at his return he found the counte-
> nances of the people all changed, melancholy, spiteful, as if
> bewitched.[1]

Dorset was not exactly seething with rebellion, but it was described by
a royalist conspirator as 'generally looked upon as a county well affected
to the King'.[2] There was even restlessness among those who had previously been faithful parliamentarians. After the execution of the King,
Henry Henley, the high sheriff said his commission had lapsed with
Charles's death, but a few months later, back in office, he was judging an
inquisition on what goods and lands were held by Richard Bingham at
Toller Porcorum. Then in January 1650 Prince Charles was secretly proclaimed King of England at night in Blandford. Two months later the
Prince, then at Breda in Holland, was contacted by Colonel Alexander
Keynes of Radipole, who had been captured during the battle of
Weymouth, and whose farm, worth £200 a year, had been sequestered
since 1645. Keynes was a Roman Catholic, and he had links with other
Dorset Catholics such as the Arundells of Chideock, as well as leading
royalists in the county.

After visiting Charles, Keynes returned to England with a plan to revive
the Western Association, and to lead an uprising if and when the new
King should return to England. Despite the failure of the attempt on
Portland and Weymouth in 1649, the seizure of the area was still considered possible and there was also 'some design upon the garrison of
Poole'.[3] Keynes visited Giles Strangways, and several other royalists, and
in April 1650 Colonel Strangways was one of the Dorset representatives at
a meeting of the Western Association at Salisbury, under the guise of a
race meeting. However the authorities rapidly clamped down, and
Captain John Holmes and three others were arrested on a charge of treason.

Nevertheless the rulers of Dorset continued to feel insecure and all over
the county royal symbols were destroyed wherever they could be found.

At Wimborne 2s. 8d. was paid 'for washing out the King's arms' and another 2s. 4d. to 'the glazier for taking down of the King's arms in the windows and mending it again'.[4] On 10 August 1650 the governors of Sherborne school agreed

that the warden do get workmen to take down the King's arms over the school door and at the south end of the schoolhouse, it being commanded and required by Captain Helyar, a Captain for the Parliament, to be done.[5]

The same year the school was given fresh statutes.

Travellers were regarded with deep suspicion. Indeed, during the next ten years, even though the nation was largely at peace, a pass was essential for those who wished to travel. In 1651 Beaminster accounts record that money was given 'to two Irish people travelling with a pass...two soldiers with a pass that came from Ireland...six Irish persons travelling with a certificate'.[6] Hugh Hodges, the Steward of Sherborne school had to go to Dorchester to 'get a license to travel to London'.[7]

In the autumn of 1650 a doubtful character, Henry Francis, was questioned at Bridport. Henry Francis, who was from Warwickshire, had been travelling all round the south coast, visiting Southampton, the Isle of Wight, Salisbury, Weymouth, and Bridport, as well as possibly sailing to Holland. These were sensitive areas, furthermore Francis possessed a certificate from the town of Gloucester declaring that his name was Richard Cooper who 'to our knowledge has been and always reputed a man of honest life' and never was 'in arms against the Parliament, but has served in arms under command of the same, and not accounted an enemy to the present government established in this Commonwealth'.[8] In the circumstances it was not surprising that Mr Francis was thoroughly investigated. Especially as on 27 August the Council of State were informed 'there are designs of mischief carrying on in several places,'[9] and in November Parliament saw complaints about the 'refractoriness' of the ministers and magistrates of Weymouth.

Early in 1651 Gillingham exploded again over the enclosures of the forest. The Commonwealth government reacted exactly the same as Charles I's had done: with soldiers. John Desborough was ordered to take a troop of horse to Gillingham and crush the riots there, which he seems to have done most efficiently as there is no evidence of any more trouble.

Most of the troops in Dorset had been disbanded, but there were still garrisons at Poole, Brownsea, Weymouth and Portland, totalling around 650 troops with their officers. The importance with which the Dorset coast was regarded is shown by the cost of garrisoning the county, over £1000 a month, which was 8.4 per cent of the cost of garrisoning the whole of England, Wales and south Scotland. Meanwhile the clearing up of the county continued. The bridge between Weymouth and Melcombe, which had played such a crucial part in the battle of Weymouth, was badly in need of repair. In April 1651 the governors of Weymouth and Portland, Colonel Heane and Lieutenant Colonel Joyce, 'made a grant to the incorporation of 30 trees of timber in the late King's forest in Hampshire'.[10]

Pirates continued to plague the county. In 1649 they were described as 'so poor and cowardly they dare not fight',[11] but the reality was more serious. The royalists, aided by Irish ships, still raided from their island strongholds, and in January 1650 Weymouth was attacked. Six months later a single parliamentary ship fought a running battle against three Irish pirates. Eventually, in April 1651, Colonel Heane sent out a boat full of soldiers to escort some vessels. When a pirate from Jersey attacked, the soldiers remained hidden until their ship was boarded, then counter attacked. The captain of the Jersey vessel was killed with 12 of his men and the boat itself barely got away. Six months later Heane and Robert Blake gathered men at Weymouth for a successful attack on the Channel Islands. There were a few losses though, notably William Wyer of Dorchester 'he having been drowned at Jersey in service under Colonel Heane'.[12] John Bingham, who stormed Castle Cornet, the fort of St Peter Port, in December 1651, became the governor of Guernsey.

Threats to the peace and stability of the Commonwealth came not only from the royalists. Several of the leading army men in Dorset had strong sympathies with the radicals who believed in the vote for all men and other extremist views. One such was Edward Sexby, a Leveller leader who in 1647 had ringingly declared, 'I am resolved to give my birthright to none.'[13]

> He had been, in the beginning, a common soldier of Cromwell's troops, and was afterwards one of those agitators who were made use of to control the Parliament; and had so great an interest in Cromwell, that he was frequently his bedfellow.[14]

In September 1647 Sir Lewis Dyve had suggested to Charles I that he meet 'Mr Sexby, agitator for the general's [Fairfax's] regiment',[15] and in 1649 Sexby was made governor of Portland, a post he held until June 1650, when he left to join Cromwell's army in Scotland.

Another radical was John Rede, a Wiltshire man and the governor of Poole from November 1647. Initially he seems to have been popular in the town, and in April 1649 the inhabitants of Poole promised to 'assist, maintain, and join with the present governor, Lieutenant Colonel John Rede, his officers and soldiers'.[16] However his political views eventually angered the old rulers of the town, men like John Bingham and the Skutts who had held Poole during the war. In March 1651 they accused Rede of making 'the city a place of refuge to exorbitant Levellers and those grand enemies to just liberty, civility and godliness, our civil rights devoured by the power of his arbitrary sword'.[17]

The complaint rang a warning bell in London. Only two months earlier Rede had been thanked for his work, but in April the council of state, having seen the:

> articles exhibited to the council against Lieutenant Colonel Rede, governor of Poole, and upon other informations

against him, we conceive it not fit to continue him any longer in that place, which is of great importance.[18]

Major George Skutt shortly arrived with a commission to take over as the new governor. However there was some doubt about the commission, and Colonel Heane the governor of Weymouth, who knew Rede well, insisted Skutt should go to Exeter to find Cromwell's brother-in-law, Major General John Desborough, so that he could clarify the matter. Desborough was away in Plymouth, so Skutt returned to Weymouth and eventually persuaded Heane to send some men with him to Poole. Rede objected, but eventually agreed to hand over to his deputy. Skutt then spoke to the garrison of around 150, demanding that they should accept him as the new governor.

Skutt's speech was not a success. The army, although purged of some leading Levellers, was still politically radical, and the same seems to have applied to the Poole garrison. They had cheered Rede, thrown their hats in the air, and wished him a swift return as he left. Now, despite Skutt's threats, they stayed resolutely silent when Skutt shouted out, 'All you that are for me declare yourselves.' Rede's deputy did give way and accepted Skutt, but the argument bubbled on for many weeks. Eventually the council of state decided that 'to proceed to further examination at this distance would be too much trouble and charge to the witnesses,'[19] and handed the whole business over to Desborough to sort out. Desborough shrewdly ignored both claimants and appointed an uncontroversial townsman, Richard Burthogge. Eighteen months later Rede was still demanding money he was owed from his stint as governor. After the Restoration he was imprisoned in the Tower of London for alleged involvement in a plot against Charles II, but subsequently returned to Dorset.

The young Prince Charles was only twenty, a man of great bravery and quick wits. As the conquering parliamentary forces had driven west in 1645, he took refuge first in the Scilly Isles, then Jersey, where the doomed Duke of Monmouth was born of his liaison with Lucy Walter (though Monmouth's father may have been Colonel Robert Sydney). After his father's execution, Prince Charles proclaimed himself King Charles II, and travelled to France and Holland searching for allies. Eventually, after a flirtation with the Irish Catholics, he accepted the Covenant and became the King of Scotland and the Scots Presbyterians. In doing so he ruthlessly ignored the fact that the very men he was accepting as his allies had, just a month earlier, put to death the Marquis of Montrose for trying to raise a royalist army for Charles. Like many exiles, Charles was to become a great, if cynical survivor. He would also need every scrap of his celebrated sense of humour.

On 23 June 1650 Charles arrived in Scotland. Less than a month later Cromwell was hastily recalled from the bloody struggle in Ireland to challenge him. At Dunbar, on 3 September 1650, he won one of his finest victories against a much larger Scots army led by David Leslie, who had helped him to the triumph of Marston Moor six years before. After Dunbar Cromwell, weakened by malaria, spent the best part of a year trying to pacify Scotland. In his army, in Haslerig's Regiment, was yet another of Dorset's famous parliamentarian family, the Sydenhams of Wynford Eagle.

John Sydenham had been too young to fight in the first Civil War, but in 1650 he was appointed a captain of foot. His brother, Thomas, advanced him the money to pay for his equipment, and on 21 May 1650 he was ordered to march to Chester for transport to Ireland. The next year, now a major, John Sydenham found himself under attack from Charles II's own horseguards near Stirling. The 'fanatical major' fought a fierce skirmish and drove his enemies back, but during the pursuit the cavaliers regrouped and turned about. Sydenham lost 60 of his men and the rest fled. Sydenham himself was wounded mortally in the groin, second of the brothers to die for Parliament:

> Thus ended the traitor, a King-Killer in as much as he espoused the quarrel of those who having already murdered the father, were seeking after the blood of the son, whom they would in like manner have sacrificed.[20]

Yet another brother, Richard Sydenham, who was buried in January 1657, was a captain in the parliamentary army.

When Cromwell advanced to Perth in August, Charles and the Scots army struck south into England. Parliament countered with a campaign to drum up anti-Scottish feeling, and dire warnings of the consequences if the English were 'to suffer this young pretender to take root again, to bring them back into slavery and monarchical bondage too heavy for England's shoulders to bear'.[21]

Long before Charles invaded England precautions were being taken against his attack. In May 1650 Parliament had resolved to demolish Christchurch Castle, and in November the governor of Southampton was ordered to do the job. Seven months later it emerged the castle was still standing. Parliament responded in something close to panic:

> There are guns mounted on it without any guard, which may give an opportunity to enemies to put their destructive designs in execution, their disaffection wanting no greater encouragement than such a hold. Demolish and remove to Poole.[22]

Meanwhile Joyce, the new governor of Portland, demanded 'money and 50 timber trees for repairing Portland Castle',[23] as well as swords, belts, bandoliers and muskets for Colonel Heane's regiment.

Many old soldiers had also been recalled to the colours, to protect the 'public peace against all insurrections, rebellions or any other designs or conspiracies',[24] including Captain Roger Bartlett who on 26 March 1651 was appointed captain of a troop of horse in Alexander Popham's regiment. Four weeks later Captain Thomas Sydenham was also given a troop of horse, and the militia commissioners of Essex were ordered to send him men 'that he being complete may attend the service of the Commonwealth to which he is commanded, and which cannot bear delay'.[25] Sydenham concentrated on securing the Midlands for Parliament then, after Charles's invasion, he joined Major General Harrison and took part in several sharp cavalry engagements in Lancashire, during one of which he was 'left in the field among the dead'.[26]

Back in Dorset the royalists remained active. That summer an agent was sent to the continent to enlist Lord Hopton's help for a plan to seize Poole. Among the royalist conspirators was Major Fry, probably Hugh Fry who ran the medieval Angel Inn at Shaftesbury between 1654 and 1686, and was active in several royalist plots during the 1650s. The design against Poole rapidly unravelled, and in August George Thompson, a merchant, was arrested and revealed everything in exchange for a payment of £130.

A great storm struck Dorchester on 22 August:

All night there was great thunder and lightning, such as has not been known by any living in this age; and there fell with it a great storm of hail, some of the stones of which were 7 inches about, with abundance of rain, and it continued all night and great part of the next morning, till eight of the clock.[27]

The same day Charles, with an army of about 16,000, arrived at Worcester, where the local people drove out the roundhead garrison. But few English royalists had risen up, and Cromwell was sweeping down the country after him. When the two armies faced each other on 3 September, a year to the day after Dunbar, the royalists were outnumbered almost two to one, although they had the advantage of the ground. Cromwell attacked, fought an almost perfect battle tactically, and the Scots and royalists were utterly defeated.

Charles's flight after Worcester is one of the most famous romances of English history. At the time the royalists were not popular in England, and of the fugitives from Worcester 'very many of those who run away were every day knocked in the head by the country people and used with barbarity'.[28] Charles was hidden by a Roman Catholic priest, climbed the celebrated Boscobel oak to escape Cromwell's soldiers, and disguised himself as a servant, William Jackson, who rode in front of a royalist lady, Mrs Jane Lane. When challenged by a republican blacksmith, Charles voiced what must have been a fairly general view when he said he hoped Charles Stuart would be found and hanged for bringing in the Scots.

After a failed attempt to find a ship in Bristol, when in spite of his disguise he was recognized by John Pope, a butler and former royalist soldier, Charles resolved to make his way down to Trent, a village near Yeovil, where Pope had told him he would find Colonel Francis Wyndham.

During the first Civil War Wyndham had held Dunster Castle for three years, until its surrender in 1646. His brother, Edmund, was married to

Christabella Pyne 'nurse to the present King, and one that, while she lived, governed him and everything else...the old King [Charles I] putting mighty weight and trust upon her'.[29] She was also famous for her behaviour at the siege of Bridgwater in 1645, when she took a shot at Fairfax himself and responded to his summons to surrender the town by melodramatically laying her hand on her breast and answering 'Tell the general we will hold it out to the last,'[30] something the royalist garrison signally failed to do.

Francis Wyndham had lost three brothers during the war, and in February 1651 he apparently engaged in an armed skirmish with one of the Sydenhams near Corfe. It was probably as a result of this that he had only recently been released from Weymouth on parole, and had moved from Sherborne to his wife's home at Trent.

Everywhere in England soldiers were hunting for 'a tall black man, six foot and two inches high',[31] but Charles and Mrs Lane reached Trent House safely on 17 September. Here they joined up with Lord Wilmot, later the Earl of Rochester, who was travelling under the name of Mr Morton. Wyndham was overjoyed at the King's arrival, having heard a rumour Charles had been killed at Worcester, and swore 'that for his Majesty's preservation he would value neither his life, family, nor fortune'.[32] He also told the King at some length that fifteen years earlier his father, Sir Thomas Wyndham, shortly before his death, had ordered his sons 'in all time to adhere to the crown; and though the crown should hang upon a bush, I charge you forsake it not'.[33] These, said Wyndham, must be the days his father warned of.

Having met various members of the household, Charles got down to business and asked Wyndham the best way to get to France. Wyndham rode over to nearby Melbury to seek help from the Strangways family. It was not the right moment. Giles Strangways may have had 'a gallant soul, a brain indefatigable',[34] and have been involved in the royalist Western Association, but on 24 February 1651 he had finally been told that he was:

> discharged of his restraint within this garrison (Weymouth and Melcombe Regis) by virtue of an order from the council of state, wherefore these are to advise you to permit and suffer him quietly to go and remain at his house at Melbury Sampford aforesaid and from time to time to travel about his affairs to such place or places as he shall have occasion.[35]

Wyndham met Giles Strangways and they walked in the park and discussed the matter, but fearful of losing his new freedom, Giles excused himself, saying:

> he knew not any one master of a ship, or so much as one mariner that he could trust, all that were formerly of his acquaintance in Weymouth being for their loyalty banished and gone beyond the sea; and in Poole and Lyme he was a mere stranger, having not one confidante in either.[36]

However he did send £100 in gold ('three hundred broad pieces', £300, according to Charles) which, in the King's own words, 'he knew were necessary for me in the condition I was now in, for I dared carry no money about me in those mean clothes, and my hair cut short'. In contrast Wilmot had refused to put on any disguise, 'he saying that he should look frightfully in it; and therefore did never put on any'.[37]

Charles's flight now became entangled with the local rivalries of Lyme Regis. For many years the two dominant figures in Lyme politics had been Anthony Ellesdon and Richard Alford. During the Civil War both men had managed a difficult balancing act with remarkable skill, despite both having sons who had been captains in the royalist army. Anthony Ellesdon, whose son William surrendered to Colonel Sydenham in December 1644, had less than a month before become mayor of Lyme for the fifth time. (Richard Alford succeeded him in August 1652, also for the fifth time.) Whether there was any hostility between the two fathers we do not know, but there certainly was between their sons.

Wyndham initially tried to contact Gregory Alford, but the young man was in exile in Portugal, so Wyndham went into Lyme and spoke to William Ellesdon, who with Wyndham's brother-in-law, Bullen Reymes, had smuggled Sir John Berkeley over to France after his failed attempt to mediate between the army and Charles I in 1647. Ellesdon immediately spoke to one of his tenants, Stephen Limbry, who had been a captain out of Lyme Regis for some years, and in 1648 paid the town 7s. 'for loading ballast'.[38] Limbry owned a small boat of about 30 tons, and agreed to take several unnamed men 'of the royal party' over to France in exchange for £60. The plan was that a longboat would meet them on the coast by 'a little obscure village',[39] Charmouth, the manor of which Ellesdon had bought two and a half years earlier. From there Limbry would take them out to the ship, which would have come from its mooring at the Cobb.

Meanwhile back in Trent Charles heard the church bells ring out and sent down a maid to find out why. The story she brought back must have made the young King smile wryly:

> there was a rogue, a trooper, come out of Cromwell's army
> that was telling the people that he had killed me, and that
> that was my buff coat which he had then on. Upon which,
> most of the village being fanatics, they were ringing the bells,
> and making a bonfire for joy of it.[40]

The next problem was to make sure the King and his friends could occupy the Charmouth inn for some time, then leave at midnight when the tide would be right, without raising suspicion. This was solved by sending Henry Peters, Wyndham's servant, to the landlady with a tale about a runaway marriage which he told her over a glass of wine. When the day came, Jane Lane had returned home, 'yet it was still thought the best disguise for his Majesty to ride before some woman'.[41] So still using his alias of William Jackson, Charles rode with one of Wyndham's nieces, Mrs Juliana Coningsby, and together with Lord Wilmot, Wyndham and Henry

Denzil Holles pins the Speaker to his chair, 1629.

King Charles demands the surrender of the Five Members, 1642.

Sir Ralph Hopton.

Roundhead soldiers.

Mercurius Rusticus was written by the Dorset-born Bruno Ryves. The picture on the lower right shows the first siege of Wardour Castle, 1643.

Sir William Waller, 'William the Conqueror', 1643.

The Earl of Carnarvon, who took the surrender of Dorchester, 1643.

Wardour Castle as it is today. The damage inflicted during the second siege was never repaired. (Photo, Penny Brown).

Prince Maurice, the King's nephew and royalist commander in the West 1643-44.

A troop of cavaliers.

The Earl of Essex, Parliament's Lord General, who relieved Lyme in 1644.

The Earl of Warwick, Admiral of the Parliamentary Fleet.

George, Lord Goring. The ravages of his troops in Dorset were still remembered a century later.

Sir Thomas Fairfax, commander of the New Model Army.

Oliver Cromwell, 'this eagle in his eyrie'.

Sir Lewis Dyve, 'a valiant gentleman, but not a little given to romance'.

Charles II escaping in disguise with Mrs Jane Lane. Lord Wilmot is in the distance.

Giles Strangways, 'a gallant soul, a brain indefatigable'.

Anthony Ashley Cooper, who shifted 'principles like shirts'.

Robert Blake, defender of Lyme Regis and Taunton, victorious Admiral, but 'of a melancholic and a sullen nature'.

The Battle of Portland, 1653.

Thomas Sydenham, roundhead officer and one of England's greatest doctors.

Penruddock's men in Salisbury, 1655.

Sir Winston Churchill, a leading Dorset cavalier.

Peters they made their way to the Queen's Head at Charmouth. The north wind that night was perfect for France, but the boat never arrived, though Peters and Wyndham waited on the beach all night. Returning to the inn in the early morning Wyndham saw a man coming, 'dogged at a small distance by two or three women', but he dared not speak to him. Next morning Wilmot stayed on in Charmouth and Peters was sent into Lyme to find out why the boat had not arrived. Ellesdon could only suggest 'in regard it was fair day, the master might not be able effectually to command his mariners out of the ale-houses to their work.'[42]

The truth emerged some time later. Limbry,

> going to his house about ten that night, for linen to carry with him, was unexpectedly locked into a chamber by his wife, to whom he had a little before revealed his intended voyage... She apprehending the persons her husband engaged to carry over to be royalists, resolved to secure him from danger by making him a prisoner in his own chamber. All the persuasions he used for his liberty were in vain; for the more he entreated, the more her violent passion increased, breaking forth into such clamours and lamentations.[43]

Eventually Limbry's wife, and daughters who had helped her, did release him, and it had been he whom Wyndham had seen on his way back.

Limbry's wife had every reason for her fears. That very day the parliamentary proclamation of 10 September was published in Lyme, warning:

> if any person shall knowingly conceal the said Charles Stuart, or any his abettors or adherents, or shall not reveal the places of their abode or being...the Parliament does declare that they will hold them as partakers and abettors of their traitorous and wicked practices and designs; and the Parliament does further publish and declare that whoever shall apprehend the person of the said Charles Stuart...shall have given and bestowed on him or them as reward for such services, the sum of £1000.[44]

A thousand pounds was enough to live on in some comfort for the rest of one's life.

Charles and the worried Wyndham had meanwhile set off to Bridport to wait for news. On the road they passed one of Charles I's servants, who pretended not to recognize the King. Bridport was totally the wrong town for the fugitive King to enter. That very day a regiment of 1500 redcoats under Colonel Heane, on their way to attack Jersey, were passing through. Wyndham, on the verge of panic, begged Charles, 'by no means to put himself into the mouth of them who gaped greedily after his destruction,'[45] but the King very logically replied, 'We must go impudently into the best inn in the town, and take a chamber there...because we should otherwise miss my Lord Wilmot.'[46]

The yard of the George in Bridport was full of soldiers, whom Charles infuriated by leading his horses straight through the middle of them. Taking off the bridles, Charles, still in his role as servant, called the ostler, a man named Horton, over to help him. As Horton was giving the horses some oats, he suddenly claimed to recognize Charles. The King swiftly asked where the man came from, and was told he had worked at an inn near Exeter. During the war Charles had stayed close by that very inn in the house of a merchant called Potter:

> therefore I told him 'Friend, certainly you have seen me then at Mr Potter's, for I served him a good while, above a year.' 'Oh!' says he, 'then I remember you a boy there;' and with that was put off from thinking any more on it; but desired that we might drink a pot of beer together.[47]

Charles refused saying he must wait upon his master who was on his way to London, but that he would return in three weeks and they could certainly drink together then. He then went in for a hurried meal of a shoulder of mutton and waited for Wilmot, but he had gone to a different inn and the two companies missed each other.

Eventually Mrs Coningsby saw Peters riding into the inn and beckoned him up to join them. They arranged to leave Bridport by the London road, and a mile or two on were rejoined by Wilmot. Wilmot told them that there had been a misunderstanding and that the ship might be ready the next night. But by now Charles was getting wary and he refused to return to Charmouth, instead turning inland. Where exactly he went off the main road is debatable; it has traditionally been considered to be up Lee Lane towards Bradpole, but more probably it was through the wooded country around Powerstock, Hooke and Wraxall. Whichever way, after several hours they ended up in a small village inn.

Had the party not taken to the back lanes of West Dorset, they would certainly have been caught, for the authorities were much closer on the fugitive King's track than anyone suspected. After the King had left Charmouth, Wilmot had his horse reshod. The smith, a man named Hamnet, asked the ostler of the inn, Henry Hull, where the party came from. He was told Exeter, at which he retorted 'this horse hath but three shoes on and they were set in three several counties, and one of them in Worcestershire.'[48] Hull was an ex-parliamentary soldier 'whose heart was soured against the King',[49] and as he told the smith about the goings-on at the inn the previous night, the two men grew more and more suspicious.

At last Hull went to the local parson, Bartholomew Wesley, who used 'a peculiar plainness of speech, which hindered his being an acceptable popular preacher'.[50] Wesley was 'a weaver who had been a soldier' and 'used to preach and utter all the villainy imaginable against the old order of government'.[51] He had taken over the parish from Samuel Norrington, who had apparently been sequestered before the outbreak of the Civil War, and 'left his wife and five children as poor as misery could make them',[52] until his widow was driven to beg for charity from the corporation for ministers' widows.

When Hull arrived at the parsonage, Wesley was saying his morning prayers, which went on so long that Hull, unwilling to miss his tip from Wilmot, returned to the inn. Some time later Wesley:

> told a good gentlewoman that he was confident, if ever the King did come in again, he would love long prayers; for had he not been longer than ordinary at his devotions, he had surely snapped him.[53]

After Wilmot had left, the ostler went out again and this time managed to speak to Wesley, who came back with him to the inn, and confronted the landlady, Margaret Wade:

> 'Why, how now Margaret! You are a maid of honour now.' 'What mean you by that, Mr. Parson?' quoth she. Said he: 'Why Charles Stuart lay the last night at your house, and kissed you at his departure; so that now you can't but be a maid of honour.' The woman began then to be very angry and told him he was a scurvy-conditioned man to go about to bring her and her house into trouble. But said she 'If I thought it was the King (as you say it was) I would think better of my lips all days of my life. And so Mr Parson get you out of my house, or else I'll get those shall kick you out.'[54]

Wesley and Hamnet then hurried to see Mr Butler, a local J.P., (possibly Edward Butler of Marshwood), but Butler refused to order a search 'fearing lest he should make himself ridiculous to all the country by such an undertaking'.[55] Captain Macey, then in charge of troops at Lyme, was less self-conscious, and after listening to the ostler, he set out with ten or 12 troopers to pursue the King along the London Road. However he did not turn off the main road, but continued on as far as Dorchester where 'with the utmost haste and diligence imaginable he searched all the inns and alehouses in the town'.[56]

It had been a close shave, but the King was about to have an even closer one. At the inn the King and his company ordered some beer and learnt they were in Broadwindsor. Then Colonel Wyndham realized he knew the innkeeper, Rhys Jones, and his wife, and that they were trustworthy people who had suffered for their loyalty to the crown. As it was late and the party tired, the King decided it was safe to spend the night there.

Wyndham told the landlord that they wanted the most private rooms in the house. He also said that Wilmot was in fact Bullen Reymes 'who very much resembled him'[57] and as, like Wyndham himself, he had only recently received parole, they were worried in case they were seen together so far from their homes. Mr Jones took them up to the attic 'where privateness recompensed the meanness of the accommodation, and the pleasantness of the host (a merry fellow) allayed and mitigated the weariness of the guests'.[58] The landlord's wife apparently knew Bullen Reymes well, and was well aware that Wilmot was not him, but she went along with the masquerade.

Out of nowhere disaster struck. The local constable arrived at the inn with 40 soldiers who were to be billeted at the inn that very night. All the lower rooms and corridors were full of these unwelcome guests, and it was impossible to get the King out of the house. He was trapped in the attic. However safety came from an unexpected quarter.

Shortly after the soldiers had taken up their quarters, one of the women who were travelling with them went into labour in the kitchen. This caused instant trouble, as the local people feared the mother and baby would remain after the soldiers left, so the parish would have to pay for the child's upbringing. The overseers of the poor of the parish hurried to the inn to deal with the matter, and a fierce argument broke out between the locals and the soldiers, an argument that lasted until it was time for the soldiers to continue their march the next morning. What happened to the baby that had unwittingly saved the King is not known.

By now the rumour that the King had been seen in Charmouth was spreading like wildfire, and all around the area soldiers were searching the homes of known royalists. Wyndham's uncle, Sir Hugh Wyndham, who lived near Charmouth at Pilsdon, was an early victim of the hunters. Just two months earlier the Whitehall council of state had written to Colonel Heane:

> being informed that there has been some design lately car-
> ried on in Lady Wyndham's house in Dorset against the
> peace. And that some persons may be privately lodged
> there, who may justly be suspected of carrying on the said
> design, we desire you to repair to the said house'.[59]

Nothing was found during that first visit. This time the old baronet, his wife, daughters and the rest of the family, were rounded up in the hall and watched over by armed soldiers, while other soldiers went through the house with a fine-tooth comb:

> not sparing either trunk or box. Then taking a particular
> view of their prisoners, they seize a lovely young lady, say-
> ing she was the King disguised in woman's apparel. At
> length, being convinced of their gross and rude mistake, they
> desisted from offering any further violence to that family.[60]

The parliamentarians had clearly not forgotten that three years before Charles's younger brother, James, had escaped from London in girl's clothes.

The very day that Pilsdon was searched, Captain Ellesdon arrived there, certain he would find the King. Gregory Alford subsequently said that Ellesdon was 'newly married to a very rich, but rigid Presbyterian', a woman named Anne, and that his older brother John, who would be the mayor of Lyme Regis in 1659, was 'a violent Oliverian'.[61] He went on to accuse Ellesdon of being more interested in the reward than in helping the King. He also claimed that Stephen Limbry failed to arrive at the Charmouth rendezvous because of an argument over money, which Ellesdon refused to pay him. The truth of this is impossible to disentangle from Gregory Alford's later and very visible loathing for Ellesdon, which included a series of savage public attacks on Ellesdon for his nonconformist religious beliefs.

On the advice of Wyndham, Charles, who had scarcely slept for two nights, hastily retired back to Trent, while Wilmot and Peters went on, via Sherborne, to Salisbury to seek out a fresh hiding place. It was not before time. Dorset was rapidly becoming too hot to hold the King.

The Sunday after the King arrived at Trent a local tailor had told Colonel Wyndham that 'the zealots, which swarmed in that place'[62] were aware the Colonel had secret guests, and were planning to search Trent House and seize them. The tailor was rewarded for his warning, and Wyndham decided it would be best if Wilmot attended Sunday worship. Wyndham himself had rarely visited the church in recent years, but he had a separate stall so his companion would not be easily visible. Eventually, on Charles's order, the reluctant Wilmot joined Wyndham in church, and thus soothed the suspicions of the local people, notably the Minister Thomas Elford, a fervent Independent, who was encouraged to believe that the Colonel was on the edge of conversion. Meanwhile Wyndham's wife, Ann, had gone to Sherborne to look for news. While there she noticed a troop of cavalry slipping silently into the town, and when her enquiries elicited no information about these new troops, she hurried back home.

The King laughed at her fears, but was eventually persuaded to hide in 'an old well-contrived secret place, long before made' as a hiding place for Catholic priests. Charles could not be kept in there long, but Colonel Wyndham kept a careful watch all night, until at two the next morning the soldiers left for the coast. Slowly the days crawled by, while Wyndham and his helpers sought for some way to get the King away. Charles was kept strictly to his room, with the priest-hole close by in case of danger, and 'his Majesty's meat was likewise (to prevent danger of a discovery) for the most part dressed in his own chamber, the cookery whereof served him for some diversion of the time.'[63]

There is a variety of other tales about Charles II's flight through Dorset which do not appear in the documents of the time, but which have long been believed in the county. Before his failed attempt to embark at Charmouth, he was said to have visited Clapton Court, where hurrying away after a false alarm, he left behind one of his gloves. As well as rumours of a brief visit to Wyld Court a few miles north of Lyme Regis, Charles is also said to have taken refuge at Coaxden Manor near Axminster, where a certain Mrs Cogan, (perhaps Patience Cogan of Lyme Regis), despite having a roundhead-sympathising husband, concealed the King under her hooped skirts while soldiers searched the house, and subsequently received a gold chain and locket from the grateful Charles.

On 28 September a new ally arrived at Trent, Edward Phelips of Montacute, with information that his younger brother, Colonel Robert Phelips, had managed to get a ship at Southampton. But once more the coming attack on Jersey foiled the King's escape plan as the ship Phelips had hired was commandeered by the army authorities to carry their soldiers.

By now it was clear that Charles must move on.

Thus his sacred majesty, taking Mrs Juliana Coningsby behind him, attended by Colonel Robert Phelips and Peters, bade farewell to Trent, the ark in which God shut him up when the floods of rebellion had covered the face of his dominions.[64]

Phelips and the former rector of Portland, Humphrey Henchman, had arranged for the King to stay with a widow, Mrs Hyde, in Hele House outside Salisbury. The journey was, however, fraught with danger even though they took back ways. According to one account the King passed through the middle of a marching regiment, and even met John Desborough, Cromwell's brother-in-law 'walking down a hill with three or four men with him; who had lodged in Salisbury the night before; all that road being full of soldiers'.[65] These soldiers were probably those of Major Ebery of Desborough's regiment of foot, who on 15 October temporarily deposited 'a purse of money in which is, as he says, £36 sealed up'[66] with Richard Savage, the mayor of Dorchester.

After a meal at the George Inn in Mere, where he drank a health to the King with the royalist innkeeper, Charles arrived at Hele in the dusk. It had not been intended to tell Mrs Hyde who she would be concealing, but the moment she saw Charles, she recognized him even though she had only ever seen him once before, during the march of Charles I's army through the West in the autumn of 1644. While there, the King paid a visit to Stonehenge because it was fair day at Salisbury and there was no one left in the house to watch over him.

By now the parliamentary command seems to have totally lost the King's trail. A tract issued that November called 'A Mad Design, or A Description of the King of Scots marching in his Disguise, after the Rout of Worcester' accurately describes the King as hiding in a wood near the battlefield, and getting help from a royalist lady. It goes on to state that the King's party 'waited on the lady in several offices and places, and the Scots King himself stood bare before her when he waited on her',[67] and that they fled to Bristol where they failed to find a ship. However rumours of the King having been in Dorset clearly never reached London, and Charles was thought to have skulked through London in women's clothes and taken a ship to France from Gravesend.

Phelips finally chartered a coal brig, the *Surprise*, with a Dorset skipper, Captain Tattersal, which in exchange for the £60 originally intended for Limbry, carried the King from Shoreham in Sussex to Fécamp in France and safety after six weeks on the run. The royalists celebrated 'we may look upon the King's escape as conducted by the hands of the Almighty, who covered him as with a shield, when his rebellious people sought his life.'[68] That one-time scourge of the royalists, William Waller, prayed for the young King:

I thought it my duty to seek God for him in that distressed condition; it pleased the Lord to enlarge my heart with much comfort, and to give me a confident assurance that I should have an answer of peace. The issue was that his royal person was miraculously delivered out of the hands of the hunters.[69]

The *Surprise*, having unloaded the King and his party, simply continued her voyage to Poole without anyone being the wiser. After the Restoration the boat was brought to London, cleaned and repainted, renamed the *Royal Escape*, and registered in the books of the Royal Navy. Tattersal remained her master and received a naval pension of £100 a year. The boat itself was only finally broken up in 1791.

On 24 October there was a thanksgiving day at Dorchester for the parliamentary victory of Worcester. It raised £2 16s., half what had been collected after Preston, and only a sixth of what would be raised a few months later for the 'relief of Milborne St Andrew which was burnt this week'.[70] Even in Dorchester enthusiasm for the parliamentary cause was declining, although that for the royalists was no greater.

⤛ *Chapter Eleven* ⤜
CONSPIRACIES AND DISCONTENT
1652–1655

A s Cromwell tightened his grip on the levers of power, the army remained prey to discontent, still influenced by the Levellers and extreme Fifth Monarchy men, like Major General Thomas Harrison, who believed the end of the world was coming and England must be made ready for it. The royalists might be 'so broken and subdued that they could scarce breathe under the unsupportable burdens which were laid upon them by imprisonments, compositions and sequestrations',[1] but they still had their hopes and plans, and Parliament itself regarded Cromwell with ever-deepening suspicion.

Nonetheless the nation was armed and prepared for war as never before. In Cromwell England had one of its most successful ever generals, the navy was about to prove it had an excellent admiral, Robert Blake, the defender of Lyme Regis and Taunton. At the time the dominant maritime power in the world was the Netherlands. On 19 May 1652, due it seems to a misunderstanding, the Dutch fleet under the celebrated Maarten Tromp unexpectedly attacked a heavily-outnumbered English fleet led by Blake. At heavy cost Blake beat them off and the two nations found themselves at war, though trade continued across the Channel, for example on 3 July 1652 the *Marcel* of Morlaix in Brittany was on route for Lyme with '4 *paquets de toile* [cloth]',[2] and a variety of other merchandise.

After an initial Dutch victory off Dungeness, the decisive battle came the next year, off Portland Bill.

> In the month of February, the most dangerous season of the year, they [the Dutch] having appointed a rendezvous of about 150 merchantmen, sent a fleet of above 100 sail of men of war to convoy them; and Blake, with a fleet much inferior in number, engaged them in a very sharp battle from noon until the night parted them; which disposed them to endeavour to preserve themselves by flight, but in the morning they found that the English had attended them so close, that they were engaged again to fight, and so unprosperously that, after the loss of above 2000 men, who were thrown overboard, besides a multitude hurt, they were glad to leave 50 of their merchantmen to the English, that they might make their flight the more securely.[3]

It was the first major defeat of a Dutch fleet in the history of that young nation, and a bloodthirsty English letter reported:

All the men-of-war who are taken are much dyed with blood, their masts and tackle being moiled [wetted] with brains, hair, pieces of skulls; dreadful sights, though glorious, as being a signal token of the Lord's goodness to this nation.[4]

The following month Weymouth fishermen were said to catch nothing but shipwreck and dead men.

During the battle Blake's flagship, the *Triumph*, had been surrounded by seven Dutch ships, and lost 100 of its crew of 350. Blake himself was wounded, and although he took part in a subsequent victory off Harwich, a chill prevented him leading the fleet into the final battle of the war at Scheveningen, where Monk, at great cost, destroyed the Dutch fleet, and Tromp was killed.

The churchwarden accounts of the time are suddenly scattered with references to sailors. At Beaminster 2s. was paid 'to two seamen coming out of the state service being sick',[5] and at Wimborne 6d. 'to two hurt sailors'.[6] At Bere Regis one of the sailors 'fell sick at Thomas Hayn's house', remained there ill for some time, and finally died, which involved the parish in further expenses 'for a shround for him' and to 'the women for shrouding him for the burial'.[7] While the great navies of Holland and England battled it out, pirates still raided the south-western coasts, Bere Regis churchwardens paid 1s. 'to three women, they held their husbands were taken by the Turks',[8] and at Beaminster some time later an unusually generous 10s. was given to 'two captains for the relief of their fathers which were in Turkey'.[9]

In London there was ferment as Parliament and Cromwell manoeuvred against each other. Even Denis Bond, soon to be a loyal supporter of Cromwells, resisted growing pressure to end the Long Parliament. But in April 1653 Cromwell finally lost patience, strode into the House of Commons with Major General Harrison and Colonel Ingoldsby 'and pulled out the members and so dissolved that Parliament. Harrison takes the Speaker by the hand and pulls him out of the Chair and this three put them all out before them.'[10]

Despite the tumults of the capital, Dorset was gradually settling down, though people were expected to swear that they would 'be true and faithful to the Commonwealth of England as it is now established, without a king or House of Lords'.[11] In Dorchester day-to-day matters had resumed their normal dominance, payments for arrears due from the war disappear and are replaced by orders like: 'that the number of children to be taught to read at the hospital shall from henceforth not exceed the number of three score',[12] or £5 to be sent immediately to Piddletrenthide 'for supply of the necessities of the poor people whose houses were burnt yesterday'.[13]

Nonetheless reminders of the past must have been everywhere. The churchwardens of Langton Long gave 1s. 6d. 'to three maimed soldiers, grievously hurt',[14] while at Beaminster 2s. 6d. was paid 'for four maimed soldiers, and another 2s. 6d. for 'three maimed soldiers were come from the Hospital of London, travelling towards Plymouth'.[15]

Dangerous sources of discord also lingered on, notably religious dissent. At Lyme Regis there was 'an assembly of Protestant dissenters who scrupled the baptising of infants', and practised full immersion or 'dipping' in the river. In 1653 this Baptist congregation was 73 people. The following year the Baptists of Lyme Regis were asked for help by a fellow Baptist from Kilmington 'whose house had been burnt down by persecutors'.[16]

One of the features of life after the Civil War had been the mass of wandering preachers, each spreading his own version of God's word to people who seemed only too willing to listen. Many of these preachers were in practice revolutionaries, launching fierce attacks on organized religion, the state, and even traditional morality. As Cromwell's rise to the pinnacle of power was matched by a swing to conservatism, he began to suppress these dangerous ideas, and the 1650 Blasphemy Act was aimed specifically at the most extreme of all these religious revolutionaries, the Ranters. The Ranters attacked virtually every tenet of Christianity, and were infamous for swearing, drinking, and practising as well as preaching sexual freedom. Some Ranters even denied the existence of sin at all, while one of the best-known of them, Abiezer Coppe, optimistically predicted 'equality, community, and universal love shall be in request to the utter confounding of abominable pride, murder, hypocrisy, tyranny and oppression.'[17]

A group of Ranters was active in Southampton in 1649, but they were tried and imprisoned the next year. Poole also seems to have been quite a hotbed of religious heterodoxy, and among the accusations against John Rede, the governor, in 1651 were: 'that he has openly declared himself against the observation of the Lord's Day by his favouring of the Ranters' and 'that he did protect and shelter Radman, the great Ranter, and his companion, after Parliament had set forth an ordinance for his apprehension'.[18] John Radman of Ingoldsby's regiment had led a mutiny demanding the immediate implementation of the Leveller programme. After Ingoldsby escaped and suppressed the mutiny, Radman fled and was never caught, last being heard of robbing the post office at Newbury.

Rede's sympathy for religious radicals was clear. In 1650 he wrote to the clerk of peace at the Wiltshire quarter sessions appealing in favour of Anne Cooper of Allington, who was in trouble for not attending church. She was a godly Christian woman, Rede said, who 'takes all opportunities to hear such as are enabled by the spirit of truth to make known what they have received from the Lord'.[19] In other words she followed unofficial preachers rather than orthodox ones. No doubt it was this attitude that had helped make Rede so unpopular with the Poole establishment, even as it made him popular with his soldiers. Rede, or more likely his children, apparently finally settled in Maiden Newton, (a pauper named James Rede was living in nearby Rampisham in 1664), and 100 years later his descendants were prominent nonconformists.

Another Dorset man who came to religious extremism was the disabled M.P., John Fry, 'who had run through most if not all religions, even to Ranterism' and whose death was said to have 'saved the hangman his labour'.[20]

The Ranters were too extreme to last, but the Puritan revolution did give birth to a religious movement that was to have a great influence in England, and later America – the Quakers. From 1646 George Fox had travelled the country, calling on men and women to trust their 'inner light' and reject all war, and often converting his listeners in large numbers. Fox was arrested in 1654 on suspicion of plotting against the government, but Cromwell received him well, talked to him for some time then sent him on his way.

The next year Fox came to Dorset, and significantly perhaps, the first town he visited was Poole:

> having set up our horses at an inn, we sent into the town to
> inquire for such as feared the Lord, and such as were worthy;
> and had a meeting with several sober people. William Baily,
> a Baptist teacher, was convinced there at that time. The peo-
> ple received the truth in the inward parts...and there is
> become a great gathering in the name of Jesus of a very ten-
> der people, who continue under Christ's teaching.[21]

From there he travelled to Dorchester, where he received an antagonistic reception, and Weymouth where 'some that had been Ranters came to own the truth and live very soberly.' At Weymouth he also met a captain of horse who was:

> the fattest, merriest man, the most cheerful and the most
> given to laughter that I ever met with; insomuch that I was
> several times moved to speak in the dreadful power of the
> Lord to him; and yet it was become so customary to him that
> he would presently laugh at anything he saw. But I still
> admonished him to come to sobriety, sincerity and the fear of
> the Lord.... He afterwards was convinced, and became a
> serious and good man and died in the truth.[22]

The following year Fox visited Dorset again, having meetings in Poole, Weymouth and Lyme. In all he preached at Poole four times over eight years. Baily became one of Fox's chief supporters, and was eventually sentenced to transportation to the West Indies in 1675, dying on the voyage.

Many Dorset justices, perhaps about half of them, were very hostile to Quakers. Edward Cheeke of Stanton St Gabriel had a woman Quaker whipped 'till the blood ran and her breasts were raw'; John Fitzjames sent many to prison who 'would not put off their hats before him'; James Dewey 'sent one to prison for speaking the word of the Lord in Blandford street', and George Fulford said, if Quakers kept meeting so near his nose he would fill the prison with them.'[23] However Cromwell, whose instincts were towards religious toleration, ordered the release of imprisoned

Quakers in Dorchester, Exeter and other places. In Bridport a shopkeeper stirred up the priest and magistrates against Fox, and set a trap for him, but Fox's friend Thomas Curtis was suspicious, and went himself.

Meanwhile I had an opportunity of speaking to some sober people that came to the inn. When Thomas was come back, and we were passing out of the town, some of them came to us and said 'the officers were coming to fetch me,' but the Lord's power came over them all, so that they had not power to touch me. There were some convinced in the town, who were turned to the Lord, and have stood faithful to the Lord ever since, and a fine meeting is there.[24]

At the time Fox was not seen as the clear leader of the Quakers, which he later became. There was also the more radical ex-soldier, James Nayler, who was closer to the Ranters. In 1656, after a tour through the Westcountry Nayler, who had long hair and a beard, entered Bristol riding on a donkey, with women strewing palms before him. He was arrested and the House of Commons spent six weeks savagely denouncing him, many demanding the death sentence. One of the few brave enough to stand up for him was William Sydenham who said that Nayler's aims were 'near a glorious truth'.[25] Sydenham resisted anti-Quaker legislation, and during an argument over parliamentary privilege he reminded the House of its fundamental commitment to freedom: 'We live as Parliament men but for a time, but we live as Englishmen always. I would not have us be so tender of the privilege of Parliament as to forget the liberties of Englishmen.'[26]

Captain John Chaffin, unusually a parliamentarian from Sherborne, also favoured toleration and may even have been Fox's merry captain of horse as he eventually became a Quaker himself.

Nayler was finally condemned by Parliament to be flogged through the streets of London, his tongue bored with a hot iron, his forehead branded with a B for blasphemy, then sent to Bristol for a second flogging, afterwards to be kept in prison until Parliament decided otherwise. He was released three years later, a broken man, and died soon after.

One of the leading religious radicals in Dorset was Captain John Arthur. In December 1656, describing himself as 'a merchant',[27] he petitioned the House of Commons that he was threatened daily with arrest for debt over £2000 that the committee of Dorset owed him, plus interest. There are several references to money owing to Arthur over the years 1646-8, notably £979 15s. 10d. 'for his service as captain and governor of Portland Castle and island, and for provisions by him laid into the said castle at his own cost',[28] and £45 'for two tuns of sack and 12 empty casks taken for use of the garrison of Weymouth in time of the siege'.[29] Although several M.P.s objected to Arthur receiving the money, Denis Bond spoke in his favour, saying he was very poor. A few months later the House of Commons resolved that because 'the petitioner has been so zealously affected to Parliament, and ready to supply the State's necessity in the low condition of their affairs',[30] he should receive the full amount he was owed. Eight years later Arthur seems to have been a well-off man, owning two houses in Weymouth, one of them a large one.

Rede and Captain Arthur were not the only men sympathetic to the religious extremists in the army. The governor of Portland from 1650 was George Joyce, the man who on 3 June 1647 had helped change English history by, on his own initiative, putting Charles I in the power of the army. He was also rumoured to have been Charles I's executioner, though there is no evidence for this. Certainly Joyce, together with such men as Harrison, Pride, Sexby and Okey, were the last Englishmen for over 200 years to be promoted to high rank in the army on grounds of talent alone, rather than birth or money. Described as 'one of the agitators in the army, a tailor, a fellow who had two or three years before served in a very inferior employment in Mr Holles's house',[31] Joyce had risen rapidly from cornet to lieutenant colonel, been given a post under Colonel Heane, and voted lands worth £100 a year for him and his heirs in perpetuity. However he was also one of the men who endangered Cromwell's steady drift back to a more conservative style of government.

Joyce, who had previously been investigated by the army commissioners but cleared, found himself in rapidly deepening trouble because of his beliefs. His lieutenant 'was sent for from Portland by General Cromwell, and by him encouraged to prosecute his lieutenant colonel again', and Joyce was accused of saying he was sorry Cromwell had not been assassinated. In September 1653 Joyce was cashiered and put in a prison 'where the lice crept up very thick', then moved to another 'where he fell sick with the filthy smells and other inconveniences'. When the lieutenant asked for his promised preferment, Cromwell told him 'you have not dealt like a Christian with your lieutenant-colonel Joyce...and thrust him out of his chamber and bade him go like a knave as he was.'[32] But it was not only the Levellers and their allies who were causing trouble.

Robert Phelips, that 'very able, well-accomplished man',[33] who had helped Charles II to escape, came back from a failed attempt to get a place at the King's court in exile and plunged into royalist conspiracies. Arrested, Phelips found himself being interrogated by Cromwell and Anthony Ashley Cooper. Cromwell was very polite, and spoke pleasantly of Phelips's father, an M.P. for Somerset in the 1620s, regretting that his son had not followed in his footsteps. However it seems to have been Cooper who did most of the talking. After revealing he was an old acquaintance of the family, and praising Phelips's character, Cooper went on

> 'But my Lord, I must confess I know him to be as ill-affected to the state as any man, and many more of the honest party as well as myself do apprehend him to be the likeliest man in all our parts to disturb the quiet of the state...' 'Sir Anthony,' said Phelips, 'You have been pleased to deal with me as the ancients did with their beasts destined to sacrifice. In the first part of your character you have adorned me with gar-

lands; in the last you have at least whet the knife to sacri-fice.'[34]

Phelips refused to confess or incriminate anyone else, and was sent to the Tower, from which, like a remarkable number of royalists before him, he soon escaped.

The stock of Anthony Ashley Cooper seemed to be rising dramatically, not least due to his remarkable ability to change sides at the right moment:

> When the Presbyterians thought themselves sure of him, 'whip, he was gone,' and in a trice commenced a brother Independent, which was in a wise part, and no trick of a changeling, to shift principles like shirts.[35]

In December 1653 he was promoted to Cromwell's council of state. Colonel William Sydenham was also doing well, and in 1650 he had been made governor of the Isle of Wight, which put him in charge of two of Charles I's children, Prince Henry and Princess Elizabeth. Sydenham was no extremist, and in February 1649 he was one of the parliamentarians who tried to keep the House of Lords, while in December 1653 he supported the minority that fought for the retention of the established church.

After Cromwell dissolved the Long Parliament he replaced it with a nominated Parliament which contained a high proportion of religious zealots. Sydenham's conservative republican views meant he had no time for this so-called Barebones Parliament, named after one of the members, a well-off London leatherseller Praise-God Barebones. As one of the two members for Dorset, (John Bingham was the other) Sydenham took the lead in proposing the Parliament's rapid dissolution, and so became one of the founders of the Protectorate. He was also appointed a member of the 13-man strong army council, and next year Cromwell made him a commissioner of the Treasury at a salary of £1000 a year, in addition to the same sum he was already receiving for his work as an army councillor.

It was probably the rapidly rising star of his elder brother that encouraged Thomas Sydenham, in March 1654, to petition Cromwell directly for money he was owed on behalf of his dead brother, John:

> your petitioner therefore most humbly prays your Highness that your Highness will please, in consideration of the faith-ful and valiant services of your petitioner's said brother, to order such satisfaction as in your Highness's piety and wis-dom shall be thought fit to be made to your petitioner, who hath likewise himself also faithfully served the Parliament with the loss of much blood, and thereby much disabled his body.

Cromwell's response demonstrated his respect for the family:

> His Highness being very sensible of the matters represented in this petition is pleased, in an especial manner, to recom-mend it to the council that they may give the petitioner due satisfaction, and that with all convenient expedition.[36]

Sydenham was granted £600, which enabled him to marry Mary Gee at Wynford Eagle, and set up as a doctor in London the next year. Shortly afterwards he was one of the first English physicians to use Jesuits' bark, the bark of the cinchona tree from which quinine would be isolated two centuries later, for the treatment of malaria. Subsequently he became 'more famous, especially beyond the seas, for his published books than before he had been for his practice'.[37] Another member of a faithful Dorset parliamentarian family, Strode Bingham, younger brother of John Bingham, was rewarded by Cromwell with a commission as a captain of foot in the army of the Commonwealth in November 1654.

The Dorset royalists were still active, though most of the last sequestrations, as for example those on Sir George Morton, were only finally taken off in 1653. January 1654 saw Bingham writing to John Thurloe, Cromwell's intelligence chief, about his fears for the safety of Poole:

> Every Tuesday we must have a cock match at Wimborne...divers unknown blades frequent the cocking game. It's near Poole, which would be made an isle, you know, in a short time.[38]

Colonel Robert Lawrence, who had defended Corfe Castle then changed sides just before its fall, held open house at his rebuilt home in Creech Grange, and threw huge Christmas parties to ingratiate himself with local people, while a variety of old royalists, including 'King' Gardiner and Bragg, the man who had betrayed Portland to the royalists in 1643, were known to be meeting secretly. There were whispers of conspiracy in Beaminster and the Blackmore Vale, and a rumour that a ship full of arms and powder had landed at Lulworth. Among the royalist plotters was a son of Francis Matthews of Woodsford, who had raised a troop for the King in 1642. However, Matthews himself was involved in writing up his plan to link London and Bristol with a state-funded canal. Later in the year he dedicated his book to Cromwell.

The clergy too, despite what amounted to a thorough purge, still contained malcontents. Anthony Sadler was given the living of Over Compton in 1654, but was then not allowed to take it up, being 'a man of rambling head and turbulent spirit'.[39] John Potter of Fontmell got into serious trouble for 'inveighing (as it was said) on a Sunday, against Oliver'.[40] Although it was proved that Potter had been in London on the day of the sermon in question, he still spent several months in Weymouth gaol, perhaps on the grounds that he had allowed his church to be used for the attack.

Fear of an uprising had led the authorities to slight most of the fortified places in Dorset, in case a sudden attack might seize strongholds from which it would be very hard to dislodge determined men. The main defences of Poole, including the battlemented gate, were broken down, and on 28 October 1653, Weymouth council sold off the stones which had been used to make the forts that ringed the port. Anything that might make money was welcome, but a year later Weymouth was complaining that through the decay of trade, and by means of the late wars, the revenue of the said town has been wholly exhausted...yet the issuing forth of monies has been far greater than in peaceable times, in that the town hath been at great charges about the soldiers and in cleansing and paving of the streets since the late siege.[41]

With the opening of the year 1655, Cromwell resolved to deal with the chief remaining radicals in the army. Several were arrested, including Harrison who was imprisoned in Portland Castle where the governor, Captain Hurst, (who had been a confidante of Joyce's) considered him a good man and allowed him to preach to the garrison. Men were also sent to catch the dangerous Sexby. His case, containing secret writings and some weapons, was seized, but Sexby himself escaped and went on the run through the Westcountry. A little over a year earlier, when Cromwell had been planning an alliance with Spain, Sexby had been promised the command of an army to invade south-west France. Nothing came of the promise and disappointment seems to have sharpened Sexby's dislike of Cromwell's regime to a savage loathing.

On 19 February the postmaster of Salisbury was closely interrogated concerning the whereabouts of Sexby. The next day troops under Captain Unton Croke arrived in Weymouth. Croke had assured Cromwell of 'the peace and quiet that was in these parts', but he also promised, 'I have not been careless in making the most curious search after Sexby, having had parties out after him both in Devonshire and Dorsetshire.'[42]

That search led Croke to Captain John Arthur's house in Melcombe, where Sexby was said to keep a mistress. One of Croke's soldiers, having put aside his weapons, knocked at the door of Arthur's house, pretending to be a countryman, and asked the maid if Sexby was in the house. The maid got Mrs Ford, Sexby's alleged mistress, who said he was not in the house but that she could get a letter to him. The soldier left, and Mrs Ford sent out Arthur's deputy to find out why soldiers were searching for Sexby. The deputy, John Dudley of Melcombe, told Croke that Sexby was indeed hiding in Arthur's house, but that it would be hard to find him as the house was so big and rambling. Undaunted Croke and his soldiers planned a late night search, but then suddenly Dudley went back on everything he had said.

Croke now found himself in trouble because the Weymouth garrison seems to have been heavily influenced by the Levellers. Arthur, who Croke described as 'a man esteemed of no good principle',[43] was an admirer of Harrison, and other officers clearly had similar views. Several of them, led by Major Harding together with the former mayor, Thomas Waltham, 'high-flown men in their principles and direct friends to Sexby and Joyce,' arrived, and demanded why Croke was trying to arrest Sexby without specific written orders:

> Major Harding said that if Sexby had been in their hands, that they having no written order, he would endeavour to

rescue him out of their hand. He said also that Sexby was so qualified, and had done such good service for my lord, that he wondered any should come to look for him in that manner.[44]

Croke and his men were disarmed and made prisoners until the matter could be sorted out, leaving Sexby plenty of time to escape. Croke, who was also trying to explain why one of his lieutenants had been 'detained upon suspicion that he did not well relish the present government',[45] later said he doubted the Leveller leader had been in Weymouth at all. Probably Croke was just trying to excuse his failure to catch Sexby and it seems likely the authorities did not believe him. Harrison apparently suspected Sexby of being an *agent provocateur*, and 'knew him to be a treacherous fellow, and would have nothing to do with him',[46] but Cromwell was taking no risks. Harrison was moved from Portland Castle to Carisbrooke on the Isle of Wight.

The continued freedom of Sexby might have cost the Commonwealth dear, for he planned an uprising to coincide with a putative Spanish invasion and negotiated with Charles, making 'such demands to the King, as if it were in his power, and his alone, to restore him'.[47] Most notoriously he master-minded two plots to assassinate Cromwell, and wrote a celebrated pamphlet *Killing No Murder* justifying the Lord Protector's assassination. The work was cheekily dedicated to Cromwell 'the true father of your country; for while you live we can call nothing ours, and it is from your death that we hope for our inheritances'.[48] In July 1657 Sexby 'in a very poor habit with an overgrown beard was taken on shipboard going out of the nation'.[49] He was put in the Tower, where he died six months later after a long sickness.

The Levellers may have been a more direct threat to Cromwell through their influence in the army, Sexby having stated 'he knows very well 'tis only we that have the power to hurt him'[50], but it was the royalists who rose in outright rebellion. Through all his vicissitudes Charles had remained optimistic and 'thought of nothing more, than how he might with the greatest secrecy transport himself into England; for which he did expect sudden occasion'.[51] But the attempt was doomed, for there was no hope of help from abroad, the Spanish and French were still bargaining for England's support against the other, and the Dutch were chastened. Charles's friend, Lord Wilmot tried to raise Yorkshire, failed and fled, this time disguised as a grazier, back to the Continent. Other planned risings fizzled out, and Francis and Sir Hugh Wyndham's attempt to secure Taunton never even started.

Only in Wiltshire did the royalists take up serious arms against the government. Led by John Penruddock, a former leader of the clubmen, 60 horsemen assembled near Salisbury on Sunday 11 March, hurried off towards Blandford to join reinforcements from Dorset, and then returned 200 strong, to enter Salisbury at five in the morning of 12 March. Two judges and Colonel John Dove, the high sheriff of Wiltshire, were dragged from their beds, manhandled and threatened with hanging. With ludicrous optimism Penruddock declared that the Duke of York was coming from France with 10,000 men, and that Thomas Fairfax with 8000 and Sir William Waller with another 4000 were also on their way to help King Charles II.

The citizens of Salisbury were unimpressed. There was no sign of the Marquess of Hertford, who Penruddock was expecting with a force of Hampshire royalists, and there were few willing volunteers except men freed from the city gaol. The royalists, now numbering about 400, left Salisbury within four or five hours and marched west, 'to reinforce their numbers what they can in that disaffected county of Dorset – than which there is not one greater in England'.[52]

Within hours of the seizure of Salisbury Cromwell was writing to Desborough warning of 'an insurrection in the West by the cavaliers who have armed themselves, and seized upon the judges of assize at Salisbury, and proceed on to commit other violences and outrages upon the people', and ordering him to 'use your best endeavours to prosecute the said cavaliers in whatever parts of the nation they shall go, and to suppress them'.[53] Other forces were gathering in Hampshire and Somerset.

Penruddock and his men had now reached 'the most rotten and corrupt places of the nation as Blandford, Sherborne, Yeovil, etc.'[54] At Blandford Penruddock allowed his hostage, Dove, to dress, but even that staunchly royalist town would not join the rebellion:

> Penruddock forced the crier to go to the Market Cross to proclaim Charles Stuart King, who made 'Oyez' four times, but...stopped, and said he could not say that word, and he was every time much beaten by them, and yet told them they might kill him, but he could not say that word, though they should call for faggots and burn him presently.[55]

Eventually Penruddock proclaimed the King himself, then led his little army on through Shaftesbury and Sherborne to Babylon Hill near Yeovil, where they arrived at one in the morning on Tuesday 13 March, and where Dove was released. There were still between three and four hundred people, but 'in Dorset, where they expected 3000 or 4000, they all refused to rise with them. So I understand most of them are the scorn of the county'.[56] Some of Penruddock's men were seen in Crewkerne and Chard, and at Dorchester they 'broke up the gaols and horsed the gaolbirds'.[57] In Poole 5s. was paid out 'for beer for the watchmen at town gates at the Insurrection', 1s. 6d. 'for fitting Mr Skutt's drum' and another 2s. for 'intelligence of the enemy's approach'.[58]

The enemy did not approach. Everywhere the Commonwealth was efficiently mobilizing its forces. On 14 March Cromwell sent a commission to John Browne, John Bingham and other leading Dorset parliamentarians, to raise the militia, 'as the enemies are raising new troubles, and now robbing and plundering the people'.[59] The same day he wrote again to Desborough that 'the enemies of the peace of this Commonwealth are still restless in their designs of raising new troubles in our own bowels'.[60]

There was no longer any coherent plan among the hunted royalists except to head for loyalist Cornwall, with its many small ports from which they might be able to escape to France. They stumbled on further west, avoiding Exeter and Taunton where thousands of volunteers had gathered to help against the disturbers of the peace. At South Molton in Devon, Unton Croke and 60 horse caught up with the bedraggled remnant and although outnumbered, forced them to surrender.

'Thus this little fire, which probably might have kindled and inflamed all the Kingdom, was for the present extinguished,'[61] remarked Clarendon. John Thurloe was far more sanguine about the whole episode, and even before Penruddock's defeat, he had written confidently

> that all the counties in England would, instead of rising for them, have risen against them; and the Protector could, if there had been need, have drawn into the field, within fourteen days, 20,000 men besides the standing army. So far are they mistaken who dream that the affections of this people are towards the House of Stuart.[62]

There were still rumours 'that Charles Stuart, Major General Massey, Lord Ormonde and Inchiquin are come for England',[63] and Desborough cautiously divided up his troops to watch Beaminster, Bridport, Crewkerne and other parts of south Somerset, but there was no need. The rebellion had collapsed into humiliating failure, and parliamentary troops scoured Dorset for die-hard royalists who had, or might have, taken part in the uprising.

Captain John Chaffin had no more to do than round up one drunken cavalier, but Major James Dewey of Bloxworth, soon to be one of the M.P.s for Dorset, had a tougher assignment. Dewey had been married to Mary Strangways, the sister of the royalist captain George Strangways, but she died before the Civil Wars began, and Dewey was a committed Commonwealth man. One evening he arrived at the parsonage of Todbere to arrest Hancock Clark, the son of the rector, Roger Clark.

Hancock leapt out of back window wearing only his drawers, shirt and one stocking, and landed in the middle of the very horsemen who had come to take him. There was a scuffle, Hancock gave Dewey a savage blow with the iron pin of an axle, and in the darkness several of the soldiers were knocked off their horses by the low branch of an apple tree. Hancock got clean away, but the furious troopers seized his seventy-year-old father, and bound him so tight that blood ran from his eyes. The old vicar was carried to Sturminster Newton where his fingers were burned with matchcord, a torture he took six months to recover from.

Hancock's brother, called Roger like his father, was the sequestered rector of Ashmore, and married to one of Lord Hopton's cousins. He had been plundered of all he had, and his young twin sons had been seized by roundhead soldiers who:

laid them stark-naked in a dripping pan with a design to roast them. But a certain woman, whose name was Pope, came, snatched them from the fire, and carried them away in her apron.[64] Subsequently he and his family fled to Herefordshire, where he was helped by an aunt of Hopton's. Nevertheless Roger Clark the younger, on whose head £100 had been placed, was imprisoned twice for having said or done something in favour of Penruddock's uprising, and died in 1658.

The leader of the rebellion had already been secured. On 17 March, from Exeter gaol, Penruddock wrote to his wife, Arundell the daughter of John Freke of Iwerne Courtney:

> My dear heart, to tell you the story of my misfortunes were too large and would but add to your afflictions... The best, it was our fortune to fall into the hands of one Captain Unton Croke, a generous and valiant officer, one that I hope will show something the better, for that we did not basely desert our soldiers as others did. That which concerns you now is that you best give your help, and make what friends you can for me.[65]

Two weeks later Desborough, who had been made Major General of the West the day Penruddock marched into Salisbury, had a list of well over 100 prisoners, of whom fewer than a quarter were from Dorset. Nearly all the rebels seem to have been skilled workmen, and the Dorset men included two husbandmen, a miller, a felt-maker, a gardener, two weavers, a tailor and a tanner.

One of the few landowners who had joined Penruddock, John Saint Lo of Child Okeford, had also been a leader of the Dorset clubmen. However Saint Lo did not have the steadfastness of Penruddock, and when questioned he claimed he had been forced to go along with the rebels against his will. Colonel William Butler remarked dismissively of him 'that in addition to joining the rising himself, he had been informed that he had sent two men and horses to assist the rebels'.[66] But somehow Saint Lo (who became a J.P. after the Restoration) got away without being tried, although Butler also wrote 'I hope His Highness will be persuaded that, next to Penruddock, scarce a man among them deserves less favour.'[67] Robert Phelips was also on the original list of men to be charged, but was never brought to trial.

Penruddock was taken to London, kept imprisoned at the Swan Inn in the Strand, questioned, then sent back to Exeter gaol to await trial. His adherents were accused of being

> false rebels and traitors against the said Lord Protector and government of the Commonwealth aforesaid, not having the fear of God in their hearts, but being moved and seduced by the instigation of the Devil.[68]

Shortly before the trial began, Thurloe was informed that 'on Friday night last, after Penruddock came into the prison, the prisoners had agreed together to make an escape, and to break through the guards that night.'[69] However the plan leaked, the guards were doubled, and the escape was foiled. Meanwhile the leaders of the Protectorate were making sure the trials would go smoothly. Desborough wrote to Cromwell from Taunton at the end of March 'I have spoke also with the sheriff of this county about the juries, and he has promised to be very careful therein,'[70] while Edmund Prideaux, the Attorney-General and M.P. for Lyme Regis, was more forthright: 'the jurors we find very well affected and willing to dispatch the cavaliers'.[71]

Compared with Judge Jeffrey's assizes of thirty years later, the trials were surprisingly fair. There was no special high court, although that had been the rule in dealing with treason since 1648; the two judges who had been seized in Salisbury did not serve in case their experiences prejudiced them; one judge, Hugh Wyndham of Silton in Dorset, a distant relative of the royalist Wyndhams of Somerset, had himself come under suspicion of royalism in 1651; and Penruddock was allowed to challenge 22 jurors before the jury was sworn in.

Fewer than 50 of Desborough's list were brought to trial, and a few like William Broadgate, a yeoman of Blandford, were acquitted. Hugh Wyndham later claimed to have done all that he could to save lives and that 'his tears at the time of judgement spoke his grief'.[72] Eventually 39 death sentences were passed, but only 14 or 15 of them were carried out.

The execution of Major Thomas Hunt was delayed 'by reason of the difficulty of procuring an axe (which must be eleven inches for such a purpose), and the preparing of a scaffold'.[73] The night before the postponed sentence was to be carried out, the scaffold 'being up and all ready for the purpose', Hunt was visited in Ilchester gaol by his sisters, Elizabeth and Margery. The gaoler had been ordered to put Major Hunt in irons, but had not done so, which may imply he had been bribed. At all events Hunt was able to exchange clothes with Margery, slipping out with Elizabeth and covering his face as if to hide his tears. That morning, still in disguise, Hunt heard the bell tolling for what would have been his own execution. Margery stayed behind in her brother's bed until she was found there, when 'hue and cry were speedily abroad for the stopping of the prisoner'.[74]

After being given a lift by a collier, Hunt discovered the man had royalist leanings, revealed himself, and was offered shelter. The following night eight or ten of Desborough's troops arrived at the collier's house and demanded to be let in. While Hunt waited, poised to fight, with the collier's wife holding his ammunition for him, the collier himself leant out of the window and pretended to be half asleep. The soldiers threatened to break down the door, but the collier said he had lost his tinderbox, so they must search in the dark. The irritated roundhead leader lost patience. 'Useless to waste time here' he snapped, 'the stupid fellow does not know his right hand from his left'[75] and he led his men away. Hunt's sisters paid for their bravery and devotion with two and a half years' imprisonment.

Penruddock's trial before Edmund Prideaux lasted five hours, and turned on his claim that Captain Croke had promised them their lives when they surrendered at South Molton. When Penruddock accused Croke of this:

> Captain Croke hereupon stood up and his guilty conscience, I suppose, advised him to sit down again after he had made this speech, that is to say he opened his lips and spoke nothing.[76]

Unlike Penruddock that fierce Dorset royalist, William Wake the younger and a few others had held out in a house against Croke, and eventually extracted written articles of surrender. After he was condemned to death, Wake, according to his son's account:

> got those articles carried up to Cromwell by one of Croke's own officers, who, ashamed of the perfidiousness of his colonel, voluntarily undertook to ride up post with them from Exeter, upon which his execution with that of others mentioned in those articles, was not only stopped but by an ordinance of Parliament, he and six others of his companions were pardoned.[77]

The accusation of Croke's perfidiousness was certainly unjust, as the captain (not colonel, though he was shortly to be promoted to major) had already written to Thurloe mentioning the men he gave articles to.

The younger Wake apparently remained in gaol for two and a half years, but it cannot have been a very close imprisonment as his son, a future archbishop of Canterbury, was born in January 1657. Nor does Wake's fidelity to the royalist cause seem to have harmed him financially, for he remained a well-off man, with £800 a year, a large house in Blandford, and enough spare money to buy an estate at Winterborne Thomson, and possibly another at Shapwick.

Penruddock's wife Arundell had responded energetically to his appeal to her to make what friends she could for him, and she made every effort to save her husband. She wrote to everyone she could think of, appealing for mercy, and even spoke personally to both Cromwell and his son, Richard. It was no use. The letters Penruddock and his wife exchanged on his last night alive reveal a devoted and loving couple, fortified by their great religious faith:

> Adieu therefore ten thousand times my dearest dear, and since I must never see you more, take this prayer: May your faith be so strengthened that your constancy may continue, and then I hope heaven will receive you, where grief and love will in a short time after, I hope, translate, my dear, your sad but constant wife, even to love your ashes when dead.

> As I am sure I shall leave none behind me like you, which weakens my resolution to part from you, so when I reflect I

am going to a place where there are none but such as you, I recover my courage. But fondness breaks in upon me, and as I would not have my tears flow tomorrow, when your husband and the father of our dear babes is a public spectacle, do not think meanly of me that I give way to grief now in private, when I see my sand run so fast, and I within a few hours am to leave you helpless and exposed to the merciless and the insolent.[78]

On 16 May John Penruddock was put to death at Exeter. Cromwell's response to the petitions had been to allow Penruddock to be beheaded rather than hanged. As for the other executions, Cromwell gave specific instruction that no one was to be hung, drawn and quartered.

John Martyn, whom Penruddock had put in as rector of Compton Chamberlayne in 1645, and was subsequently ejected for refusing to take the Covenant, was imprisoned for joining the uprising, but then released. He became the trustee for Penruddock's estate, preserved it from sequestration, and took Penruddock's family into his house.

However within months the untiring Arundell Penruddock was writing to her uncle, John Trenchard about the difficulty she had in supporting her seven children. She also appealed to Cromwell, Richard Cromwell, John Fitzjames and William Sydenham. In 1657 she received £200 out of Penruddock's estate, and thanked Richard Cromwell and Sydenham for their help, but she was soon writing to them again, pleading for more help. After the Restoration, she petitioned Charles II. It is to be hoped she received more than some of her husband's soldiers got in 1660. Puddletown paid out 'for three soldiers that had been banished and had been of Mr. Penruddock's party, one shilling',[79] while in Beaminster the churchwarden 'gave to a soldier of Penruddock's, 6d.', less than half what was given to 'John Gerard for seven polecats and one jay'.[80]

The most important result of Penruddock's rising was what it would do to destroy the comparative popularity of Cromwell's rule. Despite its miserable ending, the uprising had briefly threatened so much that

> Cromwell himself was alarmed; he knew well the distemper
> of the kingdom, and in his army and now... he could not
> imagine that such an enterprise could be undertaken with-
> out a universal conspiracy; in which his own army could not
> be innocent.[81]

The consequence was the division of England into military disticts, each under the rule of a major general. Dorset's controller was John Desborough, Cromwell's countrified brother-in-law, later described as 'the grim giant'. Desborough compiled an exhaustive list of royalist suspects in the county, which included well over 200 people in West Dorset alone. Beaminster provided 31 names, Powerstock 26, Bridport 19, Loders 14 and Netherbury 13. Some knowledge about Charles II's escape four years earlier may have finally reached the authorities, as included among Broadwindsor's 11 names was Rhys Jones, the royalist innkeeper of the George, together with Sir Hugh Wyndham of Pilsdon, while there were just two men mentioned in Lyme Regis, Richard Alford and William Ellesdon. Desborough also instituted a sharp clamp-down on anything the Puritans did not like, from sporting events to tramps.

At the same time, to pay for the newly-declared war against Spain, together with the expenses of a standing army, and of trying to control the crime wave of the time, special taxes were placed on all former cavaliers who were men of property. The tax alienated afresh large numbers of people who had been slowly, if unwillingly, coming to terms with the Protectorate. The Wyndhams must have been typical of the enraged royalists, who thought the sequestrations and compoundings of previous years had been more than enough without this new tax. Francis Wyndham had been arrested and imprisoned in Bristol after Penruddock's rebellion, but an appeal to Cromwell led to his release. When ordered to pay the new 'decimation' tax, he may have been cautious, but his uncle, Hugh of Pilsdon, felt no such restraints. He seems to have had a full-scale row with Desborough and 'showed such forwardness and averseness' that he had to be dealt with 'very plainly and indeed roundly',[82] before he submitted.

Nevertheless, there was little sign of any effective resistance. In December the commissioners of Dorset, who included Richard Lawrence, John Bingham, John Browne, Edward Butler, John Arthur, John Lea and James Dewey, wrote to Cromwell. They were ready

> to put in execution your orders for securing the peace of the Commonwealth, wherein we cannot but acknowledge the goodness and mercy of God in directing your Highness in a work so much conducing to the good and quiet of the nation.[83]

As long as Cromwell lived, the nation would indeed remain quiet.

‹‹ *Chapter Twelve* ››
THE FALL OF THE COMMONWEALTH
1656–1660

The rule of Cromwell's major-generals may not have been popular, but it did bring peace, and the people of Dorset generally found it best to be conciliatory whenever possible. At Dorchester on 18 July 1656:

> It was resolved that Mr Bury and Mr Stansby be desired to ride to Blandford on Wednesday next, to invite General Desborough to a private lodging at Mr Stansby's house, and that there be a gallon of sack and a gallon of white wine and claret and a sugar loaf presented to him from the town, together with a fat sheep.[1]

Such respect was wise, for Desborough's power extended into every facet of day-to-day life. He and the justices even set the legal price of oats and hay, and in April 1658 Dorchester town records report that:

> William Chase, lately a trooper and farrier, desired leave to dwell in town and keep a victualling house. To whom was answered that he might come and dwell in the town freely, but we should not grant him a licence for an alehouse without the approbation of General Desborough.[2]

It seems probable that Mr Chase did not receive 'the approbation of General Desborough', as six years later there was no one of his name living in Dorchester.

The Protectorate, it seemed, was well established, and even royalist Wimborne paid out 2s. 'for beer for the ringers the thanksgiving day for the proclamation of his Highness the Lord Protector'.[3] Military matters had all but vanished from the records, though in May 1658 there were references to 'two barrels of powder',[4] which made up an eighth of the mayor of Lyme Regis's entire expenses for the year. Normal day-to-day life had finally returned to the county. Local merchants and shopkeepers in many Dorset towns, including Lyme, Poole, Evershot and Milton Abbas, issued tokens for use in their shops. In Sherborne Dr Nathaniel Highmore was finding the time and leisure to write extensively on medicine and botany, discover a new duct in the testicles, and to build up a large practice, especially among the clergy whom he never charged. After the Restoration he became a J.P. and when he died left £5 a year for a poor boy to be sent from Sherborne grammar school to university for six years, and another £50 towards building an almshouse in Sherborne.

By 1658 a regular stage coach service linked London and Dorset.

Leaving from the George Inn outside Aldersgate, it took two and a half days to Blandford and Dorchester, three days to Bridport, and cost 30s. Two years earlier the churchwardens of Bere Regis had felt confident enough about the future, and well-off enough, to spend £21 2s. 6d. on a new church bell. The free school at Bere Regis was open, and in 1657/8 the schoolmaster, James Hallett, received an allowance of £10 from the tithes, while Henry Parson got £7 15s. for the school in Bridport. There was also a small free school at Cerne Abbas in the remains of the abbey. William Handley, the rector of Melbury Bubb, (and son of Richard Handley, the previous rector), had been the schoolmaster there, but the Dorset Committee had turned him out and the family was supported by his wife 'by hard working night and day'.[5]

Even under the major generals there were still plenty of roaming preachers in the land, ultra-independents who accepted no church authority of any sort. Broadwindsor was paid a visit by 'one Hine, an Anabaptist, who pretended to inspiration and was much celebrated on that account, as well as for other uncommon gifts'. Hine, who may have been a local man from Powerstock or Nettlecombe, demanded to preach in Broadwindsor church, but the rector, John Pinney, refused. Hine's supporters retaliated by calling out that all ministers were 'dull blockheads and dumb dogs that would neither preach themselves, nor suffer others to preach that would'.

Eventually the two men preached on the same text in a field nearby, and:

> they carried the prophet off in triumph... But he never came there any more; and there was this good effect of this management, that many were settled who before were wavering, and some were recovered.[6]

When Dr Fuller, the original rector, returned to take up his appointment again after the Restoration, he listened to Pinney preaching and 'told the people afterwards that he would not deprive them of such a man'. Subsequently however Pinney was ejected, twice imprisoned, and worked in Dublin for ten years, before finally returning to his own people in Broadwindsor after religious toleration was granted.

May 1658 saw a great meeting of 300 or more Anabaptists in Dorchester spread over four days. Unlike the Quakers they were not directly persecuted, and even had a formal meeting with the mayor. Nevertheless the authorities sent three spies to attend the gathering who

> came on Monday night about eight at night, delaying the time until then because we would observation in our coming, and in order to the concealment of ourselves left our swords at Bridport.

The main source of disquiet was as to whether the Anabaptists planned an alliance with the Fifth Monarchy men like Thomas Harrison, but the leading English Anabaptist, Captain William Kiffen, a very rich London merchant and M.P. for Middlesex at the time, opposed the move. Finally the meeting's resolutions were 'so empty as not worth reciting', while the messages sent out to other churches the spies 'could not understand'.[7] The main strength of the Westcountry Anabaptists remained in Somerset, and there were no other important gatherings in Dorset.

During the fifth year of the Protectorate things took a turn for the worse again, and 'a public fast or day of humiliation' was observed in Dorchester 'seeking of God to divert the calamity of extraordinary sickness in most parts of the nation'.[8] By early August fever was rife in Milton Abbas. Lyme Regis seem to have reacted to hard times by going back to a positively medieval authoritarianism. After the siege several women had been whipped and J. Brewer had been paid 17s. 6d. 'for a pair of stocks'.[9] The mayor's accounts for the late 1650s include 'for making a ducking stool, 5s. 8d.',[10] 'for a lock for the prison, 2s... for the pillory, 19s. 2d... for colouring the pillory 4s... for watching Spratt's daughter who had a bastard 4s.'[11]

On 3 September, the anniversary of the battles of Dunbar and Worcester, Cromwell died, famously remarking 'it is not my design to drink or to sleep, but my design is to make what haste I can to be gone.'[12] Just four days earlier Denis Bond had also died, on 'the windiest day that had before happened for twenty years, being then tormented with the strangury and much anxiety of spirit'.[13] A common story was that the Devil had come for Cromwell 'but not being prepared for him' took Bond to be going along with. Although 'there were few persons more disliked by the violent partisans of King Charles I than Mr Denis Bond,' even royalist supporters accepted that he had 'had very superior abilities' and only enriched his family 'without doing any private injury, and he contributed all he could to render the public such services as the times were capable of'.[14] The former woollen draper was buried in Westminster Abbey.

Other pillars of the old regime were also passing away. John Fry, the closest Dorset could offer to a regicide, died in 1657, as did Sir Thomas Trenchard. The controversial Richard Alford of Lyme Regis followed them to the grave the next year, leaving behind a will that demonstrated just how he had prospered. In 1659 John Browne of Frampton and Edmund Prideaux died. The latter had done very well out of his parliamentarianism, marrying his son to a rich ward of Alexander Popham's, Amy Francis, and even employing Inigo Jones to make changes to his great house at Forde Abbey. Many people came to admire Prideaux's coffin: 'so fine a thing that it might have served more fit for a real person of quality's chamber ornament'.[15] A friend of Clarendon's was even more cutting:

If God be pleased when men do cease to sin
If the Devil be pleased when a soul he does win
If the world be pleased when they are rid of a knave
Prideaux pleases all in going to his grave.[16]

The corporation of Lyme Regis were more respectful to their long-serving M.P. and the accounts include a charge for a horse to 'ride out and meet the corpse'.[17] Prideaux had been granted a baronetcy by Cromwell, but the title scarcely outlived the man himself, not being recognized after the Restoration.

The fragmentation of religion that had been such a feature of the Interregnum was also showing some signs of coming to an end. The Independent churches in 'Wiltshire, Dorsetshire, Somersetshire, Hampshire, Essex and others' began to move towards voluntary associations, 'in a word a great desire of concord began to possess all good people in the land, and our breaches seemed ready to heal.'[18]

Even Dorchester was no longer the Puritan citadel it had once been, and in September 1658 there was a discussion in the town council about 'the great need we have of improving the means and embracing every opportunity, to the stirring of our cold hearts, the more to be quickened in the ways of piety'.[19] The collection made to mark the Lord Protector's death raised only £2 10s., nearly all of that from the church of the aging William Benn. The year before ecclesiastical returns from Dorset had been only £2236 13s. 02d., easily the lowest in the whole of the South West.

February 1659 saw a sensational crime in London that was the direct result of a long-running Dorset family feud. George Strangways, one of the sons of Thomas Strangways of Muston (who died in 1648), had fought as a major in the King's army, had been ordered to pay £615 to compound with Parliament, and subsequently acted as a go-between, linking Lady Grace Strangways and the Dyve family. To avoid 'those vultures of a Commonwealth, sequestrators, by the calm neutrality of a discreet sister',[20] George had apparently given a bond for his farm at Muston to his sister, Mabel.

For some years the lives of George Strangways and John Fussell, a well-known royalist lawyer of Blandford, had interweaved. Both men had been in the garrison of Sherborne, and been taken prisoner when the castle fell in August 1645. Fussell then spent at least eighteen months in prison in London, before paying £268 6s. 8d. to lift the sequestration on his estate. George Strangways was probably also imprisoned as in 1646 and 1647 Sir Lewis Dyve used both of them to carry messages between himself and King Charles I. Subsequently both men were involved, to a greater or lesser extent, in royalist conspiracies.

Abruptly Mabel Strangways, whom George had been certain was a confirmed spinster, announced her intention to marry Fussell. Frightened that he would be cheated of his property, or furious at losing his sister's estate which he had expected to inherit, George Strangways, who was well-known for his 'impetuous rage',[21] threatened to kill Fussell if his sister married her. Mabel, who must have been a woman of great determination, went ahead with the marriage anyway. She also accused her brother of taking much that was hers, and of forging the bond about Muston. Not long afterwards she bore Fussell a son.

The arguments dragged on for many years. On 15 November 1652 Fussell, who had only recently taken up legal practice again, wrote from

London to Sir John Strangways, referring to 'differences between Mr George Strangways and myself'.[22] He asked for a meeting at Blandford when he was next there, and stated that he was willing to accept Sir John as an impartial judge of the dispute. But the problems remained.

Six and a half years later Fussell was murdered in London. He had been sitting writing at his desk in the George and Half Moon between nine and ten in the evening when he was shot through the first floor window. One bullet from a carbine struck his forehead, another his mouth. A third bullet was found in the window frame. His body was found by his clerk.

The quarrel must have been well known, for George Strangways was rapidly seized and arrested, but denied the crime and said he was in his room elsewhere all the time. Men were sent to all the gunsmiths' shops in and around London to search for evidence. One gunsmith who was a member of the jury, objected it would be impossible to discover any information that way. However when this very gunsmith was questioned, he admitted he had lent a carbine to another former royalist officer, Mr Thomson. Thomson was away from home, but after his wife was arrested, he hastily returned to London and confessed he had borrowed a gun on the day of the murder and given it to George Strangways 'for the killing of a deer'.

Gradually the truth emerged. A friend of Strangways, disguised, had walked up and down in his room to make it seem he was still there, while Strangways himself stole out to commit the murder. His previous service as a soldier was partly blamed for the crime. 'A legitimate war' might make the spilling of blood 'not only honest, but honourable, yet being so well versed in that killing trade',[23] Strangways was a man always more likely to commit murder.

Strangways, who was about forty-five, wrote to his brother-in-law, the M.P. for Wareham, Major Dewey, admitting the crime, but denying any intention to kill Fussell. He refused to plead at the trial, thus preserving his estate, and was sentenced to be laid on his back in the dark, naked except 'his privy parts', tied and stretched out, and then have loaded onto his body 'as much iron and stone as he can bear and more'.[24] The horror of the sentence seems to have moved even the executioner, especially as Strangways was not permitted the usual sharp piece of wood under his back that accelerated death by breaking the spine. In the circumstances everyone present in the cell at Newgate was allowed to pile on weights, and he was dead in between eight and ten minutes.

London seems to have been a dangerous place in the 1650s. One evening Thomas Sydenham:

> being in his lodging at London, and going to bed at night with his clothes loosed, a mad drunk fellow, a soldier likewise in the same lodging, entered the room, with one hand gripping him by the breast of his shirt, with the other discharged a loaded pistol in his bosom.[25]

By a miraculous chance the shot went through the assailant's own hand sideways on, and after breaking every bone in it, fell harmlessly at Sydenham's feet. As for the soldier himself, the wound grew infected and he died a few days later.

Without the guidance of Cromwell, the republican settlement rapidly began to break down. Everywhere army generals and factions began to plot and manoeuvre for their own advantage. The good-natured and popular Richard Cromwell made an attempt to fill his father's shoes, and was proclaimed Protector by, among others, William Sydenham who had been promoted to the new House of Lords in December 1657. Over half the members of Richard Cromwell's Parliament were new to the House, as were 13 of Dorset's 20 M.P.s, who included the ex-royalists Ralph Bankes and John Tregonwell. However nearly all of the county's new M.P.s had either served in the parliamentary armies, like James Dewey and John Lea, or else held office under the Commonwealth, like James Baker and James Gould. Denis Bond was replaced by two of his sons, Samuel and Elias, though the defeat of Thomas Sydenham in what had been his brother's seat at Melcombe may have been significant.

John Fitzjames had, like Anthony Ashley Cooper, pleaded with Cromwell to assume the crown, but he was fast gaining a reputation as the 'cavaliers' protector'. He and his cousin Robert Coker of Mappowder both stood in the election. Robert Coker's father, William Coker, had been commissioned by Hopton to raise a regiment of foot for the King. Robert, however, had fought on the Parliament side as a colonel, and was sheriff of Dorset in 1647. Like Fitzjames he seems to have been a moderate, against both the army and the established pre-war Puritan gentry.

As the election approached Fitzjames wrote to Coker: 'Sir Walter Erle and Bingham sit in close council at Dorchester, where I am confident (heaven bless the town) there are monstrous plots against you and myself.'[26] As it happened the old parliamentary leaders of the county, Erle, Bingham, Prideaux and John Trenchard, stayed firmly in the saddle for a little longer, and the attempt of Fitzjames and Coker to be elected as knights of the shire was beaten off. Fitzjames had covered his bets by arranging for Poole to elect him if his first attempt failed, but that wily old campaigner, Erle, immediately accused him of irregularity, and eventually Fitzjames was forced to withdraw.

As early as March 1659 Anthony Ashley Cooper considered it safe enough to launch a fierce attack on Oliver Cromwell, 'his Highness of deplorable memory to this nation'[27] in Parliament. His vindictiveness towards the man he had begged to assume the crown less than three years before, may have stemmed from a shrewd guess as to the way things were going. Or it may have been a more personal grudge relating to Cromwell's last years, when Cooper

> aspiring to become the Protector's son-in-law, Cromwell (who well enough understood him) either disdaining or not daring to take him so near into his bosom, took occasion also to quit him out of his Council.[28]

Despite his well-meaning attempts to bind up the wounds of the nation Richard Cromwell, 'Tumbledown Dick' as he was nicknamed, never had the necessary ruthlessness or prestige to control the army. He and his Parliament were expelled in May 1659, and England fell into the power of the army-controlled Committee of Safety. Among the men who led this army coup were William Sydenham and John Desborough. Sydenham became a member of the Committee of Safety and the council of state, which was no doubt why Thomas Sydenham received a government post to do with leases and rents, Comptroller of the Pipe, in July 1659 just before he went abroad for two years to study medicine in France.

A key figure in the manoeuvres of the generals was Colonel Nathaniel Whetham. Whetham was by birth a Dorset man, born in Burstock near Broadwindsor, but his family had moved to Buckinghamshire when he was still a child. He had been apprenticed to a baker before joining the parliamentary army and fighting extensively in the Midlands during the Civil War. He must have profited from the parliamentary victory, as he bought up the manor of Chard, previously belonging to the bishophric of Bath and Wells, for the sizeable sum of £3718 9s. 6d. In 1655 he was in Scotland with General Monk, and subsequently he was reappointed governor of the vital garrison town of Portsmouth. As a collapse back into civil war reared its head, he joined 450 'men of quality' who signed a remonstrance against the officers who had overthrown Parliament. His name was joined by, among others, Thomas Fairfax, Anthony Ashley Cooper, Arthur Haslerig, John Bingham, and General Monk.

The crucial meeting for Whetham had been with Anthony Ashley Cooper, 'his friend and very long acquaintance',[29] in Westminster Hall. Cooper, demonstrating what Clarendon, soon to be his deadly political foe, called 'the flexibility and instability of that gentleman's nature',[30] had decided the time had come to change sides and he persuaded Whetham to secure Portsmouth for Parliament when the right moment came. However Cooper himself was already suspected by the authorities.

Over the summer George Joyce, freed from imprisonment, had been searching the South and West for royalist conspirators, and a blacksmith was lured into indiscretion when Joyce 'showed me the King's commission, telling me that the King had given him power to raise forces for him'.[31] Another royalist uprising was indeed being planned in north Dorset. The leaders were Captain Henry Butler of Handley, who had fought for Charles I, suffered the sequestration of his farm outside Gillingham, and compounded for £568; Captain Hugh Fry of the Angel Inn; and Dr William Chamberlain, a cavalier-physician of Shaftesbury and the author of several poems including one named 'Pharonnida' which came out this same year. The day for the revolt was to be 31 July, but the projected gathering at Stonehenge was called off the day before and the uprising crumbled without ever breaking out.

The examinations of some twenty-five people at Shaftesbury in August reveal a plan that had no chance of success, and was if anything even more chaotic than that of Penruddock four years earlier. There were whispered promises that Charles II was about to arrive with an army of twenty or thirty thousand, that Bristol and Windsor were to be handed over, that £2000 would arrive any moment. However the practical preparations were feeble in the extreme. A few minor gentry and skilled workers around Shaftesbury, Stalbridge and Sherborne promised help and a handful of horses, and Chamberlain was said to have a commission from King Charles to raise a company, but there seem to have been virtually no weapons available. Chamberlain accused Luke Cave, a Shaftesbury blacksmith, of having betrayed the plot, but Cave denied it.

Nevertheless the military authorities were taking no chances. The Lyme Regis accounts include £1 10s. 10d. for 'expenses about the militia',[32] while on 10 August John Lea, Edmund Butler and Robert Butler wrote to Humphrey Weld ordering him to 'send in to us at the sign of the Red Lion in Blandford four sufficient horse with bridles, saddles, pistols, holders, swords and all other furniture'.[33] Weld would receive a similar request for troops in April 1660, but by then the situation had changed drastically.

Other royalist uprisings in Gloucester, Lynn, Shrewsbury and Exeter never materialized. The royalists did rise in Cheshire, but were swiftly defeated by General Lambert, and at Milton Abbas the bells were rung in celebration 'concerning Chester business'.[34] The royalist leader, George Booth, was caught escaping in women's clothes, and thrown into the Tower. Anthony Ashley Cooper was known to 'speak much in commendation of Sir George Booth that he was a very honest man',[35] and a boy named Nicholas testified he had carried a letter from Cooper to Booth. There was further evidence against Cooper, 'the discovery of several papers of his which were lately intercepted',[36] and he was suspected of having a party in Dorset ready to rise if Booth's revolt should go well. On 25 August Cooper was arrested by Major Dewey, and shortly afterwards found himself being questioned by the council of state, whose members included Sydenham, Haslerig and Desborough:

> He made answer so dextrously to their objections, that he
> stopped the mouths of his accusers, and most of the members,
> having a great opinion of his fidelity, did then dismiss him.[37]

The Committee's unanimous report stated: 'it does not appear to them that there is any just ground of jealousy or imputation upon him,'[38] and Cooper was released after less than three weeks.

The council had made a bad mistake. Cooper had had enough of the army and was rapidly returning to his aristocratic roots: 'we have already had too much experience how insupportable servants are when they become our masters.'[39] Other old parliamentarians had also been arrested, including William Waller, who was put in prison for two months, and Denzil Holles. Holles, 'the chief pillar of the Presbytery and who has since the suppression of that party lived privately in Basse Normandy'[40] had been sent a pass by Cromwell in May 1654, and returned to live quietly in Dorset. Even though his wife, Jane, was the stepmother of Arundell

Penruddock, Holles had not been troubled until now. However his imprisonment did not last long and on 2 September an order was sent to 'Major Dewey and Captains Lea and Chaffin to see Denzil Holles released and his horses and his arms, and what else was seized with him, restored'.[41]

The next rebellion was not by old cavaliers, or even old parliamentarians, but by men who still wielded real political and military power. In December Colonel Whetham was joined by Haslerig and immediately declared against the Committee of Safety. Goring's declaration of Portsmouth for the King in 1642 had sparked off the first Civil War. Now Whetham, who was 'devoted to the presbyterian-republican party'[42] would open the way for peace from the same place.

With the Committee of Safety's army, under Lambert, suspiciously watching the ex-royalist Monk in Scotland, the desertion of Portsmouth was crucial. It rapidly became a focus for all discontent in the South, and among those who declared for the restoration of the Long Parliament and marched there was Major Unton Croke and his men. More than half the soldiers sent by the Committee of Safety to block up the port deserted.

Meanwhile Anthony Ashley Cooper had remained in London, where his loyalty was still regarded with great misgiving. One day a man knocked on his door in Covent Garden. They spoke together for a while, then the man left, but Cooper was suspicious and 'went inwards as if he intended to go into the house, but as soon as the fellow was gone, turned short and went out, and went to his barber's, which was just by.' It was as well he did. A file of musketeers were lurking around the corner in the Strand, and the man he had just spoken to was their officer, who was making sure his quarry was at home. The soldiers burst into the house 'to seize him, but not finding him there, they searched every corner and cranny of the house'.[43]

There was every reason to arrest Ashley Cooper, as he was by then trying to subvert several leading supporters of the army regime. To Major General Fleetwood, who had helped take Sherborne in 1645, and was occasionally rumoured to have been Cromwell's intended successor, Cooper wrote that Parliament was 'the sole lawful authority' which could 'make the sword subservient to the civil interest and settle the government in the hands of the people'. However first the sword could only be fought with the sword:

> God (we trust) has raised up a deliverer, having by admirable providence put an opportunity and power into the hands of General Monk, the ablest and most experienced commander of these nations.[44]

Ashley Cooper had also 'insinuated himself into a particular friendship' with Colonel Hutchinson, the regicide:

> and made him all the honourable pretences that can be imagined, called him his dear friend, and caressed him with such embraces as none but a traitor as vile as himself could have suspected.[45]

Another of Cooper's contacts was Vice-Admiral Lawson, who was thought to be a radical republican. Suddenly Lawson joined the uprising and sailed his fleet into the Thames. It was a crucial change of sides, and Whetham and Haslerig took the chance to march on the capital. They reached it just before Christmas, Cooper was put in charge of the Tower, and the Long Parliament was reassembled. William Sydenham, who was with the army in the north, was expelled from the Parliament for helping the Committee of Safety seize power. Then on New Year's Day Monk crossed the Scottish border, and marched south.

A return to full-scale civil war loomed, but the country shied away from the possibility. Dorset, like much of the South, seems to have swung against the Committee of Safety, and the new year saw the mayor and burgesses of Lyme congratulated on disarming forces raised against the re-established Parliament. Crucially Lambert's army disintegrated, and on 3 February 1660 Monk reached London, Whetham having joined him on the way. The bells of Milton Abbas, which had rung for Lambert six months earlier, now rang for his conqueror, Monk.

The Long Parliament, back in Westminster, remained a fairly radical assembly, and gave an enthusiastic response to a petition from Praise-God Barebones and his supporters calling on a complete abjuration of all members of the royal family. Denzil Holles was said to be 'the man of greatest sway in it...but he was a haughty, stiff man and so by straining it a little too much he lost all'.[46]

In practice real power still rested with the soldiers under the command of Monk, patronizingly described by one royalist as 'the instrument to bring that to pass, which certainly he had neither wisdom to foresee nor understanding to contrive, he being a phlegmatic dull person'.[47] Monk hesitated for some weeks, and was rumoured to have told the French ambassador he planned to become the next Lord Protector, but was then dissuaded. Finally Monk took his decision, sternly reproved Parliament and formally invited King Charles to take up his throne. Among those who went to get Charles was Denzil Holles, whose career had come a long way from his violent defiance of 30 years before.

Chapter Thirteen

THE RETURN OF THE KING
1660–1665

The old Dorset cavaliers reacted to Monk's pronouncement with a declaration of 16 April 1660, which promised 'to forgive one another as we expect to be forgiven', disclaimed the extremists and 'turbulent spirits' of their own party, and swore they would submit 'to the resolves of Parliament'.[1] The signatories included Sir Hugh Wyndham, Sir Gerard Napier, Sir John and Giles Strangways, Robert Lawrence, and George Penny.

The restoration of the King was not a popular decision with most of the army officers, but the relief of the great majority of the nation was enormous. On 10 May King Charles II was proclaimed at Dorchester with a solemn procession, and a speech by the town clerk condemning the past that had 'wasted our treasure and much precious blood in the nation'.[2] Five shillings was paid to the bell-ringers at Beaminster for ringing out the town's celebrations. In Lyme Regis £16 12s. was paid out 'for entertainment at the Proclaiming of the King', which was in fact only a little more than had been spent the previous Christmas 'for entertainment of the gentry and officers'.[3]

It was at royalist Sherborne that the celebrations were most extravagant.

> Besides the melody of divers sorts of loud music, there were the martial noises of many drums and trumpets, innumerable vollies of shot, the continual ringing of bells, and loud acclamations of many thousands of men, women and children...the conduit that day and the next ran with claret, besides many hogsheads of March beer and large baskets of white loaves set out in the streets for the poor.

That veteran royalist, Sir John Strangways, read the proclamation despite 'not being able, by reason of his age, to utter it with so loud and distinct a voice as was requisite'. He then rode through the streets, telling the people of Sherborne

> that as they were some of the first people in England that appeared in arms for the defence of King Charles I, so now it did rejoice his heart to see how studious they were to transcend all other places in the expressions of their joy for the restoring of King Charles II.

Effigies of Cromwell and John Bradshaw (president of the court that had tried Charles I) were put on trial, then hung:

> they were so hacked and hewed, so gored and shot through, that in a short time but little remained...yet would not the people be satisfied till they had made a fire between the gib-

bets and burnt all they could get of their garbage or garment. The celebration continued day and night:

> At night besides the multitude of bonfires in the streets, which no doubt made the inhabitants of the world in the moon (if there be any) think there was an apparition of some blazing star, there were three huge piles of faggots fired...which were visible over all the marshes of Somersetshire, in part of Wales, and the greatest part of Blackmore.[4]

Eleven days later Charles II landed at Dover. On 29 May he was in London, surrounded by cheering crowds, and the bells of Sherborne yet again chimed the town's joy.

> In this wonderful manner and with this incredible expedition, did God put an end to a rebellion that had raged near twenty years, and been carried on with all the horrid circumstances of murder, devastation, and parricide, that fire and the sword, in the hands of the most wicked men in the world, could be the instruments of; almost to the desolation of two kingdoms and the exceeding defacing and deforming the third.[5]

A humble address of the nobility and gentry of Dorset giving thanks for Charles's restoration, with 219 signatures, was presented to the King by, among others, Anthony Ashley Cooper, Sir John Strangways, John Fitzjames and Giles Strangways. As one republican commented acidly, 'indeed it was a wonder in that day to see the mutability of some, and the hypocrisy of others, and the servile flattery of all.'[6] Among 13 Dorset gentlemen who were proposed for the order of Knights of the Royal Oak were Robert Lawrence of Creech Grange, and Giles Strangways, who was shown in Roman dress on a celebratory silver medal struck in Antwerp. On the reverse was the Tower of London with the royal banner flying over it, and underneath the dates of Strangways' own imprisonment there.

Anthony Ashley Cooper was one of the few parliamentarian nominees to be made a Privy Councillor, foreshadowing a formidable and dramatic career as the effective founder of the Whig party. He had been richly rewarded for his shrewd changes of sides. Fifteen years earlier William Strong had said:

> He that cannot spin a fine thread, carry a design subtly, speak words smoother than butter, when war is in his heart; mariner-like look one way when he rows another, and pretend to build, where especially he desires to destroy, is no politician for these times.[7]

The future First Earl of Shaftesbury was very much a politician for those times.

Denzil Holles, also a Privy Councillor and created Lord Holles of Ifield even before the coronation, was put in effective control of Dorset, and when he visited Dorchester, he received almost exactly the same presents as Desborough had been given five years earlier: 'it is ordered that my Lord Holles be presented with a gallon of sack and two gallons of French wine at his coming to town, and a sugar loaf.'[8]

Charles paid off the army as fast as he could. The regiment that Fleetwood had used against Parliament in 1659, and then changed sides after he was expelled from command, was quartered in Devon, Dorset and Somerset when it was disbanded in October 1660. A month and a half later William Williams of Dorset, a soldier in Anthony Ashley Cooper's troop of horse, was provided with a certificate stating he 'was actually in his Majesty's service...on the 25th day of April 1660 and was instrumental to the happy restoration of his Majesty to his just right of government'.[9]

But just as the Dorset Committee had had to find money for all the old roundheads, so the King had to find money for old cavaliers. There are hardly any royalist veterans listed from Dorchester, Poole, Weymouth or indeed anywhere along the coast at all except Bridport with 19, but Sherborne alone provided the enormous total of 148. Other strong royalist centres included Shaftesbury with 36 pensioners, Blandford with 34, Beaminster 21, Sturminster Newton 20, Gillingham 18 and Wimborne 15; while the villages of Motcombe with 15 and Netherbury with 14 also contributed heavily. The only Dorset settlement that was proportionately as royalist as Sherborne was isolated Powerstock, with ten royalist pensioners out of a population of around 250; presumably this was because Powerstock was owned by the fanatical royalist John Paulet. However the neighbouring village of Toller Porcorum, owned by another royalist Sir Francis Fulford, had no pensioners at all from a population of roughly 175.

Denzil Holles wrote to the mayor and corporation of Lyme Regis sternly reminding them of their new duty:

> we are informed that several persons among you, who were maimed soldiers for the Parliament, have received large pensions from you...now finding that by the complaint of John Stower [actually of Symondsbury] and John Butler of your town, who were soldiers in the King's service, that nothing is allowed them. Our desire therefore to you is that they (being maimed soldiers) may also receive such favours from you as may afford them a comfortable subsistence.[10]

Fourteen years before Holles had encouraged the House of Commons to pass the Declaration of Dislike, which defined soldiers who continually petitioned Parliament for back pay and compensation as enemies of the state.

More illustrious royalists were hastily putting in bids for the new King's favour. Just two months after the Restoration Humphrey Weld, previously a cup-bearer to Queen Henrietta Maria, was writing to the King listing out a variety of offices vacant in the west Midlands and begging Charles 'to confer the said offices upon your petitioner'. Charles's

Secretary of State, Edward Nicholas, shuffled the matter off by referring 'the consideration of this petition to the Right Honourable the Lords Commissioners of the Treasury to certify what is fit to be done'. It seems the answer was little or nothing. There were, no doubt, many more deserving cases. Just under a year later Weld was sending letters to the influential John Granville, Earl of Bath, 'containing my services to and sufferings for the late King' in an attempt to obtain 'some marks of his Majesty's favour in conferring an office about the new Queen upon me'.[11] Weld in fact did not do badly, being made governor of Portland and granted a secret service pension of £1000 a year for maintaining an underground correspondence between Charles and the French court.

William Sydenham was in a very different position. He took the oath of allegiance to Charles, but justified his previous actions and was included among 18 people who were banned from holding any office. He also had to pay a bond of £1000 not to disturb the peace of the kingdom, but fortunately for him he had amassed a 'great and plentiful estate'[12] in jewels, plate and furniture, valued at £6000, and in 1661 he was able to lend £100 to Weymouth 'for carrying on the harbour work until the grant from the customs shall come in'.[13] The same year he died, to be followed just eight days later by his wife, Grace. Their daughter Mary was the grandmother of the famous painter and engraver, William Hogarth.

Colonel Whetham soon found the Restoration was not at all what he had hoped or expected, and Charles was not going to build his government on the moderate parliamentarians who had in fact brought him back into power, but on the old royalists. From his estate in Chard Whetham wrote bitterly to Monk:

> I find all my business in a very bad posture, and all honest
> people greatly discouraged by the height and confidence of
> the Cavaliers, who have chosen one of the knights for this
> shire one that whose father was in actual service for the King
> against Parliament. Many honest men that upon the poll
> tended their voices for an honest gentleman were refused to
> have their names taken.[14]

Whetham was referring to Robert Coker who, with his ally John Fitzjames, had this time succeeded where they failed the year before. Of Dorset's 20 M.P.s in the first Parliament of Charles II, only half were newcomers, all the others had served under the Commonwealth, and two, Walter Erle and Denzil Holles, were survivors of the original Long Parliament of 1641. Erle had managed to get re-elected in Poole, the very town that he had manoeuvred Fitzjames out of only a little over a year earlier.

The Cavalier Parliament of 1661 would be very different, and except for a few former roundheads such as Henry Henley and William Penn, the father of the famous Quaker and a former admiral in the parliamentary navy, it was packed with men who had fought for the King, like Bullen Reymes, Giles Strangways, and Winston Churchill. Humphrey Weld's attempt to get elected as M.P. for Wareham failed, despite his letter to the mayor and magistrates of the town describing his 'particular inclination to that place' and assuring them of

> my good intentions towards them whom I respect not as my nearest neighbours, but also as my special friends, whose advantage and interest I shall ever seek to promote to the utmost of my power.[15]

Weld had to fall back on using influence to get himself successfully chosen for Christchurch.

It may have been the royalists' turn to taste the fruits of victory, but those fruits were not always easy to find. Ralph Bankes spent many weary months trying to trace and recover all his possessions that had been taken from Corfe Castle. In October 1660 he was told 'some of the greatest timber was carried to Sutton, to Mr Denis Bond's farm, where it remains yet unused. And not a little timber and stone was used about the George Inn.' An old servant even sent him 'a particular of goods viewed by me at Colonel Bingham's house' which included hangings, tapestry, window cushions, carpets, beds, 'a rich ebony cabinet with gilded fixtures' and 'a silk gilt carpet for the table in the withdrawing room'.[16] In August 1661 Ralph wrote peremptorily to Sir Walter Erle:

> It may perhaps seem strange to you after such an intermission that I should now demand of you that which belongs to me. I doubted not your own conscience and the justice of the thing would, before this, have invited you to make restitution or some recompense... I can, if you give me the occasion, bring those that will swear that one of the great pieces of timber (if not the greatest) in your house came from the castle, besides stone and other materials you have made use of.[17]

Erle's reply was blandly unhelpful:

> As for the things themselves, the quantity and value of them, certainly they are nothing near so considerable as I perceive you apprehend them to be – five or six load of timber and stone being in point of value no such great matter.[18]

Bingham's response to Bankes's repeated demands was far more friendly, but only a little more generous, which was scarcely surprising as he had been forced to mortgage much of his family's estate:

> I have a large bed, a single velvet red chair, and a suite of fine damask; had not the horse plague swept away my horse, I would have sent these to you...command one of your servants to come to Blandford next Friday morning by ten o'clock, there these things shall be ready for him at the Crown.[19]

This was all Ralph Bankes got back from his plundered home, and even the bed lacked its feathers which had been 'stolen out' by a maid. Nonetheless, there is no need to feel sympathy for a man who was then engaged in building the magnificent mansion of Kingston Lacy.

One of the first things most of the towns and villages did was demonstrate loyalty to the restored monarchy. At Milton Abbas the royal arms had been removed and carried off to Blandford on a plough. They were hastily rescued and set up. Langton Long had more cautiously only painted over the arms in 1651, and it cost only 6s. 8d. to repair the damage. At Wimborne there were payments to 'the masons for work done about the King's arms, labour about the two scaffolds for the masons and painters about the King's arms' and 'the painter Harding for painting the King's arms',[20] while Beaminster paid Henry Clarke 1s. 6d. 'for setting up of the scaffold about the King's arms' and William Lack £2 'in full for the arms'.[21]

Beaminster had other heavy expenses. Extensive work had been undertaken on the church in 1659, and in 1664 the town was still recovering from the disastrous fire twenty years earlier. Only one-fifth of the houses in the town were small ones, with just one hearth, while the usual figure in similar-sized towns was at least a third. As ever, it was the poorer inhabitants who had suffered the most. George Penny, whose sequestered estate had helped pay for the rebuilding of Beaminster, sued for his losses, but didn't get them despite an appeal to Charles II himself. That shrewd survivor, aware of how fortunate he had been, was being careful not to disturb the still precarious balance too much.

Superficially the remarkable thing about the English Civil War is just how little difference it seems to have made to the shape of the nation. There was still a Stuart king, a Parliament elected by the same very limited electorate as it had been before the war, and the same state religion. Nonetheless, there was never again any serious likelihood of a King of England ever trying to rule without Parliament, or using a standing army to keep him in power.

Charles II took care to keep the revenge of the cavaliers down to a bare minimum. The graves of Cromwell and some other leading parliamentarians buried in and around Westminster, including those of Robert Blake, Edward Popham, William Strode, William Strong and Denis Bond, were desecrated and their bodies thrown in a pit. John Fry, although nearly four years dead, was specifically excepted from the Act of Pardon and Oblivion, and 'the lands and estates of John Fry, which he had on 25 March 1646', were forfeited to the crown.[22] Nevertheless his son, John, must have been protected from his father's disgrace, for he was married to Ann, the daughter of the royalist Robert Napier, who in 1664 was appointed receiver of Dorset and Poole for the hearth tax.

Many of the fiercest parliamentarians and regicides fled the country. George Joyce made his way to Rotterdam, where he stayed for ten years. In 1670 the British government demanded his arrest and return to stand trial, but the Dutch magistrates allowed Joyce to escape, and he vanished into obscurity. Only 13 men were put to death including Thomas Harrison. Denzil Holles, who was among the judges of the regicides, found Harrison using the same argument that Holles himself had used at his trial in 1629, that M.P.s were responsible only to Parliament. Holles was furious and blustered, 'Do not make Parliament to be the author of your black crimes.'[23] At his execution Harrison behaved with great bravery and made a defiant speech before being hanged, drawn and quartered. Pepys, who watched, remarked that he looked 'as cheerful as any man could do in that condition'.[24]

Another unrepentant regicide, Edmund Ludlow, had gone into hiding just before Charles's return, even though Holles had advised him to give himself up. The man who gave him shelter was, remarkably, a member of the most royalist family in Dorset, the Strangways. Giles Strangways of Muston, brother of the ill-fated George Strangways, had married Ludlow's sister, Margaret, and Ludlow stayed for four days with him at East Charleton, where 'the servants [were] commanded to be silent concerning me.'[25] Ludlow subsequently fled to Switzerland, where he found himself pursued by assassins, one of whom murdered Ludlow's fellow regicide and refugee, John Lisle. In 1689, after the Glorious Revolution and the expulsion of Charles II's brother, James II, Ludlow returned to England, but within days an order for his arrest was issued. The seventy-year-old Ludlow escaped back to Switzerland, and stayed there for the rest of his life. The wounds of the King's execution had not closed in forty years, and as late as 1702 a pamphleteer could remark 'the word Commonwealth frights men like a goblin.'[26]

A few other parliamentarians suffered heavily, like John Sadler. Another son-in-law of John Trenchard, who himself died in 1662, Sadler had got on well with Cromwell, and was chosen town clerk of London. He was an expert in Oriental languages, and the man who persuaded Cromwell to allow the Jews to return to England after nearly four centuries. After the Restoration Sadler was stripped of all his offices and most of his lands, retired to Warmwell, and later 'became much disordered in his senses'. Cuthbert Bound, the rector of Warmwell, supported by Giles Strangways and Colonel Coker, later gave details of some prophecies Sadler had made in 1661, including:

> there should die in London thousands of the plague. That the city of London should be burnt to ashes and showed him St Paul's church tumbling down as if beaten with great guns. That there should be three great fights between the English and the Dutch...three little ships that should land to the west of Weymouth and put all England in a fright, and that in the year 1688 there would happen such a thing in this kingdom that all the world would take notice thereof and be astonished.[27]

Most of the families that had dominated Dorset in 1640, the Strangways, the Erles, the Trenchards, the Bankeses and so on, were still there in 1660, with the majority of their wealth intact. The extensive lands of the Paulets in west Dorset had been sold off by Act of Parliament in 1652, but after the Restoration they were returned to the family.

Inevitably there was bitterness left over, and the Weymouth court records after the Restoration include an assault on Colonel Heane, who was also called 'traitor', and the abusing of Giles Strangways. More important was the changeover among those with local power. In Weymouth the six aldermen who had resigned in 1649 were all restored in October 1662, together with Fabian Hodder, and their successors removed, while in Lyme Regis 8s. 6d. was 'paid the guards on the readmission of the secluded members'.[28] William Constantine of Poole, the lawyer who had joined the royalists in 1643, and had subsequently been imprisoned in London, was reinstated as town recorder by royal writ. Surprisingly the following year he lost his job again, though soon found a new one as recorder of Dorchester, in which post he remained until his death in 1670.

For a few years longer Dorchester remained a beleaguered citadel of Puritanism. After the Restoration several companies of actors and puppet-players were refused permission to perform in the town on the grounds that 'we have no waste of money for such idle things,'[29] and in 1664 there was a complaint that 'the town is most factious.'[30] But the Corporation Act, which limited the holding of public office to people who would receive communion by the rites of the Church of England, weeded out eight of the 11 sitting members of the Dorchester corporation.

A few Commonwealth stalwarts continued to flourish. Captain John Chaffin, who had served under Massey, became the postmaster of Sherborne in 1657, and his son, who had also 'been in arms against the King that now is and his father',[31] took up the post himself in 1660. Local people helped him to hang onto the office for a year, and he was subsequently reappointed in the 1670s. Colonel William Skutt, one of the leaders of roundhead Poole, and the man who had probably defaced the town's two silver maces by scratching his initials on them, did even better. During the great plague of London, Charles II moved his court to Salisbury and amused himself by visiting nearby towns. When the King came to Poole, Skutt entertained him to a banquet and took him on a boat trip to Brownsea Island. Charles clearly enjoyed the company of his erstwhile enemy, for Skutt, who had already been Mayor of the town in 1646 and 1657, was nominated for the office again by the King himself. Two years later Poole was granted a new and generous charter, the parliamentarian citadel had been forgiven. The King's visit to Weymouth around the same time was less lucky for the town. The celebrations got out of hand and in the subsequent fire 37 houses were destroyed.

The Independent clergy, who had flourished under the Commonwealth, were probably the greatest losers from the Restoration. This was scarcely surprising as Charles II's most trusted adviser, Edward Hyde now made Earl of Clarendon, blamed the clergy for putting the 'seditious inclinations into the hearts of men' which had caused the Civil War in the first place. Clarendon was determined to return to church government by 'learned and orthodox men',[32] and his 1662 Act of Uniformity ejected all ministers who disagreed with anything in the Book of Common Prayer, despite Charles's promises of toleration two years earlier:

> The churches and people of Christ in this land having had a long day of peace and tranquillity...lo on a sudden the scheme is changed! The infinitely wise God, who changes times and seasons, was pleased to bring a black cloud over this sunny day to alter the face of the times and to cause great changes and a strange rolling of affairs to pass over these nations upon the return of an exile prince.[33]

The long-staying Puritan William Benn of Dorchester, who had originally been chosen by John White, was replaced by Richard Wine. Wine received a pension of £3 10s. on the 1672 royalist roll of honour 'for preaching in the gaol at Dorchester',[34] presumably during the wars. Ironically Wine must have been preaching in the very place which William Benn, 'who preached gratis on a weekday to the prisoners in the gaol,' had had 'built within the prison walls in good part at least at his own charge'.[35] Subsequently Wine got into trouble for speaking against too much persecution of dissenters, and was forced into a humiliating retraction. As for Benn, he was driven to take refuge in Maiden Newton for a while, but continued to preach, despite being imprisoned several times. 'He lived to be eighty years of age, yet he never used spectacles though he read and wrote much,' finally dying in 1680, almost the last link with pre-war Puritan Dorchester.

John Sacheverell, who had been appointed to Wareham in 1643, and later moved to Wincanton in Somerset, demonstrated a remarkable lack of tact, on the day of Charles II's coronation, by preaching on the text: 'But if ye shall still do wickedly, ye shall be consumed, both ye and your king.'Several people walked out during the sermon, and shortly afterwards his effigy was dragged through the streets, shot and burnt. He and his brother, Timothy, minister of Tarrant Hinton, were ejected and retired to Stalbridge. Subsequently John, together with Peter Ince, John Hallett of Chiselborough, and others, were arrested and sent to Dorchester gaol for three years. That did not silence them and the ejected ministers preached out of a window in the gaol to large crowds outside.

Bartholomew Wesley of Charmouth lost his living, and 'is since a nonconformist, and lives by practice of physic in the same place'.[36] His son, John Wesley, the grandfather of the John Wesley who founded Methodism, had married a daughter of John White. In November 1658 on John Bingham's suggestion, John Wesley 'a godly, able young man'[37] was granted the vicarage of Winterborne Whitechurch, but with the return of Charles II, he ejected. He was imprisoned several times, once being freed through the influence of Sir Gerard Napier, who disapproved of his religious views, but apparently felt sorry for him because he had a broken collar bone. Wesley was also accused of wearing a sword in the time of the Committee of Safety, but replied that the King had pardoned all that. Eventually he was 'called in by a number of serious people at Poole to be their pastor',[38] and spent the rest of his short life, when he was not in prison, preaching to small persecuted independent congregations over Dorset and Somerset. After his death his father 'declined apace and did not long survive him'.[39]

John Brice of Netherbury was ejected from Marshwood and finally took shelter with Elinor Floyer, a widow who had lost a son at the siege of Lyme. Mrs Floyer had bought the very Charmouth Inn where Charles II had sheltered in 1651, and here she protected Brice and allowed him to preach secretly to a small congregation. Eventually Brice married her, and died only in 1716. Philip Lamb of Bere Regis laid the foundations for a congregational church in the town by holding illegal private services, but Thomas Chaplyn of Wareham was less dedicated and after being ejected he stopped preaching altogether, so that to keep him and their eight children, his wife had to start a malting business.

During the time of Charles I James Rawson had been a conforming Anglican, as well as a pluralist, holding more than one parsonage at the same time. In March 1645 he was sequestered from Child Okeford 'for his delinquency' and made to promise that 'he will relinquish his rights to the parsonages of Kingston Russell and Wytherston.'[40] Rawson moved to the rectory of Hazelbury Bryan where he got in trouble with the Dorset committee for ignoring an order to pay fifths to Mrs Clarke, the wife of the rector. Rawson preached at Hazelbury Bryan for fifteen years, but his attempt to keep his post after the Restoration was doomed when it was pointed out he had said in a sermon that 'the Queen Mother [Henrietta Maria] was a whore and all her children bastards, and had publicly prayed that God would root out the royal family root and branch.'[41]

The vicar of Sherborne from 1653 was Francis Bampfield, who had been rector of Rampisham, well known for 'his unshaken loyalty to the King...and his zeal against the Parliament's war',[42] and who publicly read out the Book of Common Prayer longer than any other minister in the county. However during the Interregnum he was converted to Independent beliefs and became 'so enthusiastic and canting that he did almost craze and distract many of his disciples by his amazing and frightful discourses'. At Sherborne he carried on his work as vicar 'among the factious people, not without great disturbance from Quakering witches'.[43] After being ejected he continued preaching and was imprisoned for nine years in Dorchester gaol. Eventually he moved to London, and in 1683 was sent to Newgate where he died, being buried at the Anabaptists' burial place.

George Thorne, offered the parsonage of Fordington in 1648, had been the minister at Weymouth since about 1650. He wielded considerable influence and with William Benn was to be one of the first leaders of Dorset nonconformism. In 1656 Thorne had been granted 'an annuity under the town seal for sixty years',[44] if he should live and preach so long. In fact the annuity lasted barely a tenth of that time. Thorne was ejected in 1662, and his farewell sermon explained:

I cannot declare an unfeigned assent and consent, as the law requires. As from the fear of my God I dare not, so from the love generally you have to me, I know you would not have me dissemble with God and men.

He also repeated almost exactly what John White had said thirty years earlier, but with a different emphasis: 'Let nothing but conscience toward God hinder you at any time from yielding active obedience to all the King's laws.'[45] Subsequently Thorne was 'prosecuted so maliciously, especially by A.L. that he was forced to sell his estate and hide from place to place.'[46] A large part of his congregation deserted their church with him, but the laws against nonconformist religious gatherings were strictly enforced in post-Restoration Weymouth, and there were frequent convictions, notably of a mariner, Henry Saunders. Elsewhere a few Independent clergy did manage to trim their sails and cling on, like Samuel Hardy, appointed to Charminster by the Trenchards, who spent years evading traps laid for him by his enemies.

The return of the Church of England was unwelcome to many not only for religious reasons, it could also be expensive. Beaminster paid out £1 for 'two Common prayer books',[47] and the village of Langton Long had to find 10s. 6d. for 'a new Common Prayer Book', £2 5s. 'for 9 ells of holland at 5s. per ell to make a surplice for the minister', and 7s. 6d. 'for making and washing the surplice'.[48] At Wimborne the expenses were similar, '20 ells of holland to make two surplices for the ministers, £3 16s. 8d...Mrs Gillingham for making of two surplices, 7s...for two Common Prayer Books £1 1s.'[49]

Some of the newly-appointed orthodox clergy were poorly chosen too. Richard Lucy of Chardstock was described as:

very much given to drunkenness, and a frequent haunter of alehouses, a very frequent curser and swearer, and a blasphemer of God's name, a stirrer-up of discord among neighbours...and would commonly quarrel, brawl and fight with those he had been drinking with.[50]

The nonconformists lamented that:

men of corrupt and carnal principles, of loose, sottish, debauched conversations, many of them filled with a spirit of bitterness, enmity and persecution...were set up and appointed by the prelates to be preachers to the people. O doleful change![51]

However the appointment of Gilbert Ironside, the previously sequestered rector of Winterbourne Steepleton, as Bishop of Bristol was a fine choice. Despite his sufferings during the Commonwealth, Ironside warned the cavaliers not to assume they were the King's most faithful servants, and was reasonably accommodating to dissenting clergy. Some of the clergy who had not defied Parliament as Ironside did, but kept their heads discreetly down, were also rewarded. Dr Walter Blandford of Melbury Abbas had submitted to parliamentary inquisition in 1648, but after the Restoration he became Edward Hyde's chaplain, and later Bishop of Oxford.

Nonconformist groups were not uncommon in Dorset in the 1660s. Lyme Regis had a congregation of two to three hundred, Beaminster one of a hundred, though they were claimed improbably to be 'people unknown, from London and places distant'.[52] Officials were often sent to report on or break up nonconformist gatherings. Thomas Rowe had been ejected from Lytchett Matravers but continued to preach in the area, often staying with Sir Thomas Trenchard's daughter-in-law Hannah. Once he was preaching in a poor parishioner's house when another parishioner 'turned informer, and bringing a constable and another with him, demanded the doors of the house to be opened'.[53] The names of everyone there were taken down and many were brought up before the justices, though Rowe himself temporarily fled the county. A similar incident involved Thomas Bampfield, who had as his chaplain another ejected Dorset minister, Humphrey Philips. Then one man 'searching after his inkhorn to take names, having a pistol in his pocket ready-cocked, shot himself in the thigh'.[54]

Christopher Lawrence who 'was born at Dorchester in 1613 at the very time when the town was in flames', and ejected from Came in 1662, had soldiers sent to his house to arrest him:

> Missing him, though he was all the time in his study, they did a great deal of mischief in the house, and broke a great number of pots and bottles full of preparations for medicine...going into an outhouse, where they supposed him to lie concealed, they thrust their swords up to the hilts in the hay and straw there, swearing they would do the rogue's business.[55]

When Lawrence's brother-in-law, a well-off Dorchester merchant Joseph Whittle, came to find out what was going on, he was clubbed to the ground with a musket-butt.

The Quakers probably suffered more than any other sect, due to their refusal to take oaths of any sort, pay tithes, use the respectful 'you' to superiors rather than 'thou', or remove their hats in the presence of authority. At a meeting at Cerne on 18 June 1659 the leaders of the Quakers of west Dorset, decided that Samuel Curtis would write down 'all faithful, innocent suffering of Friends for the truth'.[56] Curtis's records document steadily increasing pressure on the Dorset Quakers. The first physical attack had taken place the previous April. Hannah Guyer of East Coker in Somerset was returning home from a meeting at South Perrott when she was:

> set upon and most wickedly abused and dragged up and down, and much dirtied and otherwise abused after a barbarous manner...she never giving them any provocation, but because she was in scorn called a Quaker.[57]

A few months later Roger Coward of Piddletrenthide and William

Coward of Plush were put in Dorchester gaol for not paying their tithes.

Parallel to the restoration of the King came growing pressure on Quaker gatherings. On 17 April 1660 there was a meeting at Lyme Regis and 12 people from Bridport, half of them women, walked there to be met by John Ellesdon, the mayor of Lyme (and William Ellesdon's older brother), who 'in a fury took one of their hats and threw it on the ground' then sent them to prison where a crowd 'threw in many stones at the window'.[58]

It was the turn of north Dorset next, and a meeting of some 30 Quakers at Sherborne in July 1660 was broken up. The Quakers referred to Charles II's promise of religious toleration and complained they were 'peaceable men...having the word of a king that none should be wronged nor abused for their religion as long as they lived peaceably'. They got little satisfaction. The court they appeared before included three leading royalists, Winston Churchill, Giles Strangways and George Fulford, son of Sir Francis Fulford, who said the only evidence against them he needed was 'their standing with their hats on in face of the court which he said did represent his Majesty's person'.[59] Fourteen Quakers, including Edward Bound, were sent to prison and fined between 5s. and 40s. 8d. Probably this was when the Sherborne churchwardens paid 2s. to 'Thomas Gull for carrying Bounds the Quaker to prison'.[60] Over the next few weeks five more Dorset Quakers, including a woman, Elizabeth Masters of Piddletrenthide, were sent to prison for refusing to pay tithes.

When the Quakers held a meeting at Cerne Abbas next March, there was a full-scale riot. Some inhabitants of the town:

> began to rage like the troubled sea, and beat a drum about
> the town to gather men (like themselves) together with sev-
> eral sorts of weapons, guns, clubs and stands [for muskets],
> with stones, dirt, dung and other filth of the streets, shooting
> off many guns.

After the meeting the Quakers tried to leave, but they found the mob waiting for them:

> beating the drum near their horses' heads, stopping them in
> the streets...beating divers with great poles and some with
> their guns, one wicked man struck one of them violently
> upon the arm, so that with the stroke he broke the stock of
> his gun, another received a dangerous blow with a great
> stone on his ribs.

An attempt to escape across the ford was blocked by a 'wicked Belialist...with a flint stone of great bigness in his hand' who threatened to kill them, while many other people threw stones at them from several directions. Driven back into town, the Quakers were ambushed and attacked again.

> Doubtless much innocent blood had been then spilt had not
> some moderate people prevailed over them, yet many were
> so smitten by them as they were scarce able to help them-
> selves from spitting blood a long time after, their bodies

swollen, being black and blue a long time after.[61]

Three days later a Quaker meeting at Hawkchurch was broken up by John Bragg of Wyld Court who

> required the Lord's people in his Majesty's name (as he said) to depart this house (this John Bragg was formerly a captain in the Parliament's service against the King.... Thus did this envious man make use of the King's name, to whom he had been long an enemy, to utter his envy and malice against the Lord's people.[62]

Quaker influence, especially in west and north Dorset and the neighbouring counties, was widely regarded as dangerous to the state. Aubrey spoke of parts of Wiltshire as containing 'the greatest fanatics, even to spiritual madness...the strangest extravagancies of religion that were ever heard of'[63] and 'nothing but Quakers and fanatics'.[64] Not all Quakers were yet associated with pacifism, and in autumn 1662 the constant grinding persecution seems to have suddenly sparked off violent protest. On 26 October 1662 Pepys reported

> All this day soldiers going up and down the town, there being an alarm, and many Quakers and others clapped up, but I believe without any reason: only they say in Dorsetshire there has been some rising discovered.[65]

The Sherborne churchwarden accounts for the same year refer to 5s. 'paid to the widow Whitelord for beer for the soldiers at the rising of the Quakers at Camelhill'.[66]

Around 200 Quakers were imprisoned in Dorset that year. Two and a half years later, after refusing to take the Oath of Allegiance on the grounds that all oaths were unlawful, Edward Tucker was sent to Dorchester gaol, where plague was then raging. At the time there were said to be 30 Quakers at Ryme Intrinseca, and even the village of Halstock included 'one reputed Anabaptist' and two 'reputed Quakers'.[67] Despite routine intolerance and harassment Protestant radicalism remained strong through the reign of Charles II, and significant numbers of Monmouth's unlucky rebels of 1685 had connections with dissent or the Commonwealth.

The wars also caused many other, sometimes very odd, changes in seventeenth century life. Charles I had freed wild boars in the New Forest. The introduction had been highly successful and the boars 'much increased and became terrible to the travellers' but 'in the Civil Wars they were destroyed,'[68] presumably by hungry soldiers. John Aubrey mentions another example:

> When I was a child (and so before the Civil Wars) the fashion was for old women and maids to tell fabulous stories night-imes, of spirits and walking of ghosts etc... When the wars came, and with them liberty of conscience and liberty of inquisition, the phantoms vanished. Now children fear no such things, having heard not of them, and are not checked

with such fears.[69]

This was probably connected to the rapid decline in the number of people brought to trial for witchcraft. The Sherborne accounts for the time include £2 19s. 2d. 'for carrying the supposed witches to Dorchester'[70] and in September 1660 John Fitzjames was ordered to investigate 'the business concerning the witchcraft and consultation with the Devil and evil spirits in Sherborne',[71] but by 1665 such cases were very rare.

Even half a century after King Charles's execution, some people had not escaped a sense of guilt for their behaviour during the Civil Wars. In 1699 George Connington of West Stafford, formerly of Hound Street near Sherborne, died. In his will he left 20s. a year to the poor of Sherborne in perpetuity, as well as a piece of silver plate for the church 'in exoneration of my conscience regarding a horse taken from a soldier in the late civil wars'.[72]

The cost of the devastation wrought by the wars in Dorset is impossible to calculate, and some of the losses were things that could never be replaced. John Aubrey reported:

I went to Parson Stump out of curiosity to see his manuscripts, whereof I had seen some in my childhood, but by that time they were lost and dispersed. His sons were gunners and soldiers, and scoured their guns with them.[73]

Weymouth alone estimated its losses at £20,000, and the fierce fighting and destruction in and around Weymouth and Lyme would help to establish Poole as the pre-eminent port of the county. Even during the Protectorate Poole was able to afford extensive repairs to the town quay, while Lyme Regis had to appeal both to Cromwell and Charles II for large sums of money out of the Lyme customs to maintain the Cobb. Away from the main areas of fighting, the Weld estates around Lulworth and Wool were surveyed in detail in 1641 and again in 1682-4, and four of the six principal manors showed a decline in population in that time, while virtually every farm, pasture, meadow and mill had fallen in rental value.

Any figure for deaths in the county would be speculative. However one recent estimate gives the losses for the Westcountry in general as over 13,000,[74] with perhaps as many again from disease and famine. Although there were no major battles in Dorset, the vast majority of all Civil War deaths occurred during minor skirmishes and sieges, from both of which Dorset suffered more than its fair share. For most of the war Cornwall and Devon were largely or entirely under royalist control, so the losses in those two counties were probably much lower than in heavily fought-over Somerset, Gloucestershire, and Dorset. On this estimate Dorset must have suffered a bare minimum of 3000 battle deaths, quite aside from a comparable increase in mortality from other causes. With a population of the county which was probably about 85,000, that represents a total loss of over 7 per cent of the population of the whole county, a proportion well over twice as high as Britain's losses during the First World War which were said to have destroyed a generation. If we take notice of the casualty figures actually reported at the time, notably the Earl of Warwick's claim of over 2000 dead at the siege of Lyme alone, that figure could easily be doubled.

Clarendon might conclude his great history by declaring:

> after this miraculous restoration of the crown and the church
> and the just rights of Parliament, no nation under heaven can
> ever be more happy, if God shall be pleased to add estab-
> lishment and perpetuity to the blessings He then restored[75]

but Dorset had paid heavily, and the scars remained for many long years.

SELECT BIBLIOGRAPHY

Unpublished Sources

Bankes Archives, DCRO, D/BKL.
Beaminster Churchwarden Accounts, DCRO, PE/BE/CW 1/1.
Bere Regis Churchwarden Accounts, DCRO, PE/BER/CW.
Bloxworth Estate Archives, DCRO, D/BLX.
Bridport Borough Archive, DCRO, DC/BTB.
Bridport Parish Register, DCRO, PE/BTB.
Catalogue of Sherborne School, DCRO, S.235.
Charlton Marshall Churchwardens Accounts, DCRO, PE/CHM/CW.
Christchurch Borough Archive, DCRO, DC/CC.
Commission of Roger Bartlett, DCRO, D/MMD 16/JK16a.
Dorchester Borough Archive, DCRO, DC/DOB.
Folke Parish Register, DCRO, PE/FOL/RE.
Fox-Strangways Archives, DCRO, D124.
Hazelbury Bryan Parish Register, DCRO, PE/HAZ RE1/1.
Letter to Our Loving friends, the Mayor and Corporation of Lyme Regis, Dorset, 10 October 1661, DCRO, PH 184.
Letter of Sir Thomas Fairfax to his father, 4 August 1645, DCRO, PH 522.
Letter to Sir John Stawell from King Charles, 11 February 1644, DCRO, PH 665.
Letter to Sir John Browne and Sir W. Erle, knights, from the inhabitants of Stockelande, DCRO, DI/OR/1.
List of Parishes whose royalist suspects are included, DCRO, RON 22/2/15, PE/BDW OV 69.
List of Royalist pensioners, 1672, DCRO, R/GOO 2992.
List of Royalist soldiers for immediate relief and possible pensions, DCRO, D/RGB 610.
List of Royalist suspects compiled by General Desborough, DCRO, RON 22/2/14.
Lyme Regis Borough Archive, DCRO, DC/LR.
Maiden Newton Parish Register, DCRO, PE/MAD/RE.
Marriage Settlement of Amy Francis and Edmund Prideaux, 14 February 1656, DCRO, D/FAE T60.
Marriage Settlement of Giles, son and heir of Thomas Strangways of Muston, and Margaret, daughter of Sir Henry Ludlow of Maiden Bradley, 1640, DCRO, D/FRA T241.
Materials for a History of the County of Dorset, compiled by A.J.Dunkin, Dorchester Reference Library.
Milton Abbas Churchwardens Accounts, DCRO, D/RGB 631a.
Minute Book of the Dorset Standing Committee, 17 February 1646-16 April 1646, DCRO, D/BKL.
Oborne Parish Register, DCRO, PE/OBN/RE.

A Private Chronology of Denis Bond Esqre of Lutton in the Isle of Purbeck made AD 1636 and 1640 with notes by Thomas Bond of Tyneham, DCRO, D53/1 4H.
Puddletown Churchwardens Accounts, DCRO, PE/PUD/CW.
Quarter Sessions Minutes Order Books, DCRO, QSM.
Sherborne Churchwardens Accounts, DCRO, PE/SH/CW.
Sherborne Parish Register, DCRO, PE/SH RE1/1.
Society of Friends Archive, DCRO, NQ.
A True Note of George Ffoxe's Disbursements from the ninth of Ffebruarie 1643, DCRO, D/SHA/A222.
Two letters from John Bingham, Dorchester Reference Library.
Wareham Town Records, DCRO, D86/T239.
Weld of Chideock Archive, DCRO, D/WCH.
Weld of Lulworth Muniments, DCRO, D/WLC.
Will of Sir Walter Erle, 12 August 1665, DCRO, PE/SML/OV 15.
Wimborne Churchwarden Accounts 1640-92, DCRO, PE/WM CW1/42.
Winchester College Muniments Relating to Dorset, DCRO.

Published Sources

W.C. Abbott, *The Writings and Speeches of Oliver Cromwell*, 4 vols, (Cambridge, Massachusetts, 1937–47).
An Act Prohibiting Correspondence with Charles Stuart or his Party, (1651).
John Adair, *By the Sword Divided*, (1983).
John Adair, *Roundhead General: A Military Biography of Sir William Waller*, (1969).
T. Adams, *A History of the Antient Town of Shaftesbury*, (Shaftesbury, 1808).
The Apologie of Colonel John Were, (1644).
Articles of Agreement between his Excellency Prince Maurice, and the Earl of Stamford upon the Delivery of the City of Excester, (1643).
The Casebook of Sir Francis Ashley JP, Recorder of Dorchester 1614–35, (Dorset Record Society, 1981).
Stuart Asquith, *New Model Army*, (1981).
The Vindication of Richard Atkyns Esquire, As also a Relation of Severall Passages in the Western War, wherein he was Concerned, (1669).
Aubrey's Brief Lives, ed. Andrew Clark, 2 vols, (Oxford, 1898).
Aubrey's Brief Lives and Other Selected Writings, ed. O.L. Dick, (1949).
John Aubrey's Monumenta Britannica, ed. John Fowles, (Sherborne, 1980).
Aubrey's Natural History of Wiltshire, ed. John Britton, (1847).
The Axminster Ecclesiastica, ed. K.W.H. Howard, (Ossett, W.Yorks, 1976).
George Bankes, *The Story of Corfe Castle*, (1853).
Charles Edwards Banks, *Topographical Dictionary of 2885 English Emigrants to New England, 1620–50*, (Baltimore, 1957).
W. Bowles Barrett, *Weymouth and Melcombe Regis in the Time of the Great Civil War*, (Dorchester, 1911).

A.R. Bayley, *The Great Civil War in Dorset 1642–1660*, (Taunton, 1910).

William Beal, *The Fathers of the Wesley Family*, (1862).

J.H. Bettey, *Dorset*, (Newton Abbot, 1974).

Maureen Boddy and Jack West, *Weymouth, an Illustrated History*, (Wimborne, 1983).

Thomas Bond, *History and Description of Corfe Castle in the Isle of Purbeck, Dorset*, (1883).

A.M.Broadley, *The Royal Miracle*, (1912).

Joan Brocklebank, *Affpuddle in the County of Dorset, AD 987–1953*, (Bournemouth, 1968).

Louise Fargo Brown, *The First Earl of Shaftesbury*, (New York, 1933).

A Worthie Speech Spoken in the Honourable House of Commons, January the 17th 1642 by Mr. John Browne Knight of the Shire for the County of Dorset, (1642).

Sir Richard Bulstrode, *Memoirs and Reflections upon the Reign and Government of King Charles I and King Charles II*, (1721).

A.H. Burne and P. Young, *The Great Civil War*, (1959).

Edmund Calamy, *An Abridgement of Mr Baxter's History of his Life and Times, with an Account of the Ministers etc Who Were Ejected after the Restoration of King Charles II*, 2 vols, (1713).

Calendar of State Papers, Domestic.

Camden's *Britannia*, 1695.

John Cannon, *Parliamentary Reform 1640–1832*, (Cambridge, 1973).

Charles Carlton, *Going to the Wars*, (1992).

Thomas Carte, *A Collection of Original Letters and Papers Concerning the Affairs of England from the Year 1641 to 1660*, 2 vols, (1739).

The Cavaliers new Common-Prayer Booke Unclapt, (York, 1644).

Geoffrey Chapman, *The Siege of Lyme Regis*, (Lyme Regis, 1982)

Henry Chessell, *A Portrait of Lyme*, (Lyme Regis, 1974).

W.D. Christie, *A Life of Anthony Ashley Cooper*, 2 vols, (1871).

W.S. Churchill, *Marlborough, His Life and Times*, 4 vols, (1933).

Edward, Earl of Clarendon, *The History of the Rebellion and Civil Wars in England*, ed. Bulkeley Bandinel, 8 vols, (Oxford, 1826).

State Papers Collected by Edward, Earl of Clarendon, ed. R. Scrope and T. Monkhouse, 3 vols, (Oxford, 1767–86).

The Clarke Papers, ed. C.H. Firth, 4 vols, (1891–1901).

A. Lindsay Clegg, *A History of Dorchester, Dorset*, (1972).

A. Lindsay Clegg, *A History of Wimborne Minster and District*, (Bournemouth, 1960).

J.T. Cliffe, *The Puritan Gentry: The Great Puritan Families of Early Stuart England*, (1984).

Norman Cohn, *The Pursuit of the Millennium*, (1970).

Rev. John Collinson, *The History and Antiquities of the County of Somerset*, (Bath, 1791).

A Compleat Collection of Farewell Sermons, (1663).

The Compleat Statesman Demonstrated in the Life, Actions and Politics of that Great Minister of State, Anthony Earl of Shaftesbury, (1683).

T.B. Howell, comp., *A Complete Collection of State Trials*, vols, (1809–16).

A Continuation of the True Narration of the Most Observable Passages in and about Plymouth from January 26 1643 till this Present, (1644).

G. Wingrove Cooke, *The Life of the First Earl of Shaftesbury*, (1836).

Lettice Ashley Cooper, ed., *Two Seventeenth Century Dorset Inventories*, (Dorchester, 1974).

Abiezer Coppe, *Selected Writings*, (1987).

The Manuscripts of the Earl Cowper, Historical Manuscripts Commission, 12th report, (1888).

Patricia Crawford, *Denzil Holles 1598-1680: A Study of his Political Career*, (Royal Historical Society 1979).

C.D. Curtis, *Blake, General-at-Sea*, (Taunton, 1934).

F.J. Harvey Darton, *The Marches of Wessex*, (1922).

Godfrey Davies, *The Early Stuarts*, (Oxford, 1959).

The Declaration of the County of Dorset, shewing their Consent to Joyn with other Counties in this Loyall Work of Redeeming his Majesty and Setling the Kingdom, (1648).

A Declaration of the Knights and Gentry in the County of Dorset who were in His Late Majesty's army, (1660).

The Desires and Resolutions of the Club Men of the Counties of Dorset and Wilts, (1645).

The Dictionary of National Biography.

H.M. Digby, *Sir Kenelm Digby and George Digby, Earl of Bristol*, (1912).

Lettice Digby, *The History of the Digby and Strutt Families*, (1928).

C.A.F. Meekings, ed., *Dorset Hearth Tax Assessments 1662–1664*, (Dorchester, 1951).

Dorset Protestation Returns, (Dorset Records Society, 1912).

F.T.R. Edgar, *Sir Ralph Hopton: The King's Man in the West*, (Oxford, 1968).

Marie de G. Eedle, *A History of Beaminster*, (Chichester, 1984).

G.A. Ellis, *The History and Antiquities of the Borough and Town of Weymouth and Melcombe Regis*, (Weymouth, 1829).

Elizabeth Braithwaite Emmott, *The Story of Quakerism*, (1908).

E.S. de Beer, ed., *The Diary of John Evelyn Esq.*, 6 vols, (Oxford, 1955).

An Exact and True Relation in Relieving the Resolute Garrison of Lyme in Dorsetshire by the Right Honourable Robert Earl of Warwick, Lord High Admiral of England, (1644).

Allan Fea, *The Flight of the King*, (1897).

C.H. Firth, *Cromwell's Army*, (1921).

C.H. Firth and G. Davies, *The Regimental History of Cromwell's Army*, 2 vols, (Oxford, 1940).

John Fowles, *A Short History of Lyme Regis*, (Wimborne, 1982).

Journal of George Fox, 2 vols, (1852).
Antonia Fraser, *Cromwell: Our Chief of Men*, (1973).
Antonia Fraser, *The Weaker Vessel*, (1985).
E.A. Fry, *Dorset Wills*, (British Record Society, 1900).
E.A. Fry and G.S. Fry eds., *Abstracts of the Inquisitones Post Mortem*, (1894).
Thomas Fuller, *The History of the Worthies of England*, (1662).

Peter Gaunt, *The Cromwellian Gazeteer*, (Gloucester, 1987).
Samuel R. Gardiner, *History of the Commonwealth and Protectorate*, 4 vols, (1903).
Samuel R. Gardiner, *History of England from the Accession of James I to the Outbreak of the Civil War*, 10 vols, (New York, 1965).
Thomas Gerard, (published under the name of John Coker), *A Survey of Dorsetshire, Containing the Antiquities and Natural History of that County*, (1732).
G.N. Godwin, *The Civil War in Hampshire 1642–5*, (Southampton, 1904).
Richard L. Greaves and Robert Zaller eds, *Biographical Dictionary of British Radicals in the Seventeenth Century*, (Brighton, 1984).

Derek Hall and Norman Barber, *Colonel Richard Norton's Regiment of Horse*, (Leigh-on-Sea, 1989).
Ann Natalie Hansen, *The Dorchester Group, Puritanism and Revolution*, (Columbus, Ohio, 1987).
Ann Natalie Hansen, *The English Origins of the 'Mary and John' Passengers*, (Columbus, Ohio, 1985).
Happy Newes from Sherborn, and Sherborne Castle, (1642).
Harleian Miscellany, viii, (1811).
K.H.D. Hayley, *The First Earl of Shaftesbury*, (Oxford, 1968).
Sidney Heath, *The Story of Ford Abbey*, (1911).
M.F. Heathcote, *Lulworth and its Neighbourhood*, (Winchester, 1906).
Basil Duke Henning, *The History of Parliament, the House of Commons 1660–90*, (1983).
Christopher Hibbert, *Cavaliers and Roundheads*, (1993).
Christopher Hill, *God's Englishman*, (1970).
Christopher Hill, *The World Turned Upside Down*, (Middlesex, 1975).
Richard Hine, *The History of Beaminster*, (Taunton, 1914).
His Highness Prince Rupert's Late Beating up the Rebels Quarters at Post-comb and Chinner in Oxfordshire, (Oxford, 1643).
His Majesty's Resolution Concerning the Setting up of his Standard, (1642).
Historical Manuscripts Commission, 9, *Calendar of the Manuscripts of the most honourable the Marquess of Salisbury*, (1971).
Sixth Report of the Royal Commission on Historical Manuscripts, (1877).
Historical Manuscripts Commission, *7th report*, (1879).
Historical Manuscripts Commission, *13th Report*, (1891).
The Historical Passages of England Since the Beginning of this Miserable Blood-shed and Breach of All GoodLawes by Rebells, (1643).

The History of King-Killers, or the Fanatick Martyrology, 2 vols, (1720).

The Memoirs of Denzil, Lord Holles, (1699).

Gervase Holles, *Memorials of the Holles Family*, (1937).

Bellum Civile, Hopton's Narrative of his campaign in the West 1642–4, ed. Charles E.H. Chadwyck-Healey, (Somerset Record Society, 1902).

John Camden Hotten, *Lists of Emigrants to America, 1600–1700*, (Baltimore, 1962).

A Genuine and Faithful Account of the sufferings of William Houlbrook, Blackmsith of Marlborough, in the reign of King Charles I, (1744).

Roger Howell, *Cromwell*, (1977).

Pennethorne Hughes, *Witchcraft*, (1952).

The Humble Petition of the Inhabitants of the County of Dorset, presented to His Majesty at Ragland the 8th of July 1645. With his Majesties Gratious Answer thereunto, (Oxford, 1645).

John Hutchins, *The History and Antiquities of the County of Dorset*, 4 vols, (Westminster, 1861-74).

Memoirs of the Life of Colonel Hutchinson by his widow Lucy, ed. C.H. Firth, (1885).

Alex Janes and Yvonne Potter, eds., *Westcountry Voices from the Civil War*, (Okehampton, 1992).

The Journals of the House of Commons.

The Journals of the House of Lords.

Joyful Newes from Plymouth, being an Exact Relation of a Great Victory Obtained against the Cornish Cavaliers, (1643).

Laurence Keen and Ann Carreck eds., *Historic Landscape of the Weld Estate, Dorset*, (East Lulworth, 1987).

Barbara Kerr, *Bound to the Soil, A Social History of Dorset*, (1968).

P. Lemmey, *A History of Halstock*, (Halstock, 1986).

A Letter from Sir Anthony Ashley Cooper, Thomas Scot, Io Berners and John Weaver Esquiers, Delivered to the Lord Fleetwood, (1659).

A Letter from the Right Honourable Edward Lord Montagu, one of the Commissioners attending His Majesty, (1647).

A Letter from the Right Honourable Robert Earl of Warwick, Lord High Admiral of England, to the Speaker of the House of Peeres, (11 June 1644).

A Letter from Sir Lewis Dyve, Written out of France to a Gentleman, a Friend of his in London, Giving him an Account of the Manner of his Escape out of the King's Bench and the Reasons that Moved him thereunto, (1648).

A Letter sent from the Right Honourable Robert, Earl of Warwick to the Right Honourable the Speaker to the House of Peers Concerning the Present State and Condition, with the Manner of the Raising of the Siege of Lyme, (18 June 1644).

A Letter sent to the Right Honourable William Lenthall, Esquire, Speaker to the Honourable House of Commons, Concerning the Raising of the Siege of

Taunton by the Parliament's Forces, (1645).
The Works of John Locke, 9 vols, (1824).
The Lord Marquesse of Hertford, His Letter Sent to the Queen in Holland, (1642)
The Memoirs of Edmund Ludlow, ed. C.H. Firth, 2 vols, (Oxford, 1894).

Wallace T. MacCaffrey, *Exeter 1540–1640*, (Cambridge, Massachusetts, 1958).
R.Machin, ed., *Probate Inventories and Manorial Excerpts of Chetnole, Leigh and Yetminster*, (Bristol, 1976).
Arthur Weight Matthews, *A Descriptive and Historical Account of West Bay*, (1901).
William Matthews, ed., *Charles II's Escape from Worcester*, (1967).
Thomas May, *The History of the Parliament of England which began November the 3rd 1640*, 3 vols, (1647).
C.H. Mayo, *Bibliotheca Dorsetiensis*, (1885).
C.H. Mayo, ed., *The Minute Books of the Dorset Standing Committee, 23 September 1646 to 8 May 1650*, (Exeter, 1902).
C.H. Mayo ed., *The Municipal Records of the Borough of Dorchester*, (Exeter 1908).
C.H. Mayo, ed., *The Municipal Records of the Borough of Shaftesbury*, (Sherborne, 1889).
Memoirs of the Court of Charles II by Count Grammont. Also The King's Account of His Escape from Worcester, as Dictated to Pepys, and The Boscobel Tracts, (1891).
Mercurius Belgicus, or a Briefe Chronologie of the Battails, Sieges, Conflicts and Other Most Remarkable Passages from the Beginning of this Rebellion to the 25th March 1646, (1646).
Mercurius Rusticus, the Country's Complaint, Recounting the Sad Events of this Unparraleld Warr, (1646).
The Message of John Lambert Esq in Answer to the Proclamation, (1660).
Anna Milford, ed., *Eye and Ear Witnesses*, (Leigh-on-Sea 1992).
John Morrill,ed., *The Impact of the English Civil War*, (1991).
John Morrill, *The Revolt of the Provinces: Conservatives and Radicalism in the English Civil War*, (1980).
A.L. Morton, *The World of the Ranters*, (1970).
H.J. Moule, *A Descriptive Catalogue of the Charters, Minute Books and other Documents of the Borough of Weymouth and Melcombe Regis, 1252–1800*, (Weymouth, 1883).
H.J. Moule, *Old Dorset*, (1893).
Jerom Murch, *A History of the Presbyterian and General Baptist Churches in the West of England*, (1835).

A Narration of the Great Victry (through God's Providence) Obtained by the Parliament's Forces under Sir William Waller at Alton in Surrey, (1643).
Mark Noble, *The Lives of the English Regicides and other Commissioners of the Pretended High Court of Justice*, 2 vols, (1798).

George Oliver, *Collections Illustrating the History of the Catholic Religion in the Counties of Cornwall, Devon, Dorset, Somerset, Wilts and Gloucester,* (1857).

Vere L. Oliver, *Calendar of Dorset Deeds,* (Dorchester, 1932).

Carola Oman, *Elizabeth of Bohemia,* (1938).

Carola Oman, *Henrietta Maria,* (1936).

An Ordinance of the Lords and Commons Assembled in Parliament, (1 July 1644).

An Ordinance of the Lords and Commons Assembled in Parliament for the Raising of Moneys to be Imployed Towards the Maintenance of Forces within this Kingdom, (1647).

Samuel Palmer, *The Nonconformists' Memorial,* (1775).

Joseph Frank Payne, *Thomas Sydenham,* (1900).

Stuart Peachey and Alan Turton, *The Fall of the West,* (Bristol, 1994).

The Diary and Correspondence of Samuel Pepys, 4 vols, (1908–11).

Thomas Perkins and Herbert Pentin, *Memorials of Old Dorset,* (1907).

A Phanatique League and Covenant solemnly entered into by Affectors of the Good Old Cause, (1660).

The Poetry of Anna Matilda, to which are added Recollections, Printed from an Original Manuscript, written by General Sir William Waller, (1788).

Richard Polwhele, *The History of Devonshire,* (1793-1806).

F.W. Popham, *A West Country Family: The Pophams,* (Sevenoaks, 1976).

Stephen Porter, *Destruction in the English Civil Wars,* (Stroud, 1994).

J. Powell and E. Timings, eds., *Documents Relating to the Civil War, 1642–1648,* (Naval Records Society, 1963).

The Proceedings of the Army under the Command of Sir Thomas Fairfax from the 1st of August to the seventh of the Same, (1645).

A Proclamation for the Discovery and Apprehending of Charles Stuart and other Traytors his Adherents and Abettors, (1651).

A Proclamation of His Majesties Grace Favour and Pardon to the Inhabitants of His County of Dorset, (Oatlands, 1642).

R.B. Pugh, *Old Wardour Castle,* (1984).

George P.R. Pulman, *The Book of the Axe,* (Bath, 1969).

Rawleigh Redivivus: or the Life and Death of the Right Honourable Anthony Late Earl of Shaftesbury, (1683).

Joad Raymond, ed., *Making The News,* (Stow, 1993).

A Relation of the Actions of the Parliament's Forces under the Command of the Earl of Bedford, Generall of the Horse, against those which Came from Shirbourn unto Babell-hill neer unto Yerrell, (1642).

Report on Manuscripts in Various Collections, i, (1901) and iv, (Dublin, 1907).

Walter Richards, *Lyme Regis Baptists 1653–1953,* (Lyme, 1953).

George Roberts, *The History and Antiquities of the Borough of Lyme Regis and Charmouth,* (1834).

George Roberts, *The Social History of the People of the Southern Counties of England in Past Centuries*, (1856).

W. Hamilton Rogers, *Memorials of the West*, (Exeter, 1888).

W. Hamilton Rogers, *West Country Stories and Sketches*, (Exeter, 1895).

Frances Rose-Troup, *John White, the Patriarch of Dorchester*, (New York, 1930).

Frances Rose-Troup, *The Massachusetts Bay Company and its Predecessors*, (New York, 1930).

A.L. Rowse, ed., *The West in English History*, (1949).

John Rushworth, *Historical Collections*, (1692).

John Rutter, *An Historical and Descriptive Account of the Town of Shaftesbury*, (1827).

E.S. Scroggs, *A Brief Guide to the Municipal Records of Bridport*, (Bridport, 1953).

A Second Letter sent from John Ashe Esquire, a Member of the House of Commons, to the Honourable William Lenthall Esq Speaker to the House of Commons in Parliament, Concerning Divers Messages and Passages between the Marquess Hertford, Lord Paulet, Lord Seymour, Lord Coventry and Others his Majesty's Commissioners, (1642).

R.R. Sellman, *Illustrations of Dorset History*, (1960).

Edward Sexby, *Killing no Murder*, (1657).

A Sermon preached at the funeral of the right honourable Denzil Lord Holles, (1680).

Kevin Sharpe, *The Personal Rule of Charles I*, (New Haven, 1992).

Leonard J.Shaw, ed., *Borough and County of the Town of Poole, Calendar of Local Archives*, (Poole, 1958–72).

William A. Shaw, *A History of the English Church during the Civil Wars and under the Commonwealth, 1640–60*, 2 vols, (1900).

Basil Short and John Sales, *The Book of Bridport*, (Buckingham, 1980).

Bernard C. Short, *Early Days of Nonconformity in Poole*, (Poole, 1927).

Sir Thomas Fairfax's Letter to the Honorable William Lenthall Esq; Speaker of the House of Commons, Concerning the Taking of Sherborn Castle, (1645).

The Speech of Dr Robert Skinner, Lord Bishop of Bristol, at the Visitation of Dorchester, September 18, 1637, (1744).

H.P. Smith, *The History of the Borough and County of the Town of Poole*, 2 vols, (Poole, 1951).

Joshua Sprigg, *Anglia Rediviva, England's Recovery* (1854).

James H. Stark, *Dorchester Day, Celebration of the 279th Anniversary of the Settlement of Dorchester*, (Boston, 1909).

Strange, True and Lamentable newes from Exeter and Other Parts of the Western Countreyes Showing how Cruelly the Resolute Cavaliers have Dealt with the Inhabitants, (1643).

James Strong, *Joanereidos: or, Feminine Valour; Eminently Discovered in Western Women, At the Siege of Lyme*, (1674).

The Day of Revelation of the Righteous Judgement of God, Delivered in a Sermon

Preached to the Honorable House of Commons by William Stag, (1646).

G.F. Sydenham, *The History of the Sydenham Family*, (East Molesey, 1928).

John Sydenham, *The History of the Town and County of Poole*, (Poole, 1839).

Richard Symonds, *The Complete Military Diary*, ed. Stuart Peachey, (Leigh-on-Sea, 1989).

H.G. Tibbutt, *The Life and Letters of Sir Lewis Dyve*, (Bedfordshire Historical Records Society, 1948).

H.G. Tibbutt, ed., *The Tower of London Letter-Book of Sir Lewis Dyve*, (Bedfordshire Historical Records Society, 1958).

To the King's Most Excellent Majesty, the Humble Address of the Nobility and Gentry of the County of Dorset, (1660).

To the Right Honourable the Parliament of England Assembled at Westminster, the Humble Petition of Arthur Haselrig, (1659).

Dorothea Townshend, *George Digby 2nd Earl of Bristol*, (1924).

Three Severall Letters of Great Importance, (1644).

A Collection of the State Papers of John Thurloe Esq., ed. T.Birch, 7 vols, (1742).

The Tragedy of the King's Armies Fidelity since their Entring into Bristol Together with the Too Late Repentance of the Inhabitants, (1643).

G.M. Trevelyan, *England under the Stuarts*, (1904).

A True and Impartiall relation of the Battaile betwixt his Majesties Army and that of the Rebels near Newbury in Berkshire, (1643).

A True and Perfect Relation of the Barbarous and Cruell Passages of the King's Army at Old Brainceford neer London, (1642).

The True Copie of a Letter from an Inhabitant of Bridgewater in the County of Somerset, (1643).

A True Description of a Treacherous Plot intended against this Kingdom by the Lord Digby and his assistants at Sherborne in the County of Dorset, (1642).

A True Discovery of the Great and Glorious Victory of that Victorious and Ever Renowned Patriott Sir William Waller Knight, at Christ Church in Hampshire, (1644).

A True Relation of a Plot to Betray the Towne of Poole in the County of Dorset, (1643).

A True Relation of the Dorsetshire Affairs: Particularly of the Surrender of the Townes of Dorchester and Waymouth in that County: and of the Late Siege of Corfe Castle in the Isle of Purbeck, (1643)

A True Relation of the Great and Glorious Victory through God's Providence, obtained by Sir William Waller, Sir Arthur Haselrig and Others of the Parliament's Forces against the Marquess of Hertford, Prince Maurice, Sir Ralph Hopton and Others, (1643).

G. Lyon Turner, ed., *Original Records of Early Nonconformity under Persecution and Indulgence*, (1911).

J.S. Udall, *Charles II in Dorset*, (Dorchester, 1887).

David Underdown, *Fire from Heaven*, (1992).

David Underdown, *Revel, Riot and Rebellion*, (Oxford, 1985).

David Underdown, *Royalist Conspiracy in England, 1649–60*, (New Haven, 1960).

David Underdown, *Somerset in the Civil War and Interregnum*, (Newton Abbot, 1973).

The Unhappy Marksman or a Perfect and Impartial Discovery of that Late Barbarous and Unparalleled Murder Committed by Mr George Strangways formerly a Major in the King's Army, on his Brother-in-Law Mr John Fassel, an Attorney on Friday 11th February, (1659).

John Vicars, *Jehovah-Jireh, God in the Mount or England's Parliamentary Chronicle*, (1644).

John Vicars, *God's Arke Over-topping the World's Waves, or the Third Part of the Parliamentary Chronicle*, (1646).

John Vicars, *The Burning Bush not Consumed, or the Fourth and Last Part of the Parliamentary Chronicle*, (1646).

The Victoria History of the County of Wiltshire, (1955–91).

The Victoria History of the County of Dorset, (1975).

The Victoria History of the County of Somerset, (1906–85).

The Victoria History of Hampshire and the Isle of Wight, ed. William Page, (1900-12).

Thomas Wainwright, comp., *Bridport Records and Ancient Manuscripts*, taken from the Bridport News *1898–9*.

Sir Edward Walker, *Historical Discourses upon Several Occasions*, (1705).

John Walker, *An Attempt towards Recovering an Account of the Numbers and Sufferings of the Clergy of the Church of England*, (1714).

Cyril Wanklyn, *Lyme Leaflets*, (1944).

C.V. Wedgwood, *The King's Peace*, (1955).

C.V. Wedgwood, *The King's War*, (1958).

C.V. Wedgwood, *The Trial of Charles I*, (1964).

Maureen Weinstock, *Old Dorset*, (Newton Abbot, 1967).

Maureen Weinstock, *Studies in Dorset History*, (Dorchester, 1953).

Maureen Weinstock, *More Studies in Dorset History*, (Dorchester, 1960).

Maureen Weinstock, ed., *Weymouth and Melcombe Regis Minute Book, 1625–60*, (Dorchester, 1964).

William West, *A History of the Forest or Chace known by the name of Cranborn Chace*, (Gillingham, 1816).

C.D. Whetham and W.D. Whetham, *A History of the Life of Colonel Nathaniel Whetham*, (1907).

B.R. White, ed., *Association Records of the Particular Baptists of England, Ireland and Wales to 1660*.

John White, *The Planters Plea, or the Grounds of Plantations Examined*, (1630).

John White, *A Sermon preached at Dorchester in the county of Dorset at the Generall Assizes held the 7th of March 1632*, (1648).

The Troubles of Jerusalem's Restauration or the Church's Reformation, Represented in a Sermon Preached before the Right Honourable House of

Lords in the Abbey Church Westminster, November 26, 1645 by John White, (1646).

John White, *A Way to the Tree of Life, Discovered in Sundry Directions for the Profitable Reading of the Scriptures*, (1647).

Bulstrode Whitelock, *Memorials of the English Affairs*, (1732).

William Whiteway of Dorchester, His Diary 1618–1635, ed. David Underdown, (Dorchester, 1991).

W.B. Wildman, *A Short History of Sherborne from 705 AD*, (Sherborne, 1902).

Browne Willis, *Notitia Parliamentaria, or an History of the Counties, Cities and Boroughs in England and Wales*, (1716).

D.T. Witcombe, *Charles II and the Cavalier House of Commons*, (Manchester, 1966).

Anthony Wood, *Athenae Oxonienses*, 2 vols, (1691–2).

A.H. Woolrych, *Penruddock's Rising*, (1968).

T. Worthington, *Chideock Historical and other Notes*, (Bridport, 1880).

H.A. Wyndham, *A Family History 1410–1688, The Wyndhams of Norfolk and Somerset*, (Oxford, 1939).

Peter Young, *Civil War England*, (1981).

Peter Young, *The English Civil War*, (1973).

Peter Young and Wilfrid Emberton, *Sieges of the Great Civil War*, (1978).

Peter Young and Richard Holmes, *The English Civil War, A Military History of the Three Civil Wars 1642–51*, (1974).

C. Zillwood, printer, *An Historical and Descriptive Guide to the Antiquities of Dorchester*, (Dorchester, 1827).

Articles

Peter Alford, 'Richard Alford of Lyme Regis,' *SDNQ*, xxv, (1950), 195–9.

D.G. Allan, 'The Rising in the West 1628–31', *Economic History Review*, 2nd series, V, (1952–3), 76–85.

D. Allen, 'The "Weymouth" and "Salisbury" Mints of Charles I', *British Numismatic Journal*, 23, (1941), 97–117.

W.B. Barrett, 'Weymouth and Melcombe Regis in the Time of the Great Civil War,' *Dorset Proc.*, xxxi, (1910), 204–29.

R.G. Bartelot, 'Archdeacon Ironside: Two Letters from the John Walker MSS,' *SDNQ*, xix, (1929), 208–12.

R.G. Bartelot, 'Burials of Soldiers during the Civil War', *SDNQ*, xvii, (1923), 62–3.

R.G. Bartelot, 'A Dorset Civil War Pass, 1644', *SDNQ*, xix, (1929), 119.

R.G. Bartelot, 'Dorset Royalist Roll of Honour 1662–1672', *SDNQ*, xviii, (1926), 8995, 165–7, 200–3; xix, (1929), 43–6, 139–42.

R.G. Bartelot, 'The Last of the Turbervilles', *SDNQ*, xix, (1929), 5–8, 36–40, 104–6, 166–8, 248–9.

R.G. Bartelot, 'Sherborne and the Civil War', *SDNQ*, xix, (1929), 3.

George J. Bennett, 'Wareham, its Invasions and Battles', *Dorset Proc.*, xiii, (1892), 82–114.

J.H. Bettey, 'The Revolts over the Enclosure of the Royal Forest at Gillingham 1626–1630', *Dorset Proc.*, 97, (1975), 21–24.

J.H. Bettey, 'Dorset Churchwardens' Presentments in the Early 17th century', *SDNQ*, xxix, (1974), 263–5.

J.H. Bettey, 'Parish Life in Dorset during the Early 17th century', *Dorset Proc.*, 114, (1992), 9–12.

J.H. Bettey, 'A Penitent at Charminster, 1631', *SDNQ*, xxix, (1974), 257–8.

J.H. Bettey, 'Varieties of Men: Contrasts among the Dorset Clergy during the 17th Century', *SDNQ*, xxxii, (1991), 846–50.

N. du Quesne Bird, 'The Goldsmiths of Dorset', *SDNQ*, xxxiii, (1993), 235–60.

A.M. Broadley, 'The Dorset Clubmen', *SDNQ*, viii, (1903), 347–9.

A.M. Broadley, 'An Important Somerset and Dorset Civil War Letter', *SDNQ*, xi, (1909), 157–9.

A.M. Broadley, 'The Proclaiming of Charles II at Sherborne', *SDNQ*, xiii, (1913), 179–81.

A.M. Broadley, 'Robert Blake, the Siege of Lyme and the Battle of Portland', *SDNQ*, xiii, (1913), 57–8.

James A. Casada, 'Dorset Politics in the Puritan Revolution', *Southern History* iv, 1982.

James A. Casada, 'Corfe Castle: New Evidence on the Second Siege', *SDNQ*, xxix, (1974).

Benjamin G. Cox, 'Some 17th Century German Protestant Refugees at Blandford Forum', *SDNQ*, xxxiii, (1991), 53–7.

C.D. Curtis, 'Robert Blake, General-at-sea', *SDNQ*, xxix, (1974), 142–3, 166–70.

G.J. Davies, 'Early Dorset Nonconformity', *Dorset Proc.*, 97, (1975), 24–30.

P. Drake, 'Captain John Chaffin of Sherborne', *SDNQ*, xxxii, (1991), 576–8.

E.H. Fairbrother, 'Dorset Commonwealth Ministers, 1657', *SDNQ*, xiii, (1913), 233–4.

J.P. Ferris, 'The Gentry of Dorset on the Eve of the Civil War', *The Genealogist's Magazine*, (1965).

J.P. Ferris, 'Two Forgotten Dorset Authors', *SDNQ*, xxix, (1974), 155–7.

J.P. Ferris, 'The Wareham Parliamentary Garrison in 1645', *SDNQ*, xxix, (1974), 245–7.

J.M.J. Fletcher, 'Constantine Jessop, Intruded Minister of Wimborne Minster', *SDNQ*, xvii, (1923), 250–2.

J.M.J. Fletcher, 'A Dorset Worthy, William Stone, Royalist and Divine', *Dorset Proc.*, xxxvi, (1915), 16–27.

J.M.J. Fletcher, 'Wimborne Minster during the Period of the Civil War and the Commonwealth', *SDNQ*, xviii, (1926), 258–61.

J.K. Floyer, 'Mr John Brice, Minister of Charmouth', *SDNQ*, xviii, (1926), 273–6.

Michael Foster, 'Sir Troilus Turberville', *Royal Stuart Papers*, xvi, 1980.

E.A. Fry, 'Absentees from Divine Worship in Dorset, 1649', *SDNQ*, xi, (1909), 307.

E.A. Fry, 'The Augmentation Books 1650–60 in Lambeth Palace Library', *Dorset Proc.*, xxxvi, (1915), 48–105.

E.A. Fry, 'John Fry the Regicide', *SDNQ*, i, (1888–9), 53–6 and 73–4.

George S. Fry, 'Captain Hugh Fry of the Angel Inn, Shaftesbury 1654–86', *SDNQ*, xxi, (1935), 79–82.

George S. Fry, 'The Clubmen and the Leaders in the Fight on Hambledon Hill', *SDNQ*, xviii, (1926), 157–9, 169–72.

George S. Fry, 'John Fry, M.P. for Shaftesbury', *SDNQ*, xxii, (1938), 272.

George S. Fry, 'John Fussell, A forgotten Blandford Worthy, 1622–59', *SDNQ*, xxi, (1935), 15–18.

George S. Fry, 'Quakers in Dorset, 1656', *SDNQ*, xxii, (1938), 143, 165–6, 215.

T. Goodwin, 'Varying Degrees of Royalism in One Area of West Dorset', *SDNQ*, xxxiv, (1996), 49-56.

J. Elise Gordon, 'The Highmore Family of Dorset', *Journal of the Sherborne Historical Society*, iii, (1966).

T.B. Groves, 'The Dorset Colony in Massachusetts, USA', *Dorset Proc.*, ix, (1888), 100–17.

J.O. Halliwell, 'On the Municipal Archives of Dorset', *Journal of the British Archaeological Association*, xxviii, (1872), 28–31.

Helen Andrews Kaufman, 'Colonel Bullen Reymes', *Dorset Worthies*, no. 9, (Dorchester, 1964).

L.G.W. Legg, ed., 'Relation of a Short Survey of the Western Counties, 1635', *Camden Miscellany*, xvi, (1936).

J.C. Mansell-Pleydell, 'On Sorcery and Witchcraft', *Dorset Proc.*, v, (1884), 1–15.

C.H. Mayo, 'Commonwealth Levy on the County of Dorset, 1653', *SDNQ*, xi, (1909), 78–9.

C.H. Mayo, 'Langton Long, Blandford, Churchwardens' Account Book', *SDNQ*, iii, (1893), 18–24, 56–62.

C.H. Mayo, 'Migration from Symondsbury, Dorset, to New England in 1635', *SDNQ*, xii, (1911), 290–1.

C.H. Mayo, 'Sir Richard Strode's Annotated Almanac', *SDNQ*, viii, (1903), 201-6, 244-9.

G. Andrews Moriarty, 'Dorset People in New England', *SDNQ*, xix, (1929), 73–8.

J.S. Morrill, 'Mutiny and Discontent in English Provincial Armies 1645–7', *Past and Present*, 56, (1972), 49–74.

H.J. Moule, 'Notes on a Minute Book Belonging to the Mayor and Corporation of Dorchester', *Dorset Proc.*, xv, (1894), 142–63.

Hugh Norris, 'King Charles II at Coaxden Hall', *SDNQ*, iii, (1893), 306–13; iv, (1895), 6–12.

W.H. Parry Okeden, 'Dorchester, Massachusetts', *SDNQ*, xxii, (1938), 169–72.

V.L. Oliver, 'Captain Richard Yardley', *SDNQ*, xix, (1929), 178–9.

J.A.M. Overholt, 'Colonel Francis Bluett,' *SDNQ*, xxxiii, (1955), 390.

J.H.P. Pafford, 'John Clavell, 1601–43, Burglar, Highwayman, Poet, Dramatist, Doctor, Lawyer', *SDNQ*, xxxii, (1991), 549–63.

Herbert Pentin, 'Bishop Henchman: the Cavalier Rector of Portland', *Dorset Year Book*, 1958–9, 37.

Herbert Pentin, 'A Dorset Parish during the Commonwealth', *Dorset Proc.*, 65, (1944), 108–11.

T. Perkins, 'A Sketch of the History of old Wardour Castle', *Dorset Proc.*, xv, (1894), 26–35.

F.P. Pitfield, 'Articles on the History of Bere Regis', *Bere Regis Parish Magazine* (July 1961-November 1966).

F.J. Pope, 'The Adventure to New England from Dorchester in 1623', *SDNQ*, x, (1907), 107–8.

F.J. Pope, 'Dorset Seamen in the Second Dutch War', *SDNQ*, xiii, (1913), 118–21.

F.J. Pope, 'Dorset Soldiers in the Tudor and Early Stuart Periods', *Dorset Proc.*, xxxviii, (1918), 34–52.

F.J. Pope, 'Puritans at Shaftesbury in the Early Stuart Period', *SDNQ*, xiii, (1913), 160–2.

F.J. Pope, 'Sidelights on the Civil War in Dorset', *SDNQ*, xii, (1911), 52–5.

F.J. Pope, 'More Sidelights on the Civil War in Dorset', *SDNQ*, xiv, 1–3.

J.R. Powell, 'Blake and the Defence of Lyme Regis', *Mariners Mirror*, 20, 448–74.

W. de C. Prideaux, 'The Monumental Brasses of Dorsetshire', *Journal of the British Archaeological Association*, (December 1907), 209–226.

W.W. Ravenhill, 'Records of the Rising in the West', *Wiltshire Archaeological Magazine*, (1870), xiii, 119–88, 252–73, xiv, 38–67, xv, 1–41.

William Rhodes, 'The Battle for Weymouth in the Civil War', *Dorset Year Book*, (1963–4), 71.

Nelson Moore Richardson, 'The Travels of Peter Mundy in Dorset, 1635', *Dorset Proc.*, xlii, (1922), 42–50.

Ann Smith, 'A Brief Chronologie', *SDNQ*, xxxii, (1991), 759.

G.D. Squibb, 'The Civil War in Weymouth', *SDNQ*, xxii, (1938), 40–1.

G.D. Squibb, 'Dorset Incumbents 1542–1731', *Dorset Proc.*, 70, (1948), 99–117; 71, (1949), 110–132; 72, (1950), 111–128; 73, (1951), 141–62; 74, (1952), 60–78; 75, (1953), 115–132.

G.D. Squibb, 'Dring's List of Royalist Compounders for Dorset', *SDNQ*, xxii, (1938), 28–30.

Henry Symonds, 'The War in Dorset 1642–5', *SDNQ*, xii, (1911), 193–5.

Henry Symonds, 'Sandsfoot and Portland Castles', *Dorset Proc.*, xxxv, (1914), 27.

Robert Temple, 'The Massey Brigade in the West', *SDNQ*, xxxi, (1986), 437–45.

S.J.P. Thomas, 'Dorset and Parliament in the Great Civil War', *Dorset Year Book*, 1964–5, 165.

J.S. Udal, 'Charles II in Dorset', *Dorset Proc.*, viii, (1887), 9–28.

J.S. Udal, 'Charles II in West Dorset', *Notes and Queries*, 9th series, x, (1902), 141–4.

J.S. Udal, 'Dorset Seventeenth Century Tokens', *Dorset Proc.*, ix, (1888), 41–54.

J.S. Udal, 'Witchcraft in Dorset', *Dorset Proc.*, xiii, (1892), 35–56.

David Underdown, 'The Chalk and the Cheese, Contrasts Among the English Clubmen', *Past and Present*, 85, (1979), 25–48.

A.W. Vivian-Neal, 'Ship Money, Long Bredy Dorset', *SDNQ*, xx, (1930–2), 234–5.

T. Hedley White, 'Dr Thomas Sydenham', *Dorset Worthies* no. 20.

NOTES

Chapter 1

1 E.B. Emmott, *The Story of Quakerism,* (1908), 8.

2 Anthony Wood, *Athenae Oxonienses,* 2 vols, (1691–2), ii, 60.

3 W.C. Christie, *A Life of Anthony Ashley Cooper,* 2 vols, (1871), i, app. 1, xx.

4 Edward, Earl of Clarendon, *The History of the Rebellion and Civil Wars in England,* ed. Bulkeley Bandinel, 8 vols, (Oxford, 1826), 4, vii, 213.

5 *The Case Book of Sir Francis Ashley JP, Recorder of Dorchester 1614–1636,* ed. J.H. Bettey, (Dorset Record Society, 1981), 91.

6 Calendar of State Papers, Domestic, 1644–5, 216–7.

7 Clarendon, 1, i, 131.

8 *Aubrey's Brief Lives and Other Selected Writings,* ed. O.L. Dick, (1949), xix.

9 John Adair, *Roundhead General: A Military Biography of Sir William Waller,* (1969), 30.

10 *Case Book of Sir Francis Ashley,* 94–5.

11 *William Whiteway of Dorchester, His Diary 1618–35,* ed. David Underdown, (Dorchester, 1991), 87.

12 Dorset County Record office, PE/BER/CW5–6.

13 Samuel R. Gardiner, *History of England from the Accession of James I to the Outbreak of the Civil War,* 10 vols., (New York, 1965), vi, 253.

14 CSPD, 1625–49, 204–5.

15 DCRO, D1/OR 1.

16 Thomas Wainwright, comp., *Bridport Records and Ancient Manuscripts taken from the* Bridport News *1898–9,* 38.

17 C.H. Mayo, ed., *The Municipal Records of the Borough of Shaftesbury,* (Sherborne, 1889), 31.

18 C.H. Mayo, *The Municipal Records of the Borough of Dorchester,* (Exeter, 1908), 676.

19 MRBD, 677.

20 A.R. Bayley, *The Great Civil War in Dorset, 1642–60,* (Taunton, 1910), 12.

21 George Roberts, *The Social History of the People of the Southern Counties of England in Past Centuries,* (1856), 125.

22 H.J. Moule, *Descriptive Catalogue of the Charters, Minute Books and other Documents of the Borough of Weymouth and Melcombe Regis, 1252–1800,* (Weymouth, 1883), 174.

23 *The Planters Plea, or the Grounds of Plantations Examined,* (1630), 17–19.

24 Richard Eburne, 'The Pathway to Plantations', in A.J. Dunkin, comp., *Materials for a History of the County of Dorset,* ii, 35–6.

25 *Diary of William Whiteway,* 110.

26 *Diary of William Whiteway,* 113.

27 CSPD, 1629–31, 186.

28 CSPD, 1627–8, 16.

29 *Bridport Records and Ancient Manuscripts,* 40.

30 Roberts, *Social History*, 264.

31 CSPD, 1627–8, 16.

32 CSPD, 1628–9, 485.

33 T.B. Howell, comp., *A Complete Collection of State Trials*, (1809), iii, 294.

34 DCRO, D/FSI, Box 260.

35 Gervase Holles, *Memorials of the Holles Family*, (1937), 106.

36 Frances Rose-Troup, *John White, Patriarch of Dorchester*, (New York, 1930), 241.

37 *Diary of William Whiteway*, 108.

38 Bayley, 26.

39 CSPD, 1631–3, 381.

40 DCRO, D 53/1 4H.

41 *Diary of William Whiteway*, 154.

42 CSPD, 1634–5, 508–9.

43 Moule, *Documents of Weymouth and Melcombe Regis*, 141.

44 *Diary of William Whiteway*, 156.

45 DCRO, D 53/1 4H.

46 DCRO, D/BLX L10.

47 *Aubrey's Natural History of Wiltshire*, ed. John Britton, (1847), 75.

48 CSPD, 1636–7, 150–1.

49 Bayley, 5.

50 Roberts, *Social History*, 145.

51 CSPD, 1625–49, 603–4.

52 J.H. Bettey, 'The Revolts over the Enclosure of the Royal Forest at Gillingham 1626–30', *Dorset Proc.*, 97, (1975), 22.

53 John Hutchins, *The History and Antiquities of the County of Dorset*, 4 vols, (Westminster, 1861–74), iii, 623.

54 Bettey, 'The Revolts over the Enclosure', 23.

55 *Case Book of Sir Francis Ashley*, 102.

56 Thomas Gerard, (published under the name of John Coker), *A Survey of Dorsetshire, Containing the Antiquities and Natural History of that County*, (1732), 73.

57 Clarendon, 1, i, 174.

58 *Case Book of Sir Francis Ashley*, 99.

59 Mayo, ed., *Municipal Records of Shaftesbury*, 30.

60 Roberts, *Social History*, 362.

61 DCRO, DC/DOB 16/4, 27.

62 DCRO, DC/DOB 16/4, 106.

63 *Diary of William Whiteway*, 101.

64 J.H. Bettey, 'A Penitent at Charminster, 1631', SDNQ, xxix, (1974), 258.

65 J.C. Mansell-Pleydell, 'On Witchcraft and Sorcery', *Dorset Proc.*, v, (1884), 1011.

66 *The Speech of Dr Robert Skinner, Lord Bishop of Bristol, at the Visitation at Dorchester, September 18, 1637*, (1744).

67 F.J. Pope, 'The Adventure to New England from Dorchester in 1623', SDNQ, x, (1907), 107.

68 Pope, 'The Adventure', 108.

69 John Vicars, *Jehovah-Jireh, God in the Mount or England's Parliamentary Chronicle*, (1644), 11.

70 Christie, *Anthony Ashley Cooper*, i, app. 1, xvii.

71 Memorial Inscription in Steeple Church.

72 Christie, *Anthony Ashley Cooper*, i, app. 1, xv–xvii.

73 Richard Hine, *The History of Beaminster*, (Taunton, 1914), 355.

74 J.T. Cliffe, *The Puritan Gentry: The Great Puritan Families of Early Stuart England*, (1984), 122.

75 DCRO, PE/SML/OV 15.

76 DCRO, DC/BTB B3 AB81.

77 Hine, *History of Beaminster*, 184–5.

78 H.P. Smith, *The History of the Borough and County of the Town of Poole*, 2 vols, (Poole, 1951), ii, 131–2.

79 John White, *A Sermon preached at Dorchester in the County of Dorset at the Generall Assizes held the 7th of March 1632*, (1648), 8.

80 Hutchins, ii, 402.

81 Wood, *Athenae Oxonienses*, ii, 60–1.

82 White, *Sermon*, 13–14.

83 J.H. Bettey, 'Dorset Churchwardens' Presentments, Early Seventeenth Century', *SDNQ*, xxix, (1974), 265.

84 Mayo, ed., *Municipal Records of Shaftesbury*, 66.

85 Cliffe, The Puritan Gentry, 161.

86 Christie, *Anthony Ashley Cooper*, i, app. 1, xix.

87 Hine, *History of Beaminster*, 88.

88 *Report on Manuscripts in Various Collections*, (1901), 350.

89 Bettey, 'Dorset Churchwardens' Presentments', 264.

90 A. Lindsay Clegg, *A History of Wimborne Minster and District*, (Bournemouth, 1960), 94.

91 Gerard, *Survey of Dorsetshire*, 6.

92 Christie, *Anthony Ashley Cooper*, i, app. 1, viii.

93 Christie, *Anthony Ashley Cooper*, i, app. 1, xviii.

94 Christie, *Anthony Ashley Cooper*, i, app. 1, xiii.

95 Christie, *Anthony Ashley Cooper*, i, app. 1, xiv.

96 Christie, *Anthony Ashley Cooper*, i, app. 1, xx–xxi.

97 Cliffe, *The Puritan Gentry*, 193.

Chapter 2

1 Lettice Ashley Cooper, ed., *Two Seventeenth Century Inventories*, (Dorchester, 1974), 7–11.

2 *Aubrey's Natural History of Wiltshire*, 86.

3 P. Lemmey, *A History of Halstock*, (Halstock, 1986), 17–18.

4 R. Machin, ed., *Probate Inventories and Manorial Excerpts of Chetnole, Leigh and Yetminster*, (Bristol, 1976), 27.

5 Historical Manuscripts Commission, 9, p xxii, (1971), 354.

6 Charles Carlton, *Going to the Wars*, (1992), 22.

7 DCRO, DC/DOB 8/1, 275.

8 DCRO, DC/DOB 8/1, 290.

9 Christie, *Anthony Ashley Cooper*, 1, app. 1, xviii.

10 HMC, 9, p xxii, 353.

11 DCRO, DC/DOB 16/4, 59.

12 HMC, 9, p xxii, 353.

13 *State Papers collected by Edward, Earl of Clarendon*, ed. R. Scrope and T. Monkhouse, 3 vols, (Oxford, 1767–86), ii, 121.

14 DCRO, DC/DOB 16/4, 25.

15 CSPD, 1640, 55.

16 CSPD, 1640, 335.

17 CSPD, 1640, 324.

18 CSPD, 1640, 559.

19 Thomas May, *The History of the Parliament of England which Began November the 3rd 1640*, 3 vols, (1647), i, 64.

20 *Memoirs of the Life of Colonel Hutchinson by his widow Lucy Hutchinson*, ed. C.H. Firth, 2 vols, (1885), i, 129.

21 MRBD, 436.

22 Clarendon, 2, iv, 27.

23 DCRO, D 53/1 4H, 30.

24 Hutchins, ii, 402.

25 *State Papers collected by Edward, Earl of Clarendon*, ii, 133.

26 Clarendon, 1, iii, 329.

27 Bayley, 26.

28 Wood, *Athenae Oxonienses*, ii, 428.

29 Sir Richard Bulstrode, *Memoirs and Reflections upon the Reign and Government of King Charles I and King Charles II*, (1721), 193.

30 William A. Shaw, *A History of the English Church during the Civil Wars and under the Commonwealth, 1640–60*, 2 vols, (1900), i, 31.

31 Hutchins, iii, 498.

32 Vicars, *Jehovah-Jireh, God in the Mount*, 32.

33 George Bankes, *The Story of Corfe Castle*, (1853), 91.

34 *Dorset Protestation Returns*, (Dorset Records, 1912), iii.

35 Christie, Anthony Ashley Cooper, i, app. 1, xix.

36 Bankes, *Corfe Castle*, 98.

37 Clarendon, 2, iv, 103n.

38 Clarendon, 2, iv, 99.

39 *A Declaration of the House of Commons, Touching a Late Breach of their Priviledges, Set Forth by Themselves*, (1641).

40 John Rushworth, *Historical Collections*, 8 vols, (1659–1701), v, 478.

41 *Memoirs of Edmund Ludlow*, ed. C.H. Firth, 2 vols, (Oxford, 1894), i, 25.

42 *A Worthie Speech Spoken in the Honourable House of Commons, January the 17th 1642 by Mr John Browne Knight of the Shire for the County of Dorset*, (1642).

43 *The Journals of the House of Commons*, ii, 411.

44 Clarendon, 1, iii, 349.
45 DCRO, DC/DOB 16/4, 49.
46 DCRO, DC/DOB 16/4, 15.
47 May, *History of the Parliament of England*, i, 16.
48 Maureen Weinstock, ed., *Weymouth and Melcombe Regis Minute Book, 1625–60*, (Dorchester, 1964), 50.
49 DCRO, D/RGB 631a.
50 H.J. Moule, 'Notes on a Minute Book belonging to the Mayor and Corporation of Dorchester', *Dorset Proc.*, xv, (1894), 159.
51 MRBD, 544.
52 Minute Book of the Dorset Standing Committee, 17 February 1646 – 16 April 1646, DCRO, D/BKL, 25.
53 C.H.Mayo, ed., *The Minute Books of the Dorset Standing Committee, 23 September 1646 to 8 May 1650*, (Exeter, 1902), 360.
54 DSC, 253–4.
55 DCRO, DC/DOB 16/4, 53.
56 MRBD, 508.
57 Bayley, 39–40.
58 Hutchins, ii, 342.
59 *Aubrey's Natural History of Wiltshire*, 11.
60 Clarendon, 3, vi, 230.
61 *The Vindication of Richard Atkyns Esquire, As also a Relation of Several Passages in the Western War, wherein he was Concerned*, (1669), 18.
62 Clarendon, 3, vi, 550.
63 Bankes, *Corfe Castle*, 125.
64 Bankes, *Corfe Castle*, 134–5.
65 Clarendon, 3, vi, 557.
66 Bankes, *Corfe Castle*, 139.
67 CSPD, 1640, 333.
68 *His Majesty's Resolution Concerning the Setting up of his Standard*, (1642), 2.
69 DCRO, DC/DOB 16/4, 61.
70 CJ, ii, 694.
71 Clarendon, 3, v, 119.
72 Clarendon, 3, vi, 540.
73 Clarendon, 4, viii, 458.
74 F.T.R. Edgar, *Sir Ralph Hopton: The King's Man in the West*, (Oxford, 1968), 23.
75 Clarendon, 2, 2, iv, 282.
76 Rushworth, *Historical Collections*, v, 672–4.
77 Clarendon, 3, vi, 198.
78 *The Lord Marquesse of Hertford, His Letter, Sent to the Queen in Holland*, (1642), 3.
79 Clarendon, 3, vi, 191n.
80 *Hertford, Letter*, 34.
81 *Memoirs of Edmund Ludlow*, i, ed., Firth, 34.

1 L.G.W. Legg, ed., 'Relation of a short survey of the Western Counties, 1635', *Camden Miscellany*, xvi, (1936), 70.

2 John Walker, *An Attempt towards Recovering an Account of the Numbers and Sufferings of the Clergy of the Church of England during the Great Rebellion*, (1714), ii, 394.

3 Walker, *Sufferings of the Clergy*, ii, 394.

4 CJ, ii, 914.

5 *The Message of the Members of the House of Commons, and the Deputy Lieutenants, the Committee of Both Houses of Parliament, for the Preservation of the Peace of the County of Somerset*, (1642), 2.

6 *Bellum Civile, Hopton's Narrative of his campaign in the West 1642–4*, ed. Charles E.H. Chadwyck-Healey, (Somerset Record Society, 1902), 5.

7 Hopton, *Bellum Civile*, 8.

8 David Underdown, *Somerset in the Civil War and Interregnum*, (Newton Abbot, 1973), 45.

9 Vicars, *Jehovah-Jireh, God in the Mount*, 133.

10 Christie, *Anthony Ashley Cooper*, i, app., xx.

11 Gerard, *Survey of Dorsetshire*, 122.

12 Vicars, *Jehovah-Jireh, God in the Mount*, 136.

13 MRBD, 680.

14 DCRO, DC/DOB 20/1.

15 *Happy Newes from Sherborn, and Sherborn Castle*, (1642), 3.

16 Clarendon, 3, vi, 622.

17 Clarendon, 3, vi, 206.

18 *The Historical Passages of England Since the Beginning of the Miserable Blood-shed and Breach of All Good Lawes by Rebells*, (1643), 30.

19 DCRO, D/124 Box 233 (ii), FSI 41A, 8, Giles Strangways, 1.

20 HMC, *12th report*, (1888), ii, 322.

21 Hutchins, iv, 269.

22 Clarendon, vii, 4, 204.

23 *A True Description of a Treacherous Plot Intended against this Kingdom by the Lord Digby and his Assistants at Sherborne in the County of Dorset*, (1642), 3.

24 *His Highness Prince Rupert's Late Beating up of the Rebels Quarters at Postcomb and Chinner in Oxfordshire*, (Oxford, 1643), 16.

25 Hopton, *Bellum Civile*, 13.

26 *Happy Newes from Sherborn*, 4.

27 Bayley, 52.

28 *A Relation of the Actions of the Parliament's Forces under the Command of the Earl of Bedford, Generall of the Horse, against those which Came from Shirbourn unto Babel-hill neer unto Yerrell*, (1642), 7–8.

29 *Parliament's Forces under Bedford*, 4.

30 Hopton, *Bellum Civile*, 15.

31 *Happy Newes from Sherborn*, 4.

32 Christie, *Anthony Ashley Cooper*, i, app. 1, xx.
33 George P.R. Pulham, *The Book of the Axe*, (Bath, 1969), 252.
34 Hopton, *Bellum Civile*, 17.
35 Bayley, 59.
36 £18 13s. 7d. was spent on the attempt. In contrast the slighting of Corfe in 1646 cost well over £300.
37 HMC, *13th Report*, Appendix part i, (1891), i, 64.
38 DCRO, DC/DOB 16/4, 63.
39 DCRO, DC/BTB/H6.
40 DCRO, D/RGB 631a.
41 HMC, *13th Report*, app. part i, i, 64.
42 David Underdown, *Fire from Heaven*, (1992), 153.
43 R.G. Bartelot, 'Archdeacon Ironside: Two Letters from the John Walker MSS', *SDNQ*, xix, (1929), 211.
44 Wood, *Athenae Oxonienses*, ii, 357.
45 Bartelot, 'Archdeacon Ironside', 212. In Hutchins, the rector of Beer Hackett is called Hugh Strode.
46 Bartelot, 'Archdeacon Ironside', 210.
47 DCRO, D/BKL CJ2/2.
48 C.V. Wedgwood, *The King's War*, (1958), 129.
49 May, *History of the Parliament of England*, iii, 33.
50 *A Proclamation of His Majesties Grace Favour, and Pardon, to the Inhabitants of his County of Dorset*, (Oatlands, 1642).
51 DCRO, DC/DOB 16/4, 66.
52 Christie, *Anthony Ashley Cooper*, i, app. 1, xix.
53 Wedgwood, *King's War*, 182.
54 *Memoirs of Denzil, Lord Holles*, (1699), 8.
55 CJ, ii, 987.
56 Adair, *Roundhead General*, 63.
57 Wood, *Athenae Oxonienses*, ii, 298.
58 Clarendon, 4, vii, 114.
59 *Clarendon State Papers*, ii, 155.
60 Vicars, *Jehovah-Jireh, God in the Mount*, 276.
61 *Minutes of the Dorset Standing Committee*, DCRO, D/BKL, 18.
62 *Memoirs of Edmund Ludlow*, ed. Firth, ii, 133.
63 DCRO, DC/DOB 16/4, 73.
64 DCRO, DC/DOB 16/4, 68.
65 DCRO, DC/DOB 16/4, 72.
66 *The Diary of John Evelyn Esq.*, ed. E.S. de Beer, 6 vols, (Oxford, 1955), i, 54.
67 DCRO, PE/WM/CW 1/42.
68 Vicars, *Jehovah-Jireh, God in the Mount*, 303–4.
69 Hutchins, iv, 271.
70 DCRO, PE/SH/CW 1/114.
71 Bayley, 70.
72 Herbert Pentin, 'Bishop Henchman: The Cavalier Rector of Portland',

Dorset Year Book 1958–9, 41.

73 *Aubrey's Natural History of Wiltshire*, 99.

74 *Mercurius Rusticus, The Country's Complaint Recounting the Sad Events of this Unparraleld Warr*, (1646), 41.

75 *Memoirs of Edmund Ludlow*, ed. Firth, i, 51.

76 *Mercurius Rusticus*, 42.

77 *Mercurius Rusticus*, 43.

78 *Mercurius Rusticus*, 46.

79 MRBD, 509.

80 *The Journals of the House of Lords*, vi, 118.

81 Thomas Carte, *A Collection of Original Letters and Papers Concerning the Affairs of England from the Year 1641 to 1660*, 2 vols, (1739), i, 21.

82 *The Works of John Locke*, 9 vols, (1824), viii, 266–7.

83 Legg, 'Survey of the Western Counties', 69–70.

84 *Mercurius Rusticus*, 99.

85 Gerard, *Survey of Dorsetshire*, 54.

86 *Mercurius Rusticus*, 99.

87 *Mercurius Rusticus*, 101.

88 HMC, *Sixth Report*, p 1, report and app., (1877), 84.

89 Similar engines, based on Roman ideas, were used during the royalist siege of Gloucester a few weeks later, with equal lack of success.

90 *Mercurius Rusticus*, 104.

91 Clarendon, 3, vi, 560.

92 J. Powell and E. Timings, ed., *Documents Relating to the Civil War*, (Naval Records Society, 1963), 83–4.

93 *Articles of Agreement between his Excellency Prince Maurice and the Earl of Stamford upon the Delivery of the City of Excester*, (1643), 5.

94 Bankes, *Corfe Castle*, 313–4. In contrast £268 12s. 3d. was spent on powder, match and bullets.

95 *Mercurius Rusticus*, 105.

96 *A True Relation of the Dorsetshire Affaires: Particularly of the Surrender of the Townes of Dorchester and Waymouth, in that County: And of the Late Siege of Corfe Castle in the Isle of Purbeck*, (1643), 3.

97 Clarendon, 4, vii, 213.

98 Bayley, 103.

99 HMC, *13th Report*, App., part 1, (1891), i, 710–1.

Chapter 4

1 *Vindication of Captain Richard Atkyns*, 19–20.

2 Hopton, *Bellum Civile*, 47.

3 *Vindication of Captain Richard Atkyns*, 24.

4 *A True relation of the Great and Glorious Victory through God's Providence, Obtained by Sir William Waller, Sir Arthur Haselrig and others of the Parliament's forces against the marquess of Hertford, Prince Maurice, Sir Ralph Hopton and others*, (1643), 5.

5 *Mercurius Rusticus*, 204.

6 Bayley, 90.

7 Wood, *Athenae Oxonienses*, ii, 100.

8 Clarendon, 4, vii, 108.

9 *The Tragedie of the King's Armies Fidelity since their Entring into Bristol together with the Too Late Repentance of the Inhabitants*, (1643), 4.

10 May, *History of the Parliament of England*, iii, 12.

11 Carola Oman, *Elizabeth of Bohemia*, (1938), 236.

12 Oman, *Elizabeth of Bohemia*, 361.

13 Clarendon, 4, vii, 603.

14 *A True Relation of the Dorsetshire Affaires*, 1.

15 Clarendon, 4, vii, 212.

16 *A True Relation of the Dorsetshire Affaires*, 2.

17 Clarendon 4, vii, 213.

18 DCRO, DC/DOB 16/4, 74.

19 DCRO, D124 Box 233, FSI 41A, 7, Grace Strangways, 4.

20 Rose-Troup, *John White*, 312.

21 George S. Fry, 'John Fry, M.P. for Shaftesbury 1647–51', *SDNQ*, xx, (1930–2), 1867.

22 DSC, 57.

23 Bankes, *Corfe Castle*, 312–3.

24 *The Tragedie of the King's Armies Fidelity since their Entring into Bristol*, 4.

25 DSC, 31.

26 Clarendon, 4, vii, 220.

27 Hutchins, ii, 423.

28 Bayley, 103.

29 CJ, iii, 206.

30 *Strange, True and Lamentable Newes from Exeter and Other Parts of the Western Countreyes Showing how Cruelly the Redute Caviliers have Dealt with the Inhabitants*, (1643), 1.

31 *A True and Perfect Relation of the Barbarous and Cruell Passages of the King's Army at Old Brainceford neer London*, (1642).

32 Bayley, 109.

33 Bayley, 115.

34 Bayley, 113.

35 Bayley, 112.

36 Clarendon, 4, vii, 324.

37 *Vindication of Captain Richard Atkyns*, 44.

38 *A True Relation of a Plot to Betray the Towne of Poole in the County of Dorset*, (1643), 4.

39 *A True Relation of a Plot to Betray the Towne of Poole*, 4–5.

40 DCRO, PE/WM CW1/42.

41 Clarendon, 4, vii, 322.

42 HMC, *7th Report*, App., part 1, (1879), 445.

43 Hopton, *Bellum Civile*, 61.

44 Hopton, *Bellum Civile*, 63.

45 Hopton, *Bellum Civile*, 64.

46 *The Diary and Correspondence of Samuel Pepys*, 4 vols, (1908–11), i, 133.

47 *The True Copie of a Letter from an Inhabitant of Bridgwater in the County of Somerset*, (1643), 2.

48 Gerard, *Survey of Dorsetshire*, 57.

49 Camden's *Britannia*, (1695), 47.

50 John Vicars, *God's Arke over-topping the World's waves, or the Third Part of the Parliamentary Chronicle*, (1646), 82.

51 Vicars, *God's Arke*, 100–1.

52 *Memoirs of Edmund Ludlow*, ed. Firth, i, 61.

53 *Memoirs of Edmund Ludlow*, ed. Firth,i, 59.

54 *Memoirs of Edmund Ludlow*, ed. Firth,i, 60.

55 DCRO, D/RGB 631a.

56 DCRO, PE/CHM/CW1.

57 *Memoirs of Edmund Ludlow*, ed. Firth, i, 70.

58 *Report on Manuscripts in Various Collections*, (1901), 122.

59 *Aubrey's Natural History of Wiltshire*, 53.

60 *Memoirs of Edmund Ludlow*, ed. Firth, i, 72.

61 Hopton, *Bellum Civile*, 63.

62 *Aubrey's Natural History of Wiltshire*, 99.

63 *Memoirs of Edmund Ludlow*, ed. Firth, i, 78.

64 Clarendon, 4, viii, 458.

65 Vicars, *God's Arke*, 163.

66 Hopton, *Bellum Civile*, 62–3.

67 George J. Bennett, 'Wareham, its Invasions and Battles', *Dorset Proc.*, xiii, (1892), 109.

68 CSPD, 1655, 211.

69 Louise Fargo Brown, *The First Earl of Shaftesbury*, (New York, 1933), 44–5.

70 Christie, *Anthony Ashley Cooper*, i, app. 1, xxix.

71 *Rawleigh Redivivus: or the Life and Death of the Right Honourable Anthony Late Earl of Shaftesbury*, (1683), 17.

72 Christie, *Anthony Ashley Cooper*, i, app., xvii.

73 Christie, *Anthony Ashley Cooper*, i, app., xxxiii.

74 DCRO, PH 665.

75 DCRO, PE/SH/CW 1/115.

76 DCRO, D/SHA/A222.

77 F.J. Pope, 'More Sidelights on the Civil War in Dorset', *SDNQ*, xiv, (1915), 1–3.

78 Wedgwood, *King's War*, 286.

79 *A True Discovery of the Great and Glorious Victory of that Victorious and Ever Renowned Patriott Sir William Waller Knight, at Christ Church in Hampshire*, (1644).

Chapter 5

1 Bayley, 103.
2 Wood, *Athenae Oxonienses*, i, 825.
3 Clarendon, 7, xv, 216.
4 *The History of King-Killers, or the Fanatick Martyrology*, 2 vols, (1720), ii, August, 43.
5 George Roberts, *The History and Antiquities of the Borough of Lyme Regis and Charmouth*, (1834), 80.
6 W.S. Churchill, *Marlborough, His Life and Times*, 4 vols, (1933), i, 17.
7 Bayley, 130–1.
8 Walker, *Sufferings of the Clergy*, ii, 217.
9 Hutchins, iii, 396.
10 LJ, vi, 498.
11 CSPD, 1625–49, 667.
12 Vicars, *God's Arke*, 184.
13 Mayo, ed., *Municipal Records of Shaftesbury*, 30.
14 *A Continuation of the True Narration of the Most Observable Passages in and about Plymouth from January 26, 1643 till this Present*, (1644), 8.
15 Hutchins, i, 12.
16 Sir Edward Walker, *Historical Discourses upon Several Occasions*, (1705), 8.
17 Gerard, *Survey of Dorsetshire*, 19.
18 Hine, *History of Beaminster*, 118.
19 Hine, *History of Beaminster*, 119.
20 Joshua Sprigg, *Anglia Rediviva, England's Recovery*, (1854), 66.
21 The defences were levelled by order of Parliament in 1647, so there is no way of telling exactly where they were. For contrasting theories compare Powell and Timings, eds., *Documents Relating to the Civil War*, 142, and Geoffrey Chapman, *The Siege of Lyme Regis* (Lyme Regis, 1982), 11.
22 Edward Drake, 'The Diary of the Siege of Lyme Regis' in Bayley, *Civil War in Dorset*, 141–188, 142.
23 *Mercurius Belgicus, or a Briefe Chronologie of the Battails, Sieges, Conflicts and Other Most Remarkable Passages from the Beginning of this Rebellion to the 25th of March 1646*, (1646).
24 Drake, 'Diary', 143.
25 Shipton, 'Relation concerning the Siege of Lyme', in Bayley, 138–141, 138.
26 Drake, 'Diary', 144.
27 Rushworth, *Historical Collections*, vi, 678.
28 Drake, 'Diary', 149.
29 *A True and Perfect Diurnall of all Passages since Colonell Weres comming to the Towne of Lyme Regis*, (1644), 7.
30 Vicars, *God's Arke*, 231.
31 Drake, 'Diary', 149–50.

32 Rushworth, *Historical Collections*, vi, 678.

33 Drake, 'Diary', 152–3.

34 Vicars, *God's Arke*, 231.

35 Legg, 'Survey of the Western Counties', 73.

36 DSC, 226.

37 Drake, 'Diary', 161.

38 Walker, *Historical Discourses*, 12.

39 *A Letter from the Right Honourable Robert Earl of Warwick, Lord High Admiral of England to the Speaker of the House of Peeres*, (1644), 2.

40 *An Exact and True relation in Relieving the Resolute Garrison of Lyme in Dorsetshire, by the Right Honourable Robert Earl of Warwick, Lord High Admiral of England*, (1644), 2.

41 Drake, 'Diary', 168–9.

42 Bulstrode Whitelocke, *Memorials of the English Affairs*, (1732), 88.

43 Vicars, *God's Arke*, 246.

44 James Strong, *Joanereidos: or, Feminine Valour; Eminently Discovered in Western Women, At the Siege of Lyme*, (1674).

45 DCRO, DC/LR G1/1.

46 Rushworth, *Historical Collections*, vi, 670–1.

47 Vicars, *God's Arke*, 240–1.

48 Hutchins, ii, 58.

49 Powell and Timings, eds., *Documents Relating to the Civil War*, 149.

50 Drake, 'Diary', 178.

51 Powell and Timings, eds., *Documents Relating to the Civil War*, 150.

52 Clarendon, 4, viii, 522.

53 Hutchins, ii, 60.

54 Drake, 'Diary', 188.

55 Powell and Timings, eds., *Documents Relating to the Civil War*, 154–5.

56 *A Letter sent from the Right Honourable Robert, Earl of Warwick, to the Right Honourable the Speaker to the House of Peers Concerning the Present State and Condition, with the Manner of the Raising of the Siege of Lyme*, (18 June 1644), 6.

57 Vicars, *God's Arke*, 256.

58 Walker, *Historical Discourses*, 27.

59 *The Cavaliers new Common Prayer Booke Unclapt*, (York, 1644), 8.

60 *Warwick's letter concerning Lyme*, 4–5.

61 Carte, *A Collection of Original Letters and Papers*, i, 52.

62 Clarendon, 4, viii, 485.

63 Peter Young and Wilfrid Emberton, *Sieges of the Great Civil War*, (1978), 71.

64 Adair, *Roundhead General*, 155.

65 Rushworth, *Historical Collections*, vi, 683–4.

66 *Warwick's Letter Concerning Lyme*, 3–4.

67 Walker, *Historical Discourses*, 26.

68 Powell and Timings, eds., *Documents Relating to the Civil War*, 157.

69 Powell and Timings, eds., *Documents Relating to the Civil War*, 161.

70 H.G. Tibbutt, *The Life and Letters of Sir Lewis Dyve*, (Bedfordshire Historical Records Society, 1948), 57.
71 CSPD, 1625–49, 668.
72 *An Ordinance of the Lords and Commons Assembled in Parliament*, (1 July 1644).
73 Hutchins, ii, 344.
74 Wood, *Athenae Oxonienses*, ii, 638.
75 Hutchins, ii, 344.
76 Vicars, *God's Arke*, 286.
77 *Memoirs of Edmund Ludlow*, i, 95–6.
78 Rushworth, *Historical Collections*, vi, 685.
79 Powell and Timings, eds., *Documents Relating to the Civil War*, 161.
80 With the possible exception of the battle of Towton in 1461, which took place only 10 miles away.
81 *Aubrey's Brief Lives*, ed. Dick, xxxvi.
82 Vicars, *God's Arke*, 296.
83 Walker, *Historical Discourses*, 46.
84 Richard Symonds, *The Complete Military Diary*, ed. Stuart Peachey, (Leigh-on-Sea, 1989), 26.

Chapter 6

1 R.G. Bartelot, 'Burials of Soldiers during the Civil War', *SDNQ*, xvii, (1923), 623.
2 Bulstrode, *Memoirs and Reflections*, 112.
3 Edward Walker, *Historical Discourses*, 80.
4 John Vicars, *The Burning Bush not consumed, or the Fourth and Last Part of the Parliamentarie Chronicle*, (1646), 21.
5 Edward Walker, *Historical Discourses*, 75.
6 CSPD, 1644–5, 45.
7 CJ, iv, 334.
8 Clarendon, 4, viii, 572–3.
9 Walker, *Historical Discourses*, 99.
10 Adair, *Roundhead General*, 167–8.
11 Pulham, *Book of the Axe*, 479–80.
12 DCRO, PE/MAD/RE 1/2.
13 Walker, *Historical Discourses*, 100.
14 Underdown, *Somerset in the Civil War and Interregnum*, 80.
15 R.G. Bartelot, 'A Dorset Civil War Pass', *SDNQ*, xix, (1929), 119.
16 Clarendon, 4, viii, 575.
17 CSPD, 1644–5, 114.
18 Symonds, *Military Diary*, 36.
19 Hutchins, iii, 380.
20 Wedgwood, *King's War*, 350.
21 CSPD, 1644–5, 85.
22 CSPD, 1644–5, 124.

23 Vicars, *Burning Bush not Consumed*, 55.

24 Underdown, *Somerset in the Civil War and Interregnum*, 88.

25 DCRO, PE/WM CW1/42.

26 Tibbutt, *Sir Lewis Dyve*, 54–5.

27 DCRO, DC/LR G1/1, 1644–5.

28 Henry Symonds, 'The War in Dorset 1642–5', *SDNQ*, xii, (1911), 193–5.

29 *Three Severall Letters of Great Importance*, (1644), 2.

30 *Three Severall Letters*, 3.

31 *Three Severall Letters*, 3.

32 Christie, *Anthony Ashley Cooper*, i, 62–3.

33 Christie, *Anthony Ashley Cooper*, i, 69–70.

34 Vicars, *Burning Bush not Consumed*, 72.

35 Vicars, *Burning Bush not Consumed*, 73. Vicars assigns the incident to William Sydenham, but other sources say it was his brother, Francis.

36 DCRO, PE/BT RE 1/2.

37 Clarendon, 5, viii, 10.

38 *Memoirs of Edmund Ludlow*, ed. Firth, i, 107.

39 Christie, *Anthony Ashley Cooper*, i, 72–3.

40 A.M. Broadley, 'An Important Somerset and Dorset Civil War Letter', *SDNQ*, xi, (1909), 157–9.

41 Shaw, *History of the English Church during the Civil Wars*, ii, 43.

42 Clarendon, 3, v, 173n.

43 Clarendon, 5, ix, 138.

44 *Memoirs of Edmund Ludlow*, ed. Firth, i, 113.

45 DCRO, DC/CC C1/28.

46 Clarendon, 5, ix, 140.

47 Bulstrode, *Memoirs and Reflections*, 120.

48 Bulstrode, *Memoirs and Reflections*, 122.

49 Weinstock, ed, Weymouth and Melcombe Regis Minute Book, 52.

50 William Rhodes, 'The Battle for Weymouth in the Civil War', *Dorset Year Book* 1963–4, 71.

51 W. Bowles Barrett, *Weymouth and Melcombe Regis in the Time of the Great Civil War*, (Dorchester, 1911), 11.

52 Joseph Frank Payne, *Thomas Sydenham*, (1900), 42.

53 Legg, 'Survey of the Western Counties', 72.

54 Gerard, *Survey of Dorsetshire*, 35.

55 Carlton, *Going to the Wars*, 181.

56 CSPD, 1644–5, 304.

57 Clarendon, 5, viii, 68–9.

58 Barrett, *Weymouth and Melcombe Regis in the Civil War*, 12.

59 Barrett, *Weymouth and Melcombe Regis in the Civil War*, 14.

60 Powell and Timings, eds, *Documents relating to the Civil War*, 189.

61 LJ, vii, 260.

62 Walker, *Sufferings of the Clergy*, ii, 217–8.

63 Powell and Timings, eds, *Documents relating to the Civil War*, 189.

64 Wood, *Athenae Oxonienses*, ii, 638.

65 Payne, *Thomas Sydenham*, 46.
66 Rhodes, 'The Battle for Weymouth in the Civil War', 72.
67 LJ, vii, 260.
68 Vicars, *Burning Bush not Consumed*, 119.
69 Powell and Timings, eds, *Documents relating to the Civil War*, 190.
70 Clarendon, 5, ix, 139.
71 MRBD, 525.
72 Rhodes, 'The Battle for Weymouth in the Civil War', *Dorset Year Book* 1963–4, 73.
73 Vicars, *Burning Bush not Consumed*, 120.
74 Barrett, *Weymouth and Melcombe Regis in the Civil War*, 20.
75 Barrett, *Weymouth and Melcombe Regis in the Civil War*, 21.
76 G.A. Ellis, *The History and Antiquities of the Borough and Town of Weymouth and Melcombe Regis*, (Weymouth, 1829), 262.
77 Ellis, *History and Antiquities of Weymouth and Melcombe Regis*, 264.

Chapter 7

1 Hutchins, i, 12–3.
2 Carlton, *Going to the Wars*, 294–5.
3 Roberts, *History and Antiquities of the Borough of Lyme Regis*, 101–2.
4 Weinstock, ed, *Weymouth and Melcombe Regis Minute Book*, 52.
5 Moule, *Documents of Weymouth and Melcombe Regis*, 77.
6 Clarendon, 5, ix, 136.
7 Clarendon, 5, ix, 142.
8 Abbott, *Writings and Speeches of Oliver Cromwell*, i, 334.
9 *The Poetry of Anna Matilda, to which are added Recollections, Printed from an Original Manuscript, Written by General Sir William Waller*, (1788), 125–6.
10 Abbott, *Writings and Speeches of Oliver Cromwell*, i, 334.
11 Whitelocke, *Memorials of the English Affairs*, 136.
12 Clarendon, 5, ix, 197.
13 Clarendon, 5, ix, 141.
14 Whitelocke, *Memorials of the English Affairs*, 139.
15 Adair, *Roundhead General*, 181.
16 Carte, *A Collection of Original Letters and Papers*, i, 77.
17 Abbott, *Writings and Speeches of Oliver Cromwell*, i, 336.
18 Hall and Barber, *Colonel Richard Norton's Regiment of Horse*, 27.
19 Bayley, 255.
20 DCRO, PE/OBN RE 1/1.
21 Bayley, 253.
22 *Memoirs of Denzil, Lord Holles*, 36.
23 Vicars, *Burning Bush not Consumed*, 148.
24 Carte, *A collection of original letters and papers*, i, 85.
25 Sprigg, *Anglia Rediviva*, 20–1.
26 Carte, *A Collection of Original Letters and Papers*, i, 85.

27 C.D. Curtis, *Blake: General-at-Sea*, (Taunton, 1934), 54.

28 Clarendon, 5, ix, 191.

29 *The Victoria History of the County of Somerset*, ii, 212.

30 Walker, *Sufferings of the Clergy*, ii, 4.

31 J.P. Ferris, 'The Wareham Parliamentary Garrison in 1645', *SDNQ*, xxix, (1974), 246.

32 Bulstrode, *Memoirs and Reflections*, 125.

33 Hutchins, i, 13.

34 *The Desires and Resolutions of the Club Men of the Counties of Dorset and Wilts*, (1645), 1–3.

35 Sprigg, *Anglia Rediviva*, 89.

36 Tibbutt, *Sir Lewis Dyve*, 68–9.

37 Ferris, 'The Wareham Parliamentary Garrison', 246–7.

38 *The Humble Petition of the Inhabitants of the County of Dorset, presented to His Majesty at Ragland the 8th of July, 1645, with His Majesties Gratious Answer therunto*, (Oxford, 1645).

39 Pulham, *Book of the Axe*, 257.

40 Sprigg, *Anglia Rediviva*, 63–4.

41 Clarendon, 5, ix, 211.

42 Bayley, 262.

43 LJ, vii, 484.

44 Sprigg, *Anglia Rediviva*, 66.

45 LJ, vii, 484.

46 Rushworth, *Historical Collections*, vii, 52.

47 Underdown, *Somerset in the Civil War and Interregnum*, 106.

48 Sprigg, *Anglia Rediviva*, 62.

49 *A Letter sent to the Right Honourable William Lenthall, Esquire, Speaker to the Honourable House of Commons, Concerning the Raising of the Siege of Taunton by the Parliament's Forces*, (1645), 4.

50 Bayley, 38.

51 Minute Book of the Dorset Standing Committee, DCRO, D/BKL, 12.

52 Hopton, *Bellum Civile*, 17.

53 Bulstrode, *Memoirs and Reflections*, 137.

54 Carte, *A Collection of Original Letters and Papers*, i, 131.

55 Vicars, *Burning Bush not Consumed*, 191.

56 Vicars, *Burning Bush not Consumed*, 192.

57 Clarendon, 5, ix, 263.

58 Abbott, *Writings and Speeches of Oliver Cromwell*, i, 365.

59 Clarendon, 5, ix, 210.

60 *Aubrey's Brief Lives*, ed. Andrew Clark, 2 vols, (Oxford, 1898), ii, 241.

61 Clarendon, 5, ix, 223.

62 DCRO, PE/FOL RE1/1.

63 Bayley, 272.

64 DCRO, PH522.

65 Vicars, *Burning Bush not Consumed*, 196.

66 Sprigg, *Anglia Rediviva*, 86.

67 *Letter to Lenthall Concerning the Raising of the Siege of Taunton*, 4.
68 Bayley, 277.
69 DSC, 109.
70 DCRO, PH522.
71 *The Proceedings of the Army under the Command of Sir Thomas Fairfax from the 1st of August to the 7th of the same*, (1645), 2.
72 Abbott, *Writings and Speeches of Oliver Cromwell*, i, 368.
73 Sprigg, *Anglia Rediviva*, 87–8.
74 Abbott, *Writings and Speeches of Oliver Cromwell*, i, 368–9.
75 Sprigg, *Anglia Rediviva*, 88–9
76 *Proceedings of the Army under Fairfax*, 4.
77 Sprigg, *Anglia Rediviva*, 89.
78 Sprigg, *Anglia Rediviva*, 90.
79 Sprigg, *Anglia Rediviva*, 63.

Chapter 8

1 Underdown, *Somerset in the Civil War and Interregnum*, 112.
2 *Proceedings of the Army under Fairfax*, 5.
3 Bayley, 282.
4 DCRO, PE/SH RE1/1, Captain Fleming, according to Rushworth.
5 Nelson Moore Richardson, 'The Travels of Peter Mundy in Dorset', 1635, *Dorset Proc.*, xlii, (1922), 42–50.
6 J.P. Ferris, 'The Gentry of Dorset on the Eve of the Civil War', *The Genealogist's Magazine*, 1965, 111.
7 Sprigg, *Anglia Rediviva*, 92.
8 Sprigg, *Anglia Rediviva*, 92–3.
9 Tibbutt, *Sir Lewis Dyve*, 76.
10 Vicars, *Burning Bush not Consumed*, 256.
11 *Sir Thomas Fairfax's Letter to the Honorable William Lenthall Esq, Speaker of the House of Commons, Concerning the Taking of Sherborn Castle*, (1645), 5.
12 *Fairfax's Letter Concerning the Taking of Sherborn Castle*, 6.
13 DCRO, S.235, A2/1/1.
14 Walker, *Sufferings of the Clergy*, ii, 394–5.
15 Minute Book of the Dorset Standing Committee, DCRO, D/BKL, 6.
16 Vicars, *Burning Bush not Consumed*, 259.
17 CJ, iv, 257.
18 DCRO, D/FSI, Box 233 (ii), FSI 41A, 8, Howard Dyves, 1.
19 Bayley, 307.
20 Memorial Inscription, St Peter's church, Dorchester.
21 Rushworth, *Historical Collections*, vii, 177–8.
22 *The Works of John Locke*, viii, 271.
23 LJ, vi, 677–80.
24 Shaw, *History of the English Church during the Civil Wars*, i, 268.
25 John White, *A Way to the Tree of Life, Discovered in Sundry Directions for the Profitable Reading of the Scripture*, (1647).

26 HMC, *13th Report*, App. p 1, i, 279.

27 Smith, *History of Poole*, ii, 154–5.

28 John Sydenham, *History of Poole*, (Poole, 1839), 130.

29 Smith, *History of Poole*, ii, 154.

30 'To our Honoured and respected Ffriends, the Governor with the Maior and Minister of the Towne and Garrison of Christchurch there present, 12 December 1645', in Dunkin, *Materials for a History of Dorset*, ii, 353.

31 Minute Book of the Dorset Standing Committee, DCRO, D/BKL, 13.

32 Sprigg, *Anglia Rediviva*, 139.

33 Peter Young, *Civil War England*, (1981), 153.

34 Whitelock, *Memorials of the English affairs*, 191.

35 *The Day of Revelation of the Righteous Judgement of God, Delivered in a Sermon Preached to the Honorable House of Commons by William Strong*, (1646), 13.

36 *The Day of Revelation*, 35.

37 DCRO, PE/HAZ RE1/1.

38 Hutchins, iii, 565.

39 Christie, *Anthony Ashley Cooper*, i, app. 1, xviii.

40 Hutchins, iii, 566. This letter is dated by Hutchins as 29 October 1660, but its phrasing make it clearly pre-Restoration, possibly October 1659.

41 Bayley, 458.

42 Bayley, 294.

43 DCRO, PE/WM CW1/42.

44 J.M.J. Fletcher, 'A Dorset Worthy, William Stone, Royalist and Divine', *Dorset Proc.*, xxxvi, (1915), 19.

45 DCRO, PE/WM CW1/42.

46 Hutchins, i, 508.

47 CSPD, 1645-7, 270.

48 *Memoirs of Edmund Ludlow*, ed. Firth, i, 130.

49 Whitelock, *Memorials of the English affairs*, 192.

50 *Mercurius Belgicus*.

51 HMC, *13th Report*, app. part 1, (1891), i, 379.

52 Hutchins, iii, 62.

53 CSPD, 1645-7, 340.

54 CSPD, 1645-7, 341.

55 CSPD, 1645-7, 348.

56 Minute Book of the Dorset Standing Committee, DCRO, D/BKL, 18.

57 Vicars, *Burning Bush not Consumed*, 372.

58 James A. Casada, 'Corfe Castle: New Evidence on the Second Siege', *SDNQ*, xxix, (1974), 298–9.

59 Vicars, *Burning Bush not Consumed*, 373.

60 Smith, *History of Poole*, ii, 154.

61 CJ, iv, 462.

62 T. Bond, *History and Description of Corfe Castle in the Isle of Purbeck, Dorset*, (1883), 124.

63 Casada, 'Corfe Castle', 298–9.

64 Minute Book of the Dorset Standing Committee, DCRO, D/BKL, 1.
65 Bayley, 304.
66 Minute Book of the Dorset Standing Committee, DCRO, D/BKL, 19.
67 HMC, *Sixth Report*, p 1, report and App., 84–5.
68 DCRO, Minutes of the Dorset Standing Committee, D/BKL, 9.
69 Bayley, 310.
70 *The Troubles of Jerusalem's Restauration or the Church's Reformation, Represented in a Sermon Preached before the Right Honourable House of Lords in the Abbey Church Westminster, November 26, 1645 by John White*, (1646), 57.
71 *The Troubles of Jerusalem's Restauration*, 4–5.

Chapter 9

1 Bayley, 314.
2 Robert Temple, 'The Massey Brigade in the West', *SDNQ*, xxxi, (1986), 437–45.
3 Christie, *Anthony Ashley Cooper*, 1, xxxiv–xxxvii.
4 Christie, *Anthony Ashley Cooper*, 1, xliii.
5 DSC, 210.
6 Walker, *Sufferings of the Clergy*, ii, 198.
7 Walker, *Sufferings of the Clergy*, ii, 136.
8 Walker, *Sufferings of the Clergy*, ii, 230.
9 DSC, 21.
10 MRBD, 685.
11 MRBD, 686.
12 DSC, 347.
13 DSC, 146.
14 DSC, 50.
15 CSPD, 1645–7, 493.
16 DSC, 271.
17 DCRO, PE/BE CW1/1.
18 Hutchins, ii, 119.
19 Underdown, *Fire From Heaven*, 239.
20 Minute Book of the Dorset Standing Committee, DCRO, D/BKL, 14.
21 DSC, 6.
22 DSC, 8.
23 DCRO, D/124 Box 233 (ii), FSI 41A, 7, Lady Grace Strangways, 2.
24 DCRO, D/124 Box 233 (ii), FSI 41A, 8, Giles Strangways, 1.
25 Bankes, *Corfe Castle*, 223.
26 Minute Book of the Dorset Standing Committee, DCRO, D/BKL, 4.
27 DCRO, D/124 Box 233 (ii), FSI 41A, 7, Lady Grace Strangways, 3.
28 DSC, 45.
29 DCRO, D/124 Box 233 (ii), FSI 41A, 7, Lady Grace Strangways, 1.
30 DSC, 482.
31 Shaw, *History of the English Church during the Civil Wars*, ii, 491.

32 Shaw, *History of the English Church during the Civil Wars*, ii, 493.

33 C.A.F. Meekings, ed., *Dorset Hearth Tax Assessments 1662–4*, (Dorchester, 1951), xiv.

34 DCRO, D/WLC/F9.

35 *Memoirs of Denzil, Lord Holles*, 207.

36 Bankes, *Corfe Castle*, 231–2.

37 *Memoirs of Denzil, Lord Holles*, 129.

38 *History of King-Killers*, ii, December, 62.

39 Mark Noble, *The Lives of the English Regicides and other Commissioners of the Pretended High Court of Justice*, 2 vols, (1798), ii, 281.

40 DSC, 80.

41 Bayley, 349.

42 Minute Book of the Dorset Standing Committee, DCRO, D/BKL, 14.

43 Drake, 'Diary', 152–3.

44 Minute Book of the Dorset Standing Committee, DCRO, D/BKL, 14.

45 J.S. Morrill, 'Mutiny and Discontent in English Provincial Armies, 1645–7,' *Past and Present*, 56, (1972), 66.

46 Hutchins, ii, 426.

47 Bayley, 480.

48 Moule, *Documents of Weymouth and Melcombe Regis*, 76–7.

50 G.D. Squibb, 'The Civil War in Weymouth', *SDNQ*, xxii, (1938), 40–1.

51 Moule, *Documents of Weymouth and Melcombe Regis*, 78.

52 *Memoirs of Denzil, Lord Holles*, 75.

53 J.P. Ferris, 'The Wareham Parliamentary Garrison', 247.

54 Clarendon, 5, x, 486.

55 Clarendon, 5, x, 505.

56 Bayley, 344.

57 H.G.Tibbutt, ed., *The Tower of London Letter-Book of Sir Lewis Dyve*, (Bedfordshire Historical Records Society, 1958), 55, 68.

58 Tibbutt, ed., *Letter-Book of Sir Lewis Dyve*, 53.

59 Tibbutt, *Life and Letters of Sir Lewis Dyve*, 83.

60 *A Letter from Sir Lewis Dyve, written out of France to a Gentleman, a friend of his in London*, (1648).

61 DCRO, D/124 Box 233 (ii), FSI 41A 8, James Strangways, 1.

62 DCRO, D/124 Box 233 (ii), FSI 41A 8, James Strangways, 2.

63 DCRO, D/124 Box 233, FSI 41A 6, Anne Norton, 4.

64 DCRO, D/124 Box 233, FSI 41A 4, Sir John Strangways, 1.

65 DCRO, D/124 Box 263, FSI 50.

66 DSC, 402.

67 DSC, 384.

68 Walker, *Sufferings of the Clergy*, ii, 394.

69 Hutchins, i, 231.

70 CSPD, 1648–9, 36.

71 CSPD, 1648–9, 52.

72 Bayley, 413.

73 DSC, 395.

74 John White, *Way to the Tree of Life*.

75 Rose-Troup, John *White*, 375.

76 C. Firth and G. Davies, *The Regimental History of Cromwell's Army*, 2 vols, (Oxford, 1940), i, 107.

77 Abbott, *Writings and Speeches of Oliver Cromwell*, i, 606.

78 *The Declaration of the County of Dorset, shewing their Consent to Joyn with other Counties in this Loyall Work of Redeeming his Majesty and Setling the Kingdom*, (1648).

79 DSC, 408.

80 DSC, 408.

81 CSPD, 1648–9, 239.

82 CSPD, 1648–9, 248.

83 DCRO, S.235 B1/79/1.

84 DCRO, DC/DOB 16/4, 75.

85 DCRO, DC/DOB 16/4, 86.

86 James H. Stark, *Dorchester Day, Celebration of the 279th Anniversary of the Settlement of Dorchester*, (Boston, 1909), 91–2.

87 MRBD, 594.

88 *Memoirs of Colonel Hutchinson*, ed. Firth, ii, 152.

89 E.A. Fry, 'John Fry the Regicide', *SDNQ*, i, (1890), 55.

90 Wood, *Athenae Oxonienses*, ii, 247.

91 CSPD, 1648–9, 124. As William Wake the elder was arrested only 'a little time' (Walker, *Sufferings of the Clergy*, ii, 394) after the events at Blandford, it is probably his son who is referred to.

92 CSPD, 1648–9, 311.

93 CSPD, 1648–9, 345.

94 Bayley, 329.

95 Moule, 'Notes on a Minute Book belonging to the Mayor and Corporation of Dorchester', *Dorset Proc.*, xv, (1894), 157.

96 DCRO, PE/WM CW1/42.

97 DCRO, PE/BE/CW 1/1.

98 Bayley, 358.

99 David Underdown, *Royalist Conspiracy in England, 1649–60*, (New Haven, 1960), 27.

100 *Clarke Papers*, ed. Firth, ii, 132.

101 Bayley, 357.

102 *Diary of John Evelyn*, ed. de Beer, iii, 40.

103 *Diary and Correspondence of Samuel Pepys*, iii, 338.

104 *Diary of John Evelyn*, ed. de Beer, iii, 40.

105 *Diary of John Evelyn*, ed. de Beer, iii, 49–50.

106 DCRO, D/124 Box 233 (ii), FSI 41A 8, Howard Dyves, 2.

107 DCRO, D/124 Box 233 (ii), FSI 41A 8, Howard Dyves, 5.

108 DCRO, D/124 Box 233 (ii), FSI 41A 8, Howard Dyves, 6.

109 Clarendon, 6, xi, 266.

Chapter 10

1 *Aubrey's Brief Lives*, ed. Clark, i, 408.

2 HMC, *13th Report*, App. p 1, i, 588.

3 HMC, *13th Report*, App. p1, i, 577.

4 DCRO, PE/WM CW1/42.

5 DCRO, S.235 A2/1/1.

6 DCRO, PE/BE/CW 1/1.

7 DCRO, S.235 A2/1/1.

8 DCRO, DC/BTB/L8.

9 *A Collection of the State Papers of John Thurloe Esq.*, ed. T. Birch, 7 vols, (1742), i, 158.

10 Hutchins, ii, 442.

11 Bayley, 339.

12 MRBD, 687.

13 A.L. Morton, *The World of the Ranters*, (1970), 217.

14 Clarendon, 7, xv, 278.

15 Tibbutt, ed., *Letter-Book of Sir Lewis Dyve*, 90.

16 Bayley, 342.

17 Bayley, 344.

18 CSPD, 1651, 149.

19 CSPD, 1651, 195.

20 *History of King-Killers*, i, March, 48–9.

21 A.M. Broadley, *The Royal Miracle*, (1912), 230.

22 *The Victoria History of Hampshire and the Isle of Wight*, 5 vols, ed. William Page, (1900–1912), v, 89.

23 CSPD, 1650, 293.

24 DCRO, D/MMD/JK 16.

25 Payne, *Thomas Sydenham*, 77–8.

26 G.F. Sydenham, *The History of the Sydenham Family*, (East Molesey, 1928), 486.

27 Hutchins, ii, 392.

28 Clarendon, 6, xiii, 513.

29 *Diary and Correspondence of Samuel Pepys*, ii, 331.

30 H.A. Wyndham, *A Family History 1410–1688. The Wyndhams of Norfolk and Somerset*, (Oxford, 1939), 204–5.

31 *Memoirs of the Court of Charles II by Count Grammont, edited by Sir Walter Scott. Also The King's Account of His Escape from Worcester, as Dictated to Pepys, and The Boscobel Tracts*, (1891), 585.

32 Ann Wyndham, 'Claustrum Regale Reseratum,' in *Grammont/Boscobel*, 524.

33 'Claustrum Regale Reseratum', 526.

34 Tibbutt, *Life and Letters of Sir Lewis Dyve*, 83.

35 DCRO, D124 Box 233 (ii), FSI 41A 8, Giles Strangways 3.

36 'Claustrum Regale Reseratum', in *Grammont/Boscobel*, 527.

37 The King's Account, in *Grammont/Boscobel*, 434.

38 DCRO, DC/LR G1/1.

39 Gerard, *Survey of Dorsetshire*, 11.

40 'The King's Account', in *Grammont/Boscobel*, 435.

41 'Boscobel, or the History of the Most Miraculous Preservation of King Charles II after the Battle of Worcester', p II, in *Grammont/Boscobel*, 491.

42 'Letter of Mr William Ellesdon to the Earl of Clarendon', in *Clarendon State Papers*, ii, 567.

43 'Claustrum Regale Reseratum', 531.

44 *A Proclamation for the Discovery and Apprehending of Charles Stuart and other Traytors his Adherents and Abettors*, 10 September 1651.

45 'Claustrum Regale Reseratum', 532.

46 'The King's Account', *Grammont/Boscobel*, 436.

47 'The King's Account', *Grammont/Boscobel*, 436.

48 'Letter of William Ellesdon', ii, 568.

49 Clarendon, 6, xiii, 538.

50 Hutchins, ii, 217n.

51 Clarendon, 6, xiii, 537–8.

52 Walker, *Sufferings of the Clergy*, ii, 318.

53 'Miraculum Basilicon', in Broadley, *Royal Miracle*, 136.

54 'Letter of William Ellesdon', ii, 568–9.

55 'Letter of William Ellesdon', ii, 569.

56 'Letter of William Ellesdon', ii, 569.

57 'Letter of William Ellesdon', ii, 570.

58 'Claustrum Regale Reseratum', 533.

59 J.S. Udal, 'Charles II in Dorset', *Dorset Proc.*, viii, (1887), 21n.

60 'Claustrum Regale Reseratum', 535–6.

61 'Captain Gregory Alford's Narrative', in Broadley, *The Royal Miracle*, 189–90.

62 'Claustrum Regale Reseratum', 537.

63 'Boscobel', pt II, 494.

64 'Claustrum Regale Reseratum', 540.

65 Clarendon, 6, xiii, 540.

66 DCRO, DC/DOB 16/4, 164.

67 Broadley, *The Royal Miracle*, 230.

68 Bulstrode, Memoirs and Reflections, 221.

69 *The Poetry of Anna Matilda*, 129.

70 MRBD, 547.

Chapter 11

1 Clarendon, 6, xii, 431.

2 DCRO, DC/LR O4A.

3 Clarendon, 6, xiii, 606.

4 Curtis, Blake, 124.

5 DCRO, PE/BE/CW1/1.

6 DCRO, PE/WM CW1/42

7 DCRO, PE/BER/CW8.
8 DCRO, PE/BER/CW8.
9 DCRO, PE/BE/CW1/1.
10 DCRO, D53/1 4H.
11 DCRO, DC/LR A 10/1.
12 MRBD, 519.
13 MRBD, 547.
14 C.H. Mayo, 'Langton Long Churchwardens' Account Book', *SDNQ*, iii, (1893), 57.
15 DCRO, PE/BE/CW1/1.
16 Walter Richards, *Lyme Regis Baptists 1653–1953*, (Lyme, 1953), 2–4.
17 Abiezer Coppe, *A Second Fiery Flying Roule*, (1970), 330.
18 Bayley, 344–5.
19 *Report on Manuscripts in Various Collections*, (1901), 121.
20 Wood, *Athenae Oxonienses*, ii, 248.
21 *Journal of George Fox*, (1852), 2 vols, i, 222.
22 *Journal of George Fox*, i, 223.
23 CSPD, 1656–7, 123–4.
24 *Journal of George Fox*, i, 290.
25 Christopher Hill, *The World Turned Upside Down*, (Middlesex 1975), 364.
26 Sydenham, *History of the Sydenham Family*, 479.
27 CJ, vii, 473.
28 DSC, 133.
29 DSC, 361.
30 CJ, vii, 503.
31 Clarendon, 5, x, 437.
32 *Harleian Miscellany*, (1811), viii, 306.
33 Christie, *Anthony Ashley Cooper*, i, appendix 1, xx.
34 Brown, *Shaftesbury*, 57.
35 Wood, *Athenae Oxonienses*, ii, 540.
36 Sydenham, *History of the Sydenham Family*, 418–9.
37 Wood, *Athenae Oxonienses*, ii, 638.
38 Clegg, *History of Wimborne Minster and District*, 101.
39 Walker, *Sufferings of the Clergy*, ii, 356–7.
40 Walker, *Sufferings of the Clergy*, ii, 421.
41 Weinstock, ed., *Weymouth and Melcombe Regis Minute Book*, 99.
42 *State Papers of John Thurloe*, ed., Birch, iii, 165.
43 *State Papers of John Thurloe*, ed., Birch, iii, 194.
44 *State Papers of John Thurloe*, ed., Birch, iii, 195.
45 *State Papers of John Thurloe*, ed., Birch, iii, 193.
46 *State Papers of John Thurloe*, ed., Birch, iii, 195.
47 Clarendon, 7, xv, 279.
48 Edward Sexby, *Killing No Murder*, (1657), 1.
49 Bayley, 381.
50 Sexby, *Killing No Murder*, 14.
51 Clarendon, 7, xiv, 138.

52 *State Papers of John Thurloe*, ed., Birch, iii, 242.

53 Abbott, *Writings and Speeches of Oliver Cromwell*, iii, 650.

54 Bayley, 374.

55 W.W. Ravenhill, 'Records of the Rising in the West', *Wiltshire Archaeological Magazine*, (1870) xiii, 129.

56 Bayley, 374.

57 *State Papers of John Thurloe*, ed. Birch, iii, 242.

58 Leonard J. Shaw, ed., *Borough and County of the Town of Poole: Calendar of Local Archives*, 4 vols, (Poole, 1958–72), i, 45.

59 Abbott, *Writings and Speeches of Oliver Cromwell*, iii, 661.

60 *State Papers of John Thurloe*, ed. Birch, iii, 233.

61 Clarendon, 7, xiv, 144.

62 Samuel R. Gardiner, *History of the Commonwealth and Protectorate*, 4 vols, (1903), iii, 292.

63 *Clarke Papers*, ed. Firth, iii, 28.

64 Walker, *Sufferings of the Clergy*, ii, 414.

65 Ravenhill, 'Records of the Rising in the West', 132–3.

66 Ravenhill, 'Records of the Rising in the West', 147.

67 Bayley, 378.

68 Ravenhill, 'Records of the Rising in the West', 168n.

69 *State Papers of John Thurloe*, ed. Birch, iii, 381–2.

70 Ravenhill, 'Records of the Rising in the West', 142.

71 Ravenhill, 'Records of the Rising in the West', 256.

72 Wyndham, *Family History, 1410–1688*, 254.

73 Pulham, *Book of the Axe*, 487.

74 *State Papers of John Thurloe*, ed. Birch, iii, 453.

75 Pulham, *Book of the Axe*, 486.

76 T.B.Howell, comp., *A Complete Collection of State Trials*, 1809–16, v, 775.

77 Hutchins, i, 232.

78 Howell, comp., *State trials*, v, 783–4.

79 DCRO, PE/PUD/CW1/1.

80 DCRO, PE/BE/CW 1/1.

81 Clarendon, 7, xiv, 142.

82 Wyndham, *Family History, 1410–1688*, 256.

83 *State Papers of John Thurloe*, ed. Birch iv, 305.

Chapter 12

1 MRBD, 645.

2 MRBD, 681.

3 DCRO, PE/WM CW1/42.

4 DCRO, DC/LR G1/1, 1657–8.

5 Walker, *Sufferings of the Clergy*, ii, 264.

6 Edmund Calamy, *An Abridgement of Mr Baxter's History of His Life and Times with an Account of the Ministers etc who were ejected after the Restauration of King Charles II*, 2 vols, (1713), ii, 266–7.

7 B.R. White, ed., *Association Records of the Particular Baptists of England, Ireland and Wales to 1660*, 96–7.

8 MRBD, 548.

9 DCRO, DC/LR G1/1, 1645–6.

10 DCRO, DC/LR G1/1, 1658–9.

11 DCRO, DC/LR G1/1, 1659–60.

12 Antonia Fraser, *Cromwell: Our Chief of Men*, (1973), 676.

13 Wood, *Athenae Oxonienses*, i, 323.

14 Noble, *Lives of the English Regicides*, i, 101.

15 Underdown, *Somerset in the Civil War and Interregnum*, 191.

16 J.A. Casada, 'Dorset Politics in the Puritan Revolution', *Southern History*, iv, (1982), 118.

17 Cyril Wanklyn, *Lyme Leaflets*, (1944), 80.

18 Shaw, *History of the English Church during the Civil Wars*, ii, 157.

19 MRBD, 618.

20 *The Unhappy Marksman, or A Perfect and Impartial Discovery of that Late Barbarous and Unparalleled Murder Committed by Mr George Strangways, formerly a Major in the King's Army, on his Brother-in-Law, Mr John Fassel, an Attorney, on Friday 11th February*, (1659), 2.

21 *The Unhappy Marksman*, 5.

22 DCRO, D124 Box 233, FSI 41A/4, John Strangways II, 6.

23 *The Unhappy Marksman*, 5.

24 *The Unhappy Marksman*, 8–9.

25 Payne, *Thomas Sydenham*, 78.

26 Casada, 'Dorset Politics in the Puritan Revolution', 116.

27 *A Speech Made by a Worthy Member of Parliament in the House of Commons Concerning the Other House*, (1659), 123.

28 Wood, *Athenae Oxonienses*, ii, 540–1.

29 C.D. Whetham and W.C.D. Whetham, *A History of the Life of Colonel Nathaniel Whetham*, (1907), 192.

30 Clarendon, 4, vii, 222.

31 *A Genuine and Faithful Account of the Sufferings of William Houlbrook, Blacksmith of Marlborough, in the reign of King Charles I*, (1744), 10.

32 DCRO, DC/LR G1/1, 1658–9.

33 DCRO, D/WLC F9.

34 Pentin, 'A Dorset Parish during the Commonwealth', *Dorset Proc.*, 65, (1944), 108–11.

35 Bayley, 385.

36 *Clarke Papers*, iv, 48.

37 Wood, *Athenae Oxonienses*, ii, 541.

38 Christie, *Anthony Ashley Cooper*, i, 186.

39 *A Speech Concerning the Other House*, 125.

40 *Clarendon, State Papers*, iii, 224.

41 CSPD, 1659–60, 165.

42 Clarendon, 7, xvi, 376.

43 *The Works of John Locke*, viii, 276.

44 *A Letter from Sir Anthony Ashley Cooper, Thomas Scot, Io Berners and John Weaver Esquiers, Delivered to the Lord Fleetwood*, (1659), 3–4.

45 *Memoirs of Colonel Hutchinson*, ed. Firth, ii, 238.

46 *The Works of John Locke*, viii, 278.

47 Bulstrode, Memoirs and Reflections, 209.

Chapter 13

1 *A Declaration of the Knights and Gentry in the County of Dorset who were in his Late Majesty's Army*, (1660).

2 Underdown, *Fire From Heaven*, 231.

3 DCRO, DC/LR G1/1.

4 A.M. Broadley, 'The Proclaiming of Charles II at Sherborne', *SDNQ*, xiii, (1913), 180–1.

5 Clarendon, 7, xvi, 505.

6 *Memoirs of Colonel Hutchinson*, ed. Firth, ii, 245.

7 *The Day of Revelation*, 27.

8 MRBD, 646.

9 DCRO, DC/LR D66/3.

10 DCRO, PH 184.

11 DCRO, D/WLC D10/C2.

12 Sydenham, *History of the Sydenham Family*, 620.

13 Moule, *Documents of Weymouth and Melcombe Regis*, 183.

14 Whetham and Whetham, *Colonel Nathaniel Whetham*, 217.

15 DCRO, D/WLC D10/C2.

16 Bankes, *Corfe Castle*, 248–50.

17 Bankes, *Corfe Castle*, 255.

18 Bankes, *Corfe Castle*, 258.

19 Bankes, *Corfe Castle*, 259.

20 DCRO, PE/WM CW1/42.

21 DCRO, PE/BE CW1/1.

22 E.A. Fry, 'John Fry the Regicide', *SDNQ*, i, (1888-9), 55.

23 Patricia Crawford, *Denzil Holles, 1598–1680: A Study of his Political Career*, (Royal Historical Society, 1979), 193.

24 *Diary and Correspondence of Samuel Pepys*, i, 113.

25 *Memoirs of Edmund Ludlow*, ed. Firth, ii, 256.

26 John Cannon, *Parliamentary Reform 1640–1832*, (Cambridge, 1973), 24.

27 Hutchins, i, 435.

28 DCRO, DC/LR G1/1, 1659–60.

29 A. Lindsay Clegg, *A History of Dorchester, Dorset*, (1972), 77.

30 Clegg, *History of Dorchester*, 83.

31 P. Drake, 'Captain John Chaffin of Sherborne', *SDNQ*, xxxii, (1991), 576–8.

32 Clarendon, 3, vi, 230.

33 *The Axminster Ecclesiastica*, ed. K.W.H. Howard, (Ossett, W.Yorks, 1976), 6.

34 DCRO, D/GOO 2992.

35 Wood, *Athenae Oxonienses*, ii, 507.

36 'Miraculum Basilicon', 136.

37 E.A.Fry, 'The Augmentation Books 1650–60 in Lambeth Palace Library', *Dorset Proc.*, xxxvi, (1915), 81.

38 Smith, *History of Poole*, ii, 175.

39 Hutchins, ii, 217n.

40 Minute Book of the Dorset Standing Committee, DCRO, D/BKL, 18.

41 Walker, *Sufferings of the Clergy*, ii, 218.

42 Calamy, *Ministers Ejected after the Restauration*, ii, 259.

43 Wood, *Athenae Oxonienses*, ii, 571.

44 Moule, *Documents of Weymouth and Melcombe Regis*, 201.

45 *A Compleat Collection of Farewell Sermons*, (1663), 641–72.

46 Calamy, *Ministers Ejected after the Restauration*, ii, 263.

47 DCRO, PE/BE/CW 1/1.

48 Mayo, 'Langton Long Churchwardens' Account Books', 1824, 56–62.

49 DCRO, PE/WM CW1/42.

50 J.H. Bettey, 'Varieties of Men, Contrasts among the Dorset clergy during the Seventeenth Century', *SDNQ*, xxxii, (1991), 846–50.

51 *Axminster Ecclesiastica*, ed. Howard, 17–18.

52 Hine, *History of Beaminster*, 90.

53 Calamy, *Ministers Ejected after the Restauration*, ii, 272.

54 Calamy, *Ministers Ejected after the Restauration*, ii, 260.

55 Calamy, *Ministers Ejected after the Restauration*, ii, 265.

56 DCRO, NQ1/A18.

57 DCRO, NQ1/A15, 13 April 59. The entries are not set down in the accepted seventeenth century style, ending the year on 25 March. I have assumed the dates are accurate rather than their order.

58 DCRO, NQ1/A15, 17 April 1660.

59 DCRO, NQ1/A15, 16 July 1660.

60 DCRO, PE/SH CW1/131.

61 DCRO, NQ1/A15, 17 March 1660 (see above note 58).

62 DCRO, NQ1/A15, 20 March 1660 (see above note 58).

63 *Aubrey's Natural History of Wiltshire*, 12.

64 *Aubrey's Brief Lives*, ed. Dick, xxxvi.

65 *Diary and Correspondence of Samuel Pepys*, i, 339.

66 DCRO, PE/SH/CW1/132.

67 Lemmey, *History of Halstock*, 40.

68 *Aubrey's Natural History of Wiltshire*, 59.

69 *Aubrey's Brief Lives*, ed. Dick, xxv.

70 DCRO, PE/SH/CW1/130.

71 J.S. Udal, 'Witchcraft in Dorset', *Dorset Proc.*, xiii, (1892), 37.

72 Bartelot, 'Sherborne and the Civil War', *SDNQ*, xix, (1929), 3.

73 *Aubrey's Natural History of Wiltshire*, 79.

74 Carlton, *Going to the Wars*, 204–7.

75 Clarendon, 7, xvi, 506.

INDEX

Cooke, Colonel Edward, 121
Cooper, Anne, 162
Cooper, Sir Anthony Ashley, 18-20, 47, 55, 59, 62-3, 67, 102-4, 115-7, 120-1, 126, 136, 165-6, 182, 188-9
joins parliamentarians, 63
leads parliamentary forces in Dorset, 82, 85-8, 100
works for the restoration of Charles II, 182-6
Cooth, Josias, 45
Coppe, Abiezer, 162
Corfe Castle, 2, 18, 21, 24, 28, 30, 36, 62, 77, 87, 108, 116, 121, 124, 128-9, 131, 151, 167, 191
first siege of, (1643), 47-9
second siege of, (1645-6), 119, 121-4
Cornwall, 5, 39, 49, 67, 76, 80-2, 99, 107-8, 110, 116, 118, 171, 201
Corporation Act, (1661), 194
Corporation for Ministers' Widows, 154
Corscombe, 5
Cotswolds, 76
Cotton, Henry, 4
Courtney, William, 97
Coventry, Margaret, 19-20
Coventry, Thomas, Lord, 19
Coward, Jane, 13
Coward, Roger, 198
Coward, William, 198-9
Crabbe, John, 128
Cranborne, 56, 66, 84
Cranborne Chase, 11
Crawford, Ludovick Lindsey, Earl of, 56-7, 61
Creech Grange, 48, 131, 167, 188
Crew, Ann, 13
Crewkerne, 38, 77, 90, 99, 101-2, 106, 170-1
Croke, Major Unton, 168-9, 171-2, 174, 185
Cromwell, Colonel, 121-2
Cromwell, Oliver, 2, 24-5, 52, 62, 75, 79, 82, 84, 91-2, 100, 102, 107,

116, 118, 121, 136-7, 139-43, 145, 147-50, 152, 158, 160-3, 165, 187, 192
campaigns in Dorset, 98-9, 108-111, 113, 118
as Lord Protector, 166-77, 179-80, 182, 184-5, 193, 201
Cromwell, Richard, 100, 174-5,182-3
Crook, John, 131-2
Cropredy Bridge, Battle of, (1644), 79, 103
Cross, John, 21
Crouch, James, 33
Cumberland, 36, 62
Curtis, Samuel, 198
Curtis, Thomas, 164

Dartmouth, 83, 105, 118
Davenant, Edward, 103
Day, Nicholas, 3
De Salanova, Peter, 27-8
Denmark, 1
Derby, John, 14
Derby, Richard, 14
Derby, Roger, 15
Derby, William, 14
Desborough, Major-General John, 107, 109, 146, 148, 158, 170-3, 175-7, 183-4, 189
Devonshire, 5, 39, 42, 49, 56, 65, 67, 75-8, 81-2, 90, 93, 99, 107-8, 110, 116, 118, 121, 168, 171, 189, 201
Dewey, Major James, 102, 163, 171, 176, 181-2, 184-5
Digby family, 15, 45, 128-9
Digby, Ann, 37, 39
Digby, George Lord, 2,24-7, 29, 37, 44, 84, 107, 111
Digby, John, brother of George, 33-4, 39
Digby, John, brother of Sir Kenelm, 25, 107
Digby, Sir Kenelm, 30-1, 107
Doddington, Sir Francis, 61, 78-80

Fairclough, Samuel, 127-8
Fairfax, Lord Ferdinando, 51
Fairfax, Sir Thomas, 51, 79, 100,
102, 104-8, 118-9, 121, 125, 139-40,
143, 147, 151, 170, 183
  campaigns in Dorset, 100-2, 105-
6, 108-14, 118, 122
Falmouth, 83
Faringdon, 22
Farnham, 58, 89
Fawne, John, 135
Fécamp, 158
Fiennes, Nathaniel, 45, 52
Fifehead Magna, 117
Fifth Monarchists, 160, 178
Fisher, Giles, 5
Fitzherbert, Richard, 102
Fitzjames, Colonel John, 40, 62, 78,
84, 118, 122-3, 136, 163, 175, 182,
188, 190, 201
Fleet, 112, 127
Fleetwood, Colonel Charles, 108,
185, 189
Flewell, Henry, 133
Floyer, Elinor, 196
Folke House, 108
Fontmell, 167
Ford, Captain, 120
Ford, Mrs, 168
Forde Abbey, 179
Fordington, 11, 18, 21, 99, 118, 196
Forward, Samuel, 103
Fox, George, Quaker, visits Dorset,
163-4
Fox, George of Hermitage, 64
Foy, Walter, 102, 127
Frampton, 2, 16, 25, 72, 179
France, 1,4-5, 51, 80, 83, 95, 103,
105, 116, 141, 143, 148, 151, 153,
158, 168-70, 183, 186, 189-90
  French troops in Dorset, 68, 77-8,
83, 85, 91, 96
Francis, Amy, 179
Francis, Henry, 146
Frederick, King of Bohemia, 4
Freke, Sir John, 9, 12, 112, 172

Fry, Hugh, 150, 183
Fry, John, 54, 102, 136, 163, 179,
192
  at Charles I's trial, 142
Fry, John junior, 192
Fulford, Sir Francis, 11, 189, 199
Fulford, George, 163, 199
Fuller, Thomas, 178
Fullerton, Sir James, 10
Fussell, John, 105, 137, 142, 180-1

Gallot, Mrs, 143
Galpin, Eleanor, 13
Gardiner, John, 10
Gardiner, 'King', 33, 143, 167
Gardiner, William, 143
Gee, Mary, 167
Gerard, John, 175
Germany, 52, 56
Gillingham, 10-11, 46, 52, 103, 183
  royalist pensioners in, 189
Gillingham forest, riots in, 10-11,
46, 146
Gillingham, Edward, 13
Gillingham, John, 13
Gillingham, Mrs, 197
Glorious Revolution, (1688), 193
Gloucester, 146, 184
  siege of, (1643), 57-8, 118
Gloucestershire, 96, 121, 201
Godmanstone, clubmen at, 96
Goffe, Nicholas, 64
Gollop, Colonel Thomas, 124
Goodridge, Richard, 144
Goring, Lord George, 32, 35, 89-90,
97-102, 104-8, 116, 185
  campaigns in Dorset, 90-6, 99
Gould, James, 10, 182
Gould, John, 118
Gower, Nicholas, 17
Grand Remonstrance, 26
Gravesend, 158
Green, Giles, 30, 128
Green, Hugh, 35
Greene, Ursula, 13

Gregory, Richard, 132
Grenville, Sir Richard, 77, 99, 101, 105
Gresley, Mary, 144
Guernsey, 147
Gull, Thomas, 199
Guyer, Hannah, 198

Hallett, James, 178
Hallett, John, 195
Halstock, 20, 200
Hambledon Hill, fight at, (1645), 109-10
Hamnet, Mr, 154-5
Hampden, John, 24, 26, 51
Hampshire, 8, 43, 52, 58, 63-4, 89, 99, 116-7, 121, 132, 147, 170, 180
  clubmen in, 96, 108, 110
Hampton Court, 139
Hancock, John, 125
Hancock, Robert, 10
Handley, 183
Handley, Richard, 178
Handley, William, 178
Harbin, Henry, 34, 58
Harbyn, Christopher, 13
Harding, a painter, 192
Harding, Major William, 123, 135, 168-9
Hardy, Samuel, 197
Harrington, Major, 70
Harrison, Major General Thomas, 150, 160-1, 165, 168-9, 178, 192-3
Hartford, Connecticut, 14
Harvey, Captain, 134
Harvey, William, 58
Harwich, sea fight off, (1653), 161
Haslerig, Sir Arthur, 26, 43-4, 81, 149, 183-6
Hastell, Mark, 10
Hastings, George, 58
Hastings, Henry, 15, 58, 84, 89
Hastings, Sir Walter, 83
Hawkchurch, 200
Hawkins, Robert, 90, 97

Haye House, 69, 74
Hayn, Thomas, 161
Hazelbury Bryan, 55, 93, 119, 196
Heane, Colonel James, 93, 128, 138, 146-9, 153, 156, 165, 194
Hele, Sir John, 2, 19, 42, 53, 107, 112, 131
Hele House, 158
Helyar, Captain, 146
Hemyock Castle, 67
Henchman, Humphrey, 45-6, 158
Henley, Henry, 69, 78, 140, 145, 190
Henley, John, 40, 45, 55
Henley, Mrs, 40
Henley-on-Thames, 91
Henrietta Maria, Queen, 13, 25, 32, 51, 53, 63, 76, 80, 189, 196
Henstridge, 6
Herefordshire, 172
Hermitage, 64
Hertford, William Seymour, Marquess of, 19, 31-7, 39, 44, 46, 48-9, 55, 57, 170
Hertfordshire, 36
Highmore, Abraham, 36
Highmore, Nathaniel, 177
Hiley, Haviland, 117
Hill, John, 13, 28
Hill, Roger, 133, 142
Hillard, Thomas, 41
Hine, a preacher, 178
Hinton Martel, 33
Hoble, Agnes, 7
Hodder, Anne, 90
Hodder, Fabian, 3, 90-1, 95, 129, 194
Hodder, John, 85
Hoddinot, Captain, 61
Hodges, Hugh, 45, 146
Hogan, Thomas, 134
Hogarth, William, 190
Holborne, Major-General James, 88, 98-99
Holland, 14, 26, 89, 145-6, 148, 161
Hollar, Wenceslas, 116, 145
Holles, Denzil, 7-9, 23-7, 30-1, 36-9,

4, 139-40, 142, 151-3, 155, 157, 160,
173, 177, 179, 184, 186-7, 189, 194,
201
  siege of, (1644), 68-76, 81, 118,
128, 133-4, 142, 160, 196, 202
  women of, 72-3, 75, 78, 127
  royalist suspects in, (1655), 176
  religious radicals in, 162-3, 198-9
Lymington, 89
Lynn, 184
Lytchett Matravers, 198

Macey, Captain, 155
Maiden Bradley, 18
Maiden Newton, 10, 82-3, 85, 162,
195
Maine, 14
malaria, 149, 167
Manchester, 33
Manchester, Edward Montague,
Earl of, 84, 100, 102
Mappowder, 22, 69, 182
Marlborough, 32
Marshall's Elm, skirmish at,
(1642), 34
Marshwood, 143, 155, 196
Marston Moor, Battle of, (1644), 79,
83, 149
Martyn, John, 175
Mason, John, 5
Massachusetts, 14-5
Massachusetts Bay Company, 14
Massey, Major-General Edward,
106, 118, 121, 123, 126, 171, 194
Masters, Elizabeth, 199
Masters, Humphry, 128
Matthews, Francis, 24, 167
Maumbury Rings, 35
Maurice, Prince, 21, 51-6, 58, 61,
64-5, 67-8, 76-8, 80, 83
  at the siege of Lyme, 68-71, 73-5
Mayor, Richard, 100
Melbury Abbas, 197
Melbury Bubb, 178
Melbury Sampford, 131, 138, 151

Melcombe Regis, 16, 21, 62, 85, 97,
120, 123, 127, 138, 141, 146, 151,
168, 182
  falls to royalists, (1643), 55
  retaken by Parliament, (1644), 77
  besieged by royalists, (1645), 91-
5, 128, 146
Mercurius Rusticus, 41
Mere, 46, 158
Methodism, 195
Middlesex, 29,178
Middleton, Lieutenant-General
John, 80-1, 85
Milborne St Andrew, 15, 159
Mills, John, 95
Milton Abbas, 18, 27, 40, 61, 110,
118, 177, 179, 184, 186, 192
Minehead, 39, 59
Minge, Valentine, 3
Mintern, John, 127
Minterne Magna, 43
Mitchell, Bernard, 16
Monckton Wyld, 143
Mohun, William, 22-3
Moizer, a seaman, 72
Monk, General George, 161, 183,
185-7, 190
Monmouth, James, Duke of, 148,
200
Montacute, 157
Montague, Colonel, 106
Montrose, James Graham, Marquis
of, 148
Moon, Mr, 33
Morden, 16
More Crichel, 118-9, 132
Morgan, Major John, 79
Morlaix, 160
Morton, Sir George, 15, 27, 38, 112,
167
Morton, Robert, 33, 67
Motcombe, 46, 131, 189
Munden, Richard, 106
Munster, 59, 80
Murphy, Maurice, 128
Muston, 18, 180

Uxbridge, peace negotiations at, (1645), 92

Verney, H., 58
Vincent, John, 85

Wade, Farmer, 132
Wade, Margaret, 152, 155
Wade, Thomas, 132
Wake, William the elder, 33, 111, 114-5, 119, 123, 138-9
Wake, William the younger, 33, 119-20, 139, 142, 174
Wake, William, Archbishop of Canterbury, 174
Walcot, Sir John, 44-5, 87, 111
Waldegrave, Sir Edward, 82
Wales, 39, 44, 96, 131, 140, 188
Walker, Clement, 52
Wall, Elizabeth, 90
Waller, Sir William, 21, 42-4, 50-3, 55-8, 61, 64, 69, 76-7, 79-80, 90-1, 93, 100, 118, 141, 158-9, 170, 184
  in Dorset, 4, 42-3, 64, 67, 81-2, 84, 87, 99-100, 103
Walter, Lucy, 148
Waltham, John, 135
Waltham, Thomas, 10, 168
Wambrook, 66
Ward, Colonel, 20
Wardour Castle, 21, 46, 58
  first siege of, (1643), 45-6, 55
  second siege of, (1643-4), 60
Ware, Mr, 33
Wareham, 8, 13, 16, 33, 35-36, 40, 62, 77-8, 87, 98, 102, 111, 119, 121, 124, 128, 138, 181, 191, 195-6
  taken by parliamentarians, (1643), 59-60
  retaken by royalists, (1644), 67
  retaken by parliamentarians, (1644), 80, 82
  skirmish at, (1646), 121-2
Warmwell, 133, 193

Warwick, 1
Warwick, Robert Rich, Earl of, 30, 48-9, 66, 75-8, 100, 141-2
  at siege of Lyme, 71-2, 74-5, 202
Warwickshire, 146
Way, Henry, 45
Weld family, 201
Weld, Humphrey, 130, 132, 184, 189-91
Weld, Lady, 130
Wells, 183
Were, Colonel John, 49, 66-7, 69, 72, 77, 81
Wesley, Bartholomew, 154-5, 195
Wesley, John of Winterborne Whitechurch, 195
Wesley, John, 195
West Indies, 163
West Stafford, 201
Western Association, 76, 98, 145, 151
Westhay, 71
Westminster, 57, 73, 183, 186
Westminster Abbey, 125, 179, 192
Weymouth, 1, 3, 6, 9-10, 12-4, 16, 21, 27, 33, 36, 39, 43, 45, 49, 52, 59, 62, 66-7, 69, 75, 79-84, 86, 90, 97, 99, 116-7, 120-4, 127-9, 134-6, 139, 142, 146-8, 151, 161, 165, 167-8, 189-90, 193-4, 196-7, 201
  falls to royalists, (1643), 55, 65
  retaken by Parliament, (1644), 77
  Battle of, (1645), 91-6, 130, 145-6
  royalist designs on, 141, 143, 145
  radicalism in, 163, 168-9
Weymouth Bay, 93
Whetham, Colonel Nathaniel, 183, 185-6, 190
Whitaker, William, 136
White, Ignatius, 60
White, John, 3, 8, 13-4, 16-7, 40, 54, 116, 119, 125, 139-41, 195, 197
White, William, 40
Whitelord, widow, 200
Whiteway, John, 140
Whiteway, William, 6, 9, 13